# International Real Estate

## An institutional approach

Edited by

## William Seabrooke

Professor of Real Estate and Director of the
Research Centre for Construction and Real Estate Economics
The Hong Kong Polytechnic University

## Paul Kent

Associate Professor, Department of Building and Real Estate
The Hong Kong Polytechnic University

and

## Hebe Hwee Hong How

Lecturer, Department of Building and Real Estate
The Hong Kong Polytechnic University

**Blackwell**
Publishing

Editorial offices:
Blackwell Publishing Ltd, 9600 Garsington Road, Oxford OX4 2DQ, UK
  Tel: +44 (0)1865 776868
Blackwell Publishing Inc., 350 Main Street, Malden, MA 02148-5020, USA
  Tel: +1 781 388 8250
Blackwell Publishing Asia Pty Ltd, 550 Swanston Street, Carlton, Victoria 3053, Australia
  Tel: +61 (0)3 8359 1011

First published 2004 by Blackwell Publishing Ltd

Library of Congress Cataloging-in-Publication Data
International real estate: an institutional approach / edited by William Seabrooke, Paul S.
  Kent, Hebe H.H. How.
    p. cm.
Includes bibliographical references and index.
  ISBN 1-4051-0308-6 (Pbk. : alk. paper)
  1. Real estate investment. 2. Institutional investments. 3. Real estate business. 4. Real
  estate development. 5. Real property--Foreign ownership. I. Seabrooke, W. II. Kent, Paul
  S. III. How, Hebe H. H.

HD1382.5.I58 2004
332.63'24--dc22

ISBN 1-4051-0308-6

A catalogue record for this title is available from the British Library

Set in 10/13 pt Trump Mediaeval
by Sparks, Oxford, UK – http://www.sparks.co.uk
Printed and bound in India
by Replika Press Pvt. Ltd, Kundli 131028

The publisher's policy is to use permanent paper from mills that operate a sustainable
forestry policy, and which has been manufactured from pulp processed using acid-free
and elementary chlorine-free practices. Furthermore, the publisher ensures that the text
paper and cover board used have met acceptable environmental accreditation standards.

For further information on Blackwell Publishing, visit our website:
www.thatconstructionsite.com

**RICS FOUNDATION**

The **RICS Foundation** was established by the Royal Institution of Chartered Surveyors to promote and highlight the importance of the built and natural environment. The RICS Foundation supports and develops programmes of research to explore the key issues relevant to the way in which we manage, finance, plan and construct our built and natural environment, to make best and most effective use of the resources available to us.

## Real Estate Issues

**Series Managing Editors**
*Stephen Brown* RICS Foundation
*John Henneberry* Department of Town & Regional Planning, University of Sheffield
*David Ho* School of Design & Environment, National University of Singapore

*Real Estate Issues* is an international book series presenting the latest thinking into how real estate markets operate. The books have a strong theoretical basis – providing the underpinning for the development of new ideas.

The books are inclusive in nature, drawing both upon established techniques for real estate market analysis and on those from other academic disciplines as appropriate. The series embraces a comparative approach, allowing theory and practice to be put forward and tested for their applicability and relevance to the understanding of new situations. It does not seek to impose solutions, but rather provides a more effective means by which solutions can be found. It will not make any presumptions as to the importance of real estate markets but will uncover and present, through the clarity of the thinking, the real significance of the operation of real estate markets.

## Books in the series

Guy & Henneberry *Development and Developers*
Adams & Watkins *Greenfields, Brownfields and Housing Development*
O'Sullivan & Gibb *Housing Economics and Public Policy*
Couch, Fraser & Percy *Urban Regeneration in Southern Europe*
Allen, Barlow, Léal, Maloutas & Padovani *Housing and Welfare in Southern Europe*
Leece *Economics of the Mortgage Market*
Evans *Economics and Land Use Planning*
Evans *Economics, Real Estate and the Supply of Land*
Byrne & Matysiak *Real Estate Investment*
Seabrooke, Kent & How *International Real Estate*
Ball *Markets and Institutions in Real Estate and Construction*
Dixon, McAllister, Marston & Snow *Real Estate in the New Economy*
Adams, Watkins & White *Planning, Public Policy and Property Markets*
McGough & Tsolacos *Real Estate Market Analysis and Forecasting*

# Contents

# Contributors

**Andrew E. Baum**
Professor of Land Management, University of Reading; Managing Director, Oxford Property Consultants, Reading, UK

**Yat Hung Chiang**
Associate Professor, Department of Building and Real Estate, The Hong Kong Polytechnic University, Hong Kong SAR

**Mark J. Eppli**
Professor of Finance and Robert B. Bell, Sr., Chair in Real Estate, College of Business Administration, Marquette University, Milwaukee, WI, USA

**Chang Chun Feng**
Professor, Faculty of Urban and Regional Planning; Director of Research Centre of Real Estate Studies, Peking University, China PRC

**Michael A. Goldberg**
Herbert R. Fullerton Professor of Urban Land Policy, Faculty of Commerce and Business Administration, Associate Vice President International, The University of British Columbia, Canada

**Hebe Hwee Hong How**
Lecturer, Department of Building and Real Estate, The Hong Kong Polytechnic University, Hong Kong SAR

**Eddie Chi Man Hui**
Associate Professor, Department of Building and Real Estate, The Hong Kong Polytechnic University, Hong Kong SAR

**Professor Yu Ichiro Kawaguchi**
Professor of Real Estate Finance, Waseda University, Graduate School of Finance, Accounting and Law, Tokyo, Japan

**Paul Kent**
Associate Professor, Department of Building and Real Estate, Faculty of Construction and Land Use, The Hong Kong Polytechnic University, Hong Kong SAR

**Derek C. Nicholls**
Director, Cambridge International Land Institute, Fitzwilliam College, University of Cambridge, United Kingdom

**William Seabrooke**
Professor of Real Estate; Director, Research Centre for Construction and Real Estate Economics, Department of Building and Real Estate, Faculty of Construction and Land Use, The Hong Kong Polytechnic University, Hong Kong SAR

**Sujeet Sharma**
Research Associate, Research Centre for Construction and Real Estate Economics, The Hong Kong Polytechnic University, Hong Kong SAR

**C. Tsuriel (Tsur) Somerville**
Associate Professor, Real Estate Foundation Professorship in Real Estate Finance, Director, UBC Centre for Urban Economics and Real Estate, University of British Columbia, Canada

**Bo Sin Tang**
Associate Professor, Department of Building and Real Estate, The Hong Kong Polytechnic University, Hong Kong SAR

**Charles C. Tu**
Associate Professor, Department of Finance, College of Business Administration, California State University, Fullerton, USA

**Bernard Winograd**
President, Prudential Investment Management, Gateway Center 3, 15th floor, Newark, NJ 07102, USA

**Stanley Chi Wai Yeung**
Associate Professor, Department of Building and Real Estate, The Hong Kong Polytechnic University, Hong Kong SAR

# Foreword

Everyone who works in real estate and understands their own market is at one time or another tempted to apply what they know further afield. Whether it is the small local investor trying to expand into the next door town, the large institutional investor diversifying overseas, or the successful consultant – the opportunity and temptation always materialises. After all, we reason, real estate is essentially the same everywhere. Sadly, the world is awash with the epitaphs of those in property whose temptation overcame their reason! One thinks of British investors in Continental Europe in the 1970s, Swedish investors in Britain in the 1980s and Hong Kong investors in China in the 1990s.

Grosvenor has been active outside Britain for 50 years and though some may say we have thrived, we have the wounds to prove our long service! During this time we have invested or developed in 16 countries, each one very different in law, custom, technique, transparency and language – all vital ingredients of the market, if you think about it. Culture is never easily defined but an outsider is always dangerously unaware of history and gossip; these things contribute strongly to the psyche of people who collectively react to events to make a market. Sometimes it is true that the outside observer of a market can see the big picture clearer than the local but I believe that the only route to long-term success is to become a local. Early on this might be mimicked by finding a truly compatible local partner, but eventually it means making decisions locally, using local expertise and local culture.

At all stages, knowledge is essential and the route to good knowledge is the humility to learn something new. This book is a wonderful contribution to greater knowledge and I look forward to making much use of it. It may hold out the promise of fewer acts of self-destruction in our industry but it is also a fascinating insight into the disconnection between rational analysis and action. I fear not everyone will heed its lessons!

Jeremy Newsum
Group Chief Executive
Grosvenor Group Holdings

# Preface

Hong Kong has offered a grandstand view of three strands of economic development over the past decade that has demonstrated an urgent need for a better understanding of international real estate transactions. The first arises from the opaque yet frenetic behaviour of real estate markets in south and east Asia during the 1980s; followed by the second: the wasteful consequences of an uninformed rush of international capital into Asian real estate markets that were patently too immature (institutionally) to stand the strain of such rapid expansion; and third, the burgeoning interest in investing in the emerging (but still immature) market economy of the People's Republic of China (PRC). The need for a more informed way of analysing and investing in unfamiliar real estate markets gave rise to this book.

Three notable themes have emerged from this three-stage phenomenon. The first is the reality of international investment: international capital can travel like a tidal surge, arriving suddenly, with irresistible force. It then moves on, leaving a certain amount of economic debris in its wake. The second theme is the aftermath of this 'flush' of capital. As the surge arrives, almost universally a significant proportion gets channelled into real estate development. Capital, the most transient and fluid lubricant of production, is converted into the most fixed and illiquid factor of production, land and buildings. The enhancement in the value of land by the addition of buildings depends on the active presence of capital. When the capital moves on, it leaves the physical as well as economic debris of obsolete expectations. The third theme is the essentially urban nature of these capital flows, in particular, what makes some cities more successful in holding on to international or 'footloose' capital?

This highlights the twenty-first century emergence of the Renaissance equivalent of 'city-states'. The East Asian region accommodates two of the most famous twentieth-century city-states: Hong Kong and Singapore. The phenomenon of the city-state metaphor developed in the PRC as it rolled out the economic reforms of the 1990s. Economic reforms tend to be introduced in one or two cities at a time and, if successful, spread further afield. Typically they are introduced in the coastal cities of China including Hong Kong, Guangzhou, Shenzhen, Shanghai, Nanjing and Beijing. (Apart from Shenzhen, which in 1978 was little more than a frontier village between the then British colony of Hong Kong and the PRC, the other five cities have long histories of international commerce and trade.)

The important lesson relating to sustainable real estate investment to be learned from this brief period of modern economic history is 'know the rules before playing the game'. When international capital gets sucked into poor real estate investments, not only do the subsequent failures become non-performing loans, they quickly become physically obsolete, causing lasting damage to the social, economic and environmental fabric of the cities in which they mushroomed into existence.

One may ask why those advising on real estate investment fail to grasp this obvious principle. In many of the institutionally mature and robust economies of the world, real estate professionals receive high-quality training in appraisal and the economics of asset management: are they ignored or do they just get it badly wrong? Sometimes they are ignored by the movers and shakers of the capital markets but they also get things wrong, especially when called upon to give advice about investments in real estate markets with which they are unfamiliar. The level of unfamiliarity with Asian real estate markets among western advisers is profound. Even Hong Kong suffered from a high degree of complacency about the problems of real estate investment in mainland China.

Universally, real estate investment is a complex matter. The traditional training of real estate professionals tends to be strongly based on a single sovereignty. Real estate professionals themselves prefer to focus their advice on markets with which they are familiar. As the demand from international clients or local clients with international interests becomes increasingly significant to professional advisers, the old-fashioned narrow approach is inadequate for the modern needs of the international business community and for city governments.

This book introduces a new way of looking at real estate investment that is more relevant to the challenge of international advice. First and foremost it focuses on 'transactions', developing a new understanding of how real estate transactions work and how this understanding can be tailored to the needs of individual transactions in any sovereignty. The book is structured in three parts: part 1 introduces the transaction-based approach; part 2 addresses contextual issues relating to city planning and large-scale project analysis; part 3 consists of individual perspectives from six authors of five different real estate markets around the world. There has been little attempt on the part of the editors to dictate a particular format for the invited contributions contained in parts 2 and 3. The broad focus of the book emphasises the importance of the rules of the game that affect real estate transactions from one sovereignty to another. The differences between the issues that individual contributors have chosen to emphasise illustrate the degree to which perceptions vary from market to market.

Almost all the topics which form part of this book require further detailed study in order for the reader to acquire sufficient depth of knowledge to produce detailed, professional advice.

The importance placed on property rights indicates that the broad philosophy of the book is based on a 'conventional', western economic approach, three characteristic features of which are:

- The existence of property rights that form the subject of market transactions;

- A price mechanism for allocating scarce resources;

- Freedom of enterprise to generate profit and wealth which is retained by its creator.

All three factors and capitalism itself are human creations and, therefore, imperfect. These institutional arrangements provide incentive to individuals and corporate bodies to generate wealth, secure in the belief that they can exercise their enterprise in good faith without the risk of losing the fruits of their efforts. However, the extent of that security depends on the clarity and strength of property rights, the power, rigour and fairness of their enforcement, and the transparency of the institutions which give formal structure to market mechanisms.

The pillars of capitalism do not oblige those exercising their entrepreneurial capabilities to apply any moral or social regard to other members of society. Market economies require checks and balances in order to counteract the establishment of injustice and inequality. These checks and balances are not naturally occurring phenomena; they have to be designed and created, clearly expressed and enforced. They are the rules of the 'game': participants must be familiar with them and should be aware of the consequences if they fail to abide by them.

Nevertheless, the market system is robust and has proved durable. Many nations which are more familiar with different economic and political conditions are now looking at the price mechanism as the best, though imperfect, means of allocating resources. However, the price mechanism as it operates in western economies cannot be isolated from property rights. Without property rights, capitalism would not exist. This book attempts to show how the institutional features of real estate determine the manner in which it is integrated into market economies that vary in form from sovereignty to sovereignty.

# Part 1

## Analysis of Real Estate Transactions in Unfamiliar Markets, Using an Institutional Approach

## Introduction

Chapter 1 establishes a transaction-based perspective as the analytical focus for international real estate. It introduces the rise of transaction cost concepts and their relevance to real estate decisions. It highlights the dangers and uncertainties associated with the creation and capture of 'value' and the influence of indirect stakeholders on value creation. It explains how a transaction-based perspective supports an institutional approach to the analysis of international real estate transactions.

Chapter 2 explores the relationship between rule structures, institutional arrangements and transacting. It identifies a framework that enables foreign investors (and their advisers) to evaluate the institutional uncertainty associated with investing in foreign real estate markets in a critical and systematic manner. It provides a new analytical tool to facilitate navigation through a web of institutional arrangements from a transaction-based perspective. The application of institutional analysis to real estate transactions is illustrated by the use of case studies.

Chapter 3 focuses on the subject matter of real estate transactions using an institutional approach. A comparison of vendor and purchaser transactions in the Hong Kong Special Administrative Region with the acquisition of land-use rights in the People's Republic of China reveals how the quality of title to real estate is contingent upon institutional arrangements prevailing during the transacting process. This underlines the importance of systematic determination of the property rights actually transferred in a transaction.

# 1

# Real Estate Transactions: an Institutional Perspective

## William Seabrooke and Hebe Hwee Hong How

## The international real estate phenomenon

The physical appearance of towns and cities is self-evident; how they function is not. A visual image of international real estate created by the urban development that is one of the distinguishing global features of the last half of the twentieth century gives an impression of consistency, even uniformity, which is misleading. The manner in which urban development is achieved varies substantially from city to city and, particularly, from country to country. Visual cues that indicate international consistency conceal underlying rules of the game that are far from international.

Much of the development that characterises the 'modern' appearance of towns and cities has occurred over the past 50 years. The 1950s marked a watershed in urban development. The urban fabric of countries that had been at the forefront of the Industrial Revolution had been ravaged by war. The (new at the time) developments associated with the early Industrial Revolution laid the foundation for the development of urban real estate markets. By the 1950s real estate markets in these economies had become well established. But, apart from war damage, the urban fabric had in many respects become obsolescent. The 1950s witnessed a boom in redevelopment but more particularly rapid increases in new development associated with the expansion of urban areas; a trend that has become a world-wide phenomenon. However, within this pattern of global development some markets had become institutionally mature, while others in developing or transition economies were newly formed and immature.

In the United Kingdom the physical appearance of many town and city centres was reshaped by entrepreneurs who saw profitable opportunities for urban expansion and comprehensive redevelopment of urban fabric that had become technically and economically obsolete. They sought capital from sources with greater interest in long-term lending than most banks, and they worked with the post-war town planning agencies to provide a new force in comprehensive urban development. Less obvious were corresponding changes in the structure of property ownership and tenure that accompanied the new urban development. For example, financial institutions became increasingly dominant as landlords for prime commercial property. The pre-war tradition of industrial organisations building factories and offices for their own use and housing for their workers gradually disappeared as they were compelled by market pressures to re-evaluate the fixed capital necessary to run their businesses. The rules of the game that governed the development and evolution of urban centres for the first half of the twentieth century had changed.

The globalisation of economic activity stimulated widespread urban development, even in cities and sovereignties with ramshackle and undeveloped rule frameworks. Yet, investors and developers were reluctant to venture beyond markets with which they had grown familiar and in which they could exert some influence. Prior to the global economic expansion of the 1980s and 1990s, private international investment was largely limited to shareholdings in multinational companies and foreign government bonds. Rapid economic growth in Asia prompted wealthy individuals and corporations to sponsor private investment in real estate development in their region. By the 1990s, many cities in many countries displayed their share of high-rise concrete and glass.

Prudent investors recognised that 'prime' real estate was not confined to London and New York, or even to the UK and North America, but could be found in cities throughout the world. The pressure to seek out investments showing better than average returns remained a compelling reason for them to monitor apparent opportunities for profitable investment in foreign real estate markets. 'Horror' stories about overseas real estate developments and investments that had 'gone wrong' were countered by evidence of exceptional successes. The true significance of such anecdotal evidence is more dependent on the particular circumstances surrounding individual real estate transactions than for almost any other class of investment.

## Real estate transactions and transacting

Transactions represent exchanges of value between vendors who own property of some kind (goods, services, intellectual property, land, buildings) and purchasers who offer equivalent value in return. Dictionary definitions of 'transaction', 'transact' or 'transacting' are curiously vague but imply a process leading to a conclusive event involving some form of trade, exchange or transfer of value. The conclusion of an economic transaction marks the point at which ownership rights are assigned or exchanged. Transactions occur because what a purchaser wishes and is able to buy a vendor wishes and is able to sell. As a general rule, a transaction may be expected to proceed if the value of the subject matter to the purchaser is not less than the price that the seller will accept (at least to the extent that the price also covers the cost of undertaking the transaction).

In order to reassure themselves of this, the parties incur the cost of engaging in a process of 'transacting' (normally designed to lead to consummation of the transaction) to secure information that tests the viability of their intention to transact the exchange. For many transactions involving goods other than real estate, the parties are sufficiently well informed for the process of transacting to be of minor significance. In contrast, the process of transacting plays a central role in the consummation of real estate transactions because of the value and complexity of the subject matter. Thus, the analysis of individual transactions constitutes the foundation for understanding international investment in or development of real estate.

Traditional microeconomic analysis focuses on transactions (i.e. events) rather than transacting (i.e. a process, the successful completion of which results in transaction events). Furthermore, it does not focus on all transactions but only those that represent market behaviour. It pays little regard, for example, to subsidiary or 'quasi' transactions (usually undertaken within an organisation, firm or household) contributing to market transactions. The impact of 'quasi' transactions on 'market' transactions tends to be treated as organisational management rather than economics. Collectively, a pattern of similar market transaction events represents actual (revealed) market behaviour. If goods or services are relatively homogeneous, analysis of aggregated patterns of transactions ostensibly results in clear trends which, other things being equal, may be extrapolated to forecast future behaviour.

For transactions involving the acquisition of simple goods or services, uncertainty, which forms an implicit part of transacting, may appear to be largely resolved when a transaction is completed. If the expected outcome (1) can be evaluated soon after its completion and (2) is not fulfilled, the result is simple disappointment. For more complex transactions involving property rights giving entitlement to an income flow, the completion of a transaction does not end the risk that the expected long-term outcome may not be achieved. The transacting process must incorporate a proper assessment of these future uncertainties.

Although the conclusion of a transaction for the sale or purchase of real estate is important, it may be less significant in understanding buyer behaviour than the transacting process (see Commons 1934). Real estate transactions can be individually complex, prolonged and distinctive (non-homogeneous). Unlike transactions relating to conventional goods or services, which can be completed in minutes, hours or days, those relating to real estate normally extend over weeks or months, in which time the terms of any transaction can change significantly. The transacting process leading to the transaction event becomes a source of considerable uncertainty. The aggregation of data relating to real estate transactions can give a misleading impression of uniformity of thought and action among participants in the market.

For example, in Hong Kong, when real estate prices were rising rapidly interests in land were often treated as market commodities. What appears to be one transaction disguises the existence of a number of intermediate agreements to acquire the property between the vendor and the ultimate purchaser. The intermediate agreements are made by 'confirmors' or sub-purchasers, each selling on to the next person in the chain. The head vendor eventually assigns the property to the last sub-purchaser in the chain. Such transactions may be relatively instantaneous and ostensibly resemble transactions for goods insofar as they concertina the linked agreements into a single transaction.[1]

The value of the subject matter to be exchanged is one of the primary clauses of a contract for sale. In the case of urban land and buildings, this is a function of (1) the profitability of the use to which it can be put and (2) the strength and duration of the right to exclusive enjoyment of the benefits deriving from that use. Value is portable because it attaches to the property rights that enable the use of land to occur while the land accommodating the use remains fixed and non-portable. A landowner holds rights that include:

- Physical possession of the land;

- The right to derive an income from its use;

- The right to sell or transfer some or all of those rights and to retain the value of that transfer.

These rights represent the benefits associated with land and buildings in a particular spatial location, together with any enforceable burdens. They constitute the formal subject matter of a real estate transaction. The popular perception that real estate means 'land' is misleading. It is important to remember that real estate is not defined simply by the physical characteristics of the land or the buildings on it, although these are important, but by the enforceable rights that allow the use of land (and buildings fixed to it) to be exercised, protected and transferred. Even at this early stage of our introduction, we draw a distinction between the rights associated with exclusive possession of land, the exercise of its existing use, and the development of new, more valuable uses. We highlight for later consideration (chapter 3) the distinction between the rights and obligations associated with 'title' and the use rights that enable development to take place.

## Appraising value

Estimating the market price of real estate for sale and purchase transactions is largely based on analysis of previous comparable transactions, although estimating the general state of real estate markets is based on aggregated transaction data. When assessing the market value of land and buildings, appraisers or valuers rely on methods that appear mathematically crude but are widely accepted by their professional peers. They incorporate into their appraisals qualitative factors relating to physical characteristics such as the attractiveness of property or the popularity of the location. They also incorporate the terms (benefits and obligations) of the property rights that they are valuing and, when appropriate, their estimate of the probability that consent for a beneficial change of use may be obtainable. These non-physical characteristics may be likened to 'rules of the game' which, in addition to formal rules, include informal practices, self-justifying beliefs, fashions and rules of thumb, which influence behaviour.

The methods of appraisal rely on the conventions of practitioners that incorporate heuristic (experience-based) rules of thumb, modified implicitly and pragmatically in response to shifts in the market. Heuristic rules are expedient but selective, providing short cuts at the expense of objective rigour and open to many of the common errors of subjective inference. Appraisers tend to focus their attention on those factors that they believe to be significantly 'out of the ordinary' for the type, class and location of real estate that they are evaluating. In familiar markets they take for granted rules of the game that affect in similar fashion all transactions for similar types of property in that market. Individual transactions become amenable to comprehensive, objective analysis, including the heuristics used in the appraisal, only if they develop into a *cause célèbre* (usually in the form of legal or quasi-legal proceedings).

Despite the differences between the aggregative approaches of mainstream economists and the comparative approaches of valuers, they share an assumption that the framework of rules, conventions, practices and customs that structure similar transactions is relatively constant. This assumption is broadly valid if a transaction is considered to be an event rather than a process. Although the prolonged nature of real estate transactions tests the credibility of this assumption, the assumption may remain valid in a pragmatic sense. The rules relating to real estate transactions are so much more complicated than for other classes of goods and services that to undertake a full analysis for every transaction would be impractical. In markets in which the rules of the game are transparent, robust, stable and familiar, the impact of all variants of the 'rules' on any transaction is relatively predictable and capable of being reflected in the terms of the transaction (contract). But this presumption is unlikely to hold true in unfamiliar sovereignties.

## Rules of the game

Urban environments and the transactions that mould them function according to rules, conventions, social norms, customs and practices, sometimes referred to collectively as 'rule regimes' (Bromley 1991) or 'institutions.' (Douglass North 1995 in Breit & Spencer 1995). Such institutions create complex economic and social operating systems, many aspects of which are not readily apparent. Rule regimes create a framework within which transactions take place. Institutional arrangements form sinews connecting the rule regimes to transactions. The application and interaction of rule regimes and institutional arrangements constitute 'the rules of the game' with which developers must interact.

The institution of property rights, central to all market transactions but particularly significant in the case of real estate transactions, is connected to other institutions such as local governance of land use and development, the judicial system for settling civil disputes, and the economic system. The value of a legitimate ownership interest owes much to the extent to which (1) the range of permitted uses attaching to it can be extended by public approvals and (2) it is recognised and enforced by an independent judicial system, backed by the power of government.

Successful development is achieved by negotiating transactions involving property rights and quasi-transactions relating, for example, to use and development permits. Each transaction is the outcome of a transacting process involving a variety of participants, which enables 'value' to be identified, realised and captured. The value passes across a 'decision landscape' strewn with obstacles that seldom allow decision routes to follow a path that is straight and smooth. The decisions leading to successful investment and development in familiar markets are complex enough: adding an international dimension means that many of the rules of the game that are taken for granted (because, in a familiar context, they are stable and settled) can no longer be assumed. This adds a degree of uncertainty over and above intrinsic market uncertainty.

## Institutions

The philosopher David Hume, a contemporary of Adam Smith, singled out three 'institutions' as being fundamental to human progress and civilised society, namely:

- Guaranteed property rights;

- Free transfer of property by voluntary contractual agreement;

- Keeping promises made in relation to social transactions.

In a personal account of his own work, the economic historian and winner of the Nobel Prize for economic science, Douglass North, explains:

> In a world of uncertainty they (*institutions*) have been used by human beings in an attempt to structure human interaction. They are the rules of the game of a society and in consequence provide the framework of incentives that shape economic, political, and social organization. Institutions are composed of formal rules (laws, constitutions, rules), informal constraints (conventions, codes of conduct, norms of behaviour), and the effectiveness of their enforcement. Enforcement is carried out by third parties (law enforcement, social ostracism), by second parties (retaliation), or by the first party (self-imposed codes of conduct). Institutions affect economic performance by determining, together with the technology employed, the transaction and transformation (production) costs that make up the total costs of production. Since there is an intimate connection between the institutions and technology employed, the efficiency of a market is directly shaped by the institutional framework.
>
> Breit & Spencer (1995)

This use of the term 'institution' is by no means exclusive. Other usage can refer to a persona (e.g. 'the King'), a characteristic group (e.g. 'developers', landowners, financiers), a practice (e.g. surveying, accountancy), a process (e.g. town planning, the process of law), a building that has a special, well-established place in society (e.g. a hospital, school, prison), a characteristic grouping of organisations (e.g. financial institutions, the Church), a socio-logical phenomenon (e.g. the institution of marriage), an enduring body of settled doctrine employed to regulate different legal relations, as in the 'institution of property'.

Nevertheless, the definition adopted by North refers to usage within economics, particularly transaction cost and institutional economics. For example, Kasper and Streit (1998) define 'institutions' as 'widely known, man-made rules that are meant to constrain possibly opportunistic human behaviour'. The application identified by North is consistent with that adopted by other researchers in the area of property rights systems (Ostrom 1990; Oakerson 1992; Oakerson & Walker 1997). It is particularly apposite in this context because it effectively groups together a cumbersome and sometimes unstable raft of formal and informal rules, conventions, practices and customs that influence and sometimes govern transacting behaviour.

'Institution(al)' has become a term of art in the area of law and economics. In this area in particular, much attention has been paid by writers such as Posner (1973) to the 'efficiency' of institutions, particularly formal institutions such as legal rules. The 'efficiency' criterion is not the only, nor necessarily the primary justification for institutions; for example, 'stability' may have greater importance than 'efficiency'. Such differences can be the source of profound differences in the perceptions of investors in taking institutional criteria from one sovereignty and applying them in another.

In stable capitalist economies the intimacy of the relationship between urban development and the right to exclusive possession of the land on which buildings are fixed is so axiomatic that it appears to be a tautology. Indeed it can be argued (de Soto 2000) that the success of capitalism is tied to strong property rights systems. In these economies, real estate investment exemplifies the importance of trust and confidence in a predictable future. However, de Soto (2000) draws attention to 'extralegal' property rights existing among the 'under-classes' in many urban communities across the world. Although 'extralegal' properties can command substantial prices, their value is largely unrecognised by government agencies, banks and conventional lending organisations. By contrast, in the planned economies associated with the 'traditional' Communist regimes, the institution of real estate was non-existent; there was no open market for land, which officially had no intrinsic value.

Rule regimes have a ubiquitous and important influence on the nature of investing in or developing real estate. They are individually complex and vary significantly from one sovereignty to another. Although their content, form, even their purpose, are considered normal and familiar by local market participants, they often appear alien to foreign investors or developers. Furthermore, a foreign participant in the market has little means of directly assessing what is and what is not 'normal'. The 'rules of the game' differ significantly even in sovereignties that share common roots to their system of governance.

For example, Hong Kong, British Columbia and England share a system of governance based on English common law. To outward appearances, the central business districts of the cities of London, Hong Kong and Vancouver appear to share many characteristics of any modern, international business district. Under the surface, however, institutions of ownership, tenure and use differ significantly. Freehold ownership of land in the City of London is largely in the hands of financial institutions, such as pension funds, for the purpose of long-term investment. Leases are granted for relatively long periods (up to 21 years). The government of the United Kingdom has, effectively, no role in its management and development although the local government plays an active role in encouraging effective and efficient use of land in the City. Land within the Hong Kong Special Administrative Region (HKSAR) is the property of the State (the People's Republic of China). The government of the HKSAR is responsible for its management, use and development, and has power to lease or grant such property to individuals, legal persons or organisations for use or development. Until 1997, the government sold land on long leases for a substantial premium and nominal rent, typically for periods of 75 to 99 years. Since the transfer of sovereignty from the United Kingdom to China on 1 July 1997, the practice has been to grant land for development on 50-year leases, at a rent equivalent to 3% of its rateable value (often a considerable sum). The size and value of government leases has resulted in their accumulation in the hands of a small number of property development companies that are, ostensibly, public listed companies but which are in fact controlled by particular families. Sub-leases of land for commercial use tend to be for relatively short periods of less than 4 years. In Vancouver freehold ownership applies although ownership rights pre-dating English colonial rule still have significance in some areas. The provincial government is a prominent landowner, working in partnership with private developers to develop government-owned sites. Land is held on a variety of terms of tenure but, in general, the duration of leases is typically between 4 years and 21 years.

All three cities have systems of land-use planning and control that create an impression of similarity, yet they differ in significant ways. The City of London has a system based on planning policy statements including some land-use zoning principles that form a basis for negotiated consents between developers and the planning authority. Hong Kong has a tradition of land-use regulation achieved by specific terms contained in government leases, now augmented by a 'conventional' planning system running in parallel with the government lease system. Vancouver has a land-use planning system based heavily on zoning plans but which gives very strong weight to the opinions of local residents who, in turn, place heavy emphasis on the quality of their local environment.

## The building blocks of economic behaviour in real estate markets

Transactions are the building blocks of economic behaviour. They are the outcome of private bargaining or ordering. Conventional analysis of economic behaviour in market economies assumes that economic activity takes place within and is constitutive of markets. Emphasis is placed, therefore, on recorded transactions that represent evidence of actual or revealed economic behaviour occurring between firms and households. Transactions of similar types are aggregated to yield a picture of market behaviour that diminishes the significance of individual transactions, which are seldom the focus of economic analysis. Until the advent of transaction cost economics, relatively little analysis was undertaken of the 'anatomy' of transactions and even less analysis of the transacting process. Neo-classical economists largely assumed, among other things, that (1) the process of transferring resources was more than justified by its conclusion and (2) the cost of this process was negligible.

Transactions do not have to be organised and executed through a market. The simplest way of organising transactions is by agreement between the parties based on trust and mutual benefit. This is prevalent within organisations that are able to set their own rules for compliance with and enforcement of any transaction. Recorded transactions are typically the product of a sequence of minor ('quasi') transactions that take place behind closed doors and build the transactions that are considered to represent economic behaviour. Williamson (1975) examines the mechanisms that give effect to transactions and focuses on the distinction between formal contracts and less formal arrangements within firms or other organisations (leading into the area of organisational behaviour). Contract-based transactions are the preferred mechanism for real estate transactions. Indeed, it can be claimed that the contract mechanism is intrinsic to real estate transactions based on common law principles.

When there is a danger that agreements may give rise to disputes or when informal agreements become too complex for every detail to be recalled accurately and without ambiguity, they may be recorded in a written form (although it may be difficult to record the 'letter' and spirit of complex transactions). Within an organisation this may consist of operating procedures and protocols. Outside an organisation the form is typically a contract. Contracts are employed to record the stated or implied intentions of the parties to a transaction but they also introduce rules relating to enforcement of the agreement. Indeed, confidence in and reliance on contractual agreements may, in part at least, be seen as a reflection of confidence in and reliance on the rule of law.

Among the universe of transactions constituting economic behaviour, real estate stands out as a discrete 'population' largely at variance with conventional perceptions of transactions between firms or households. Furthermore, real estate markets are not readily amenable to the conventional application of neo-classical microeconomic analysis. Most real estate transactions consist of individual contractual agreements between buyers and sellers. They are distinctive because the 'event' may be less significant in explaining behaviour than the process that precedes it. This may seem trivial in a general sense but, in the case of real estate transactions, it is highly significant in understanding the transaction itself and its significance in relation to market behaviour. Individual transactions give form and structure to real estate markets.

Uncertainty, arising from the unknown effects on the outcome of transactions of the formal and informal 'rules' that govern the transacting process, has a significant bearing on the risk premiums that investors apply to decisions involving the acquisition or disposal of real estate. International real estate transactions are particularly vulnerable to such uncertainty and this is compounded where development is involved. Risk premiums that are unnecessarily high, as a result of a misleading perception of adversely asymmetric knowledge, are a self-imposed barrier to entry into foreign markets. It is implicit in a transaction-based approach that assessing the risks associated with investing or operating in a particular market should include an analysis of the costs and uncertainties of transacting, which may or may not culminate in a transaction.

Real estate is a complex commodity possessing high financial value and a significant element of uniqueness (asset specificity). Real estate transactions are, by nature, abnormally lengthy and far from instantaneous. Once a transaction has been properly agreed (and despite the fact that it may be completed at a later date) escape strategies may be few and expensive. Prudent purchasers undertake substantial preliminary investigation in order to minimise the uncertainties associated with the acquisition of real estate. This investigation can be complex, time consuming and expensive. Within familiar trading environments, investigations focus on those aspects of the rules of the game that differ from normal expectations. This is clearly inadequate for transactions in unfamiliar territory. A local party to the transaction will possess valuable information concerning the trading environment and the rules of the game that the foreign party lacks (asymmetric knowledge).

## Transaction cost concepts

Transaction cost economics, which has gained increasing recognition over recent decades, challenges some of the extravagant assumptions on which orthodox, neo-classical microeconomic analysis is based. It recognises that (1) most transactions do not occur with perfect knowledge of all factors relevant to their outcome and (2) the process of transacting incurs costs in order to overcome information deficits.

The basic principles for the analysis of economic behaviour were introduced in the eighteenth century and substantially developed in the nineteenth century. In *The Wealth of Nations* (1776) Adam Smith asserted that competitive advantage is governed by 'the invisible hand of the market'. In 1838, the economist Cournot published the 'theory of the firm'. In 1898, Leon Walras published the most renowned 'general theory of equilibrium'. Although based on exaggerated assumptions about the behaviour of markets, these theories continue to have a powerful influence on economic analysis that focuses on economic behaviour between firms and households rather than on individual transactions. It also relies heavily on concepts of market equilibrium, which assume that an economic system in perfect equilibrium contains no 'friction' or inefficiency costs. The costs of conducting transactions are viewed as a form of inefficiency that rational individuals, firms or markets will eliminate.

In 1937 Ronald Coase questioned the purpose of 'firms'. His seminal paper entitled 'The Nature of the Firm' advanced the question: 'If the purpose of the market is to coordinate the allocation of goods in the most efficient manner possible, why is it necessary for a firm to do much the same thing?' His thoughts were developed in another seminal paper entitled 'The Problem of Social Cost' (Coase 1960), in which he pointed out that orthodox general theories of market equilibrium hold true only if transactions are cost-free. This pioneering work was slow to gain full recognition. (Coase was awarded the Nobel Prize for economic science in 1991 for his insights into the costliness of market transactions.) There is now widespread acknowledgement among economists that the process of transacting is a significant element of economic behaviour, which incurs costs.

Transaction costs are analogous to 'friction' in the physical environment: both represent inefficiency – transaction costs represent market inefficiency and friction represents mechanical inefficiency. The day-to-day experience of those responsible for resource allocation decisions confirms that perfect market knowledge is as much a theoretical abstraction as a physical world without 'friction'. Deficient market knowledge is prevalent and ubiquitous, generating uncertainty associated with the value of goods and services within prevailing market conditions. Uncertainty is increased by (1) deficiencies in relevant information about the present and (2) asymmetric distribution of information between the participants in a transaction. Overcoming such information deficits incurs transaction costs.

If transaction costs were trivial in relation to the value of each transaction, the assumption of a 'friction-free' economy might be sustainable. But they are not trivial: a study by Wallis and North (1986), measuring the economic significance of transaction costs, estimated that more than 45% of national income was devoted to transacting.

> Thus the resources of the economy consumed in transacting are of considerable magnitude and growing. Because transaction costs are a part of the costs of production, we need to restate the traditional production relationship as follows. The total costs of production consist of the resource inputs of land, labour and capital involved both in transforming the physical attributes of a good ... and in transacting – defining, protecting and enforcing the property rights to goods ...
>
> Wallis & North (1986)

We might add 'value of' to that last phrase, i.e. 'defining, protecting and enforcing the *value of* the property rights to goods'.

Adopting the assumption that economic transactions are not cost-free inevitably leads to questions of definition and measurement. Broadly speaking, transaction costs are distinct from and additional to the value of the property being exchanged. They are incurred in bringing the parties in a transaction to the point of committing themselves to an exchange of value (reallocation of resources). Economists do not hold a consistent definition of transaction costs. A narrow definition over which there is consistent agreement may be expressed as the cost of rectifying a perceived information deficit for making rational resource allocation decisions. Broader definitions treat transaction costs as the residual difference between the full cost of a transaction and the price of the resources that result from the transaction. This definition also includes externalities and marketing costs. The cost of an information deficit is common to all definitions.

In general terms, transaction costs include:

- Searching for and collecting information (to minimise uncertainty by correcting a significant information deficit);

- Bargaining, drafting and negotiating agreements;

- Insurance and bonding (to 'hedge' against risk);

- Identification of regulatory constraints that may enhance or diminish the value of an income flow.

However, they do not include all ancillary costs associated with a transaction. For example, real estate transactions are a particular target for taxes of one form or another. These are not transaction costs, but costs incurred in minimising the burden of such fees and taxes may be classed as transaction costs. Despite their ubiquity, relatively few studies involving real estate examine the form and nature of transaction costs and their practical effect on resource allocation decisions.

Systematic and accurate identification and measurement of transaction costs is a 'slippery' topic, analogous to counting fish in the sea. Although they may be hidden from view, we know they exist and can be located, identified and measured. Nevertheless, just as the size and composition of each 'catch' varies, the size and composition of transaction costs varies according to the nature of each transaction. Experience helps us to judge the likely nature, size and significance of transaction costs in classes of transactions with which we are familiar. If transactions occur with sufficient consistency and frequency, 'rules' or 'practices' can be put into place to minimise their impact. The transaction-specific nature of transaction costs encourages heuristic rather than theoretical analysis of this phenomenon.

Douglass North comments: 'Once we recognize that the costs of production are the sum of transformation and transaction costs, we require a new analytical framework of microeconomic theory' (North 1990). Transaction cost economics presents a perspective of economics that may not be 'mainstream' but is, nevertheless, widely accepted as tenable and highly relevant to the economics of real estate decisions. It explicitly incorporates into theories of rational economic behaviour recognition that participants in the transaction process operate under conditions of relative ignorance. It rejects the assumption of perfect knowledge of market transactions or even a presumption of equal distribution of ignorance. Recognition of the effects of human ignorance inherent in this approach to explaining economic behaviour creates important bridges to other behavioural disciplines. These include law (particularly the law of contract) and organisational science, particularly ways in which organisational structures and procedures are designed to minimise the transaction cost component of overall operating costs.

The neo-classical view of market utopia is a resource allocation environment in which perfect competition prevails, in which the perfect and instantaneous reconciliation of all factors affecting supply and demand enables their smooth and harmonious mutual adjustment expressed as a price relationship, devoid of the drag of 'friction'. This utopian view is spoiled by the transaction cost economists' inversion of the utopian assumption in favour of one that acknowledges inherently imperfect markets in which 'friction' expressed as transaction costs is ever present.

An ordinal concept of market utopia is very different from the neo-classical, cardinal concept. Market 'players' or participants may argue that a utopian market is one that is perfectly familiar. This is another way of saying that the 'best' market has the least degree of uncertainty. The responsiveness of investments to market uncertainty plays a prominent part in investment analysis. Generally speaking, market or systematic risk is the result of the impact of macroeconomic factors on all investments in a particular class or sector. In the case of international real estate investment, systematic risk is more complex: it is the product of:

(1)  Macroeconomic factors;

(2)  Cyclical fluctuations caused by the substantial time lag between the responsiveness of supply to expansion and contraction of demand;

(3)  The prevalence of transaction costs associated with institutional uncertainty.

## Transacting costs in real estate transactions

Relatively little work on transaction cost economics has focused on real estate transactions. As a general rule, economists seldom address the institutional implications of property rights, preferring to adopt an implicit assumption that if a transaction takes place, the property rights are adequate to allow an exchange of value to occur. This issue is explored further in chapter 3. Some transaction cost economists, notably Alchian (1977), Cheung (1983) and Barzel (1997), have recognised some of the transaction cost implications of property rights but remain largely silent on the important implications that they have on real estate transactions.

Real estate transactions are inescapably costly. Even in markets that are open, stable and transparent the costs of transacting remain stubbornly high. The imperfections of real estate as an investment include obvious physical factors such as indivisibility and lack of portability (fixed location). They also include imperfections that relate to its institutional characteristics and have a profound effect on its liquidity as an asset or investment. These include the form and application of the rules that define and govern the value of real estate, for example:

- The formal rule-based nature of real estate;

- The rigour with which those rules are enforced;

- The impact of extrinsic institutional factors that affect its use and exploitation;

- Uncertainties associated with the definition and interpretation of the rights and obligations associated with real estate;

- The legal requirements necessary to formalise transactions;

- The time taken to effect a transaction;

- The security and duration of the income flow;

- Deficient and asymmetric knowledge on the part of the parties.

Each of these inefficiencies has a cost associated with it. In the context of real estate transactions, the cost of transacting cannot be eliminated. In a competitive environment, this can have a critical effect on decisions at the margin of acceptability.

Imperfect knowledge, the product of deficient information and incomplete comprehension of existing, relevant information, introduces uncertainty that can be reduced or contained (but never eliminated) by transaction-specific knowledge. Reducing uncertainty incurs costs; accepting uncertainty carries risks. The costs associated with relatively simple acquisition/disposal transactions in familiar environments are universally and persistently high and affect both vendor and purchaser. The net proceeds of sale received by the vendor are less than the selling price of the property and the purchaser bears the cost of professional fees and the opportunity cost of his or her own time in addition to the purchase price. In most real estate markets these additional transaction costs are accepted as normal practice. In unfamiliar sovereignties, transaction costs increase substantially, to the detriment of the value of the transaction.

Most participants in real estate markets prefer to minimise their exposure to abnormal risk by a form of 'muddling through'. They stay within a clearly defined 'comfort zone', attempting to contain transaction risk within acceptable limits by limiting transaction activity to familiar market environments in which changes are modest and gradual, and the 'rules of the game' are stable and transparent. Then, they rely on heuristic adjustments to tried and trusted solutions in order to maintain a consistent standard of analysis. This approach does not eliminate transaction costs but keeps them at a predictable and tolerable level. However, additional transaction costs must be incurred in order to overcome the bargaining asymmetry of operating in someone else's comfort zone. This upward pressure on transaction costs must be balanced by the value of knowledge that may bring the inherent uncertainties of transacting back to a tolerable and competitive level. Overcoming the uncertainties associated with the rules of the game in unfamiliar markets adds an additional layer of cost to the 'normal' costs associated with transacting in familiar markets.

## Transacting costs in real estate development

Real estate development represents a contingent sequence of transactions and quasi-transactions that results in the release and capture of latent value, over and above the value attributable to existing use. The transacting process implicit in this sequence is institutionally complex, even in familiar markets. From the point of view of a potential purchaser of real estate for development, the transacting sequence typically consists of:

- Identifying potential value;

- Obtaining the property rights to which that value attaches;

- Securing any use permits that apply to the land to which the property rights are attached;

- Releasing the potential value by the addition of capital;

- Capturing the value of the development.

All stages in the sequence carry risks and uncertainties that are proportional to the accuracy, reliability, relevance and comprehensiveness of the many sources of information that affect the development process and the realisation of latent value.

The value of urban land is derived from use entitlements that attach to it. Ownership rights only empower the existing, legitimate use of land but this may not necessarily be its most valuable potential use. If land possesses potential for change to a more valuable use, that change is normally contingent upon approval(s) of the change of use from relevant local public authorities. Public approvals relating to development may be considered as quasi-transactions. The probability of obtaining all necessary approvals (and, therefore, the value of the land) may be uncertain at the time that terms for the acquisition of the relevant property rights are being negotiated. In these circumstances, information deficits in the form of incomplete or ambiguous knowledge can have a critical effect. If the pattern of information deficits shifts as a transaction progresses, the intention of one or both of the parties may switch from a desire to complete the transaction to a wish to withdraw and search for an exit strategy.

The development process is triggered by activating rules relating to the use of land that are largely unrelated to the rules relating to transfers of title (although the transaction value may be contingent on the outcome of the former rules). An outcome in favour of development enables latent value to be accurately quantified and facilitates the immediate release of some but not all of it. In order to be fully realised, the development must be completed, commissioned and either used or disposed of. The institutional arrangements that largely determine the form and content of transactions making up this sequential process have distinct characteristics. The nature of the uncertainties associated with each of these stages is also quite distinct.

(1) *Stage 1 transactions:* Acquisition of transferable rights to exclusive possession of the land upon which the development takes place. (In cases where successful development could release substantial latent value, but the probability of securing development approval is modest, developers prefer to secure an option to purchase the development rights once the 'chance' element has been resolved.)

(2) *Stage 2 (quasi-) transactions:* Acquisition of the use consents that permit development to proceed.

(3) *Stage 3 transactions:* A discrete sub-set of transactions collectively comprising the construction process from design to procurement.

(4) *Stage 4 transactions:* Use or disposal of the completed development.

Acquisition transactions may be characterised as high-value but procedurally relatively simple. In contrast, the construction process contains a multitude of relatively low-value transactions arranged in a largely contingent sequence (i.e. one part of the construction is contingent upon the successful completion of another). It consists of numerous individual transactions, spread over a relatively lengthy period, incorporating asset specificity; asymmetric information (mainly associated with trade skills); free-riding; opportunism and shirking behaviour, which makes the construction phase difficult to control and relatively inefficient. Construction also creates physical permanence: mistakes are difficult to remedy without incurring substantial additional cost.

The final value of a development is released by use or disposal. Use releases value as a stream of benefits, either by disposal of part of the ownership interest (e.g. by granting a lease) or by direct management. Both options introduce new transactions and rules of the game. Disposal of the ownership of the development releases value as a capital payment.

Transaction costs often take the form of professional fees. Even simple acquisition transactions involve significant legal and agency fees. Subsequent development incurs additional fees associated with the construction process including fees for architects, quantity surveyors, engineers and often more. Fees for professional advice payable as a means of controlling transaction costs may, typically, amount to 5–15% of the face value of the asset that is finally developed. This is a conservative estimate of total transaction costs; often the client spends time and effort on researching the quality and reliability of professional advisers.

Within the construction process, individual transactions may be relatively small but numerous, fitting together like the pieces of a jigsaw. Although professional advisers such as a quantity surveyor may be hired to minimise transaction and transformation costs, their fees are likely to amount to a significant percentage of the cost of the building. In many industries and commercial contexts, similar sequences of small but numerous 'transactions' are dealt with within the organisation (by vertical integration rather than by separate contracts). The construction industry steadfastly relies on elaborate systems of contracts and sub-contracts, often incurring high transaction costs 'managed' by professional advisers.

## The interaction of public and private ordering

Transactions associated with title and those associated with use highlight the distinction between private ordering (based on market criteria) and public ordering (based on welfare criteria) of resources. Private ordering is undertaken by the acquisition or disposal of private property through the market mechanism. This implies that the parties to a transaction arrange matters for themselves, to their mutual benefit within a predetermined socio-economic context applying to a particular location. Public ordering relates to the function of the government and other public bodies in ensuring an equitable distribution of resources between relevant stakeholders.

This is achieved by making, implementing and enforcing rules that affect relations between the parties. This enables public authorities to interfere with the free operation of the market in order to achieve greater welfare for the greatest number. However, unless the criteria for such interference are transparent and enjoy adequate public support, public ordering lays itself open to accusations of inefficiency, incompetence and corruption. Notwithstanding these dangers, public authorities can claim to (1) represent a broader constituency than the direct participants in a market transaction; (2) have greater concern for the distribution of the benefits of development within that constituency; (3) have greater recognition of the environmental and social costs of development that are largely ignored in the market price. It is not difficult for planning authorities to claim that they can 'improve' the operation of a highly imperfect market by encouraging and facilitating appropriate development to an appropriate standard, in the most appropriate locations.

Public approvals for the use of land and buildings introduce an additional element of economic uncertainty and extend the timescale for acquisition and disposal transactions that are contingent upon the outcome of public ordering decisions. They seldom satisfy the basic requirements of a common-law contract, yet they have a highly significant bearing on acquisition or disposal transactions, particularly where there is an intention to 'develop' the site. If the criteria upon which public ordering decisions are made lack clarity, uncertainty increases and this, in turn, adversely affects the value of the transaction. Public ordering systems are costly and susceptible to their own inefficiencies – considerations that must be weighed against the inefficiencies of private ordering.

The institutions that apply to the acquisition of a fully performing real estate investment differ from those applying to the exploitation of development potential. In the former case, the rules relating to acquisition of title to the property and the modification of the relationship between the new owner and existing users of the property are of paramount importance. Although the transaction may be prolonged, in particular because of legal formalities, the number of participants is small. Transactions to acquire property rights for development simply represent an early stage in the development process. The price to be paid for the acquisition of title is contingent upon the nature and extent of enhanced use rights that might be unlocked, subject to the approval of a public land-use agency. In such cases it is not unusual for the resolution of enhanced use rights to overshadow the issue of title until the use value can be clarified.

These two categories of real estate transactions highlight the uncertainties associated with the different rules of the game that apply to private ordering and public ordering decisions. In acquiring title, the parties to the transaction (vendor and purchaser) are broadly free to agree whatever bargain they wish. Transactions involving a modification of the use rights attaching to ownership of real estate invariably involve public agencies responsible for planning, organising and controlling land use within the urban environment. In other words, there is a combination of private and public ordering and the final outcome may become clear only after a prolonged period of discussion and negotiation forming part of the transacting process.

Owners may hold the key to development decisions becoming operational, but in most urban environments the use of land is not solely the decision of its owner or user but is constrained by the land-use decisions of governmental agencies. Views differ as to the appropriate balance between public and private ordering. One view is that private ordering through the market mechanism is the most economically efficient means of developing urban areas. A market-sceptic argument views the primary focus of urban development as building communities, without social or environmental cost. This means (1) achieving an equitable distribution of the benefits of development among all relevant stakeholders and (2) ensuring that developers cover the full social and environmental costs generated by the development.

The influence of decisions from public governance bureaux on operational-level transactions is complex, widespread and sometimes inconsistent with the short-term wishes of developers and landowners. Considerations that are applied to permission to develop a site tend to emphasise social and broad economic benefits rather than commercial profitability. They typically focus on the impact of development on communities, the environment and the urban infrastructure. However, there are numerous ways in which this balance can be achieved, based on an understanding that commercial development will release added value.

A more pragmatic view encourages collaborative partnerships between private and public interests. For example, a publicly planned and developed urban infrastructure can provide the capacity and framework into which private development fits, to create the urban environment. 'Private' in this context may include public agencies and organisations working within a private-ordering property rights framework. However, uncertainty is inherent in this 'collaborative' view because collaboration between private entrepreneurs and public agencies is imprecise and the transaction costs are significant.

The issues that generate uncertainty for the landowner or developer concern the amount of added value that can be created, and how it will be 'captured' and distributed to the main stakeholders. In addition to the development team, other stakeholders in this context include:

- The local community seeking some environmental enhancement to offset the environmental or social impact of the development (planning gain);

- Infrastructure providers (e.g. utility companies) and owners (taxpayers or shareholders in the local district or at national level) seeking some financial contribution towards the cost of increasing the capacity of their systems in order to accommodate the additional development.

Property taxes may be related to other issues such as the need for the community to raise revenue, while tax breaks may be used to stimulate policy initiatives such as industrial development.

Because approvals governing the permitted use that gives enhanced value to property rights are not necessarily well integrated with transactions for the acquisition of property rights, they add an additional layer of uncertainty to the outcome of the transaction. The contingent effect of these ancillary approvals introduces substantial uncertainty into the market value for land and buildings that are believed to possess development potential. They play a key role in the transacting process associated with primary transactions such as site acquisition and implementation of development. A transacting period prolonged by obtaining regulatory approvals and consents allows presumptions upon which original terms of the transaction were based to shift, sometimes quite dramatically.

## The capture and distribution of value released by development

The aim of real estate development is ostensibly clear and simple: it is to identify, realise and capture the total value of real estate effectively and efficiently (preferably, without making others materially worse off in the process). In fact, the implications of this aim are neither clear nor simple. To begin with, different stakeholders may hold different values or, prioritise shared values in different ways. The parties to transactions involving the acquisition of property rights that empower development are direct stakeholders. However, those property rights may not include the right to develop, which is often reserved by the State by legislation. In these circumstances, individuals or organisations, other than the direct stakeholders, will participate in the decision to permit changes in use of the land and buildings to which the property rights relate. Although these 'others' are not party to the property rights being transferred, they are indirect stakeholders because they are able to influence the grant or non-grant of development rights.

Direct and indirect stakeholders may agree on the broad constituents of 'total' value but disagree on the ranking of its components. The developer may place financial value first on the list, the planner may put social welfare first and the environmentalist puts environmental value first. Few stakeholders adopt a sophisticated weighting: most prioritise one value as paramount. The others become secondary and may be treated as constraints rather than targets. Conflicts between stakeholder values complicate the transacting process and generate transaction costs.

Reconciling differing perceptions of 'value' and entitlement to its capture lies at the heart of real estate development. Reconciliation is possible if the sum of the perceived value of each participant in the game is less than or equal to the total value in the project. Whether or not it is possible, each stakeholder believes that he or she is entitled to 'their' share. This dilemma can resemble that faced by monkeys grabbing cookies from a jar. If all put their hand in at once, they end up fighting; the jar smashes, resulting in a wasteful mess. If one grabs all the cookies it can't get its hand out of the jar without surrendering some of the cookies. Apes with foresight may agree a 'picking' order; apes with greater foresight may agree, in advance, the number of cookies to which each of them is entitled. Then, of course, they have to have rules about entitlement to participate, as well as the cookie count and a system to prevent cheating. But it is only worth devising rules if the event is more than a one-off occurrence and the prize is sufficiently valuable.

Even if entitlement can be established and enforced, potential value still has to be realised and captured and, as the ancient Greek proverb says, 'there's many a slip between cup and lip'. These are complex issues that stimulate opportunist self-interest, shirking and acrimonious disputes, all of which dissipate potential value as it becomes released. Participants who work hard and openly to build strategies designed to create enhanced value may expect to be entitled to profit from their effort. Meanwhile, others seek opportunist gains arising from better (asymmetric) knowledge about some aspect of a development. The phenomenon of asymmetric information, endemic within the development process, linked to high-value unique assets, provides a fertile source of opportunist gain and is a significant contributor to financial failure in real estate projects.

The task of realising and capturing total value may be aided or frustrated by the various stakeholders. Their involvement is seldom a matter of choice but their respective roles may be collaborative, adversarial or even subversive. Nevertheless, the relationships that link them are important because the outcome of transactions (successful or otherwise) that collectively constitute a project is influenced by the actions and reactions of these other participants. Other than the vendor and purchaser, other stakeholders, who do not hold a legal interest in the property, include those who:

- Possess statutory authority to plan, organise and control land use in the area affected by development;

- Have a general interest in the land to which the property rights apply;

- Will be directly affected by the impact of the development;

- May be indirectly affected by the development.

Not all deserve equal recognition but unravelling these relationships is important in assessing how 'total value' will be realised and distributed. Although the market mechanism re-allocates value through the vendor–purchaser transaction, other institutional mechanisms, such as statutory planning systems, affect the distribution of value among stakeholders.

A project that maximises one form of value at the apparent expense of others may encourage those who consider that the outcome of the project will make them worse off to argue that, because they are adversely affected by it, they have some say in the matter. This happens, for example, with projects such as waste incineration plants where local residents may approve of the use but not the location, giving rise to the NIMBY (not in my back yard) phenomenon. Not all objectors deserve to be heard, and some will be free-riders (people or organisations who benefit from a public good without contributing to the cost of its provision), but distinguishing between valid and invalid opinions may not be simple. Individual voices may be weak but they may lobby for action by more powerful stakeholders such as a land-use authority with statutory power to influence land-use decisions; they may exercise collective action to form a like-minded group that may generate the power to affect the outcome of the decision. For example, the voice of local opinion is a powerful influence on land-use decisions in cities such as Vancouver where public participation in the land-use process is strongly encouraged.

More powerful stakeholders possess authority, granted and supported by the power of the law, to interfere in or contribute to the transacting process. This degree of authority is typically associated with public agencies deriving their authority from legislation. They owe no special responsibility to the transacting parties but are able to influence the financial outcome of the transaction. Transactions between property owners are affected by the impact of public agencies that have an obligation or power to influence resource allocation decisions (normally on the basis of public welfare). This is particularly relevant to real estate where public agencies have the power or duty to approve, modify or reject proposals to develop individual sites. Although the value of a transaction may be contingent on the outcome of public approval for a change of use, it is not unusual for such approvals to be contingent on the provision by the developer of social or environmental enhancement to the locality of a proposed project.

Such quasi-transactions are susceptible to ethical risks ranging from adverse prejudice to outright corruption. Although abuse of the power to issue approvals provides an opportunity for planning approvals to be a 'saleable' commodity, this would not constitute a legitimate economic transaction. Nevertheless, in some sovereignties such practices are considered normal and as important as legal rules at the operational level at which transacting takes place. If local social norms fail to comply with international standards of business, the rules of the game will need to be modified and strengthened by other rules capable of overriding delinquent practices. This may require not only new rules but clear signals that rules will be effectively enforced.

In summary, the task of realising and capturing value is complicated by a multiplicity of stakeholders and rules of the game, which are complex for reasons that include:

- The number and variety of interested parties and stakeholders;

- The diversity of rules and conventions that govern urban development;

- Major discrepancies between formal and informal rules of the game;

- The relative size and importance of transactions;

- The length of time between commencing and concluding transactions and the uncertainty that this generates;

- The relatively infrequent occurrence of real estate transactions in the day-to-day life of most individuals and organisations.

## A transaction-based approach lends itself to institutional analysis

All economic activity is based on a complex interaction between rule regimes (forming a framework of institutions) and institutional arrangements connecting the rule regimes with each transaction. The institutional framework that governs real estate transactions happens to be more complex than most. Douglass North (1990) pointed out that the predictable occurrence of transaction costs that have a significant impact on economic behaviour stimulates the development of 'institutions'. However, institutions are not mutually consistent: some are designed to achieve economic efficiency and are conducive to the participation of a broad range of participants; others are designed to encourage social stability (implying different definitions of efficiency). It is not uncommon for national and local governments to attract 'foreign' investment, yet rules of the game, particularly at the operational level, may discourage participation. The net result is a confusing picture of 'welcome' mixed with hostility and apparent obstruction.

The effects of uncertainty generated by the likelihood of an ambiguous outcome from major transactions are regressive. They cause investors and developers to increase the discount that they apply to investment and development decisions. Uncertainty also causes governments to fear social unrest and instability.

All institutions implicitly favour participants with knowledge of the local rules of the game, which may be formal or informal, in the public domain or known only to a few key players and undisclosed to outside observers or new participants to the game. The purposes of creating rules, conventions or practices in response to predictable transacting costs are complex and not necessarily mutually consistent. The governments of democratic market economies facilitate the operation of markets to allocate resources but regulate markets to encourage competition; they discourage pursuit of monopoly power by participants in the market and redistribute the wealth created by economic behaviour. Governments in some developing economies encourage social stability and distribute the benefits of economic growth by maximising employment in government or quasi-government organisations. Encounters with the inefficient bureaucracy that this generates can be a source of great frustration and cost. Thus, governments may create institutions that are designed to maximise stability or to maximise efficiency and occasionally both. This illustrates an unpredictable interface between politics and economics.

At the transaction level, the parties to transactions may be expected to minimise transaction costs that they see as excessively unproductive and inefficient. It is naive to assume that all participants in a market wish to encourage perfect competition. Established operators may find some pretext to maintain transaction costs. Once established in a market, many if not most prefer to stifle competition and may wish to maintain transaction costs that inhibit the entry of new competitors into the market.

Nevertheless, for reasons of stability or efficiency, most stakeholders in a market economy see benefits in bringing some sense of order to the infinite variety of transaction costs. The rules and conventions of the market facilitate allocation decisions taken by the owners of all types of property wishing to acquire or dispose of their interests. The term 'market economy' is used in a generic way; there are more variations of the market economy than there are sovereignties. However, if market transactions are perceived by government, quasi-government or regulatory agencies as indicating that the market is not functioning in a way that achieves a publicly acceptable allocation of resources, then the market may be considered to have 'failed'. This notion of market 'failure' may be used to justify additional or alternative resource allocation arrangements such as collective choice or public ordering. Within a public ordering system hierarchies of formal institutions enable, control and enforce public ordering arrangements. These, of course, are neither cost-free nor without their own inefficiencies.

Thus, the very institutions that are developed in response to the costs of transacting may generate uncertainty through lack of knowledge or understanding about the rules of the game. In other words, institutions that are relatively unfamiliar may not reduce transaction costs, but simply shift the information deficits from the analysis of supply and demand to analysis of the rules of the game: institutional analysis.

Although boundaries of national, regional or local sovereignty may be the width of a line on a map, the institutional changes that occur as a result of crossing those boundaries can be critical. For example, the meaning of concepts as fundamental as land 'ownership' varies from sovereignty to sovereignty; the mechanisms for and conditions under which use rights can be modified vary from locality to locality; the ways in which and conditions under which buildings are designed, constructed and used varies from place to place. The search for new opportunities forces developers and investors to move into markets in which familiarity is superficial and unreliable. Many property markets remain localised but new, international players and the demands of the global economy have increasing influence on local, regional and national real estate markets.

The differences between international and local real estate activity can be likened to a comparison between international football and 'beach' football. The aim of both games is to score a winning goal. The ball represents potential value (of an investment or development). Possession (of the ball) is essential for scoring a goal (capturing value). The ball is helped on its way by one team but knocked away by the other team (trying to put the ball into a different goal). The rules of the game determine how the game is played and the pitch on which it is played.

*Summary of the key characteristics of beach football:*

- The teams can be unknown to each other;

- Most of the rules are 'flexible', largely determined as the game goes on;

- Refereeing is based on majority consensus and may be tolerant of flagrant infringement of the 'rules';

- The pitch is uneven and non-regulation size;

- There are few spectators;

- The sea may eventually wash the game away.

*Summary of the contrasting characteristics of the international match:*

- The players are selected by careful evaluation of their performance;

- The rules and teams are clearly known and understood;

- The refereeing is impartial, open and professional;

- The pitch is permanent, flat, level and 'regulation' size;

- The match is under the constant scrutiny of spectators;

- The decision of the referee is final and binding on all participants;

- Flagrant infringement of the rules is met with severe sanctions (formal or informal).

Rules of selection mean that the 'beach' player cannot just turn up and join in an international match. These rules do not apply to the beach match. The international player joining the beach match discovers that the game is not what he expected. To his surprise, he ends up on the losing side – let down by his fellow players, the absence of proper refereeing, and the bumpy, sloping, energy-sapping pitch. Of course, he can become expert at beach football but has to learn how to adapt his skills to the new rules of the game and steer his play over the bumpy, sloping pitch.

Real estate transacting in sovereignties where the institutional framework is unfamiliar draws attention to three problematic areas that contribute substantially to the difficulty of achieving success. They consist of figuring out:

- The aim and purpose of the task (which can vary substantially, according to the perspective of its participants);

- The actual rules of the game including local variations. Sometimes the variations are quite obvious, for example, differences in the public control of land-use planning; sometimes they are not, particularly if they result from informal rules understood only by local participants;

- The nature of the transaction environment through which any linked sequence of transactions passes. A highly controlled and regulated environment, with a comprehensive set of rules effectively enforced, presents limited opportunity for opportunist players. A loosely regulated environment provides opportunities for gains and losses.

Underestimating these differences can have a disastrous impact on the expected outcome of real estate investment decisions in unfamiliar territory. Navigating a transacting 'landscape' that becomes more complex and unfamiliar as it crosses national and regional boundaries requires powerful decision-making tools based on careful analysis of the sequence of transactions leading to a successful development.

Confidence in the robustness and effectiveness of basic techniques for evaluating investment and development decisions in a familiar environment may be unjustified when applied as a foreigner in an alien environment. When faced with the challenge of unfamiliar markets, practitioners typically seek a local 'guide' (preferably the closest approximation to their 'double') in the unfamiliar market. The market that is unfamiliar to the foreigner is expected to be familiar to the 'guide', yet the guide may not comprehend the full extent of the client's information deficit sufficiently well to deliver perceptive and relevant guidance. It is difficult to escape the conclusion that failure to understand why and how things work in a particular way and produce the consequential results has a critical bearing on the quality of investment advice.

Unfamiliar markets generate uncertainty arising from imperfect and asymmetrically distributed information and differences in the standards of behaviour and veracity between the parties. This leads to lack of mutual understanding, trust and predictability. Unfamiliar markets that are also institutionally immature are characterised by:

- Weak property rights;

- Preponderance of informal operating procedures and practices;

- Immature national governance (particularly the rule of law and stability of the political system);

- Powerful officials with limited accountability in local government, public utilities and non-governmental organisations;

- Elaborate bureaucratic controls that inhibit entry into the market;

- Anti-competitive practices designed to inhibit entry into the market;

- Costly, informal short cuts providing accelerated access to quick decisions;

- Weakness in the independence, fairness, transparency and accessibility of the administration of justice and the rule of law;

- Ambiguity of interpretation and enforcement of the rules of the game;

- General lack of transparency and accountability.

Presence of these factors indicates that the capture and retention of the value associated with transactions can be uncertain and unprotected.

However, constantly researching the rules of the game for all markets, to the point where the understanding of a 'foreigner' is as good as the understanding of a competitor, is a daunting prospect (see Stigler 1961). A more viable analytical approach is one that facilitates the rapid accumulation of transaction-relevant information in any market. The route to overcoming the uncertainty of transacting in unfamiliar environments lies in mapping the information deficits, and constructing the most efficient and effective route through them and a risk profile of the opportunities and threats that lie ahead. The next chapter indicates a robust and systematic approach to resolving the overwhelming complexity of undertaking investment and development decisions in foreign real estate markets.

# References

Alchian, A.A. (1977) Some Economics of Property Rights. In: *Landmark Papers in Economics, Politics and Law*, pp. 12–34. Edward Elgar, Cheltenham, UK.

Barzel, Y. (1997) *Economic Analysis of Property Rights*, 2nd edn. Cambridge University Press, Cambridge, UK.

Breit, W. & Spencer, R.W. (eds) (1995) *Lives of the Laureates: thirteen Nobel economists*, 3rd edn. MIT Press, Cambridge, MA.

Bromley, D. (1991) *Environment and Economy: Property Rights and Public Policy*. Blackwell, Oxford, UK.

Cheung, S. (1983) The Contractual Nature of the Firm. *Journal of Law and Economics*, **17**, 53–71.

Coase, R.H. (1937) The Nature of the Firm. *Economica*, **4**, 386–405.

Coase, R.H. (1960) The Problem of Social Cost. *Journal of Law and Economics*, **3**, 1–44.

Commons, J.R. (1934) *Institutional Economics: Its Place in Political Economy*. University of Wisconsin Press, Madison, WI.

de Soto, H. (2000) *The Mystery of Capital*. Bantam Press, London.

Kasper, W. & Streit, M.E. (1998) *Institutional Economics*. Edward Elgar, Cheltenham, UK.

*Kensland Realty Ltd* v. *Whaleview Investments Ltd & Anor* (2001) FACV No. 10 of 2001, Hong Kong Court of Final Appeal.

North, D.C. (1990) *Institutions, Institutional Change and Economic Performance.* Cambridge University Press, Cambridge, UK.

North, D.C. (1995) Douglass C. North. In: Breit, W. & Spencer, R.W. (eds) *Lives of the Laureates: thirteen Nobel economists,* 3rd edn. pp. 251–67. MIT Press, Cambridge, MA.

Oakerson, R.J. (1992) Analyzing the Commons: a Framework. In: Bromley, D.W. *et al.* (eds) *Making the Commons Work: Theory, Practice and Policy.* Institute for Contemporary Studies Press, San Francisco, CA.

Oakerson, R.J. & Walker, S.T. (1997) Analyzing Policy Reform and Reforming Policy Analysis. In: Brinkerhoff, D.W. *Policy Studies and Developing Nations, Vol.5: Policy Analysis Concepts and Methods: An Institutional and Implementation Focus,* JAI Press, Greenwich, CT.

Ostrom, E. (1990) *Governing the Commons: the Evolution of Institutions for Collective Action.* Cambridge University Press, Cambridge, UK.

Posner, R.A. (1973) *Economic Analysis of Law.* Little Brown & Co, Boston, MA.

Stigler, G.J. (1961) The Economics of Information. *Journal of Political Economy,* **LXIX** (3), 213–55.

Wallis, J.J. & North, D.C. (1986) Measuring the Transaction Sector of the American Economy, 1870–1970. In: Engerman, S.L. & Gallman, R.E. (eds) *Long-Term Factors in American Economic Growth.* University of Chicago Press, Chicago, IL.

Williamson, O.E. (1975) *Markets and Hierarchies: Analysis and Antitrust Implications.* Free Press, New York.

## Further reading

Eggertsson, T. (1990) *Economic Behaviour and Institutions.* Cambridge University Press, Cambridge, UK.

Furubotn, E.G. & Richter, R. (1998) *Institutions and Economic Theory: the Contribution of the New Institutional Economics.* University of Michigan Press, Ann Arbor, MI.

Liebecap, G. (1989) *Contracting for Property Rights.* Cambridge University Press, Cambridge, UK.

Menard, C. (1997) *Transaction Cost Economics.* Edward Elgar, Cheltenham, UK.

Pitelis, C. (ed.) (1993) *Transaction Costs, Markets and Hierarchies: the Issues.* Blackwell, Oxford, UK.

Williamson, O.E. & Masten, S.E. (eds) (1999) *The Economics of Transaction Costs.* Edward Elgar, Cheltenham, UK.

## Note

1  See *Kensland Realty Ltd* v. *Whaleview Investments Ltd & Anor* (2001) FACV No. 10 of 2001, Hong Kong Court of Final Appeal.

# 2

# Resolving Institutional Uncertainty in International Real Estate Decisions

## William Seabrooke and Paul Kent

## The institutional nature of transactions

Transactions give effect to the transfer of property rights in exchange for the value attaching to them. They take place within economic, social and political structures that are elaborate, dynamic and complex, forming a variety of rule regimes that collectively constitute an institutional framework. Each transaction is the outcome of a transacting process, which is influenced by institutional arrangements. Market transactions take the form of contracts, which are recognised within common-law systems as legitimate institutional vehicles. The terms of the contract are determined partly by considerations that are intrinsic to the transaction and partly by the influence of extrinsic rule regimes.

Transactions do not necessarily take the form of contracts. If they take place within an organisation, their form will be determined by the rules of that organisation (Williamson 1971). Organising transactions by internal, quasi-contractual controls rather than by externally enforceable contracts offers the prospect of lower transaction costs, for example, in relation to the rigour of enforcement. This is particularly relevant where the value of the transaction is low in relation to the transaction costs. 'Firms' attempt to take advantage of savings on transaction costs by internalising relatively minor 'transactions' that contribute to but do not represent the final outcome of economic activity between the organisation and the outside world. For this they rely on internal rather than external control and enforcement mechanisms. This organisational framework has a significant impact on the performance of the 'firm'.

The terms of a transaction reflect the strength and nature of many individual institutional arrangements connecting the transaction to the institutional framework within which it occurs. The relative importance of these individual connections is reflected in the negotiation of the terms of the transaction. The robustness, predictability and transparency of the institutional arrangements that bear on a transaction will influence the trust and confidence with which it is undertaken by the parties and other 'intrinsic' stakeholders, such as financiers.

If, in the event of disputes, the terms of an agreement are intended to be settled or enforced by external adjudication, they should comply with rules of recognition employed by appropriate adjudication bodies such as courts of law. In many of the world's wealthier nations there is a widely held presumption that courts of civil law should maintain an impartial balance of fairness between parties contesting their respective obligations under a contract for the provision of goods or services. However, this presumption is not universally valid: in some jurisdictions the law is seen as an instrument of the State. Thus, the interests of 'the State' may override the interests of individual parties to a dispute. In particular, the effectiveness of the enforcement of court decisions may be dependent on the interests of 'the State'. Consequently, court decisions may be strongly influenced by political considerations (Wang 2001).

Contracts, which are intended to bind the parties to the terms of a transaction, exemplify a common institutional arrangement in institutionally mature market economies. However, in loosely organised and regulated markets or markets in a state of flux, a contractual obligation to one person may be no more than an expression of intent to another. In such cases, the convention of relying on enforceable contracts as the basis for a transaction may be deliberately or unwittingly ignored (Wang 2001). Arrangements under which it is possible for the parties to hold conflicting views of their respective obligations are potentially unstable and unreliable. The resulting uncertainty is exacerbated if adjudication and enforcement mechanisms are biased or ineffective. Weak formal institutional arrangements encourage alternative arrangements that may *appear* informal but which rely on strong personal networks such as the powerful and ubiquitous *guanxi* system in China (Wang 2001). Institutional arrangements that, to 'outsiders', appear vague, ambiguous, poorly communicated and weakly supported by rudimentary enforcement procedures generate high levels of uncertainty for new market entrants.

In some countries, property rights may appear to be robust but are weakened by ambiguity or inconsistency of constitutional support. Arrangements that are opaque, uncertain, accompanied by weak rules of enforcement and applied in an unreliable manner inhibit secure and reliable private ordering behaviour. Sovereignties wishing to encourage international real estate investment in order to develop urban land have a vested interest in adopting institutional arrangements that enable the value of finished developments to be accessible, transferable and 'portable' (i.e. marketable). This is important to investors who are accountable to shareholders or trustees and for whom property rights must be certain, enforceable and transferable.

## Real estate transactions

Devoid of institutional characteristics such as 'ownership', land could hardly function as a market commodity. The immovable nature of land and buildings presents serious commercial shortcomings. They can be overcome by socially recognised rules that make ownership of the exclusive right to the use of land and buildings enforceable yet portable. A market for immovable assets, such as land, is much more limited than a market for portable assets, such as property rights to land. Property rights are institutional arrangements that enable 'value' to be created, captured and transferred by transactions.

Owning the right to exclusive possession of land does not imply unrestricted freedom of use. As a general rule, use rights are limited to existing uses that do not cause a nuisance within the locality. Extending these use rights requires additional approvals that introduce 'extrinsic' stakeholders with no direct ownership interest in the land. Examples include (1) public agencies with the power to grant approval for developing the use of the land and (2) financiers with the ability to supply capital to fund subsequent development.

Transaction arrangements that enable the trading of property rights in land and buildings to occur may also be determined by rules of the market within which the property is traded. Markets represent a framework of 'rules' (sometimes based simply on custom and practice) giving order and recognition to transactions of a comparable type. Real estate transactions of an international nature normally occur in a market setting. (Transactions also occur in barter economies and in planned economies.) Generally, markets are organised in ways that maintain an acceptable and stable level of transaction costs to both buyers and sellers.

Although (real) property rights may be portable and tradable, the location of the land and buildings to which they relate is firmly fixed. Moreover, the physical characteristics of this location are normally of central importance

in real estate transactions. Inevitably, real estate transactions are location-specific and the markets within which they occur reflect this. The
geographic dispersion and fragmentation of real estate markets makes them
less amenable to simple analysis than most other goods and services and
contributes to high transaction costs.

## Analysing rules of the game

> The logic of institutional analysis assumes that individuals make choices
> among alternatives and that these choices are influenced by incentives
> that derive jointly from (1) attributes of the physical world and (2) insti-
> tutional arrangements. Together, the physical world and institutional
> arrangements create a 'decision space' inside which individuals make
> choices.
>
> Oakerson & Walker (1997)

Real estate combines the physical features of land and buildings (notably
its fixed, unique physical location) with the institutional attributes of ownership and use rights (that largely determine its current value), plus other
institutional arrangements that can affect future value. Thus the 'decision
space' that characterises real estate transactions consists of institutional
arrangements that apply to a specific geographic location. Because many
institutional obstacles encumber and obscure the 'decision space' for real
estate transactions, it may be more appropriate to depict this as a 'decision
landscape'. Unfortunately, however, there is no readily available classification of the institutional arrangements for real estate or the transactions that
affect its allocation in a market system.

The institutional framework that governs the operation of discrete areas of
political, social and economic behaviour may be characterised as a 'rulebook'.
But 'rules of the game' extend beyond the rulebook: in particular, they include
the connections between rules and the action of the players. These connections can be characterised as institutional arrangements. When the game
becomes complicated, as it does with real estate transacting, it is important
to distinguish between discrete types of institutional arrangements.

Applying this structure to real estate: the 'game' consists of transaction
sequences within an institutional framework consisting of discrete 'groups'
of rules. Mapping individual rules quickly becomes hopelessly complicated.
The problem can be simplified by creating generic groups representing the
largely formal rules that govern real estate transactions. For example, there

may be numerous rules relating to property rights forming a cohesive group with a distinctive bearing on real estate transactions. If the institutional framework governing individual transactions is stable, the rule 'groups' should be robust and apparent. We refer to these groupings as 'rule regimes', a term coined by Bromley (1991).

We reserve the term 'institutional arrangements' for arrangements that dictate the ways and means by which interactions between rule regimes and transactions take place. They are the sinews connecting transactions with each layer of a multi-layer framework of rule regimes and have a profound influence on transacting behaviour. Institutional arrangements are essential for practical implementation of policy or 'formal' rules. They are also the manifestation of informal and hidden 'rules' that are not evident by scanning the formal rule regimes. This latter category of arrangements presents particular hazards for inexperienced participants because, although some arrangements may be attributable to informal rules of practice, others may be false or misleading, designed simply to take advantage of the ignorance of the inexperienced party.

The approach that we advocate for real estate transactions draws a deliberate distinction between rule regimes, transactions and the institutional arrangements that connect them. It is important to be clear on this point because the institutional arrangements connecting rule regimes to transacting behaviour form a source of great uncertainty for international real estate transactions – particularly because some become apparent only once play commences, at other times remaining largely dormant or latent. In these cases they are easy to overlook in initial analysis of the rules of the game.

## The institutional transformation of land into real estate

Owners of labour or capital must question the wisdom of investing their resources to enhance the capacity of land unless they can reap the benefits of their investment. The first requirement for securing such benefits is to inhibit the free-rider phenomenon associated with open access to land. This can be achieved by physical territorial exclusion but greater social acceptability is achieved by creating rules of exclusive possession, recognised and enforced by society.

Externally enforceable rules that confine access to land (or buildings) to one or more users (i.e. to the exclusion of rival users) for a defined use create property rights for the permitted users. If rights of access to land are restricted to members of a defined group (who have the right to exclude access by others), the land to which those rights apply is usually referred to as common property. In such circumstances, if the sum of individual use rights exceeds the capacity of the land to support the demands capable of being made upon it, short-term exploitation could lead to eventual destruction of the resource, characterised as the 'tragedy of the commons' (Hardin 1968). Owners of common property rights respond to this problem by collective action, organising the exercise of their rights in ways that limit their selfish propensity for opportunist gain in favour of long-term collective benefit, reflecting the principle of Pareto efficiency. Arrangements that enable such mutually beneficial practices to be sustained are called 'collective-choice' arrangements (Kiser & Ostrom 1982; Oakerson 1992).

While common property rights may be adequate for maintaining simple, primary land uses, they have limited value as a market commodity and are inadequate for encouraging the investment of capital required for modern urban development. The ability to release the capital value of property rights, in order to repay or recycle the capital invested in the initial development, highlights the importance of rights to possession and use of land being absolutely exclusive (i.e. capable of being limited to a single entity), and transferable without restriction. This requires rule regimes that support the creation, realisation and capture of value, in particular the right to transfer ownership in exchange for the market value. Transferable rights to exclusive possession of land become a portable and tradable commodity, characterised as private real estate.

As a general rule, the value of land as a tradable commodity is proportional to: the range and intensity of use; duration of entitlement to the benefits of use; freedom to transfer entitlement, wholly or partially; rigour and consistency of enforcement of entitlements. Conversely, it is inversely proportional to limitations on: use; freedom to transfer entitlement; rigour and consistency of enforcement. The most powerful combination is represented by rights that are perpetual, unrestricted, transferable and rigorously enforced by the governance agencies of society. Thus, private real estate is created by powerful rule combinations protecting exclusive, individual, transferable ownership.

The premium placed on enforceable rights to exclusive possession in capitalist market economies is reflected in the willingness of financial institutions to lend money against its value, particularly to fund its further development. Property rights that distinguish private real property from lesser forms of shared possession are:

- Enforceable exclusive possession;

- Portability (enforceable entitlement to rights to possession, use and transfer irrespective of the location of the owner).

The implications of these differences are extensive. For example, they facilitate the attachment of a much higher quantum of value by securing additional use rights. This draws in other rule regimes if enhancing the value of urban land is contingent upon the rules for achieving change of use.

## Incorporating institutional arrangements into real estate transactions

Real estate transactions do not arise fully formed; they are usually made up of a two-stage process consisting of:

(1) Formation (which leads to agreement of the terms of the transaction, usually in the form of a contract);

(2) Completion of the contract (at which point the parties demonstrate their full compliance with the terms of the transaction).

'Formation' may start very tentatively, with little more than an inclination on the part of potential parties to explore the possibility that a transaction may be capable of being created. It ends with an enforceable agreement to an exchange of value.

A fully formed real estate transaction addresses and combines (1) the physical characteristics of land and buildings and (2) the institutional arrangements that largely determine the terms of the transaction. The part played by the physical characteristics of the land and buildings in accommodating one or more uses is a major factor in the formation of a transaction that transfers ownership. The most important physical characteristics of urban land are spatial (location, area, boundary layout, topography). The initial formation stage of a transaction tends to focus, therefore, on the economic behaviour that can be anticipated in a particular arrangement of space at a particular location. Typically, assumptions are made about institutional arrangements that will affect the terms of the transaction. Provided that the physical considerations relating to the potential transaction are consistent with the expectations of the relevant parties, institutional arrangements tend to be given secondary consideration. Despite this and despite the fact that they may be encountered at a relatively late stage in the formation of a transaction, they have a profound effect on the value of the real estate to which they relate (see chapter 3).

Proper investigation and negotiation of institutional arrangements is complicated by the fact that the rule regimes forming the institutional frameworks that govern real estate transactions are not neat, orderly and homogeneous. They can be informal, disorganised, concealed, contingent (upon events or circumstances), susceptible to obsolescence, inconsistent and ambiguous. The 'impact boundaries' of rule regimes are often fuzzy and overlapping. In summary, individual rule regimes have differential effects on different transactions in different locations.

In practice, proponents of real estate transactions (and their advisers) rely heavily on familiarity with the 'normal' pattern of institutional arrangements prevailing in a particular location. If and when they venture beyond their area of professional familiarity, the transaction costs associated with investigating an unfamiliar pattern of institutional arrangements quickly escalate. The net effect of these issues generates uncertainty about the future reliability of the flow of benefits upon which the 'value' (the nucleus of real estate transactions) is based.

The number of variables that any analyst can simultaneously and effectively apply to the evaluation of a complex problem is limited. As problems increase in number and complexity, analysts need to increase the efficiency of their search for relevant information, which can result in them becoming increasingly selective. In order to maintain an understanding of the effects of the institutional dynamics of the markets in which they operate that is sufficiently detailed yet manageable, practitioners 'frame' their search for information according to that which they consider most relevant.

The ability to recognise which institutional arrangements have a significant impact on any given transaction is critical to success in determining the terms of any real estate transaction. Market analysts frame their search for this information according to their judgement of its relevance to (1) their general understanding of the market and (2) specific transactions. Familiarity reveals patterns of interaction between transactions sharing similar characteristics (such as similar properties with similar ownership types, in similar locations) and the rule regimes that have significant impact on them.

This topical knowledge is gained largely by heuristic methods based on the adage 'fool me once; shame on you: fool me twice; shame on me'. This involves observing and evaluating the trial-and-error results of practical experience and sharing similar experience from other practitioners to discover which factors have a significant bearing on transactions in a given market. Heuristic methods for framing and evaluating the uncertainties associated with the application and enforcement of the arrangements of the market are, by nature, market-specific. However, they often lack transparency because, despite a short 'shelf-life', high-quality confidential information is thought to have commercial value. They are also susceptible to the errors associated with popular inference.

Heuristic knowledge relies on familiarity. In unfamiliar markets it becomes unreliable. 'Foreigners', outside the local quasi-social networks on which local participants rely, lack the social and cultural cues and connections that enable 'locals' to structure and apply their heuristic understanding. For example, information concerning the existence of relevant arrangements, or the degree of discretion available in the application and enforcement of the 'rules', may be inaccessible. This knowledge deficit results in adverse asymmetry of information relating to a transaction and severely reduces the reliability of the framing process. This is a particular handicap when facing international (cross-border) transactions.

In attempting to overcome this disadvantage, 'foreigners' may be tempted to assume that the interaction between institutional arrangements and the transactions that take place should conform to a rationality that they associate with familiar markets. This might be plausible if the purpose of institutional arrangements was simply to minimise the transaction costs of participation in the market, but this is an extravagant assumption. Particularly in immature or developing economies, institutional arrangements reflect more locally relevant economic objectives such as social stability rather than economic efficiency. It is hardly surprising, therefore, that the nature, purpose and philosophy of institutional arrangements can be confusing to 'foreign' participants in a market. Consequently, there is a need to find appropriate and systematic ways of establishing the relevant impact of the institutional arrangements that apply to a specific transaction.

This is particularly significant with regard to:

(1)  Quality of title and use rights (see chapter 3);

(2)  Potential use rights;

(3)  Financial arrangements for the transaction;

(4)  The operation and regulation of the market;

(5)  The nature of the business environment.

Heuristic approaches based on experience of a familiar market provide an unreliable foundation for identifying 'action pathways' in unfamiliar markets. The uncertainty produced by an appearance of chaos and lack of transparency diminishes competitiveness and should be overcome if investment decisions are to be made in a rational manner.

## Boundaries of self-determination

Notwithstanding the relative freedom of participants in open-market transactions to determine the terms of private ordering transactions, they are subject to extrinsic influences such as settled practices of the market, the law of the land, and the influence of other stakeholders. In the case of real estate transactions, the transacting process takes place within the influence of numerous rule regimes, which can be thought of as 'orbiting' each transaction. Some rule regimes, such as the rule of law, are so powerful that their influence is felt on every transaction; others, such as land-use policy, influence some transactions but not others.

Even the most open of markets operates according to settled practices, which can have a close and direct bearing on the formation of individual transactions in that market. Such arrangements are largely of the market's making, to facilitate smooth and efficient exchanges of value transacted in that particular market. They are designed to maintain stability and certainty and sometimes to reduce transaction costs. Although these rules may occasionally be considered as a constraint on the transacting process, they are ostensibly intended to be in the best interests of all participants in that market. They are essentially operational in nature.

Other rule regimes are designed to safeguard wider categories of public welfare against adverse impacts resulting from short-term, profit-maximising transactions. These instruments of policy circulate around broad categories of social behaviour, including (sometimes coincidentally) real estate transacting. They may appear largely reactive, affecting a transaction only if its particular circumstances trigger a reaction, such as land-use control or taxation provisions. They may also have a proactive function in establishing incentives to encourage particular outcomes from the transacting process. Whereas market rules may be of the market for the market, these broader rule regimes may be considered of a constituency for a constituency. They are, in other words, an extension of public governance.

Rule regimes do not have equal impact on all transactions. It is an oversimplification to assume that a transaction will lie neatly at the centre of the orbit of every rule regime – some orbits will pass close to the transaction, others will be remote with less direct significance. Several key questions arise for any given transaction:

- Which rule regimes apply?

- What is the relative influence or impact of a given rule regime?

- What is the nature of the institutional arrangements that arise from relevant rule regimes?

- To what extent should they be reflected in the terms of the transaction?

Answers to these questions will determine the form, nature and strength of the institutional arrangements that enable players to exploit opportunity or guard against threats and uncertainties. It is difficult to map or visualise all the institutional interactions that could occur for a complex transaction. The picture would be at least three-dimensional and quite irregular. Figure 2.1 (the juxtaposition of a transaction within its institutional context) attempts to depict a regular form of the institutional framework that might contain and yet interact with a particular transaction. Figure 2.1 is three-dimensional, indicating the orbits of rule regimes around the transacting decision space. (The figure shows the orbits with simple circular orbits: this is figurative. In practice the orbits may sometimes come very close to the transaction; at other times they may be remote from it.)

**Fig. 2.1**   The juxtaposition of a transaction within its institutional context.
T = transaction decision space.

In stable environments, institutional arrangements should appear to be in relative harmony, with conflicts being relatively predictable. In unstable environments, the institutional arrangements are likely to be out of harmony, creating conflict, ambiguity and uncertainty. In unfamiliar markets, the orbits encircling each transaction may at first sight seem chaotic and impenetrable. 'Foreign' participants cannot rely on familiarity to reveal patterns of interaction.

The orbits that the rule regimes describe around a transaction constitute a 'zone' within which those rule regimes are arranged. For most practical purposes, the rule regimes forming the constitutional zone form the outer boundaries of self-determination. They have the potential to affect all transactions but, in practice, are more likely to have a significant impact only in particular circumstances. For example, legal systems indicate the power of governments to create and enforce powerful institutional arrangements. These overarching (constitutional) rules form the boundaries of self-determination and freedom of action. They include:

- Fundamental statements of law, policy and political responsibility within a national jurisdiction;

- Legislative rules determining the rights and duties of citizens and organisations in relation to individuals, society and the State.

Some policies, such as land-use policy, may be expressed in legislation but lack sufficient specificity to enable constitutional policy to be interpreted in sufficient detail to be applied effectively and efficiently at the operational level. Furthermore, the capacity for avoidance, evasion or misinterpretation is great. To bridge the gap between constitutional rules and the operational behaviour of owners and users of real estate, an intermediate tier of rule-making and rule-interpreting is necessary. Implementation of 'constitutional' rules is largely delegated to local 'governance' agencies. They plan what are perceived to be durable combinations of resources in a coordinated way and function within a distinct 'governance zone' of rule regimes. They rely on authority from the constitutional zone to interpret constitutionally derived 'rules' and to generate policies and implementation strategies in order to influence the manner in which private property is used.

Complex societies exhibit second, and sometimes third, tiers of local governance between the constitutional and operational zones. The tiers include:

- The executive branches of national government;

- The courts;

- Local government agencies;

- Other public bodies.

In stable open market democracies, their powers and accountability should be transparent. Unless they are essentially an instrument of the State, they should be accountable to their constituency for the degree of discretion associated with the exercise of their powers. This includes devolved powers for making and implementing policy in their area of authority and responsibility. These imperative conditions may be deficient in institutionally immature sovereignties.

Without relying on the ownership of property rights, governance agencies are able to affect the behaviour of owners of real estate, by manipulating their inclination to prioritise their own private utility over incompatible social welfare. They are able to influence, directly, the value of property rights by their public ordering decisions using many policy measures including:

- Land-use zoning;

- Development control;

- Building codes;

- Provision and maintenance of public infrastructure, e.g. communications, transport, power supply, water supply, sanitation.

In common with many areas of national policy, land-use policy is hierarchical in the sense that it is determined within the constitutional zone, developed and applied within the governance zone, and acted upon (or not) within the operational zone by owners of use rights in accordance with market priorities. In other words, transacting behaviour is conducted in the 'shadow' of the rules (see Mnookin & Kornhauser 1979).

In property-owning democracies, public policy-makers are reluctant to resort to compulsory acquisition (of the ownership of private property) in order to implement their policies. This significantly inhibits their ability to act directly in transforming the use of land, particularly for commercial purposes. Instead, they rely on their power to affect economic incentives that motivate real estate owners. On the other hand, the reluctance of private landowners to assume responsibility for the social and environmental costs of using land provides public policy-makers with justification to exercise substantial public control over private ordering decisions. Thus, public control of land-use and private control of the right to develop land are locked together in a complex relationship. Those who engage in real estate transactions may be rule-makers at the operational level, but rule-takers in relation to the governance and constitutional rule regimes.

## Classifying institutional arrangements

Institutional economists have developed analytical frameworks for examining the institutional arrangements derived from the collective action of the owners of common property rights to avoid the 'tragedy of the commons' identified by Hardin (1968). Kiser and Ostrom (1982) refer to three distinct institutional levels, which they identify as 'operational', 'collective choice' and 'constitutional'. The structure suggested by Oakerson and Walker (1997) substitutes 'governance' for 'collective choice'. This includes the element of self-governance implicit in collective choice behaviour but enables a broader notion of extrinsic governance to be introduced. The three levels respectively consist of rule configurations (regimes) that can be broadly classified as operational, governance or constitutional in nature. They are arranged in a hierarchical structure, with governance arrangements, which form the central element of their analysis, sandwiched between constitutional arrangements at the 'top' and operational arrangements at the 'bottom'.

A similar taxonomy is broadly applicable to the analysis of transacting behaviour involving private property rights. However, the rule regimes and institutional arrangements of the constitutional and governance levels do not simply bear down on the operational level but interact with it in more complex ways. They create a public ordering context within which private ordering decisions occur. Relationships between rule regimes and the 'transaction decision space' are manifested in the form of institutional arrangements that reflect the impact of a rule regime on the transaction. They are reflected in market transactions, particularly real estate transactions.

In order to understand real estate transactions involving the acquisition or disposal of private property rights (i.e. private ordering) we have previously advocated the adoption of a transaction-centric analysis, in which a transaction is the catalyst for and a reflection of institutional dynamics. Real estate transactions occurring within an open market environment can generate complex institutional interactions:

(1)  Within the practices of the operational zone (which largely dictate how the value released in the transacting process can be captured); and

(2)  Between the operational zone and constraints imposed by constitutional and governance rule regimes.

In unfamiliar markets, the identities of the rule regimes that are relevant to any given transaction are not immediately self-evident. They are brought into focus by the commencement of the transacting process, which, sooner or later, brings to light those rule regimes that have some influence on the transfer of value under consideration. In familiar markets the existence and relevance of rule regimes are predicted in advance of a transaction. In unfamiliar markets, these matters do not become apparent as soon as the transacting process commences; they become evident as it progresses, preferably sooner rather than later.

For the analysis of private ordering transactions, the hierarchical structure associated with the analysis of common property rights is less appropriate than a framework consisting of concentric zones of rule regimes centred on the transaction. In this model of reality, rule regimes 'orbit' transactions to which they are relevant. Each rule regime remains essentially 'constitutional', 'governance', or 'operational' in nature and can be located within one of the three discrete 'zones' corresponding to this classification. The terms of an exchange of value are strongly influenced by the institutional arrangements that connect the transaction to the 'orbiting' rule regimes. The rule regimes define the (formal) institutional framework within which the transacting process occurs.

### The operational zone

Rule regimes that have the most positive and intimate impacts on individual transactions are those that facilitate and organise transactions within a market. They comprise an inner set of orbits. A distinguishing characteristic of the operational zone surrounding market transactions is the freedom of sellers and buyers to generate and retain the benefits from private ordering transactions.

Many of the rule regimes constituting the 'operational zone' appear to be informal, although the effect of the institutional arrangements to which they give rise may appear formal. The existence of 'hidden' rule regimes may become apparent only as institutional arrangements feed their effect into a transaction. For example, organisations that have some form of market dominance may impose a strong influence on the terms of a transaction, often expressed as a formal contract. In the UK market for prime commercial property, the dominance of financial institutions as landlords of the majority of such properties enables them to exert strong influence on the terms of leases. This is 'settled practice' creating an operational rule.

Wherever possible, the operational orbits remain independent of the rule regimes of the constitutional and governance zones. If, however, operational 'rules' are allowed to hinder the entry of new participants into the market, they inhibit freedom to compete in the market. In institutionally mature markets the persistence of such restraints stemming from settled practice becomes a target for investigation and external regulation imposed from governance rule regimes. In this case, operational 'rules' may be required to adapt to meet the compliance requirements of such regulation.

Further interaction between the transacting process and constitutional or governance rule regimes occurs if the value contained within a transaction is contingent upon public permissions or compliance with protocols. Operational compliance may generate additional costs, including transaction costs, which may have the effect of discouraging equivalent transactions in an unregulated environment. Institutional arrangements resulting from extrinsic regulation that is over-complicated will encourage market participants to seek informal short cuts in order to avoid the transaction costs of excessive or unaccountable bureaucracy.

Real estate transactions dispel any expectation that market transactions are relatively free from the influence of extrinsic institutional arrangements. The importance of clearly documented, enforceable property rights has already been touched upon and is developed further in chapter 3, but it is worth restating the importance that international investors attach to the guarantee of rights to exclusive possession and exclusive use. In common-law systems this can be gauged by the strength of protection afforded by the rule of law to real property rights. The only credible alternative to confidence in the rule of law is a guarantee of recognition by the State in the form of registered property rights. Weaker forms of property rights may be satisfactory for local transactions in the 'grey' or 'black' economy found in every urban society (de Soto 2000) but they are inadequate for international transactions.

Freedom to acquire or dispose of property rights is balanced, in the case of real estate transactions, by obligations of 'ownership'. Thus, property rights may bestow entitlement to the exclusive exercise of an existing use but not the right to inflict the impact of that use on other stakeholders. In some countries there may be an obligation on owners to assume responsibility for the impact of previous uses. In any sovereignty, the use and development of land may precipitate a raft of 'latent' obligations. For example, in countries such as the UK or the US the owner or occupier of sites that have supported industrial uses in the past are liable for the effects of previous contamination of the site. In China, developers are responsible for what is referred to as 'site formation', which can consist of many items that international investors may not expect, including the rehousing of previous occupants of the site, and payment of indeterminate costs for connections to the urban infrastructure, which may entail enhancement of basic infrastructure capacity such as upgrading the power-generating capacity in exchange for connecting to the power system.

The rules of the game within the operational zone can differ dramatically from one market to another. Operational issues that must be addressed if a developer wishes to qualify as a participant in the development 'game' include:

- 'Ownership', particularly the extent to which the rules bestow enforceable exclusive possession. It is not uncommon for foreign investors to believe that they have acquired exclusive possession of a development site only to discover that there is a major defect in the title. For example, the vendor may not own what the purchaser thought that they were buying, or there might be restrictions on the exercise of property rights, such as a restraint on alienation (see the 'Carfax Developments' case study).

- Right to occupy a development site or building that is 'owned'. It is not uncommon in many developing markets to discover that ownership of a site or building does not carry an automatic right to possession – existing occupants may have to be rehoused at the 'owner's' expense.

- Right to use (a site or building), for example, in China ownership of the site does not bestow an automatic right to build or operate a building without a multitude of contingent consents and approvals from public authorities.

- Obligations of ownership.

A particular example of a rule regime within the operational zone that is ubiquitous but often overlooked concerns the conduct of business and commerce. This is best illustrated by an example.

The case of Landline Investments

Mr Lee, an Australian developer, discovers that land on an island close to the coast of Tasmania has been offered for sale by the receivers of the logging company that owned it before going into liquidation. He believes that the land would be suitable for development as a leisure resort and forms Landline Investments Ltd as a vehicle for the development. He is encouraged to pursue his plans by the chief executive of the local Economic Development Office, Mr Brown.

Mr Lee estimates that the revenue generated by selling the standing timber will be sufficient to cover the cost of purchasing the site so that the net cost to him should be nil. However, the best price that he can negotiate for the timber proves to be insufficient to cover the purchase price of the land, so he has to resort to seeking funding from a merchant bank and arranges to meet Mr Handel, a director of the merchant bank. Mr Brown is also present at the meeting. He has no direct financial interest in the project but has agreed to act as agent for Landline. Mr Brown informs Mr Handel about the proposed plans and says that the information should be treated in confidence.

The merchant bank offers its services subject to a fee to be paid on signing a contract for services with Landline Investments Ltd. When Mr Lee sees the terms of the contract, he decides that they are unacceptable and no contract is signed. Having received no reply, the merchant bank notifies Mr Brown that it is withdrawing its offer to act and subsequently provides its services to another company which eventually acquires the land.

The supply of information about the project clearly made Mr Lee and Landline vulnerable to disclosure of project details to competitors. In the absence of any contract with the merchant bank, they were implicitly relying upon institutional arrangements deriving from operational-level rule regimes of banking practice rather than governance-level rules for enforcement of contracts. Landline seems to have assumed that once a financial adviser receives information about a proposed transaction, no action that is adverse to the client's interest could be taken at any time without the client's consent. They got it wrong. They misunderstood the informal rules of commercial negotiation between a client and a merchant bank in this sovereignty.

The uncertainty of the circumstances and the need for a comprehensive search for information is exemplified by a court case on broadly similar facts. In *Maclean* v. *Arklow Investments Ltd* [1998] 2 NZLR 680 and *Arklow Investments Ltd.* v. *Maclean* [2000] 1 WLR 594 (PC), the potential purchaser unsuccessfully sought compensation in reliance upon formal legal rule regimes from the law of torts and the law of equity. Both the New Zealand Court of Appeal and the Privy Council decided against him, but for different reasons.

Private ordering transactions are undertaken 'in the shadow of' constitutional and governance rule regimes.

### The constitutional zone

For most practical purposes, the constitutional zone rule regimes define the ultimate rules and boundaries of acceptable economic behaviour. They represent national laws and policies and create an institutional 'perimeter fence' representing the most powerful level of institutional authority. Although some institutional arrangements originating from constitutional rule regimes may be intended to facilitate rather than inhibit economic activity, greater emphasis tends to be placed on the extent to which they constrain and limit the potential value of market transactions.

The constitutional zone should not be confused with 'the State', which represents the identity of its sovereignty, incorporating the concept of 'nationhood' and ultimate 'ownership' of the territory of the nation. This may be largely symbolic, as in the case of England and Wales, but in some countries, ownership of real estate (and, therefore, the power to transfer ownership) is restricted. In countries adopting a state leasehold system, state ownership may be more than a simple technical issue. There can be a direct and often ambiguous link between the operational and constitutional levels. For example, Hong Kong adopts a leasehold system in which the government, on behalf of the State, maintains a more or less active role as the head landlord.

Apart from taxation the impact on transacting of rule regimes within the constitutional zone is more likely to be general than specific. For example, the rule of law may operate in a way that is unfamiliar to the appraiser. (This may include the general approach to civil disputes, standards of enforcement of the rule of law, accessibility to the courts, and standards of impartiality exercised by the courts.) In these circumstances, the general implications may apply to all transactions.

More specifically, constitutional rules governing property rights will provide an indication of the robustness of the property rights system, the clarity of the distinction between ownership rights and use rights, and the general safeguards available to property owners. Specific land-use and development policies and disputes relating to a particular transaction are normally resolved within governance rather than constitutional zones unless they carry national significance. The rigor and consistency with which constitutional and governance rules are enforced may be as significant as the rules themselves.

### The governance zone

In large, plural societies, constitutional rules expressing national policy tend to be broad-brush in nature. In order to allow for local interpretation and implementation, constitutional rules establish second or tertiary tiers of governance, including:

(1)  Local government agencies with a high degree of independence from the national government;

(2)  Other executive agencies with local responsibilities for implementing government policy.

This distinct area of institutional authority lying between the constitutional and operational zones corresponds to Oakerson's 'governance' level.

There can be extensive interaction between constitutional and governance rule regimes, particularly if a governance organisation possesses rule-making powers within its delegated authority. Interaction between governance and operational rule regimes can be extensive but, as a general rule, the governance rule regimes usually lack the ultimate power of implementation held by the owners of property rights, relying instead on power to manipulate incentives, sanctions and penalties. (Bodies or agencies within the constitutional or governance zones may possess authority to participate in market transactions by the acquisition of private property rights.) The organisational structure of national or local government agencies has a significant bearing on how rule arrangements are implemented and, therefore, the impact that they may have on transactions.

Organising land use at the local level exemplifies an area of responsibility delegated from constitutional to governance rule regimes. Land use is typically determined in principle and in detail by local government agents (officers and elected or nominated representatives charged with this responsibility). Transactions involving changes in the nature or intensity of the permitted use of real estate (development) set in motion a chain of events in which the governance zone, in particular, has a direct influence. Furthermore, the generation of revenue or added value from real estate sets in motion a set of institutional interactions relating to the sharing and capture of value between the owner of the relevant private property rights (e.g. in the form of profit) and the public sector (e.g. in the form of planning gain).

In their own respective ways, the constitutional and governance zones have substantial power to influence the size and distribution of the benefits that flow from the utilisation of land. The rule regimes within these zones and the institutional arrangements connecting them to market transactions should be clear and stable and enforced in a manner that is rigorous, impartial and just.

By and large, participants at the operational level are reluctant to take an active role in modifying the rules of the game determined by the constitutional or governance zones. But for large and complex transactions, they may seek ways of simplifying the process and reducing transaction costs inherent in the interaction between the operational and constitutional/governance rule regimes by using informal avenues of influence. These may also have a distinct institutional form; in China, for example, the use of informal connections (known as *guanxi*) has become institutionalised. Institutional arrangements that enjoy widespread local recognition yet appear to have little or no connection to formal rule regimes represent a major barrier to the entry of new market players and the long-term efficiency of the market.

## A scoping template for 'mapping' the institutional 'landscape' within which a real estate transaction takes shape

For the purposes of a transaction-centric analysis, it is appropriate to consider the rule regimes typically relevant to a transaction (see Table 2.1). The majority of rule regimes are capable of being arranged in three concentric zones according to whether they are essentially constitutional, governance or operational in nature. This gives an indication of the nature of the rule regimes that generate the institutional arrangements that are incorporated into the transacting process. Figure 2.2 represents a two-dimensional cross-section through Fig. 2.1 (see page 45). It also represents a 'scoping' template for identifying and evaluating formal rule regimes that might be considered typically relevant to the majority of real estate transactions. But this is not a one-size-fits-all template: the precise identity and composition of the rule regimes that are relevant to a given transaction will vary from sovereignty to sovereignty and according to circumstances.

The impact of any rule regime depends on its power to invoke institutional arrangements. Sometimes, this power is ubiquitous, for example, the

**Table 2.1**   Issues, framed by formal rule regimes, considered typically relevant to real estate transactions (tabulated according to the institutional zone from which they originate).

| Constitutional rule regimes | Governance rule regimes | Operational rule regimes |
| --- | --- | --- |
| Rule of/by law | Enforcement | Contractual obligations |
| Property rights | Registration of ownership | Security/duration of ownership |
| Land use policy | Land-use planning and control | Use rights |
| Environmental regulation | Environmental control | Ownership restrictions |
| Delegation of governance | Building regulation | Financial obligations |
| Market regulation | Governance structure | Business environment |
| Fiscal policy | | |
| Building codes | | |

*Note:* Political environments (at constitutional and governance levels) are not shown because their 'formal' rule regimes seldom have a direct impact on real estate transactions. The formal nature of the political system may indicate a propensity for or against political stability which, in turn, may indicate a propensity for or against the operation of 'informal' rules and will determine the nature of the institutional arrangements that affect a transaction. On the other hand, the business environment *is* shown as one of the operational rule regimes because it can normally be defined by rules of settled practice.

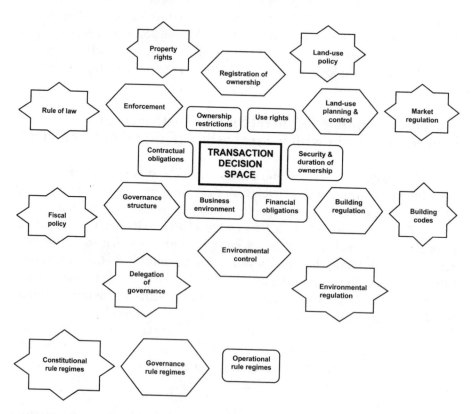

**Fig. 2.2**   Seabrooke–Kent scoping template. The 'periscope' template for 'scoping' the institutional 'landscape' surrounding real estate transactions in order to identify critical institutional uncertainties.

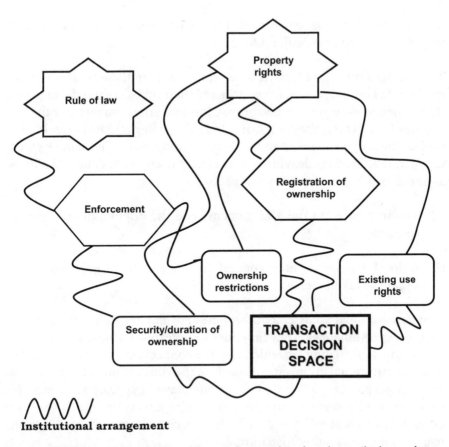

**Fig. 2.3** The 'telescope' application of the scoping template, focusing on the issue of property rights, and indicating institutional arrangements connecting relevant rule regimes with the transaction. (In this context, 'relevant' means 'having a direct impact on the value upon which the transaction is based'). *Notes:* (1) The constitutional-level support of the rule of law is strongly connected to the recognition of property rights. This connection manifests itself in institutional arrangements linking the rule regime relating to property rights with the rule regime relating to the rule of law. (2) Other institutional arrangements connect the rule regime relating to property rights to other regimes at the governance level relating, for example, to rules relating to registration of ownership, other legal interests and enforcement of property rights. (3) Getting closer to the transaction, the property rights rule regime directly affects the operational rules and practices relating to obligations of ownership, use rights, and the security/duration of ownership. (4) All the institutional arrangements that arise as a result of the rule regimes within the constitutional, governance and operational 'zones' must be taken into account in the formation of the transaction decision.

constitutional rule of law, operating through governance mechanisms to influence operational practices; in other cases, the power is more specific, for example, the rules relating to property rights bring constitutional rule regimes directly into the transacting process (see Fig. 2.3). The influence of rule regimes is manifested in the arrangements that connect them to a transaction and are taken into account in the transacting process. Some of these institutional arrangements are routine; but others have a critical impact on the outcome of a transaction because of the particular circumstances linking the transaction to a particular rule regime.

This can be a most problematic area for investors in unfamiliar real estate markets. In familiar markets, investors and their advisers should understand the connections between relevant institutional arrangements and the rule regimes from which they originate. Indeed, greater attention tends to be paid to the arrangements than to the originating rules. The same happens in unfamiliar markets, leaving the 'foreigner' open to the danger of adverse asymmetric information in two respects:

(1)  The link between the arrangements and the originating rule may be spurious;

(2)  A local transactee may conceal 'inconvenient' arrangements that should be taken into account.

Some institutional arrangements become apparent only when the transacting process commences. They may, for example, result from a discretionary element in a rule regime (in which case the connection can be made). Sometimes, institutional arrangements such as the convention of long leases on commercial property in the City of London may not appear to be connected to a formal rule regime. However, their significance indicates the clear existence of a latent rule regime, which is concealed largely because the rule regime is informal rather than formal.

The scoping template facilitates a systematic review of the factors affecting complex transactions in any jurisdiction or market. Its primary function is to identify and highlight connections between a transaction and rule regimes relevant to that transaction. The connections that are most relevant are the institutional arrangements that have a critical impact on the transacting process, whether or not they are formally reflected in documentation of the transaction itself. (In this context, 'relevant' means 'having a direct impact on the value upon which the transaction is based'). At this stage of analysis the 'transacting process' may be characterised as the development of 'action pathways' leading to the decision to commit to a transaction. The development of action pathways is illustrated in the 'Carfax Developments' case study below.

The template relies on a transaction to bring to light the many informal arrangements and rule regimes that remain hidden or obscure until a transaction brings them into focus. Its primary purposes are to identify:

- Action pathways in unfamiliar market environments that are reasoned, informed and appropriate;

- The critical institutional uncertainties associated with transactions in an unfamiliar sovereignty.

The template

- Is centred on a proposed transaction.

- Presents an analytical tool for investigating institutional structures and arrangements that have a significant effect on the outcome of real estate transactions in any market.

- Alerts appraisers to the significance of critical institutional arrangements that affect the transaction but appear to have little or no connection to an obvious rule regime.

It provides:

- An alternative to location-sensitive heuristic approaches that become unreliable in unfamiliar institutional settings;

- A structured approach for navigating the institutional landscape within which real estate transactions take place in any jurisdiction;

- A foundation for asking the right questions to identify critical institutional uncertainties: the first step in finding the right answers.

It enables 'foreigners' to:

- Reconfigure their own experience and structure their search for transaction-relevant information within a generic institutional framework;

- Identify critical differences between the pattern of threats posed by a new institutional environment and familiar comparable environments;

- Identify and investigate latent threats arising from unfamiliar aspects of the 'rules of the game'.

The template identifies and 'maps' major rule regimes that represent landmarks in an institutional 'landscape'. The relative significance of landmarks in a 360° landscape depends upon the position and orientation of the viewer. Similarly, the relative significance of rule regimes depends on the nature of the transaction. The template provides an aid to scoping and testing, centred on a proposed transaction in an unfamiliar investment 'landscape'. It enables the evaluator of a transaction to undertake a systematic search and analysis of the institutional arrangements that have a significant effect on the outcome of the transaction. In so doing it provides the evaluator with a more coherent basis for evaluating the critical uncertainty associated with that transaction. Its application as a template for testing will already have a focus – an investment proposal. The viability of the proposal can be tested by using the template as a structured checklist. Both applications are based on a structured search for information.

The scoping function becomes particularly relevant in the assessment of development decisions that are intended to unlock and capture latent value. The transformation process of development gives rise to a 'value trail' – starting with identification, passing through an institutional 'landscape', and leading to eventual capture. The template enables this 'landscape' to be investigated in a systematic manner. Mapping the value trail enables 'action pathways' to be charted. 'Action pathways' consist of sequences of transactions designed to achieve the release and capture of latent value, responding to the many opportunities for leakage or evaporation of the value upon which a development or investment proposal is based.

The scoping template should encourage objective investigation of latent threats, adopting the cautionary principle that latent opportunities may be illusory and that latent weaknesses may be the tip of an iceberg. Given sufficiently specific requirements, the template can also be used for testing the assumptions and information on which viability of a proposal is based.

The information upon which the template is based can be adapted for the purpose of general evaluation of the institutional characteristics of a particular market. Table 2.2 identifies potential risk factors, adding information relating to the probability of occurrence, the frequency of occurrence and the probable consequences of occurrence (i.e. degree of impact). Combining these factors heuristically enables the appraiser to develop a systematic assessment of the institutional risk associated with that market.

Heuristic judgements are often based on data that is not amenable to rigorous, statistical analysis. However, in recent years analytical techniques have been developed that enable relatively subjective and limited data relating to a particular set of circumstances to be 'mapped' or charted in order to illustrate comparisons, patterns and trends in data. For example, 'radar charts' were developed by the SkyMark Corporation in the late 1990s, to investigate several

**Table 2.2** A market scorecard for evaluating the institutional parameters of a particular market.

| Critical rule regimes | Probability of unexpected | Frequency of unexpected | Consequences | Risk assessment |
|---|---|---|---|---|
| Rule of/by law | | | | |
| Property rights | | | | |
| Land-use rules | | | | |
| Environmental regulation | | | | |
| Delegation of governance | | | | |
| Market regulation | | | | |
| Fiscal policy | | | | |
| Building codes | | | | |

different factors all related to one item. Each factor has its own axis of uniform length radiating from the same origin. The risk 'score' for each factor is plotted on its respective axis. (Since the origin is common, and normally represents 'zero', all scores should be of the same sign, i.e. positive or negative.)

Radar charts can be useful when the level of knowledge of the occurrence, frequency and consequence of potential risk factors is limited, for example, transaction decisions in unfamiliar markets. They enable a visual representation of identifiable risk factors and a relational component to be depicted as an 'interaction polygon'. Although the relational component may appear to be spurious, provided the chart is presented in a consistent format, differences in the shape of the polygon serve as a visual check on institutional differences in the structure of different markets.

The 'radar chart' for a particular real estate market takes each of the key institutional factors as an axis. The risk factor for each factor is plotted on the relevant axis and the 'interaction polygon' results from connecting each point in rotation sequence. The resulting polygon can be compared with a familiar comparable market with a different institutional structure. The differences between the two polygons provide heuristic clues to the areas of particular disparity between the risk profile of the respective (i.e. familiar and unfamiliar) scenarios. This approach may be useful for depicting comparable categories of investments in different markets, for example, prime commercial real estate investments in different cities.

## Using the 'scoping' template

The first, most general, 'scoping' stage corresponds to the sweep of a periscope. Viewing the investment landscape in a 'sweep' identifies (1) significant landmarks and (2) features warranting closer inspection (because they appear to be an opportunity or threat). A telescope is used to investigate these features in greater detail and can also be used in a 'sweeping' motion to pick up features missed by the periscope. Particularly significant features may warrant more detailed examination under the microscope.

The template is designed to facilitate first-stage evaluation of a real estate transaction in an unfamiliar environment. It presents an analytical framework for systematically identifying (1) rule regimes that have an impact on intended transactions and (2) institutional arrangements that connect a potential transaction to relevant rule regimes. The form and nature of institutional arrangements may require significant modification to 'normal' expectations of risk associated with a comparable project in a familiar market environment.

Heuristic understanding of a familiar institutional structure can be reconfigured into a generic structure that is appropriate for general application. Indeed, the rule regimes indicated on the template are based on heuristic experience of rule regimes that are commonly encountered in real estate transactions. This represents the conversion of experience-based heuristic knowledge into generic search criteria that are suitable for application in an unfamiliar sovereignty. The 'scoping' tool provides a template for applying experiential knowledge to generic criteria, rejecting those components that simply do not apply to the new environment and modifying those that do.

The primary qualification for the inclusion of rule regimes corresponding to Table 2.1 is their potential impact on a particular transaction. They each represent, in an abbreviated form, rule regimes that give rise to institutional arrangements that must be taken into account in framing a real estate transaction. Some rule regimes, such as those relating to property rights, apply to all transactions (see Fig. 2.3). Other rule regimes will only have a bearing on certain transactions, for example, rules relating to land-use permits will apply to those transactions in which the value of the transaction is dependent on a change of use (see Fig. 2.4). Institutional arrangements that are identified as being applicable to a transaction, apparently without connecting to an obvious rule regime, highlight the existence of latent rules of the game. Latent rule regimes are often informal and represent potential problem areas that are likely to warrant further investigation, depending on the circumstances of the transaction.

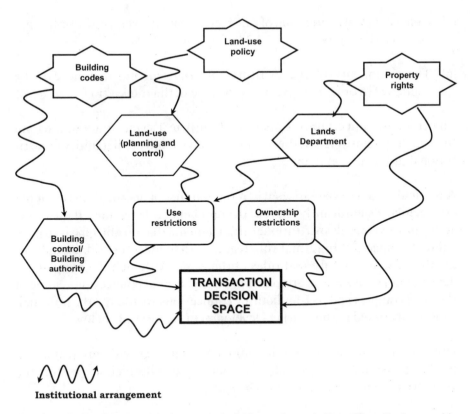

**Fig. 2.4** 'Carfax Developments' case study. Action pathway 1. *Note:* The critical ownership restriction under this action pathway is the inability of an owner to transfer the right to change the use of the land.

Considerations that are critical to interpreting the 'institutional landscape' from a transaction-centric viewpoint include:

(1) The number and diversity of rule regimes that have a significant bearing on the transaction;

(2) The frequency with which relevant rule regimes have affected comparable transactions and have generated identifiable transaction arrangements;

(3) The severity of the consequences of ignoring potentially relevant rule regimes;

(4) The proximity of institutional orbits to the transaction and each other;

(5) Consistency of application of rule regimes and the degree of 'oscillation' between the orbits;

(6) The complexity of the institutional arrangements that need to be addressed in order to maximise the value of the transaction.

The risks and uncertainties associated with real estate transactions are likely to be proportional to the number, diversity and predictability of institutional influences on them.

A particular danger sign arises when the number of accepted institutional arrangements significantly exceeds the number of rule regimes. If the transacting process reveals institutional arrangements that do not appear to have a direct connection to formal rule regimes, they may, instead, be indicating the existence of informal rules of the game. Although the template as depicted in Fig. 2.2 draws attention to strong, formal connections, some of the most complex and risk-harbouring connections are likely to be informal. This is illustrated in the 'Carfax Developments' case study below.

Users of the template need to be sufficiently familiar with any real estate market to be able to assemble the appropriate rule regimes within the appropriate zones. They must also be ready to:

(1) Discover additional or different rule regimes and institutional arrangements to build into the template;

(2) Review the relative significance of those rule regimes and institutional arrangements on transaction outcomes.

The template is transaction-specific; each new transaction requires the template to be checked, revised and re-formatted. This applies to the composition of the rule regimes and, equally, to the zones of interaction between them. In markets that are institutionally immature (emerging markets) or markets in transition (typically from centrally planned to open markets), the orbits and the zones of interaction may be fuzzy. In these circumstances, transactions may be highly susceptible to institutional arrangements that do not appear to have a direct connection to formal rule regimes.

## Putting it all together

Transacting is the process by and through which the information necessary to determine whether or not to transact is obtained. The following case illustrates how the scoping template can be used to identify institutional arrangements that play a critical part in developing 'action pathways' that culminate in a transaction or 'set' of transactions. It develops two action pathways, illustrating:

(1)  The kind of uncertainty faced by a willing but 'foreign' investor in an unfamiliar real estate market (in this case a Canadian investor in the Hong Kong real estate market);

(2)  The result of employing local (supposedly expert) knowledge to overcome excessive transaction costs created by following the 'formal' rules of the game.

'Carfax Developments' case study

Historically the value of residential property in Hong Kong has made residential development an attractive proposition. However, the ability of 'foreign' investors to participate in development opportunities is limited by the institutional peculiarities of the Hong Kong market and the market power of established local developers. So, although potential returns are attractive, breaking into the market and securing development rights present major hurdles to foreign investors. Despite this, to outside observers, the largely rural areas of the New Territories of the Hong Kong Special Administrative Region (HKSAR) do appear to offer investors limited opportunity to invest in the development of residential accommodation. The case study that follows is a fictionalised account of a proposed development project involving land in the New Territories of Hong Kong.

The case starts with the involvement of 'P', a Canadian pension fund, which wishes to invest in real estate in Hong Kong. P has been looking for high-return real estate opportunities and has heard that there are opportunities for residential development in the New Territories. P is unfamiliar with the Hong Kong real estate market. An initial scoping of the decision landscape indicates that a development proposal will be contingent upon acquisition of title to the land, and obtaining necessary approvals for change of use of the land. Beyond this, the links between these formal rule imperatives and the transaction(s) that enable development to proceed are revealed through 'action pathways', which will be determined in the light of the critical institutional arrangements identified in the course of the search for information.

Action pathway 1 (see Fig. 2.4, page 63)

Initially, P approaches the Hong Kong office of an international firm of development advisers 'F', and explains its objectives. As a result of the information from F, P is able to develop action pathway 1, which reflects the path for prudent compliance with the formal rule structure, as follows.

As part of the periscope sweep based on the scoping template, P is able to confirm the constitutional formal rule regimes that facilitate the transfer of land in Hong Kong. There is no restriction on foreigners owning land so there is no apparent uncertainty to be plotted on the constitutional zone. Title to land in Hong Kong is not currently recorded on a Land Register administered by institutions functioning within the governance zone. A register of instruments is maintained by the Land Registry, but this does not inhibit the arrangements for transferring title. The parties are therefore free to negotiate the terms of the contract for the sale of the land in the 'shadow' of formal rules of transfer plotted on the operational zone.

Bearing in mind that the use of the template as a periscope is intended to map only the critical rule regimes and institutional arrangements that might cause uncertainty, there appears to be no real difficulty with acquisition of the land. As explained in chapter 3, the courts have removed the uncertainty that might result from the fact that land in Hong Kong is held upon leasehold tenure. The critical uncertainty in this case results from the inability of a landowner to transfer the right to change the use of the land. This limitation is plotted on the operational zone since it functions as an inhibition to the parties' freedom to decide for themselves how the transaction will proceed.

Change of land use brings in another set of rule regimes and institutional arrangements. The rule regimes regulating a proposal to change the existing land use are derived from constitutional zone legislation implemented via the governance zone. This represents a source of uncertainty, attaching to the governance zone. The arrangement involves application to the Town Planning Board under the Town Planning Ordinance (Cap 131). In addition, building plans and permission to commence building works have to be approved by the Building Authority under the Buildings Ordinance (Cap 123). In other words, applications involving construction introduce institutional arrangements deriving from the separate policies and practices of the authorities and agents empowered to control the construction process, in addition to the arrangements involving land-use regulation.

A further source of uncertainty (explained in greater detail in chapter 3) which attaches to (and, with regard to the template, is plotted on) the operational zone arises from the fact that in the HKSAR, the lease (on which the land is held from the government) usually contains restrictions on the use of the land, which in this case is currently for agricultural use. Consent to a change of use must therefore be obtained from the government's land agent (the Lands Department), in addition to consents from planning and building authorities. In the case of the Lands Department, consent is usually subject to the payment of a premium based on the enhancement in value of the land. This premium may be substantial. A set of institutional arrangements in the form of policies and procedures of the Lands Department comes into play. Failure to take account of these arrangements has proved to be costly in previous cases.

The uncertainty generated by the range and variety of rules and institutional arrangements involved clearly necessitates a more focused search for specific information. F explains that this next level of investigation, again based on the scoping template, will involve further search costs and bureaucratic delays (transaction costs). At this stage P is losing interest in pursuing its development proposals in Hong Kong and is about to switch its search to Shenzhen, just across the border with mainland China. F is unfamiliar with the mainland market but, rather than lose business, introduces P to another client 'D', a development company which has successfully undertaken some residential development in the New Territories.

D advises P that there is another, less bureaucratic action pathway to securing profitable development, which will minimise the transaction costs associated with negotiating with governance bodies and maintain the greatest freedom of action. P and D form a joint venture, 'Carfax Developments Ltd' (C), to acquire the property and to carry out residential development in the HKSAR.

Action pathway 2 (see Fig. 2.5, page 68)

The strategic question that derives from the factors plotted on the template for the first action pathway is: How can the search and transaction costs implicit in conventional applications for change of land use and for consents to building works be minimised?

D immediately draws attention to a scheme, known as the 'Small House Policy', implemented in 1972, under which male indigenous villagers are entitled to build a small house for personal occupation. The policy is implemented by the Lands Department operating within the governance zone. P is encouraged to progress (at little apparent cost) to the telescope level of investigation and is reassured to read a pamphlet produced by the

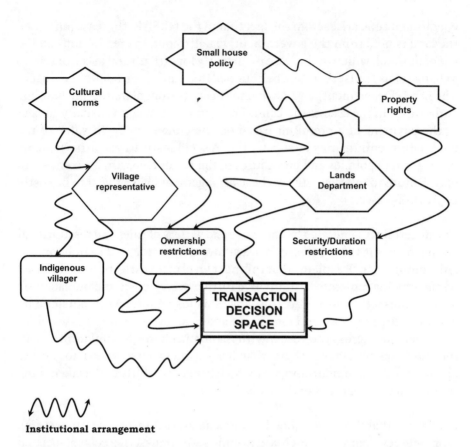

**Institutional arrangement**

**Fig. 2.5** 'Carfax Developments' case study. Action pathway 2. *Notes:* (1) The critical ownership restriction under this action pathway is the restraint on alienation (i.e. restriction on transfer within five years without the consent of the Lands Department). (2) The institutional arrangements shown in this action pathway appear to be more complicated than for action pathway 1. Two points need to be emphasised: (a) The diagram shows most of the institutional arrangements that might have a bearing on the transaction decision. However, they are not all equally critical: the one that makes the difference is that between the village representative and the indigenous male villager(s). (b) Despite the apparent complexity of the diagram, the transaction costs associated with action pathway 1 are, in the estimation of the parties, significantly higher than in this case.

Lands Department entitled *The New Territories Small House Policy, How To Apply For A Small House Grant*. The application form is a standard form obtainable from any New Territories District Office.

If an application is successful, the male indigenous villager obtains a building licence and three certificates of exemption from certain building controls under the Buildings Ordinance (Cap 123). The premium that would normally be payable to the Lands Department as a result of a beneficial change of use does not apply because the indigenous villager is not required to pay a premium for the development rights, and the building control process is considerably simplified. (Of course, these cost advantages are not lost on most villagers.)

In undertaking 'due diligence' research, P is a little concerned to discover a condition of the scheme restraining the indigenous villager from alienating his ownership rights within five years of the grant without consent of the Lands Department, which would require payment of a premium for their permission. Sale without consent means that the government would have a right to re-enter and terminate the lease (i.e. render the title potentially defeasible).[1] P notes this as a critical factor to be mapped on the operational zone of the template, having a close bearing on the transaction decision. This produces uncertainty and necessitates an inquiry as to the likelihood of re-entry by the government. (See chapter 3 for an explanation of how this uncertainty is resolved.) A further worry is that under rules of procedure established by the Lands Department an applicant must declare that he has never made, and has no intention at present to make, any private arrangements for his rights to be sold to other individuals or to a developer.[2]

P has identified that this institutional arrangement carries significant uncertainty associated with the probability of enforcement by the Lands Department. P should resolve this uncertainty to his own satisfaction. D informs him that, according to settled practice, the type of enforcement exercised by the Lands Department would not involve demolition or removal of the dwellings but may result in payment of a premium (not necessarily by P).

Despite the worries, this route appears to offer a window of opportunity for C to obtain the right to develop but only with the active assistance of male indigenous villagers. We can refer to each male indigenous villager as 'V'. Acting within the operational zone of the rules of the market, C and V enter into a contract under which, in return for a fee, V agrees to make the necessary application to acquire the special privileges outlined above, and to transfer title to the land with the completed buildings to purchasers. (Of course, in order to create a viable development project a number of Vs would be involved.) The contract also provides for the value of the overall development project to be shared between the parties to the joint venture.

The transaction necessitates the transfer of legal title to V, which would expose C to the risk that V might then renege on the deal. Determining how to respond to such a risk calls for more detailed analysis (using the template as a microscope). One possibility, relying upon the rule regimes of contract law and trust, would be to insert a term in the contract that V should hold the land on trust for C. But this also carries a risk that the courts would not uphold the agreement. If the transaction could only be performed by procuring V to make the application for the special privileges, as would appear to be the case, it is probable that the courts would strike it down as void and unenforceable as being contrary to public policy.[3] Proceedings to establish an interest in the property on some other basis[4] would simply result in further transaction costs.

Since the outcome of reliance upon formal rule regimes and institutional arrangements associated with them is uncertain, C would have to look elsewhere to secure performance of V's obligations. Are there any other rule regimes or institutional arrangements that might provide a sanction against V? The search for a solution to this question leads to institutional arrangements that connect the transaction with informal rule regimes deriving from cultural norms. As a member of a village, V will be subject to the rules of village life. This might suggest a need for collective action on the part of the villagers but, in fact, one member of the village has power to compel observance of those rules. This is the village representative, (Vr), whose authority is derived from custom and practice, and is now endorsed in legislation.[5] Vr may, on behalf of the villagers, negotiate benefits from C, thereby enabling other stakeholders to capture some of the value of each transaction. This would result in additional cost to C but less than the transaction costs associated with action pathway 1.

This analysis puts C in possession of information that enables it to decide whether, and if so how, to proceed. It illustrates the institutional dilemma faced by P via C which, in this case, consists of the extent to which P is ready, willing and able to invest in a scheme that is based on informal rules, accompanied by a significant degree of certainty, that are designed to overcome the transaction costs and additional land premium costs associated with constitutional and governance rule regimes.

## Conclusion

The proposition advanced in this chapter is that institutional uncertainty is the primary contributor to the extra uncertainty faced by investors in unfamiliar real estate markets. Conventional real estate appraisal methodologies tend to ignore serious analysis of the uncertainties associated with investing in unfamiliar markets. The pragmatic response of professional investors is to incorporate an additional risk premium uniformly within a country. Thus one country may be rated as being inherently more risky than another, but the same additional risk premium is applied to all investments in that country. This approach is systematic but insensitive to the individual parameters of transactions. The scoping template described in this chapter and the analysis upon which it is based offers a systematic approach to analysing the sources of institutional uncertainty. It is a tool for enabling investors to avoid some of the pitfalls associated with lack of familiarity with country-specific rules of the game and, more particularly, to avoid unnecessarily expensive mistakes.

# References

Bromley, D. (1991) *Environment and Economy: Property Rights and Public Policy.* Blackwell, Oxford, UK.

de Soto H. (2000) *The Mystery of Capital.* Bantam Press, London.

Hardin, G. (1968) The Tragedy of the Commons. *Science*, **162**, 1243–8.

Kiser, L. & Ostrom, E. (1982) The Three Worlds of Action: a Metatheoretical Synthesis of Institutional Approaches. In: Ostrom, E. (ed) *Strategies of Political Inquiry.* Sage, Beverley Hills, CA.

Mnookin, R. & Kornhauser, L. (1979) Bargaining in the shadow of the law: The case of divorce. *Yale Law Journal*, **88**, 950–97.

Oakerson, R.J. (1992) Analyzing the Commons: a Framework. In: Bromley, D.W. *et al.* (eds) *Making the Commons Work: Theory, Practice and Policy.* Institute for Contemporary Studies Press, San Francisco, CA.

Oakerson, R.J. & Walker, S.T. (1997) Analysing Policy Reform and Reforming Policy Analysis. In: Brinkerhoff, D.W. *Policy Studies and Developing Nations, Volume 5: Policy Analysis Concepts and Methods: An Institutional and Implementation Focus.* JAI Press, Greenwich, CT.

Wang, H (2001) *Weak State, Strong Networks.* Oxford University Press (China), Hong Kong.

Williamson, O.E. (1971) The Vertical Integration of Production: Market Failure Considerations. *American Economic Review*, **112**.

# Further reading

Barzel, Y. (1997) *Economic Analysis of Property Rights*, 2nd edn. Cambridge University Press, Cambridge, UK.

Eggertsson, T. (1990) *Economic Behaviour and Institutions.* Cambridge University Press, Cambridge, UK.

Furubotn, E.G. & Richter, R. (1998) *Institutions and Economic Theory: the Contribution of the New Institutional Economics.* University of Michigan Press, Ann Arbor, MI.

Lawson, F.H. & Rudden, B. (1982) *The Law of Property*, 2nd edn. Oxford University Press, Oxford, UK.

Libecap, G. (1989) *Contracting for Property Rights.* Cambridge University Press, Cambridge, UK.

Menard C. (1997) *Transaction Cost Economics*. Edward Elgar, Cheltenham, UK.

North, D.C. (1990) *Institutions, Institutional Development and Economic Performance*. Cambridge University Press, Cambridge, UK.

Ostrom, E. (1990) *Governing the Commons: the Evolution of Institutions for Collective Action*. Cambridge University Press, Cambridge, UK.

Pejovich, S. (ed.) (1997) *The Economic Foundations of Property Rights*. Edward Elgar, Cheltenham, UK.

Richardson, G.B. (1998) *The Economics of Imperfect Knowledge*. Edward Elgar, London.

Tanzi, V. (1999) *Policies, Institutions and the Dark Side of Economics*. Edward Elgar, Cheltenham.

Twining, W. & Miers, D. (1991) *How to Do Things with Rules*. Butterworths, London.

Voigt, S. (1999) *Explaining Institutional Change*. Edward Elgar, Cheltenham, UK.

Williamson, O.E. (1985) *The Economic Institutions of Capitalism: firms, markets, relational contracting*. Free Press, New York.

## Notes

1 *Sung Wai-kiu & Anor* v. *Wong Mei-yin* [1997] 1 HKC 288.
2 *Li Pui Man* v. *Wong Mei Yin* [1998] 1 HKLR 84.
3 *Chung Mui Teck and others* v. *Hang Tak Buddhist Hall Association Ltd and another* (2001), CACV 20/2001.
4 *Wa Lee Finance Co Ltd* v. *Yau Tak Wah* (2002) HCMP 1316/2001.
5 Heung Yee Kuk Ordinance Cap 1097.

# 3

# An Institutional Analysis of the Subject Matter of Real Estate Transactions

## *Paul Kent*

This chapter focuses on the subject matter of real estate transactions using the institutional approach to analysis explained in chapter 2. Title to real estate in the Hong Kong Special Administrative Region is compared with land-use rights in the People's Republic of China (PRC). The comparison reveals how the *quality* of title to real estate is contingent upon institutional arrangements prevailing during the transacting process. This underlines the importance of systematic determination of the property rights actually transferred in a transaction, a process that applies even in the most developed legal systems.

The Hong Kong/PRC comparison is pertinent because it enables an evaluation to be made of two property rights systems under a single sovereignty. This has applied in Hong Kong twice in the last 100 years: first under British sovereignty, second under the sovereignty of the PRC. It is particularly significant because Hong Kong has migrated from one sovereignty to another but has been permitted to retain, largely intact, the rule regimes of the former sovereignty.

## Property rights in institutional analysis

Real estate transactions involve the transfer of value, which is manifested by property rights. The nature and extent of property rights, and therefore the ability to maximise value, depends upon institutional arrangements (Eggertsson 1996). The term 'property rights' in the literature on the economics of institutions is defined by reference to a person's ability to use valuable resources (Alchian & Demsetz 1973; Barzel 1997). Within this paradigm, ability is a function of the system or structure of property rights in a particular society. Property rights are thus social institutions, bundles of rights which are recognised and enforced, not natural products. Like all institutional arrangements they are not fixed or absolute assignments of rights by the state, but are susceptible to change.

This notion of property rights subsumes issues of ownership within the concept of use. It is implicit in the notion of a right that there must be an owner or owners with power to control the resource. Rights are specified in general terms as rights of use, income and alienation (Demsetz 1967). Normative studies of property rights do not challenge this broad description but focus instead upon justifications for property rights regimes (see, for example, Paul *et al.* 1994).

The property rights paradigm is based upon, if not necessarily intended to represent, common-law systems of private property. The institutional framework has evolved over a period of more than 700 years. In terms of the Seabrooke–Kent scoping template (see chapter 2), the constitutional zone rule regimes are relatively certain. The political institutional arrangements are comparatively stable and unlikely to be altered by revolution. Formal, state-endorsed enforcement rules, administered by an independent judiciary within the governance zone, underpin the constitutional position. Judges give effect to constitutional-level arrangements. These fundamental institutional arrangements (North & Thomas 1971) enable the parties to contract, confident that their agreements will be recognised and enforced (Alston *et al.* 1996). The consequence of this is that the attention of scholars has been directed, in the main, to institutional rules of transfer existing within the operational zone.

The property rights paradigm implies a clear separation between the three layers of the institutional framework, which appears to be generally true where the subject matter of the transaction is personal property, or where land is treated as a commodity. In the absence of circumstances justifying the imposition of a trust, or some other proprietary right or remedy, the courts will generally not interfere with obligations agreed between the parties. Tradability matters more than title. Obligations determined by market rules generally prevail. Compensation in money is a ready substitute for rights in the asset, thereby avoiding the necessity to specify too closely the subject matter of the transaction. It is sufficient to specify the obligations of the parties. Ownership issues arise only rarely, as where a company is liquidated and it becomes necessary to identify the company's assets. Institutional arrangements link rule regimes in the constitutional zone with rule regimes in the operational zone, the governance rule regimes existing largely as a set of 'default rules' that function only when something goes wrong.

What matters within this paradigm is 'value' (normally based on income flow), not the transfer of title to the property rights giving rise to that value. The 'bundle of rights' notion implies that the particular asset to which the rights attach is largely immaterial (see Dwyer & Menell 1998). Exchange of property rights is seen primarily as a matter of contracts. The decision space of the parties to the transaction is large and operates within a relatively static set of formal institutional arrangements. Risks and uncertainties may be minimised and controlled by individual choice. A party to a transaction is free to insure against loss, without inhibiting the freedom of the other party. Measurement is thus largely calculative (Williamson 1993) and the parties can transact in the confidence that judicial remedies are available if the contractual arrangements break down.

The property rights paradigm tends to take for granted the institutional characteristics of property. This may not be entirely appropriate to real estate transactions, at least in the urban context, given the idiosyncratic nature of real property. It will be a rare case where real estate can be treated as a commodity, with one piece of land being substituted for another. This is manifested for example by the fact that, by contrast with other contracts, the primary remedy for enforcing contracts for sale of land is specific performance and not damages. Specific performance is an equitable remedy and therefore discretionary, but the exercise of the discretion is institutionalised to such an extent that it will be granted so long as the applicant is ready, willing and able to perform his or her contractual obligations. The institutional characteristics of real estate also necessitate more precise specification of property rights than is the case with personal property. For instance, the distinction between ownership and use is crucial in real estate but seldom an issue in respect of personal property.

Empirical studies in institutional change focusing on the acquisition and security of property rights in frontier land and native title recognise the distinction between title and use rights (see, for example, Alston *et al.* 1999). Use rights within the operational zone are contingent upon a secure title. It follows from this that, in addition to identifying what rights are capable of existing in real estate and who owns those rights (Alchian & Demsetz 1973), an investor in real estate must evaluate carefully the *quality* of the rights being acquired in a transaction.

Focus on quality, particularly security of title, brings governance zone rule regimes into play. These include but are not limited to formal rules of adjudication and enforcement that are outside the control of the parties to the transaction. The decision space of the parties to a real estate transaction may therefore be more limited than has been otherwise assumed, necessitating closer analysis of the institutional arrangements affecting the transacting process. The 'Carfax Developments' case study in chapter 2 suggests that the relationship between the different elements of the institutional framework is more dynamic than the property rights paradigm might imply.

The transacting process itself is also more complex for real estate than for other property transactions, adding a further dimension to the analysis. The transfer of legal title to real estate is effected at a date subsequent to the agreement manifested in a contract for sale of land. In the interval, institutions may change, or new institutional arrangements may come into play.

These factors cumulatively imply the necessity of careful analysis in every case of the institutional determinants of the nature and extent of the property rights being transferred, particularly in respect of international real estate transactions.

## Institutional determinants of title to real estate in Hong Kong

*The nature and extent of property rights in land in Hong Kong*

The rule regimes within the constitutional zone relating to property rights prescribe those rights that are capable of being transferred with the sanction of the State. Ownership of land and natural resources vests in the State. Individuals cannot demand state enforcement of transactions whose purpose is the transfer of ownership of land. Attempts to transfer ownership might operate for a time, in the same way that 'extralegal' (de Soto 2000) transactions are practically possible, but they are relatively insecure.

The HKSAR government has constitutional authority to manage state-owned land, including the power of sale. While it is theoretically possible for land to be granted on freehold tenure to be held for an unlimited period of time, the constitutional relationship between the HKSAR and the PRC renders the likelihood so remote that it can be ignored. The post-1997 administration has continued the policy of selling land on long leaseholds.

Purchasers of land in Hong Kong, as in other common-law jurisdictions, acquire an estate in the land. Leaseholds, like the greatest freehold estate known to the common law, the fee simple absolute in possession, confer a right to exclusive possession of the land on the holder of the estate. Subject to the exercise of powers of eminent domain (which in Hong Kong is referred to as 'resumption'), or the exercise of the power to terminate the lease in the grant itself, the right will endure for a period of time specified in the grant. Historically this included some 999-year terms, but current practice is to limit duration to 50 years from the date of the grant.

## Institutional implications of leasehold tenure

Leasehold tenure implies that constitutional zone rule regimes have the potential to influence every real estate transaction in Hong Kong. Insofar as the government is a party to the lease, government policy is clearly a relevant factor in determining the content of property rights assigned to a purchaser of land held on a long lease. The uncertainty that would be caused by a high incidence of government activity in the market has however been diminished by the refusal of the courts, operating within the governance zone, to allow constitutional rules to affect the relationship of landlord and tenant. The lease is regarded as an ordinary commercial contract subject to private law.[1]

In similar vein, the courts have refused to allow landowners to claim a perpetual interest in land based on Chinese customary tenure, one consequence of which would have been an ability to develop land without restrictions.[2]

This emphasis upon formal legal rules suggests the following institutional arrangements. First, the governance level, as represented in this instance by the courts, upholds a traditional separation of powers by giving legal effect to constitutional-level policies. Government intervention is through governance zone rule regimes which implement the generalised policies of the rules of the constitutional zone. This in turn provides a framework for decisions to be made by the parties in the light of rule regimes and institutional arrangements within the operational zone of the market. Second, the theory of a liberal state is confirmed by supporting contractual arrangements freely entered into at the operational level of a transaction.

These arrangements do not differ markedly from those applicable to other types of asset. However, despite the apparently clear demarcation between the three zones of influence, the possibility of other less formal institutional arrangements cannot be ruled out. The following section illustrates how the quality of title to real estate is dependent upon the presence of such arrangements, necessitating a re-evaluation of the meaning and effect of rights specified in a contract for sale of land in Hong Kong.

## The quality of the vendor's title

Purchasers of real estate for investment, whether for the purposes of yield or capital appreciation, desire a secure title. Under common-law rules security of title is always a matter of degree, since there can be no question of an absolute title even in the case of freehold land. Questions of degree introduce uncertainty. Evaluating uncertainty and how to respond to it is an inherent part of the assessment of the subject matter of real estate transactions. The degree of security is measured by the extent to which other persons have interests in the land that would be enforceable against the purchaser. Enforceable adverse interests, such as easements, reduce the value of the property rights. Other claims may threaten the title to the land itself as, for example, where the property rights may be taken away by the exercise of a right to forfeit a lease, or where title is extinguished under doctrines of adverse possession.

The following case study illustrates how different institutional arrangements affect the assessment of uncertainty of the subject matter of real estate transactions, and the resolution of such uncertainty.

In the absence of agreement, the parties must submit the matter to judges

---

### Case study

'V', the owner of land held on a government lease, agrees to sell it to 'P'. The lease gives the government the right to terminate the lease if the lessee fails to comply with any of the covenants in the lease. Inspection of the property reveals illegal structures erected on the property in breach of a covenant to comply with building regulations. V wishes to proceed with the sale but is unwilling to remove the structures before completion. The property market has now fallen and P wishes to withdraw from the contract. In support of this 'exit strategy' P alleges that V cannot give a good title to the property.

---

operating within the governance zone. In accordance with constitutional theory, judges are required to decide the issue according to rules of law. On the given facts V's title is potentially defeasible, that is, it may be taken away without compensation if the Lands Department chooses to exercise the government's right of termination under the lease. Alternatively the title may be defeated by the exercise of a power of sale to enforce a charge against the property. This would be possible, for example, if the Building Authority registered a charge to recover the cost of demolition of the illegal structure and the landowner refused to pay the cost.

A defeasible title is not a good title. The key task therefore is to assess the degree of risk of enforcement by the government. To resolve this issue, V might rely upon the legal principle that if there is no real risk of (1) a successful assertion against the purchaser of an encumbrance,[3] or (2) the title being held defeasible,[4] the court may declare a title to be good, and dismiss the purchaser's objections to title. If this power is exercised, the court is, in effect, solving the problem for the parties. The institutional significance of this is that governance zone rule regimes are dominant.

P, on the other hand, might rely upon a different legal test, namely, whether a prudent and experienced solicitor could properly advise the purchaser that he may safely disregard the risk.[5] The institutional implication of this approach is that the parties must resolve their own differences or, to put it another way, operational zone arrangements should dominate. This is entirely consistent with the accepted constitutional relationship between the courts and citizens in civil disputes. However, governance zone rules may still have a significant impact on the outcome of the case, especially if judges indicate what the result would be if the matter were brought before them. This is precisely what happened in *Spark Rich* where it was said that it would be a rare case where there was no real risk of enforcement by the Building Authority in the case of an illegal structure.

This legal analysis suggests that P could withdraw from the contract, particularly since the Building Authority has a statutory duty to enforce the building laws. The institutional significance of this is that the vendor would not be able to rely upon the governance zone to compel P to go through with the transaction. The courts would not grant specific performance where there was a real risk of enforcement, even if the risk were low. Sale at a price that discounts the defect in title would be a matter for agreement between the parties, that is, an operational zone matter, a matter of money, not title.

On this analysis a high proportion of titles in Hong Kong are defective, given the large number of illegal structures evident from only the briefest of inspections of Hong Kong's high-rise buildings. The logical implication is a stagnant market. But this is not the case. One is driven to ask: why?

One explanation may be that, in implementing the legal rules, judges have adopted institutional arrangements that favour the market. Further research is needed to test this hypothesis, although there are some notable judgments whose effect has been to overcome the consequences of a purely technical application of formal legal rules.[6]

Another untested proposition might be that Hong Kong purchasers are more willing to take risks than purchasers in other jurisdictions. A propensity to gamble might be cited in support. But it is doubtful whether this can explain market behaviour in real estate, particularly in view of the very high prices often paid for property in Hong Kong.

A further possibility is that the players in the game rely upon a different set of institutional arrangements. If, for example, it is apparent that the government is highly unlikely to exercise its right to re-enter and terminate the lease despite having the technical right to do so, then the parties may perceive the risk as minimised if not completely removed. Similarly, if the policy of the Building Authority is not to enforce charges by order of sale except in very rare cases, parties may regard this as a low risk.

At first sight, this appears to indicate discretion rather than institutional arrangements. However, if a discretion is exercised in a similar way in a substantial number of cases, then it could evolve into an institutional arrangement (see, for example, North & Thomas 1971). If this is in favour of the vendor, then the purchaser may decide to take the risk knowing it to be so remote as to be virtually non-existent. Analysis of authorities over a 40-year period reveals only one reported case in which the government has forfeited a government lease for breach of covenant. The practice in such cases is to offer a modification of the lease subject to the payment of a premium. A similar conclusion may be drawn in respect of building authority charges. The charge acts as a threat of enforcement, a powerful incentive on the part of landowners to pay the Authority's costs. In both cases, therefore, the matter becomes one of economic behaviour rather than a simple matter of title according to law, enabling transactions that would otherwise be at risk to go ahead.

If the above analysis is correct, it suggests that in order to evaluate the quality of the title being offered for sale, and therefore the value of the property rights dependent upon the security of that title, it is necessary to determine whether there are institutional arrangements other than the contract for sale that might influence the transaction.

## Institutional determinants of property rights in real estate in the PRC

*Nature and extent of property rights in land in the PRC* [7]

As in Hong Kong, land in the PRC cannot be owned by individuals. Owner-ship of urban land in the PRC vests in the State, while rural or suburban land vests in collectives except for those portions which belong to the State in accordance with the law.[8]

The principal interest in land which may be acquired by individuals, including a foreign-investment enterprise (FIE), is a 'land-use right'. Land-use rights confer the right to use the land for particular purposes, which may be very specific or more general, such as 'for residential purposes' or 'for commercial purposes'.

Land-use rights on state-owned land may be either 'allocated' or 'granted' by the Land Administration Bureau of the People's Government at or above county level. Collectives cannot create granted land-use rights but may acquire them by applying to the state to requisition their land and re-grant the land to the collective (Randolph & Jianbo 2000).

Allocated land-use rights normally endure for an indefinite period, but those allocated to an FIE will be for a specified period. In this respect they resemble granted land-use rights, which are for a fixed period not exceeding 70 years. Allocated land-use rights are not transferable, even if allocated to an FIE, whereas the owner of a granted land-use right may transfer it subject to com-pliance with the law.[9] This difference is not as significant as it appears since an allocated land-use right may be converted into a granted land-use right, thereby enabling the right to be transferred, leased or mortgaged.[10]

Land-use rights do not create the relationship of landlord and tenant between the grantor and the grantee. They do not confer ownership of the land or any right to exclusive possession of it. While there is a right to the surface of the land in connection with the agreed use, this does not extend underground and does not confer any right to the air space above the land beyond what is necessary for carrying out the agreed purpose.

Land-use rights must be registered in a land register maintained by land administration bureaux at or above the county level.[11] A certificate of reg-istration is issued on registration, but it is the record in the register not the certificate that is proof of ownership. Title to the land-use right is distinct from ownership of any buildings erected on the land to which the right attaches. Building ownership must be separately registered.

## Quality of title to granted land-use rights

The primary determinant of the quality of title in a common-law system is the extent of freedom to transfer title without state interference. As the previous section illustrates, formal and informal institutional arrangements in Hong Kong guarantee a high degree of autonomy by supporting operational decision-making through market rules and contractual arrangements.

Granted land-use rights are a manifestation of the movement towards a market economy in the PRC. But it does not follow that market rules prevail. The progression to a system of private property is not a simple transition from public to private control (see Oi & Walder 1999). The evaluation of the quality of title to a granted land-use right, and therefore of its value, is more difficult than in Hong Kong or other common-law jurisdictions because of institutional uncertainty in the PRC, as the following case study demonstrates.[12]

---

**Case study**

Hang Lung Enterprises, a Guangzhou-based company, and Mok Properties, based in Hong Kong, have formed a joint venture company (the company) to develop a site in Li Wan District, Guangzhou. The site has been approved for development. The Land Administration Bureau of Guangzhou City (the grantor) and the company (the grantee) have signed a contract under which the grantor grants a land-use right on the site to the grantee for a term of 30 years. The land is to be used for residential purposes only. The land use cannot be changed without the consent of the grantor. During the course of construction the partners to the joint venture decide to transfer the land-use right and the development rights to another developer.

---

An analysis of this transaction in terms of the Seabrooke–Kent scoping template indicates that the boundaries between the three zones of influence is unclear. The Land Administration Bureau, a governance zone institution, is a party to a contract which in a market system would be located within the operational zone. The contract implies that change of use is a matter for the grantor, but permission of the Zoning Administration of the county or city is also required.[13] The permitted land use is determined by governance-zone rules in the form of zoning laws. The land-use right is subject to rights in the public interest, held by the State and by constitutional zone organs of government; and to judicial and administrative powers authorised by law (see contract in Randolph & Jianbo 2000: 379). The nature, extent and quality of title rights are thus determined in part by formal rule regimes and institutions operating within the governance zone, rather than by market rules.

If this were the only source of uncertainty it would be comparatively easy to resolve. A search of the relevant rules would produce a relatively clear picture of the quality of property rights. However the landscape is more confused than the above account suggests. The uncertainty is primarily systemic in character. All international real estate transactions confront systemic uncertainty. Systems in transition are inherently less certain than evolved structures, but the differences are of degree, not of type. The transitional state of the PRC makes it difficult to identify rule regimes and institutional arrangements, and to determine which arrangements provide the best guarantee of the quality of property rights. Three categories of uncertainty are particularly pertinent.

### Doctrinal immaturity

Doctrinal immaturity refers to the lack of any authoritative definition of the nature and quality of the granted land-use right. What kind of right is it? In particular, is it enforceable against persons other than the grantor, including the State?

In legal systems based upon either the common law or the civil law, investors may make rational predictions as to the nature and extent of their property rights by referring to relatively accessible formal rule regimes. Doctrinal sophistication in a common-law system evolves to a large extent through interpretation and application of legal rules by a judiciary independent of the legislative and executive branches of government. In civil law systems doctrine is also expounded by jurists whose 'authority' may have considerable impact on how general legal formulations are given specific content.

By contrast, judicial institutions which guarantee a high degree of predictability in western-style legal systems are lacking or undeveloped in the PRC. For example, there is no independent judiciary, and judges are largely untrained. Procedural institutional arrangements tending to produce a high degree of certainty in the application of formal legal rules, such as the doctrine of binding precedent, do not exist. The highest court, the Supreme People's Court, provides 'opinions' as to the law which may guide lower courts, but these are not legal precedents in the western sense. The institutional vacuum caused by the absence of such institutions tends to be filled by highly localised judicial rules, which may produce varying interpretations of the property rights acquired in a real estate transaction.

Even if these deficiencies did not exist, the courts would still have to determine which system of rules to apply. The development of doctrine is shaped to a large extent by legal tradition. Rules of civil law systems, developed under the influence of Roman law, were different from those of the common law of England. The extent to which the common law has been influenced by Roman law is a matter of debate (Evans-Jones 1999) but differences undoubtedly exist (Zimmermann 1996). The search for doctrine in the PRC may be likened to that for a common tradition among the member states of the European Union. The result will almost certainly be a hybrid system, a 'legal tapestry of many different shades and nuances' (Zimmermann 2001: 158).

In the meantime, commentators are driven to approximations between concepts established in other systems and those applicable in the PRC. For instance, Chinese law distinguishes between credit rights and rights *in rem* but provides no clear definition of the difference. Randolph and Jianbo (2000) argue that there is a 'rough correspondence' with the distinction between equitable rights and legal rights in the common-law world, but there is no official justification for such a view. Moreover, it assumes a uniformity of concepts within common-law systems which does not exist. The scope of equity in England and Wales is not the same as that in Canada, Australia or New Zealand. Furthermore, equitable rights are not necessarily enforceable as property rights: they may be rights *in rem* for some purposes and personal rights for other purposes.[14] The distinction is important since *in rem* rights enjoy greater state protection than credit rights, at least in theory. Investors would be unwise to rely upon approximations, however authoritative the source.

The risk of error is especially significant in respect of the most important property right in land, the granted land-use right. It is similar to the common-law ground lease in that it endures for a fixed period of time and is subject to user restrictions. But a lease in China is not an *in rem* right, merely a contractual right. It confers a right to use land, but not the right to possess it to the exclusion of the State. It is 'exclusive possession' that justifies a lease as an estate in land. The lessee is 'able to exercise the rights of an owner of land, which is in the real sense his land albeit temporarily and subject to certain restrictions'.[15] The holder of the land-use right is in no sense the owner of the land, which remains vested in the State. Beyond this, the nature and extent of land-use rights depends upon institutional arrangements within the governance zone (see below).

The lack of doctrinal certainty may be remedied in part by authoritative legislation within the constitutional zone. Section 25 of the Law on Urban Real Estate Administration (1994) specifies the pre-conditions for transfer of granted land-use rights. In particular the 'right' to transfer depends upon how far the development has proceeded. Under the Provisions on Managing Idle Land, issued by the Ministry of Land and Resources (1999), the Land Administration at county or city level is entitled to 'notify' the land user to 'consult' with it on how to deal with the problem (see Randolph & Jianbo 2000: 130–1 for details). Transfer of ownership is not therefore a right exercisable in accordance with operational zone rules, but is dependent upon the policies and procedures of an agency of government operating within the governance zone.

The uncertainties of doctrine have two significant institutional implications. First, informal institutional arrangements are likely to develop in advance of doctrine. Zimmermann cites the example of the testamentary executor which was unknown to Roman law but which developed as a matter of legal practice (Zimmermann 2001). Similarly land-use rights were traded in Shanghai prior to the formal recognition of granted land-use rights (Ho & Co. 1998). Second, there is a risk of conflict between officially sanctioned property rights, supported by formal enforcement mechanisms, and culturally evolved rights enforceable as a matter of custom and practice. These institutional arrangements may inhibit acquisition of maximum value, despite official recognition of private property rights.

## Dissonance of form and substance

Dissonance in this context denotes conflict between formal rules and reality. The most fundamental example of institutional dissonance in the PRC is that between the express provisions of the Constitution and the role of the Communist Party. The Constitution contains detailed provisions on the exercise of political power, at both national and regional levels. In theory legislative power vests in People's congresses. But in practice the Communist Party is the highest authority with representatives at all institutional levels (Otto *et al.* 2000). Actual institutional arrangements may thus vary significantly from those indicated by formal rules, with 'guidance' of the Party carrying greater weight than enacted laws (cf. Keller 1994; Chen 1998).

In the context of property rights in land, institutional dissonance creates a significant risk to an investment. Consider, for example, section 19 of the Law on Urban Real Estate Administration which requires the State to pay 'appropriate' compensation for premature revocation of a granted land-use right. This assumes that if the State refuses to pay, the holder of the right would be able to execute judgment against the State. The degree of security of this right is measured by the existence of a machinery of enforcement within the governance zone, and by the power of the judiciary to compel observance of its decisions. This is, of course, an issue in all legal systems. In western systems the rule of law, a constitutional zone institution, is sufficiently entrenched to give confidence that the State would abide by court decisions. In the PRC doubts about the independence and competence of the judiciary (see, for example, Otto *et al.* 2000; Wang 2001) are fuelled by the political nature of judicial interpretation which has been described as 'primarily interpretation of government policy as embodied in the statutes' (Randolph & Jianbo 2000: 32). Ultimately problems of interpretation are referred back to the relevant government agency: even the highest court, the People's Supreme Court, has no power to strike down legislation as being contrary to the Constitution.

This political approach to problem-solving is consistent with the view of law as an instrument of the state, 'rule *by* law' rather than 'rule *of* law' (Wang 2001: 51, original emphasis) and reinforces the concern about differences between form and substance. In this situation gaps in the formal rule regimes may be filled by non-judicial agencies and officials (Keller 1994: 731). In the absence of a truly independent judiciary, political institutional arrangements for enforcement matter as much as, if not more than, judicial institutional arrangements. Even the rights expressly granted in the contract itself may be uncertain, given an attitude that treats contracts as non-binding arrangements subject to change. The problem of contract enforcement has been described as the 'most serious institutional problem for investment operations in China' (Wang 2001: 69). The enactment of a new detailed contract law in 1999, under which the remedy of specific performance is available, is no guarantee of security of rights. Formal laws do not dictate changes in attitude, or guarantee impartial adjudication.

A similar problem exists in respect of access to the land and building registers that are supposed to be maintained by local authorities. In theory, the registers are open to inspection, but in practice access may be refused by officials.[16] This could undermine transactions in real estate because title to a granted land use derives from its registration, not from the contract creating it. Ownership of buildings must also be registered but practice may vary because local authorities are permitted to adopt their own implementing regulations.

The institutionalised preference for informal methods of dispute resolution gives no greater comfort. Mediators may well be members of government departments also engaged in the business, for example as a partner to the joint venture. Arbitration awards depend upon court enforcement, which takes us back to the problem of an ineffective judiciary. Once again, property rights come to depend on institutional arrangements rather than on formal rule regimes.

### Institutional diversity within the governance zone

The institutional uncertainty resulting from the presence of governance-zone authorities in determining property rights is aggravated by the diversity of agencies with power to affect the transaction and the transacting process.

The range and diversity of rules, together with the absence of criteria for determining priority between conflicting provisions, present significant difficulties for the foreign investor in the PRC. The titles or designations of legislation often give no clue to their status or effect (Chen 1998: 88). In addition, problems of priority may not be resolved by the formal rules. Otto *et al.* (2000: 14–15) cite five particular problems of priority. Conflict between provisions promulgated by organs without any legislative competence, 'such as on a district level with people's congresses, permanent committees and administrative authorities' (Otto *et al.* 2000: 14–15) is of particular relevance to real estate transactions, given the fact that land-use rights are granted at the district level. The power of local government agencies to devise their own rules raises the prospect of inconsistency, ambiguity and conflict in the formal rules (Wang 2001: 52). In addition, the speed of change in laws can pose particular problems, especially if constitutional rights to compensation for interference with existing rights are not effectively enforced by the courts.

### *Responses to systemic uncertainty*

One might suppose that the high degree of systemic uncertainty outlined above, together with transactional uncertainties associated with local partners in the real estate development game, would deter investors. But investment in the PRC is increasing. According to one commentator, the 'answer to this apparent puzzle lies in the efficacy of informal networks in China'

(Wang 2001: 87). Confidence is manifested in informal institutions, notably *guanxi*, rather than the guarantees of impersonal laws. While *guanxi* is itself a source of risk, because it is based upon personal connections, it is an example of the importance of informal institutional arrangements in determining the subject matter of property rights in an uncertain world.

## Conclusion

The thesis of this chapter is that title to real estate, exemplified by Hong Kong and the PRC, is contingent upon the institutional arrangements that determine the subject matter of a particular transaction. However, it should not be assumed that this applies only to Hong Kong, the PRC or emerging systems. Even in the most comprehensive systems that accommodate freehold ownership, the quality of title may be dependent as much upon informal institutional arrangements as on the formal legal rules. Consider the following scenario from England.

H is a housing association that acquires a patch of bare land located in an area of high environmental value, in fact, a conservation area. H proposes to develop the land for 'affordable housing'. An application for planning permission to change the use of the land from 'open space' to 'residential' encounters rule regimes within the governance zone. The application process entails uncertainty and significant transaction costs, especially in view of the local authority's known reluctance to accept further development. On the other hand, the local authority also wishes to reverse the effects of market pricing, which has led to a loss of affordable housing for local residents in favour of holiday cottages for wealthy 'outsiders'.

In order to improve the chances of planning approval, H accepts planning obligations imposed by agreement with the local planning authority under section 106 of the Town and Country Planning Act 1990. The 'section 106 agreement' limits the occupation of buildings on the land to local residents in need of assistance. The development is completed and all of the houses become occupied by local residents (in accordance with the wishes of the local authority).

Several years pass, then one of the original owners, V, is offered a good price by a London-based stockbroker, P. P is aware of the occupation restriction, and knows that it is enforceable by the local planning authority against successors in title of H. In theory, therefore, P's title would be adversely affected by the restriction. But what would the local planning authority do if P bought the property and used it as a holiday home? How real is the risk of enforcement? This question ultimately depends upon rule regimes and institutional arrangements established by the local planning authority, despite the formal power of enforcement by injunction from courts operating within the governance zone. Even with the restriction on the freehold title to the property, P decides that the title is 'good enough' for his purposes, as a holiday home: precisely the situation that the section 106 agreement was intended to prevent.

The institutional analysis adopted in this chapter indicates that title to real estate does not depend simply upon formal rule regimes or upon formal institutional arrangements manifested in the terms of a contract, even in Hong Kong. What is visible or known is not necessarily the dominant influence on the transaction or upon the transacting process, even in well-established markets. Other, often hidden, institutional arrangements are part of the way things are done. This implies a need for a thorough and systematic analysis of institutional arrangements in every real estate transaction, wherever the land is situated.

# References

Alchian, A.A. & Demsetz, H. (1973) The Property Rights Paradigm. *Journal of Economic History* **33**(Mar),16–27.

Alston, L.J., Eggertsson, T. & North, D.C. (eds) (1996) *Empirical Studies in Institutional Change.* Cambridge University Press, Cambridge, UK.

Alston, L.J., Libecap, G.D. & Mueller, B. (1999) *Titles, Conflict, and Land Use: The development of property rights and land reform on the Brazilian Amazon frontier.* University of Michigan Press, Ann Arbor, MI.

Barzel, Y. (1997) *Economic Analysis of Property Rights,* 2nd edn. Cambridge University Press, Cambridge, UK.

Chen, A. (1998) *An Introduction to the Legal System of the People's Republic of China,* 4th impression (2002). LexisNexis Butterworths, Hong Kong.

de Soto, H. (2000) *The Mystery of Capital.* Bantam Press, London.

Demsetz, H. (1967) Toward a Theory of Property Rights. *American Economic Review,* **57**(May), 347–59.

Dwyer, J.P. & Menell, P.S. (1998) *Property Law and Policy: A Comparative Institutional Perspective.* The Foundation Press, New York.

Eggertsson, T. (1996) A Note on the Economics of Institutions. In: Alston, L.J., Eggertsson, T. & North, D.C. (eds) *Empirical Studies in Institutional Change.* Cambridge University Press, Cambridge, UK.

Evans-Jones, R. (1999) Roman Law in Scotland and England and the Development of One Law for Britain. *Law Quarterly Review* **115**(Oct), 604–30.

Ho, D.Y.H. & Co (1998) *Real Estate in China.* Butterworths Asia, Hong Kong.

Keller, P. (1994) Sources of Order in Chinese Law. *American Journal of Comparative Law* **42**(4), 711–60.

North, D.C. & Thomas, R.P. (1971) The Rise and Fall of the Manorial System: A Theoretical Model. *Journal of Economic History*, **31**(Dec), 777–803.

Oi, J.C. & Walder, A.G. (eds) (1999) *Property Rights and Economic Reform in China.* Stanford University Press, Stanford, CA.

Otto, J.M., Polak, M.V., Chen, J. & Li, Y. (2000) *Law-Making in the People's Republic of China.* Kluwer Law International, The Hague, Netherlands.

Paul, E.F., Miller, F.D. & Paul, J. (eds) (1994) *Property Rights.* Cambridge University Press, Cambridge, UK.

Randolph, P.A. & Jianbo, L. (2000) *Chinese Real Estate Law.* Kluwer Law International, The Hague, Netherlands.

Wang, H. (2001) *Weak State, Strong Networks.* Oxford University Press (China), Hong Kong.

Williamson, O.E. (1993) Calculativeness, Trust and Economic Organization. *Journal of Law and Economics*, **36**, 453.

Zimmermann, R. (1996) Savigny's Legacy: Legal History, Comparative Law, and the Emergence of a European Legal Science. *Law Quarterly Review*, **112**(Oct), 576–605.

Zimmermann, R. (2001) *Roman Law, Contemporary Law, European Law, The Civilian Tradition Today.* Oxford University Press, Oxford, UK.

# Notes

1 *Hang Wah Chong Investment Co Ltd* v. *Attorney General* [1981] 1 WLR 1141 (PC); *Canadian Overseas Development Co Ltd* v. *Attorney General* [1991] 1 HKC 288; *Secan Ltd* v. *Attorney General* [1995] 2 HKC 629; and *Polarace Investments Ltd* v. *Director of Lands* [1997] 1 HKC 373.

2 *Winfat Enterprises (HK) Ltd* v. *A-G of Hong Kong* [1988] 1 HKLR 5 (PC).

3 *MEPC* v. *Christian Edwards* [1981] AC 205; *Woomera Co Ltd* v. *Provident Centre Development Ltd* [1985] 1 HKC 257.

4 *Kan Wing Yau* v. *Hong Kong Housing Society* (1987) HCMP No 2436 of 1987; *Chi Kit Co Ltd & Another* v. *Lucky Health International Enterprise Ltd* [2000] 3 HKC 143 CFA.

5 *Spark Rich (China) Ltd* v. *Valrose Ltd* (1999) CACV 249/98; *Chi Kit*, above.

6 See, for example, *Active Keen Industries Ltd* v. *Fok Chi Keong* [1994] 2 HKC 67.

7 Much of this section is based upon the law as expressed in Randolph & Jianbo (2000) *Chinese Real Estate Law*, Kluwer Law International, The Hague, to whom the author is indebted.

8 Constitution 1982 Article 10, Land Administration Law 1986, Article 2.

9 Law on Urban Real Estate Administration 1994, s38.

10 Law on Urban Real Estate Administration 1994, s39.

11 Land Administration Law 1986 sections 9 & 10; Rules for Land Registration 1996.

12 The terms of the contract are derived from the Official Forms of contract for granting land-use rights reproduced in Randolph & Jianbo (2000: 363–87).

13 Land Administration Law s56; Law on Urban Real Estate Administration, Article 17.

14 See, for example, the differences between the majority and minority judgments in *Tinsley* v. *Milligan* [1993] 3 All ER 65.

15 *Street* v. *Mountford* [1985] AC 809, per Lord Templeman.

16 See section 3 of the Implementing Regulations of the Land Administration Law 1998 and commentary in Randolph & Jianbo 2000: 166.

# Part 2

## Evolution of the Institutional Context of International Real Estate

# Introduction

Each chapter in this part has been contributed by a different author or authors. The purpose of grouping them together is to illustrate the nature of the rules of the game within which real estate decisions occur in different places and under different conditions.

Chapter 4 explores the notion that in the face of growing global competition and integration, cities and urban regions are no longer helpless in shaping their own futures. It explains that cities and networks of cities can be a locus of economic power and progress, but in a global context, traditional urban policy mechanisms and property market institutions can become ineffectual, requiring new modes of thought, active strategies, active policies, and property market institutions. It highlights the growing connectedness between global cities and their property markets, emphasising the importance of the role of property market institutions in developing competitive strategies. It argues that sound property market institutions and supporting infrastructure are critical to the competitiveness of the urban region.

Using Hong Kong as an example, chapter 5 examines the relationship between urban planning and property development. In achieving the objective of distributing scarce land uses and property rights to different groups, organisations and social classes in cities, urban planning relies on powerful rule regimes that form part of the institutional framework within which urban social interactions are managed and accommodated spatially. This welfare role, which has been characterised as 'collective action pertinent to decisions concerning the social utilisation of urban land', certainly affects private real estate interests. It attempts to answer the key questions that concern property developers, namely: What are the rules? How are they set? How can they be changed? How much can they be changed? What are the costs of pursuing such changes?

Chapter 6 examines the evolution of an institutional framework that is supra-national, but not federal – a pan-European market area, free of barriers (physical or institutional) between the member states. The potential for reductions in the transaction costs associated with free trade within the European Union is clear. However, the chapter highlights many of the questions and uncertainties generated by this evolution, contrasting this with the relative maturity (stability and robustness) of the prevailing institutions of the member states. Using the UK as an illustrative case study, it provides a contrast between the national uniqueness of land tenure systems in each member state and the introduction of pan-European policies on environmental protection.

Chapter 7 explores the institutional influences at work at the operational level of real estate investment appraisal. It argues that the nature of global capital markets creates their own rules of the game, which have a direct impact on the computation of the value of investments or large-scale projects. It also examines the appraisal process associated with the testing of project proposals. The selection and implementation of methods for project appraisal is strongly influenced by rules of a constitutional and governance nature. This is exemplified by the constitutionally derived powers of international funding agencies such as the World Bank and the Asian Development Bank. They in turn establish their own rules for project appraisal, with a marked preference in favour of conventional appraisal methods such as discounted cash-flow analysis and cost-benefit analysis, reflecting a bias in favour of consistency (in the application of methods that have become settled practice) rather than project-specific accuracy. This is illustrated by a case study relating to projects funded by the Asian Development Bank.

# 4

# Local Property Markets and Effective Flexible Market Institutions

## Michael A. Goldberg

## The issues

### Flexible and adaptive property market institutions and infrastructure

This chapter begins by exploring 'global (or world) cities' to set the stage for a larger discussion of the policy institutions needed to manage them successfully where cities are both a cause and effect of globalisation. Property markets in these cities and the institutions and policies that guide urban development are special concerns here. The globalisation of property markets is both a metaphor and a mechanism for globalisation processes. Understanding globalisation in general and globalisation of real property markets is vital for crafting and implementing effective future urban policy. Flexible, responsive and competitive property market institutions and good infrastructure are central elements for urban regions to prosper in the global city network. Accordingly, this chapter begins by reviewing briefly the evolution of global cities as both outcomes and shapers of globalisation. It then sketches how their property markets are becoming integrated. It closes with a discussion of property market policy and regulatory institutions and the need for flexible and adaptive policies and guidance mechanisms combined with appropriate infrastructure development.

### Global cities

Global (or world) cities are those urban centres at the nexus of global economic decision-making (Hall 1984). These cities are integrated and functioning elements in a global network. Global cities, individually and through their network partners, increasingly make key economic decisions that allocate capital (both human and financial); influence governments world-wide directly and by their investment decisions; and host global corporations, international organisations and cultural institutions. In short, global cities are emerging as the crossroads for people, capital and information, the grist for today's global economic mill.

As King (1990) documents thoroughly, many researchers broadened the global or world city concept by adding one or more important specific functions or traits to characterise these cities. Friedmann and Wolff (1982) are particularly concerned about the network of global cities and its impact on the spatial organisation of production and product and service markets. Subsequently Friedmann (1986) focuses on the importance of financial functions, the presence of global and regional headquarters and international institutions, and business services in describing world cities, while Dunning and Norman (1983) focus on multinational enterprises (MNEs), their location in world cities and their ability to direct the location of branch plants and offices around the world, particularly in developing nations.

There is an ongoing and heated debate in the literature about the competitiveness of cities and their ability to make explicit strategies for competing globally (Budd 1998; Maskell & Törnqvist 1999). This chapter sides with those who argue that cities can influence their competitiveness through crafting and implementing appropriate strategies (see Goldberg (2000) for a more complete statement of the argument). Moreover, a key theme below is that effective and flexible property market institutions need to be part of any effective competitive strategy.

## Global forces introduced: an overview

### Financial markets: leading the globalisation wave

One of the first forces globalising cities was the integration of capital markets dating from the 1950s when the Soviet Union held its US dollar balances outside the US to avoid possible seizure of these assets (Levi 1989). This was a progenitor of the eurodollar market, the foundation of modern international banking. From about $110 billion in 1970, the Eurocurrency market is now estimated to exceed $4.0 trillion. Trade imbalances (e.g. 'petro-dollars' and 'samurai bonds') have also been important contributors to the growth in international lending and Eurocurrency activity.

Another force behind the internationalisation of financial markets is, in part, the breakdown of the Bretton Woods agreement with the move to floating exchange rates after 1971. Floating exchange rates increased foreign exchange risks, leading to a proliferation of financial instruments (e.g. currency futures and options) as hedges. Internationalisation of finance would have been impossible though without the use of advanced technology, particularly in telecommunications and computers (Hamilton 1986). In 1970 the 'clearing house interbank payments system' (CHIPS) was created. In 1972 the Society for Worldwide Interbank Financial Telecommunications (SWIFT) was formed for international payments instructions. Starting in May 1977, it carried some 800 banking transactions daily and now numbers in the millions each day.

Telecommunications progress has enabled stock, option and commodity exchanges to trade globally. Since 1984, the Singapore International Monetary Exchange (SIMEX) and the Chicago Mercantile Exchange (CME) have been linked to offer financial futures and options, allowing market players to take a position on one exchange and liquidate it on the other, creating a 24-hour trading day. Technology created the possibility of a truly global financial market, leading to more competition. Technology has fostered new financial instruments and, arguably (Kaufman 1986), greater efficiency via instantaneous global flows of information.

A final key factor in financial market globalisation was the deregulation and liberalisation of financial markets in the 1970s and 1980s. Deregulation led to the integration of domestic financial systems into a single global financial market, where no country could regulate its financial sector in isolation (Hamilton 1986). Deregulation is self-propagating, forcing global harmonisation of financial rules and regulations. Globalisation will intensify as borrowers seek the lowest cost funds no matter where they are located, while investors use liberalised financial markets for portfolio diversification, yield enhancement and new investment opportunities.

## Property markets: latecomers but large players in globalisation

Yield enhancement and diversification are also thrusting urban property markets onto the global business stage (Gordon 1991). Local housing markets now operate in a truly global context, suggesting that urban housing policy must increasingly be aware of the international forces impacting their local setting (Goldberg 1985, 1990).

The collapse of real estate markets in North America, Europe and Japan in the early 1990s has clearly slowed the pace of international real estate investment in and from these countries (McCoy 1991). The Asian crisis of the late 1990s also slowed the pace of investment into and out of Asia. However, the initial real estate investment frenzy of the late 1980s led to the present irreversible state of widespread foreign ownership of real property in virtually all global cities, and the emergence of a truly global real estate market, particularly among global and soon-to-be-global cities.

## Background forces and trends

Real estate markets are becoming linked along lines that were so clearly noticeable in financial markets. As information becomes global, cities are being forged into a powerful network of financial and managerial functions. Financial and economic information flows essentially instantaneously among these cities. As more transnational corporations, especially international banks and financial firms and their clients, locate regional and branch offices in global cities, information about the cities themselves and their property markets is poured into the information networks linking global cities (McGee 1984). This free flow of urban economic and property information combines with the free flow of capital that was so essential to the globalisation of financial markets to create the basis (i.e. the necessary conditions) for a truly global property market.

The potential for globalisation of real estate markets started to be realised with the accumulation of huge capital pools that could flow among the cities of the network in response to economic information about these cities and their property investment opportunities. These large pools of capital arose from several sources. First, trade surpluses have been significant sources going back to the nineteenth century with British mercantilist surpluses leading to widespread real estate investment in North America; secondly, the petrodollars of the 1970s flooded London's property market; and thirdly, Japanese trade surpluses of the 1980s flooded North American and Australian property markets (Edgington 1988).

Large pools of real estate investment capital also can be traced to the burgeoning coffers of pension funds in North America, Southeast Asia, Japan and Europe. The gargantuan Japanese postal savings system, worth some US$3 trillion, poses the most dramatic possibility for global real estate investment. The registered pension funds of Canada and the US also total some US$3 trillion and, should as little as 10% of those funds find their way into real estate investment, they must quickly start spreading around the globe so as not to overheat any specific North American urban market. Indeed, it has been suggested (Hamilton & Heinkel 1994) that pension funds should place up to 20% of their assets into real estate, implying an even more dramatic global search for suitable properties.

Among the most frequently cited sources of investment capital seeking global outlets in property markets are the Southeast Asian ethnic Chinese who have benefited from and been at the centre of the economic explosion of the Asia Pacific region. Through their extensive world-wide family networks, the ethnic Chinese have spanned the globe looking for sound real estate investment opportunities to diversify their portfolios and provide safety for future generations of their extended families (Goldberg 1985). While the Southeast Asian ethnic Chinese and the Japanese have received the most media attention, a substantial pool of capital amassed by European families over centuries has quietly, and out of the limelight, been acquiring extensive real estate holdings for decades in North America, Australia and South America. Though less visible than recent Asian investment, British, Dutch and German investors have enormous holdings of property throughout the New World, and in many ways were the precursors of today's global real estate market.

## Indications of global integration in urban property markets

Against this backdrop we can explore some specific evidence of the global movement of real estate investment capital, which began on a large scale in the 1980s and 1990s. First, in the US, a remarkably sheltered and isolated place despite its international pre-eminence, the mass and professional media frequently focus on foreign investment in real estate, even during the 1980s collapse of most US markets (Bacow 1988; *Shopping Centers Today* 1991, 1992; Rodman 1992). The passage of the North American Free Trade Agreement (NAFTA) has created significant interest in trans-border real estate investment (Foster 1991; Robaton 1994). The development of global real estate pools like the US$2 billion global fund by the Prudential Insurance Company (Miles 1994) and the US$400 million Government of Singapore Investment Corporation purchase of a Seoul office tower (*Asiaweek* 2000) are evidence that real estate investment is global, and likely to stay global. The creation of new investment instruments based on underlying real estate assets makes it possible for real estate-based securities to be traded globally and further integrates property markets and ties them to global financial markets (Ryland 1993; Cooperman *et al.* 1994).

The Canadian situation is very similar, as is that in Australia, Asia and Europe. Given the growth in globally integrated activities (e.g. multinational firms and international finance) it is obvious that all these firms need urban space. Thus, more and more market information flows around the world instantly. Combine this global market information explosion with the need for space and geographic diversification of investment capital and a decade of inflation in the 1980s, the global real estate boom that resulted, and a world property market follows logically. Despite the decline and even the disintegration of some local and regional real estate markets, real estate markets were so thoroughly globalised during the 1980s boom that there is simply no turning back now. The Asian crisis of the late 1990s was largely the result of the globalisation of real estate with enormous flows of funds into overheated, and subsequently oversupplied, urban and resort real property markets.

Hard and fast numbers on the dollar value of offshore investment are extremely difficult to obtain since much investment is done by small investors, nominees, family members, or through corporations. Accordingly, it is necessary to rely on more fragmentary, but relatively abundant, qualitative evidence to paint a picture of offshore investment in North American real property. Also, much foreign real estate investment in North America is associated with immigration and family relationships from the originating country. Thus, it is often difficult to ascertain whether or not an investment is foreign or whether it is really a domestic investment on the part of a Canadian or American family member.

Looking specifically at the United States, Canada is not surprisingly the largest investor, followed by Europeans and then Asians (*Land Use Digest* 1991). The Japanese were very active during the late 1980s (*Land Use Digest* 1990), but the decline of the Tokyo market in the 1990s dampened their enthusiasm for North American property (Leventhal 1990). In Canada, the US is the largest investor, followed by the British, Dutch and Germans (*Canada Yearbook* 1990). A great deal of investment has also been made by ethnic Chinese families and by Japanese businesses (Goldberg 1985).

## The global/world city and the new international division of labour

The 'new international division of labour' (NIDL) argues that production is organised and managed on a global scale, tying previously independent rural agrarian economies directly into the global marketplace (Frobel *et al.* 1980; Cohen 1981). This global production is tied to the emergence of global corporations which can internalise many specific product markets, allocate capital globally to the most profitable locales, and gather, process and communicate information globally to carry out its functions (Taylor & Thrift 1982; Thrift 1983). These functions almost force global corporations into cities, creating global cities which reinforce the rise of global corporations (Hall 1991), a process that has accelerated with the growth of regional trade blocs like the EU and NAFTA (Kresl 1992; Epstein *et al.* 1993).

## Local, regional and national forces impinging on global cities

### Forces deriving from structural economic change

The new international division of labour represents one important facet of structural economic change facing cities. A related change is the dominance of the services in advanced economies and the relative (and often absolute) decline of goods production, due in part to higher wages in developed countries, in part to growing environmental controls, and in part to rapid technological change reducing employment in goods-producing industries. Service activity is much less dependent on the location criteria of the industrial era. These activities are essentially footloose and location of services is increasingly quality of life-driven since employees and managers of service firms prefer living in high-quality and secure surroundings (Blomquist *et al.* 1988). The physical environment is also important as an attractor of the highly skilled labour pool needed to drive service (particularly knowledge-based) industries: clean air, clean water, and recreational activities linked to high-quality natural and built environments do matter and will likely play a larger future role in changing urban and global economies.

The move to services also suggests (and in part helps to explain) that there will be a bimodal distribution of job opportunities in developed nations, typified by higher paying managerial and professional jobs and lower paying semi-skilled or unskilled jobs. Resulting housing demand should be bimodal, as in Hong Kong, Vancouver and Toronto where high-priced condominiums are being built simultaneously with smaller, more affordable units.

Likely the greatest driver, though, of urban economic change is the highly open and cyclical nature of urban economies – a key differentiator of urban and national economies. As a result of their high volatility and their openness to external shocks, cities must be highly adaptable and flexible because they cannot diversify themselves very greatly (as compared with national economies). This forces cities to be more accommodating than larger state/provincial and national economies. Their smaller scale and greater degree of openness to competition and economic forces imposes on them a discipline that is usually lacking at more senior government levels. The inability of cities and urban regions to provide large subsidies to inefficient private sector firms suggests that the private sector must be more competitive and adaptable, a point made by Jane Jacobs very powerfully in 1969 and again in 1984 (Jacobs 1969, 1984).

The urban public sector must also be more competitive. Urban residents are quite efficient users of urban public services. As cities are the lowest level of government, they are best able to equate marginal costs of public services (i.e. local taxes) with marginal benefits of the bundle of public goods preferred locally. In contrast, national and provincial governments have to provide public goods that span the interests of all residents in the jurisdiction. The resulting bundle becomes quite large and complex. It becomes very difficult to price properly the costs and benefits associated with each of the national state/provincial bundle's attributes.

Cities are under pressure to equate marginal costs of providing goods (prices and taxes) with marginal benefits and revenues. This pushes cities, more than larger government units, to seek, and in many cases achieve, allocation efficiency. The pressure on cities to change, adapt and be efficient is greater than that felt by other levels of government, and represents a force that cannot be overlooked. Also, cities are the level of government with the least ability to delude citizens about the service bundle provided. They exhibit a similar inability to shield residents from external economic and political pressures. These factors force cities to be adaptive à la Jacobs above. This need to respond to external forces provides cities with their essential economic and evolutionary 'fitness'. As Peirce et al. (1993) argue, it is time to rethink notions that cities are the tail of the global economic dog, and replace them with older city-state ideas that saw the global economy as the result of city-states and federations and networks of city-states. Such a view clearly turns conventional wisdom on its head, but it has intellectual appeal and is in keeping with earlier arguments and illustrations made by Jacobs a quarter of a century ago.

## Forces deriving from demographic change

In countries of the Organization for Economic Co-operation and Development (OECD), where most global cities are located, increasing average age of population, slowing birth rates and the increasing importance of international (both legal and illegal) and interregional migration are all facets of the demographic forces shaping these cities and their property markets.

Accommodating new immigrants and changing tastes (both from new and existing residents) will require alterations to current development and land-use regulation, leading to new land-use forms and densities that are not possible at present. In emerging global cities like Bangkok, Beijing, Shanghai, Sao Paolo, Rio de Janeiro, Buenos Aires and Mexico City, rapid population growth and youth are still the rule, with large numbers of rural migrants. Thus, in both OECD global cities and those of the developing world, immigration drives population growth.

International immigration is a very important issue for global cities as they receive the greatest numbers of international immigrants and they further internationalise and connect global cities to other global cities undergoing analogous change as a result of international immigration (Heenan & Perlmutter 1978). Global cities extend their reach because of such international immigration and stimulate more immigration given their role in the flow of global economic information, managerial decisions and capital (Friedmann & Wolff 1982; Friedmann 1986). Vancouver, Los Angeles, San Francisco, Sydney and Melbourne all provide interesting and quite different examples of the extent to which international migration has helped propel them into the ranks of global cities and caused them to receive additional international immigration and thus solidify and shape their niche in the global city network.

## Forces associated with protecting the biophysical environment

Environmental protection will profoundly affect the growth and future of all cities, but especially global cities, given that growing environmental concerns force policy decisions that do not degrade the physical environment. Policy-makers will be called upon to remedy past sins through renewed emphasis on public transportation and land-use policies which decrease air, water and noise pollution, while protecting and expanding open spaces for public use and enjoyment.

## Summarising the global city urban development and policy-making context

All the foregoing factors will reinforce and exacerbate the open and cyclical nature of urban economies. Urban areas will increasingly be impacted by economic shifts occurring in other areas. These shifts will impact urban economies directly through the demand for goods and services produced locally and also through shifts in global real estate investment patterns. Migration flows, themselves not unrelated to global economic forces, will also subject urban areas to cyclical fluctuations and instabilities. International population flows are increasingly difficult to monitor and influence, as recent refugee issues and family reunification policies are proving in Canada. The confluence of urban economic growth and change, and demographic growth and change largely resulting from international immigration, combine to subject local property markets to stresses and strains only hinted at during the real estate boom of the late 1990s. As economic and demographic pressures move around the world, global cities and their property markets can be expected to be particularly sensitive to these ebbs and flows because cities are at the centre of the international flow of people, capital and information.

## Globalisation of world city property markets: observations and caveats on volatility

### *An institutional aside on why property markets are inherently volatile*

Investment capital flows unceasingly, if unevenly, into world cities, responding to the forces noted above. This influx has not been without its costs though, as can be seen from the heightened volatility that has typified property markets during the 1990s. The cyclical behaviour of real estate markets needs to be treated explicitly here as the erratic behaviour of property markets interacts with the volatility of open urban economies to provide policy-makers and investors with some real challenges for making sound policy and investment decisions concerning world city property markets. An exploration of the dynamics of global city property markets is in order, therefore, if we are to set the appropriate context for seriously considering new and more effective modes of policy-making and property investing in our global economy.

Real estate, as students in introductory courses are taught, has some unique and defining traits that differentiate it from other assets (Wurtzebach & Miles 1994). It is durable. Thus, the supply of real estate includes this year's production and also the standing stock that has accumulated over decades or centuries. It is highly regulated. Thus, producing new buildings takes time. Real estate production is capital intensive and heavily reliant on the availability of high debt financing both for developers of real estate and for purchasers. Finally, the demand for real estate is a function not only of the volatile availability of capital noted below but also of the demand fluctuations brought on by the ups and downs of the local and open urban economy discussed previously.

These features when taken together suggest that real property markets will be highly cyclical in their traditional localised setting. The long production time means that there are significant leads and lags in property markets that create volatility. Periodic spurts in demand, resulting from good economic times and the availability of capital to both producers and purchasers of real estate, combine with the lags resulting from regulation and long production times, implying that it takes several years before an observed increase in demand can be translated into increased supply. During this construction period prices continue to rise, encouraging more supply to be started. Several years of active building ensue and supply begins to rise and keep rising, even after the initial demand spurt has been met, leading to oversupply and falling prices and a downturn in the property cycle. This is worsened considerably by the already noted close and highly sensitive link to monetary policy and urban economic cycles.

## Real estate cycles and world cities: vulnerability through connectedness

The foregoing dynamic and causal chain has been documented too frequently in too many cities around the world to list here. The real estate cycle in its purely local traditional form has perplexed and challenged lenders, developers, local planners and policy-makers for a very long time. Placing property markets in a global context does nothing to reduce the volatility of these once purely local markets and their cycles. As argued below, globalising property markets is likely to make them considerably more volatile and heighten the already substantial challenge of managing them.

It is vital, therefore, that we understand some of the sources of this added volatility if we are to manage effectively global city property markets in their global context. Much of the increased volatility facing world city real estate derives from the same forces that have made financial markets so much more unpredictable than previously. This should be no surprise since the fluctuating flow of international capital is itself one of the causes of real estate market instability. Modern telecommunications and computing technology enable information to move, unrestricted, across the globe at electronic speeds and financial capital to flow in response to this information, also at electronic speeds. The technology of financial instrument design has also added to market instability by creating highly specialised new instruments whose markets are extremely sensitive, not only to underlying information from the real estate sector but also to financial information, creating positive feedback loops that aggravate market volatility so that financial flows are affected by information about these same financial flows.

Deregulation of financial institutions and the removal of international barriers to financial flows have greatly aided the flow of financial capital. They have also removed a former buffer, greatly speeding the responsiveness of national capital markets. The benefits of these near instantaneous financial market reactions are improved market efficiency and enormous increases in the volumes of transactions that can be handled. Capital can move anywhere to find its highest risk-return use. Real estate markets benefit from this improved efficiency of global capital markets because they can now obtain needed equity and debt financing from a much wider global market rather than having to rely on local or national sources.

The benefits, however, are not without the costs of volatility and vulnerability. Connecting local property markets, especially those in world cities, to global information networks and capital markets can move capital in vast quantities around the world and into (and out of) world city property markets, heightening property market peaks and deepening slumps in the process. Daly (1982) noted this in Sydney over 20 years ago. Through global integration of urban property markets, local enclaves are tied to the global economic system for good and bad. Restoring resilience, flexibility and longer-term stability to the global system is one of the principal tasks facing global city policy-makers in both the public and private sectors.

## Vancouver: an emerging world city facing prototypical issues in the global economy

Vancouver, British Columbia provides an example of an emerging world city grappling with ways to transform itself, and manage this transformation, from a western Canadian centre to a Pacific Rim world city. Vancouver's efforts, and the challenges that it has encountered along the way, are reviewed here. They are likely to be instructive for urban policy-makers who find that they too must govern and make decisions in the context of (1) the global economic reality and (2) the network of global/world cities within which they must function in order to prosper. It is particularly useful to examine Vancouver's much publicised property market and how the market and policy-makers have dealt with becoming international.

*Vancouver in an international context as an emerging international city*

Vancouver, 135 miles north of Seattle, Washington, is a metropolitan area of slightly more than 1.5 million people. It is a surprisingly international city for its size. It has the second busiest international airport on the Pacific Coast, for example, handling three times as many international passengers as does Seattle-Tacoma (Sea-Tac) Airport, despite having a total passenger volume only two-thirds that of Sea-Tac.

Its global world-view is instructive because of its success in attracting global investment, tourism and immigrants. Eighteen foreign banks have branches in Vancouver; two more have representative offices. Six foreign securities dealers and eight leading global investment managers have branches in the city. Additionally, a total of 16 foreign language newspapers are published in the Vancouver region, consistent with the presence of 45 foreign consulates.

Foreign language speakers are also commonplace. For example, more than 50% of Vancouver public school pupils have English as a second language (ESL). There is a three-year waiting list for French immersion programmes (the longest wait in Canada) and the highest participation rate of any English-speaking province. Moreover, secondary school students now take Japanese or Mandarin for graduation purposes. Such openness to foreign languages is in keeping with the ethnic mélange that is the Vancouver regional population. Early post-World War II immigrants came largely from western Europe. There are some 130,000 people of German ancestry, roughly 80,000 people of Dutch and Greek ancestry, some 60,000 Italians, 40,000 Portuguese and several thousand each of Yugoslavs, Danes and Swiss. Since 1970, there has been a dramatic shift to Asian immigration led by ethnic Chinese from Hong Kong and secondarily Singapore and Malaysia. In the 1990s, Taiwan and the People's Republic of China were at the top of the list of source countries for immigrants. In the province, roughly 400,000 people have Chinese ancestry, of whom some 300,000 live in the Greater Vancouver region. There is a large Indian community in excess of 150,000 people, of whom 75% are Sikhs from the Punjab. There are also some 50,000 ethnic Koreans and 30,000 ethnic Japanese, mostly third and fourth generation Canadians, with some 10,000 Japanese business people and their families.

Given such a diverse population, and a location mid-way between Europe and Asia, it is not surprising that more than a dozen foreign business associations are active in Vancouver. In fact, the second largest business group in the province is the Hong Kong–Canada Business Association with nearly 1,000 members, second only to the Vancouver Board of Trade.

Lastly, Vancouver is home to provincially sponsored initiatives designed to promote international finance (the International Financial Centre), international shipping (the International Maritime Centre) and international commercial arbitration (the International Commercial Arbitration Centre). All have been successful in attracting new international business activity to Vancouver, which broadens its economic base and its range of international customers. Vancouver also houses the federally chartered Asia Pacific Foundation patterned after the Asia Society in the US. These activities have been the result of federal, provincial and urban/regional policy initiatives directly aimed at expanding the international scope of Vancouver's economy so that the city is truly a global city and an important link in the growing network of Pacific Rim managerial and financial centres. Finally, the Vancouver International Airport Authority was created in 1992 as a local operating authority. It rents the airport (identifying code letters YVR) from the federal government that owns all airports in Canada. Under its new, more independent management structure, YVR is working to greatly expand the airport facilities and improve existing ones to bring the entire airport infrastructure up to the highest international standards so that YVR can become the principal gateway between Asia and North America. The May 1995 'Open Skies Treaty' greatly expanded cross-border travel and has made YVR a trans-Pacific hub (exceeded only by Los Angeles) and a powerful building block for global city status and functioning (Goldberg 2000, 2001).

## Local, provincial and federal actions aiding Vancouver's emergence as a global city

The internationalism illustrated above is the result of conscious actions by both governments and the private sector. The British Columbia economy is highly reliant on international trade (nearly 40% of provincial income derives from trade). The US accounts for roughly 80% of exports today, with Asia another 15% and Europe 5%. Tourism is now well ahead of mining as the province's number two industry. Vancouver hotel occupancy topped North America in 1992, 1993 and 1994, and is still among the highest.

The British Columbia provincial economy has historically been resource-based and highly cyclical. Vancouver, as the province's principal city, has similarly experienced its booms and busts. In order to broaden the economic base of the province and city, numerous initiatives have been introduced to expand the service sector, particularly related to such internationally traded services as finance, tourism, health and education. There are several key elements involved in the strategy to make Vancouver a major Asia Pacific urban centre. To begin, in the late 1970s the City of Vancouver formed the Vancouver Economic Advisory Commission (VEAC) to help develop an economic strategy for the city. The strategy evolved through a series of public meetings and several drafts to the point where it was formally adopted by the City of Vancouver in 1983. It sought to build on the region's strengths in retail, business and public services to British Columbia and Western Canada (Vancouver Economic Advisory Commission, various years).

At the same time, the province was building EXPO '86 and doing post EXPO planning. Developing an international financial services centre in Vancouver was a primary provincial concern, building on the Vancouver Stock Exchange, the several university business schools in the region, the existing regional financial infrastructure, and the absence of any history of exchange controls or freezing of foreign assets in Canada. This combined with excellent airline access to Asia and Europe (subsequently improved considerably), moderate living and office costs, good accounting and consulting support services, and a high-quality physical environment to suggest that the idea was worth pursuing further. Thus, in 1986 the province created 'IFC Vancouver' to promote Vancouver as an international financial centre and build on the following federal activities.

In February 1986 the governments of Canada and British Columbia signed a 'Memorandum of Understanding' (MOU) to establish Vancouver as a 'Pacific Rim centre for trade, tourism and finance'. Over C$6 million was allocated to research, policy development and implementation, to achieve the objectives of the MOU (Asia Pacific Initiative 1988). Also in the February 1986 federal budget, Vancouver and Montreal were designated as 'international banking centres' where financial institutions could make offshore loans with offshore deposits, free of Canadian income tax. This federal measure was complemented by legislation in British Columbia to exempt a broader range of international financial transactions from provincial tax, further spurring international financial business in Vancouver (Ministry of Finance and Corporate Relations 1987). The provincial measures passed in October 1988 and created IFC Vancouver, a provincially sponsored agency, to foster Vancouver as an international financial centre (Goldberg 1990).

These conscious attempts to internationalise Vancouver's economy and population have been successful in positioning Vancouver globally. This success has not been without actual and perceived costs, virtually all of which have related to housing issues. As a result, Vancouver provides a useful example of the need for urban housing and development policy to consider the global context when making local housing policy (Edgington & Goldberg 1992).

# Vancouver's globalised property market: the cycle of the late 1980s

## *Asia Pacific migration and investment: its local impacts*

Paralleling government efforts to attract East Asian immigration and investment to move Vancouver into world city networks, concern emerged during a modest housing boom in the late 1980s that immigration and investment were driving up housing prices and destroying traditional neighbourhoods. Vancouver was changing and local citizens had little control over what was happening – really a core issue for managing a world city in a global economy. This sense of loss of control to international forces was manifested in Vancouver's housing market: Asian money and migration were blamed for rising house prices. Average prices for single detached homes in Vancouver's desirable west side rose from about C$250,000 to C$350,000 in 1987–1988 (Vancouver Planning Department 1989).

Analyses of this tight housing situation in metropolitan Vancouver have pointed not to overseas immigration *per se*, but to a more general mismatch between the demand for and supply of housing units (Baxter 1989; Schwann 1989). Apart from Asian migration and investment, the strong demand for housing was a result of both the general attractiveness of Vancouver as a place to live and the relative prosperity of the local job market (Vancouver Planning Department 1989). Thus in 1988, net migration to British Columbia was estimated to be 46,580 people, an increase of about 45% over 1987 and the largest population increase since the 1940s. In particular, net interprovincial migration from the rest of Canada rose sharply in 1988 by 53%, after five years of overall decline consequent to the recession of the early 1980s, whereas net international migration increased by only 32.5% in the same period (Schwann 1989).

Compared with the high levels of housing demand, only about 6,000 additional single-family lots were added to supply in the Vancouver area in 1988, well below what was needed. The policy implications of these studies are clear: with or without in-migration, demand for well-located housing in Vancouver will grow, placing pressure on prices unless the supply of units keeps pace. This will mean increased densities in highly accessible existing suburbs as well as in new developments in more distant suburban locations.

The belief lingered for several years of a direct link between overseas investment and local housing prices. This was heightened by price increases and redevelopment pressures, which occurred in areas favoured by affluent migrants from Hong Kong (e.g. Vancouver's west side). Education was tied to clustering of Asian migrants, given their penchant for quality schools. In some of the best primary and secondary schools, ethnic Chinese form the majority.

Throughout 1989, demand increased for the City Council to down-zone parts of the city subject to strong redevelopment pressure. This was resisted, but in recognising the local community's apprehension and reluctance to accept rapid rates of change, the Council introduced demolition controls contingent upon six months' notice being given to tenants, or their relocation to another property, thus hoping to slow the demolition–rebuilding cycle in particular neighbourhoods. With hindsight, neither the provincial nor city government has shown any enthusiasm for controls on real estate which may adversely affect the flows of investment to Vancouver from the Asia Pacific region. In the longer term, it is already apparent that many investors and immigrants from Asia (and elsewhere) are shifting their investments from 'passive' real estate acquisitions into new development and beyond real estate into sectors such as light manufacturing, food processing and trading, all of which fit better the strategic economic objectives described earlier.

Also since the beginning of the 1990s, housing demand and supply have balanced and prices are stable. There has been little if any talk of Asians making housing unaffordable. Rather, there seems to be a growing and surprisingly widespread understanding of the roles that immigrants from Asia are playing in plugging Vancouver into the global city network, helping the urban economy restructure, and allowing the provincial economy to skirt the late 1980s recession that plagued North America. In short, Vancouver is exhibiting many of those key characteristics that Heenan (1977) cited as concomitants of success for the global city.

## Vancouver: the metaphor

Vancouver is a Pacific Rim city still undergoing profound change. The city is moving from a regional centre built on natural resources to an international city built on its location and high-quality living environment. Recent demographic change associated with Asian immigration is more modest than the economic change. Immigration patterns really continue those established long ago. The economic shifts are new. It is the rapid shift into uncharted economic waters that is likely the most stressful issue facing the city. This manifests itself in changed land uses (e.g. luxury high-rise condominiums and deluxe Asian hotels) and in higher residential and office densities. These physical manifestations catch the public eye and ire, while underlying economic changes and opportunities elude the public view.

Vancouver is still changing rapidly, which is stressful. People want to understand their world, and Asian migration and investment can be a (scapegoat) explanation. More helpful is understanding structural and global change and working with people to see how change can provide opportunities and not just losses. This is ultimately what Vancouver seems to have done and is now sharing with the world, illustrating how a city can cope with economic and demographic change while becoming a new prototype: a North American Pacific Rim global city (Edgington & Goldberg 1992; Goldberg 1998). Flexible property institutions have helped.

## Policy issues and flexible institutional responses for global cities when they are both determinants and outcomes of globalisation

Vancouver illustrates nicely the central point being made in this chapter: as a city moves into the league of global cities, both the public and private sectors must review their strategies for doing business, since both are affected by economic and investment decisions made in other countries and other global cities. This applies particularly to decisions dealing with real estate investment and the future of the global city's real estate markets. Because of their network connections (and resultant information), capital and population flows, global cities can take advantage of opportunities not available to other urban areas. Their external connectedness forces them to be open and flexible to possibilities for economic and physical growth and development that would not normally confront small, unconnected cities. This connectedness also implies volatility, and therefore a need to absorb potentially volatile change in ways that others, again, would not have to handle.

Additionally, internal connectedness and the agglomeration economies they can bestow need to be carefully considered and cultivated. This internal and external connectedness needs to be explicitly recognised, developed and accommodated simultaneously, in a balanced manner. After all, one of the great economic strengths and secrets of cities lies in their ability to provide external economies of scale and scope through clustering and infrastructure provision. Yet these very economies can be so successful as to generate congestion, pollution and ultimately diseconomies. Thus, urban regions must manage their agglomeration assets carefully and be particularly mindful of the property market development institutions (such as flexible and appropriate zoning controls) and infrastructure investments that created these agglomeration assets and external economies in the first place.

Elsewhere, the author has addressed broader issues of strategy making for cities in the global economy in considerable detail (Goldberg 2000). There the emphasis was on strategy making *per se* and building the appropriate strategy processes and ideas to be successful in the highly competitive global economy. Here the focus is narrower, being on property market and urban development institutions and infrastructure and their roles in enhancing or maintaining the competitiveness of cities in the global era. Accordingly, the policy ideas considered here can all be seen as approaches to dealing with the need for global cities to craft property market institutions that are more flexible, adaptive and resilient.

Given the foregoing, it is necessary to develop more flexible land use, and housing and real estate development policies, which can absorb the changes facing global city policy-makers in future. Changes in tastes, in technology, and in global and national economic, political and cultural forces will have to be taken into account and dealt with successfully by urban policies. As cities become better plugged into the global economy, they will need housing and land-use policies that are capable of satisfying the increasingly diverse tastes of the international populations that will come to settle within their boundaries.

Of special note is that buildings are durable and capable of providing useful housing and commercial services for decades, if not centuries. They must be upgraded, modified and adapted continuously to meet changing tastes and requirements of the global economy. New stock also needs to be built that is better suited to the diverse needs of an increasingly global real estate market. This implies developing new housing and commercial (office, industrial and retail) forms, and being able to modify existing housing, offices, retail and in-dustrial buildings capable of catering to changing demographics, economic needs and tastes.

The changes and pressures above necessitate new ways to regulate land use and a willingness to accept higher land-use densities through better planning and design. There is a much greater need to coordinate land-use and infra-structure policies, both for 'hard services' (such as roads, mass transit, water and sewers, and energy) and 'soft services' (such as education and recreation). National and state/provincial governments also need to be linked since the higher levels of government often make policies with major implications for the global cities in their midst (e.g. immigration and trade policy).

Transportation is the most critical of all of the infrastructure services: it virtually complements land use perfectly. Transportation must be seen as a critical tool of land use and development policy and vice versa. Hong Kong's

Mass Transit Railway (MTR) used dense housing and commercial development near MTR stations to attract the capital and customers it needed. Transport investments and policies need a diversity of modes and a much denser set of connections among nodes to foster developing innovative and diverse real estate opportunities.

There is also a need to equate the marginal costs and marginal benefits of urban housing development. Thus, governments should consider shifting marginal costs onto the private sector through proper pricing of land-use controls and development permits. The Lions Gate Bridge connecting Vancouver and its northern suburb West Vancouver is a fine example. The bridge was completed in 1938 by the Guinness family to open up large tracts of land owned by the family in West Vancouver. They built the bridge and developed one of Canada's most prestigious residential areas: British Properties. The Lions Gate Bridge principle can be expanded, namely that the private sector, given suitable incentives (e.g. development rights), can provide both property and transportation infrastructure in an integrated way so that the housing and transportation needs of urban areas can be met efficiently and in a coordinated way without having to draw solely on scarce public funds. Public–private partnerships (P3s) are now doing this frequently and very effectively (Province of British Columbia 1996).

In our present global framework, external transportation infrastructure such as gateway ports and airports linking the urban region with the world must also be seen strategically. The foregoing marginal benefit and cost principles still hold, with the caveat that the benefits can extend well beyond the gateway city to its region and nation. There is also a critical need to integrate these gateway ports and airports with local land-use and development policies because of their immense influence on the future shape of the urban region and its economy.

## Public attitudes to cope with change

Perhaps the biggest change required of urban policy analysts and decision-makers will be their own attitudes and those of the public. There will be a much greater need for open-mindedness with a willingness to entertain and implement wider ranges of housing and urban development policies than in the past. The public and its policy-makers will have to be more aware of the systemic and societal consequences of local actions (e.g. the 'not in my back yard' (NIMBY) phenomenon) and be more willing to share the burden locally, of needed systemic developments such as innovative and denser housing and transportation modes, catering to a greater diversity of residents, and of denser commercial and industrial real estate development. The global city will need to supply all forms of residential, commercial and industrial property in adequate quantities to keep prices globally competitive so that it can successfully lure the residents and jobs it will require to remain a global city.

## Policies for local/regional and state/provincial governments

Each of the policies presented argues for (1) greater cooperation between the public and private sectors and (2) greater understanding of market forces and willingness to work with them.

Public–private joint housing ventures should increasingly be sought where the public could contribute density or land-use change bonuses, public land, fast-track and simplified approvals processes, reductions in development cost. For its part, the private sector could contribute its capital, development, marketing and management expertise. Residential and commercial density should be employed as a bonus for desired public goods. In particular, bonuses could be granted for creating social, rental and special needs housing and could be tied to fast-track and simpler approval processes and reduced development charges. Other 'bonus' or specially approved works might include public open space and civic art, and public recreational facilities and formal P3 agreements to provide both housing and support activities on contract.

The public should contractually link density bonuses and fast housing development approvals to the provision of desired public goods (e.g. social, rental and family housing, parks and open space, schools and community centres). A bond could ensure that the developer's obligations will be met. This would replace present growth controls and regulation, which limit development and the public goods developers can provide.

More than 20 years ago the province of British Columbia pioneered a land-use planning device called a 'land use contract' (LUC). LUCs were essentially spot zonings sold to developers by municipalities, which agreed to certain uses, densities and approval schedules. Developers agreed to an array of public goods ranging from schools and community centres to road improvements. LUCs were flexible and administratively viable. Sadly, early excesses and bureaucratic abuse by municipalities led to their ban in the British Columbia Municipal Act in 1977. After their demise, developers realised what they had lost. The idea was well suited to the housing and development needs of a changing and growing region. LUCs in some form need revisiting to help finance the growing public need for roads, bridges and transit, and more local infrastructure (community centres, parks, schools, public art and social housing).

Local councils might actively encourage periodic overbuilding of housing during market upswings. Such consciously cyclical housing policies can help reduce pressure on local housing markets and provide ample supplies of diverse housing. Once again such an approach stands in marked contrast to present growth control and supply-limiting regulatory policies. However, global cities will require substantial buffer stocks, of housing especially, but also of office and industrial space, to respond to periodic spurts in demand that arise from their global connectivity. There is a downside: such policies can limit capital appreciation of housing assets and run the risk of incurring the wrath of local homeowners, as has occurred in Hong Kong as a result of a similar policy (Crowell & Chung 2000). It is still worth trying.

Periodic housing oversupply conditions provide the public and non-profit sectors with opportunities to purchase and/or finance housing purchase for (or by) low-income households counter-cyclically. This would work with market forces to achieve public ends in contrast to present crisis-based pro-cyclical panic policies that build in tight markets at the cycle peaks when it is most costly and hard to do, and can boost prices and values, gaining public support.

With limited supplies of serviced, well-located and properly zoned land, it is imperative that better use be made of these scarce urban resources. Much greater efforts need to be expended by all levels of government to educate the public about the virtues of density. Governments also need to take a much more proactive stance in developing high-quality denser living and work environments so that the public comes to see well-designed denser housing and offices as providing new residential and work opportunities that do not exist today. I am not suggesting Hong Kong densities, just higher densities than those existing in global cities today. Greater density allows the land used in housing development to drop, by functionally expanding the supply of land available. Density increases need to be systemic and not limited to small areas since it is only through large-scale, broadly based density increases that significant increases in potential housing supplies can be achieved, to reduce the price of building rights and the cost of housing. They also must be closely tied to transport investment.

Excellent transportation is critical for building competitive cities. Without adequate transportation investment it will be difficult to develop new outlying residential and commercial areas. Without public mass transportation urban air and water quality are likely to deteriorate rapidly. Finally, without careful coordination of urban transportation and land-use policy, costly transportation improvements may find themselves facing inadequate demand. Increased density of development near public mass transit nodes encourages use of the transit system. Increased sprawl and low demand density, as is currently the case in Vancouver and other west coast cities (Goldberg 2000), lead to low levels of use on public transit systems.

This last point is vital. Transportation and land-use policy go hand in hand and imply greater densities. Transportation and land use are complementary. More fundamentally, they can be substitutes to deal with issues facing each other. Complementarity implies that, not only will transportation and land-use development reinforce each other, but also that each can be used to support policies originating in the other. Two decades ago the Toronto Transit Commission (TTC) observed that its Yonge Street Subway line was at capacity inbound in the morning and outbound in the evening while reverse travel was under-utilised. The TTC solution to its capacity constraint (a transportation problem) was to encourage office employment in North York to promote counter flows to use this excess capacity. This was achieved by working with North York municipality to rezone the present North York office corridor and by putting in an additional station between Finch and Lawrence. Regrettably, this is one of the few instances where land development was explicitly used to treat a transportation issue.

At the other end of the spectrum, failure to account for land-use and transportation interactions can have serious negative impacts. The Rand Corporation found in a study of St. Louis (Enns & de Leon 1973) that freeways were mainly responsible for central city decline, as freeways robbed the central city of its primary attribute: centrality. Freeways also had the effect of greatly increasing the supply of readily accessible land in the metropolitan area, driving down prices in the central city and setting in motion a series of highly negative expectations about land prices, which led to disinvestment and heightened decline in the core.

Finally, the positive and reinforcing impacts of transportation investment can be readily used by the public sector to finance transportation improvement and thus help to realise the benefits of the investment at little or no public cost. Allowing the Hong Kong Mass Transit Railway (MTR) to extract the increase in land values created by the improved accessibility due to the MTR made a substantial contribution to its development. There was actually a two-way impact: MTR made density possible and density paid for MTR. The positive impacts of the MTR on housing opportunities are particularly noteworthy since the MTR enabled the building of massive housing estates directly on top of or in very close proximity to its stations. The key was providing high densities. The resulting affordable *and* accessible housing provides an excellent model to be emulated elsewhere by housing policy-makers wishing to create large increments to housing supply that are also located where low and middle income households can readily purchase them. Thus, the MTR and its associated housing and land development policies are a powerful example of the virtues of linking transportation investment, land use and urban housing policy.

## Possible national government roles in urban policy in a global setting

National governments will need to be more proactive in monitoring and influencing local and regional property markets. Their most important role will be to provide systemic and contextual overviews of these local markets that no local or regional agency can provide.

### *Monitoring local and regional property supplies*

To overcome the NIMBY fallacy of composition, it is imperative that a higher-level perspective be provided so that the systemic consequences of local actions can be ascertained. By monitoring local housing and property markets, and aggregating local supply potential, the national government can help local policy avoid the outcomes of NIMBYism where the actions of local areas can aggregate to yield significant negative consequences for the global city region.

The NIMBY phenomenon can be pernicious as it is often tied to issues of density and transit investment. When local entities argue against higher density housing and commercial development in their area, the effects can impact the entire urban region and even the nation. It may appear rational for a neighbourhood to argue for demolition control and down-zoning to try to preserve lower cost, older rental housing. But such policies usually wind up having the reverse effect when aggregated with similar policies and NIMBY demands from other areas. There is thus an unintended, undesirable and counterproductive link between neighbourhood decisions and larger urban and regional housing issues such as periodic housing and transport shortages. The harmful effects can be particularly notable when considering the need to be globally competitive by providing ample and appropriate stocks of real property and transport.

Sydney, Australia, in the late 1980s is a striking example of NIMBY at work. Local areas in Sydney consistently fought housing and office development with obvious adverse effects on the supply of both in a period of rapid growth. The state government removed the local councils and replaced them with an appointed triumvirate. The state argued that the Sydney economy was just too important state-wide and nationally to have it held captive by parochial local interests. The state broke the fallacy of composition by imposing broader state and national needs on top of the localised interests (Laurence 1987; Simper 1987).

NIMBY policies to limit demolition and curtail new housing development in the name of affordability and liveability can have the reverse effect by lowering potential supply, raising housing prices and thus lowering liveability in a metropolitan region. Not only can such actions lead to less affordable housing, they can also have negative impacts on the job market as national and international firms by-pass the region because of its limited and costly housing. Growth control advocates should be wary of the larger negative regional consequences of their local actions. In their bid to improve living quality, they may in the aggregate lead to restrictions in housing supply and higher prices, which make the area less liveable (price clearly being an important determinant of liveability and quality of life). NIMBY fallacies of composition can be overcome. It requires commitment from senior governments which must take positive action, as Sydney showed. Unicity, Winnipeg, is a Canadian case where 16 local governments were abolished in 1972 to create a unified urban region. Lastly, five Toronto municipalities were merged in 1998 to form one vast city.

## Make housing and infrastructure assistance available counter-cyclically

National social housing funds should be offered counter-cyclically to encourage the purchase of excess units when the market is glutted, prices are moderate and public pressure for action is minimal. The same is true for infrastructure, which should be built when there is slack in construction. This contrasts with present, and costly, pro-cyclical approaches. Furthermore a range of local counter-cyclical federal decentralisation activities would nicely complement local pro-cyclical forces such as NIMBY growth control efforts. Such local market-cycle-sensitive federal policies could greatly help to stabilise urban economies.

## Document local property effects of national policies

National governments almost routinely embark upon national policies (such as defence and energy development), which have enormous and highly localised (spatial) impacts on local property markets. In such cases national measures are needed to mitigate adverse price and availability consequences of these policies. The impacts of national immigration policy needs to be singled out, given the disproportionate impacts of immigration on global cities and because of our concern here with policy issues arising from the new global context within which cities, especially world cities, operate.

## Craft incentives and penalties to counter NIMBY

Servicing or density grants or bonuses should be considered to help local governments deal with growing infrastructure expansion and replacement. In return, density increases and more flexible land-use controls would follow, which could reduce local objections by stemming the need for higher local taxes. Local residents might be more willing to accept actual or perceived local pain associated with higher residential densities and innovative land uses in return for senior government infrastructure aid. Local groups seldom see the link between their actions and systemic responses. By letting local citizens face the trade-off of lower taxes (for infrastructure upgrading) in return for higher densities, the decision goes back to where it belongs, on the local taxpayer. This will be particularly noticeable in the critical transportation area where local and even provincial governments find it increasingly difficult to fund massive investment needed for public transportation and road improvements. To ensure the viability of the public transportation investment, national governments can readily tie cost-sharing arrangements to land-use plans and densities. Infrastructure spending in general might be linked to more flexible controls and denser land uses.

More frequent use of surplus or marginally used national government lands could be considered as part of the P3 activities cited above. The national government could become a joint venture partner by offering its land on the condition that the local global city government re-zone to higher residential densities and/or innovative housing opportunities. Again, linking a benefit (national lands for local use) and local actual or perceived pain (re-zoning) needs to be done so local residents appreciate their negative stances incur costs (the loss of national lands).

# Growing vulnerability of cities in the connected global environment

There is no need to repeat the earlier discussion here only about growing vulnerability through connectedness. We do need to remind policy-makers that this vulnerability is a new element in the urban policy that needs to be dealt with in future. It may also be necessary to seek buffers that de-couple somewhat the global city from the global system to provide it with greater stability and lessen the vulnerability to transmitted global shocks. Creating buffer stocks of real property could help here, as might analogous buffer stocks of appropriately zoned neighbourhoods and better linking of transportation investment with these zoning decisions.

# Conclusions

Flexibility is needed to absorb changes in tastes, technology and global and national economic, political and cultural forces, in urban housing and development policies and related land-use controls. And transport investments can no longer be carried out as they have been in the past. The setting in which these policies must be made and implemented has simply changed too dramatically. Urban and housing policy must simultaneously address two powerful and often conflicting forces.

First, the macro policy environment spans regional and national economic, political and social forces, and is increasingly international (witness the Asian crisis and its urban impacts). Globalisation of financial and property markets suggests that urban housing policy-makers must heed global capital and information flows and global economic and political factors in policy-making. Macro changes in demographics and tastes require new, more varied, denser forms of housing and urban development. Institutional flexibility is essential to deal with such changes.

Second, simultaneous with the macro pressures on urban development policy, there are growing local pressures reflecting the narrowest, highly localised neighbourhood and citizen group interests. This NIMBY syndrome flies in the face of the growing global reality. It is also most likely self-defeating since the larger systemic consequences of NIMBY actions often aggregate to create the reverse of the locally intended result.

Thus, whether housing and urban development policy and institutions are local, regional, provincial/state or national, they will have to accommodate and build upon these conflicting pressures. Central to the formation of effective urban housing and land development institutions is an understanding of system-wide consequences of local actions. Policy-makers must be cognisant of inconsistency between local actions and desired outcomes. The burden will fall largely on senior governments, the states or provinces and the national government to overcome the fallacies of composition brought on by NIMBY-based local policies. Only senior governments have the necessary systemic overview and policy tools to challenge and overcome the negative effects of NIMBY.

## Closing the loop and thinking globally again

In the global city there is a need to understand and monitor the nature of global forces. Specifically, there will be the need to monitor global property and investment flows, perhaps on a world-wide basis through such global agencies as the World Bank and/or the International Monetary Fund. There will certainly be a need to understand the magnitude and sources of these fund-flows at the global city level, as the Asian crisis made apparent.

Seeing cities as key actors in today's highly competitive global economic environment suggests that cities must be competitive if they are to survive, let alone prosper. Competitiveness will be achieved and maintained by acting vigorously in those areas that are the purview of the global city. First, high-quality infrastructure must be in place and maintained to a high standard. Second, maintenance of living quality will be of growing importance as the most profitable and important economic activities are so-called knowledge-based and require skilled knowledge workers who are footloose and seek high-quality living and work environments. Thus, heightened liveability can attract profitable economic activities and talented and energetic people who will be able to pay for the additional public goods that maintain and enhance the liveability of the global city's living and work environment. In the final analysis, liveability (including affordability of housing and office space) may well be the ultimate competitive weapon for global cities in the future.

Governments can and do play a centrally important role in competitiveness. By providing needed social and physical infrastructure (education, health care, parks, streets, etc.) governments present the global city with a powerful ability to attract and retain people and economic activities that can compete globally. Governments must be aware of their capacity to enhance their own global competitiveness through providing high-quality services at reasonable and stable prices (i.e. taxes). This balance between taxes and services must be 'front and centre' if global cities are to remain competitive in the future.

Traditionally, urban policy-makers, even in the world's leading urban centres, have focused their attention on local issues of land-use regulation, education, parks and recreation, and on the provision of hard engineering and infrastructure services. They have usually seen these issues as being local and unrelated to global competitiveness of their urban region. Now and in the future, world city policy analysts and decision-makers will have to see these and the entire panoply of issues addressed above in a broader context of global competitiveness. Competitiveness, particularly in a global setting, will have to be one of the principal strategic objectives of urban policy and be 'front and centre' in the planning and delivery of public services and the design of urban governance institutions, especially those relating to property.

Cities can, and must, be designers of their destiny. Global city policy-makers need to see that as the global city adapts to, and in the process changes, the network of global cities, the global economy will change as well, since it is largely based in and built upon global cities (Peirce *et al.* 1993). The proactive strategic city will be the prosperous city, and to prosper in the twenty-first century, a city will unavoidably have to be global in outlook, planning and outreach (Gappert 1989; Knight 1989b). In this vein Peirce *et al.* (1993) note:

> Citistates that hope to prosper in the international economy need to plan as carefully as the smartest corporations. They need to decide what they're good at and seize their comparative advantages. They have to keep on strategizing to stay afloat in the volatile global economy.
>
> Peirce *et al.* (1993: 292)

Jean Gottmann (1989) talked about the 'delocalised' city to denote much of what has been discussed here, dealing with the connectedness of global cities to the world economy and to each other. This raises a useful paradox: a 'delocalised' city is really a more independent entity, freed up to be proactive and international and no longer tied solely to the whims of its national and state/provincial policies. Instead we see the global city evolving rapidly where dependence and independence are inseparable (Knight 1989a).

Elkins (1995) in his seminal work on nation-states and territoriality noted something very similar about the role of cities in the face of the territorial decline of nation-states:

Just to be fair, in the long run the cities may have lost the battle [for domin-ion over nations] but won the war. As they were subordinated politically to state functions, they became even more economically essential to nations because of their crossroads status, their value to hinterlands, and the vast reservoir of voters (when voting became common) attached to them.

Elkins (1995: 49–50)

Going with the flow (more and more information, capital and population flow) will be the order of the day, the decade and the century. The helpless hapless city is dead: long live the strategic global city.

# References

Asia Pacific Initiative (1988) *Backgrounder*. Asia Pacific Initiative, Vancouver, BC.

*Asiaweek* (2000) SIC Makes a Buy in Seoul. p.13, 30 June 2000.

Bacow, L.S. (1988) *Internationalisation of the US Real Estate Industry*. Working Paper #16, M.I.T. Center for Real Estate Development, Cambridge, MA.

Baxter, D. (1989) *Population and Housing in Metropolitan Vancouver: Changing Patterns of Demographics and Demand*. Laurier Institute, Vancouver.

Blomquist, G.C., Berger, M.C. & Hoehn, J.H. (1988) New Estimates of Quality of Life in Urban Areas. *American Economic Review*, **78**(1), 89–107.

Budd, L. (1998) Territorial competition and globalization: Scylla and Charybdis of European cities. *Urban Studies*, **35**, 663–85.

*Canada Yearbook* (1990) Minister of Supply and Services. Ottawa, Ontario.

Cohen, R.B. (1981) The new international division of labour, multinational corporations and the urban hierarchy. In: Dear, M.J. & Scott, A.J. (eds) *Urbanisation and Urban Planning in Capitalist Society*. Methuen, London.

Cooperman, J.M., Gagnon, H., Hinkle, P. & Kearns, R.V. (1994) *Mortgage Securities: Canada Mortgage and Housing Corporation and Its Securities*. Goldman Sachs, New York.

Crowell, T. & Chung, Y. (2000) Chief Executive under Fire. *Far Eastern Economic Review*, p. 25, 7 July 2000.

Daly, M.T. (1982) *Sydney Boom, Sydney Bust*. Allen & Unwin, Sydney, Australia.

Dunning, J.H. & Norman, G. (1983) The theory of the multinational enterprise: an application to multinational office location. *Environment and Planning A*, **15**(4), 675–92.

Edgington, D.W. (1988) *Japanese Business Down-Under: Patterns of Japanese Investment in Australia, 1957–1985*. Trans-national Corporations Research Project, University of Sydney, NSW.

Edgington, D.W. & Goldberg, M.A. (1992) Vancouver: Canada's Gateway to the Rim. In: Blakely, E. & Stimson, R. (eds) *New Cities of the Pacific Rim*, Monograph #43, Chapter 7, pp. 7-1–7-29, University of California, Institute of Urban and Regional Development, Berkeley, CA.

Elkins, D.J. (1995) *Beyond Sovereignty: Territory and Political Economy in the Twenty-First Century*. University of Toronto Press, Toronto.

Enns, J. & de Leon, P. (1973) *The Impact of Highways on Metropolitan Dispersion: St. Louis*. RAND Report P-5061, The RAND Corporation; Santa Monica, CA.

Epstein, G., Graham, J. & Nembhard, J. (eds) (1993) *Creating a New World Economy: Forces of Change and Plans for Action*. Temple University, Philadelphia, PA.

Foster, M.B. (1991) New World Economic Integration. *Urban Land*, **50**(12; Dec), 2–6.

Friedmann, J. (1986) The World City Hypothesis. *Development and Change*, **17**, 69–83.

Friedmann, J. & Wolff, G. (1982) World city formation: an agenda for research and action. *International Journal of Urban and Regional Research*, **6**(3; Sept), 309–44.

Frobel, F.J., Heinrichs, J. & Kreye, B. (1980) *The New International Division of Labour*. Cambridge University Press, Cambridge, UK.

Gappert, G. (1989) Global Thinking and Urban Planning. In: Knight, R.V. (ed.) Cities in a Global Society, Vol. 35, *Urban Affairs Annual Reviews*, pp. 305–11. Sage Publications, Newbury Park, CA.

Goldberg, M.A. (1985) *The Chinese Connection: Getting Plugged in to Pacific Rim Real Estate, Trade and Capital Markets*. University of British Columbia Press, Vancouver, BC.

Goldberg, M.A. (1990) 'Foreign Capital Flows and the US Property Market: A View Primarily from Asia.' Presented at Prudential Realty Investors Conference, Pinehurst, NC, 30 April 1990.

Goldberg, M.A. (1998) *The British Columbia Economy into the Millennium: Perspectives and Possibilities*. Business Council of British Columbia, Vancouver, BC.

Goldberg, M.A. (2000) Transportation and Land Use and the Future of the GVRD: Getting It Right. *Vancouver Board of Trade Sounding Board*, Winter/Spring, p. 2–3.

Goldberg, M.A. (2001) *Determining the Comparative Advantages of Greater Vancouver as an International City Region: A Retrospective Review and Update of Issues and Opportunities*. Greater Vancouver Economic Partnership, Vancouver, BC, May.

Gordon, J.N. (1991) The Diversification Potential of International Property Investments. *The Real Estate Financial Journal*, Fall, 42–8.

Gottmann, J. (1989) What Are Cities Becoming the Centers of? Sorting Out the Possibilities. In: Knight, R.V. (ed.) Cities in a Global Society, Vol. 35, *Urban Affairs Annual Reviews*, pp. 56–67. Sage Publications, Newbury Park, CA.

Hall, P. (1984) *The World Cities*, 3rd edn. Weidenfeld & Nicolson, London.

Hall, P. (1991) Cities and Regions in a Global Economy. Paper given at *Multilateral Co-operation for Development in the Twenty-first Century: Training and Research for Regional Development*, UN Centre for Regional Development, Nagoya, November 1991.

Hamilton, A. (1986) *The Financial Revolution*. The Free Press, New York.

Hamilton, S.W. & Heinkel, R.L. (1994) *The Role of Real Estate in a Pension Portfolio*. Bureau of Asset Management, Faculty of Commerce & Business Administration, University of British Columbia, Vancouver.

Heenan, D.A. (1977) Global cities of tomorrow. *Harvard Business Review*, pp. 79–92, May-June.

Heenan, D.A. & Perlmutter, H. (1978) *Multinational Organization Development: A Social Architecture Perspective*. Addison-Wesley, Reading, MA.

Jacobs, J. (1969) *The Economy of Cities*. Vintage Books, New York.

Jacobs, J. (1984) *Cities and the Wealth of Nations*. Vintage Books, New York.

Kaufman, H. (1986) *Interest Rates, the Markets, and the New Financial World*. Times Books, New York.

King, A.D. (1990) *Global Cities*. Routledge, London.

Knight, R.V. (1989a) The Emergent Global Society. In: Knight, R.V. (ed.) Cities in a Global Society, Vol. 35, *Urban Affairs Annual Reviews*, pp. 24–43. Sage Publications, Newbury Park, CA.

Knight, R.V. (1989b) City Building in a Global Society. In: Knight, R.V. (ed.) Cities in a Global Society, Vol. 35, *Urban Affairs Annual Reviews*, pp. 326–34. Sage Publications, Newbury Park, CA.

Kresl, P.K. (1992) *The Urban Economy and Regional Trade Liberalization*. Praeger, New York.

*Land Use Digest* (1990) Trends in Japanese Real Estate Investment. p. 2, Vol. 23, No. 9, Sept 1990.

*Land Use Digest* (1991) Report on World Property Performance, Costs, p. 1; and Offshore Investors See US Markets as Exceptional, p. 2, Vol. 24, No. 7, July 1991.

Laurence, M. (1987) What the city's new rulers are up to. *Sydney Morning Herald*, 27 June 1987.

Leventhal, K. & Company (1990) Japanese investment in U.S. real estate declined nearly 11% in 1989, mainly because of reduced office investment. *Real Estate Newsline*, Vol. 7, Nos. 3 and 4, Mar/Apr 1990.

Levi, M. (1989) *International Finance*, 2nd edn. McGraw-Hill, New York.

Maskell, P. & Törnqvist, G. (1999) *Building a Cross-Border Learning Region: Emergence of the North European Øresund Region*. Copenhagen Business School Press, Copenhagen.

McCoy, B.H. (1991) Why Foreign Capital Flows into US Real Estate are Drying Up. *Urban Land*, **50**(7; July), 34–5.

McGee, T.G. (1984) *Circuits and Networks of Capital: The Internationalisation of the world economy and national urbanisation*. The Institute of Asian Research, University of British Columbia, Vancouver.

Miles, M. (1994) The Prudential Global Real Estate Fund. A Talk to the Urban Development Institute, Vancouver, B.C., 18 February 1994, Prudential Realty Investors, Newark, NJ.

Ministry of Finance and Corporate Relations (1987) Backgrounder: International Financial Business in Vancouver. Province of British Columbia, Victoria, BC.

Peirce, N.R., with Johnson, C.W. & Hall, J.S. (1993) *Citistates: How Urban America Can Prosper in a Competitive World*. Seven Locks Press, Washington, DC.

Province of British Columbia (1996) *Building Partnerships: The Final Report of the Public-Private Partnerships Task Force*. Ministry of Finance and Corporate Services, Victoria, BC.

Robaton, A. (1994) 'Wealth of Opportunity: US developers' and 'Retailers getting on with business in Mexico', *Shopping Centers Today*, Vol. 15, Issue 3, Mar, p. 1 and 5–7.

Rodman, J. (1992) Investors returning to US real estate markets are potential capital sources for developers. *Real Estate Newsline*, Vol. 9, Nos. 3 and 4, March/April, p. 1, 4–7.

Ryland, S. (1993) Property Futures. *International Real Estate Institute*. Spring p. 9–12.

Schwann, G.M. (1989) *When Did You Move to Vancouver? An Analysis of Migration and Migrants into Metropolitan Vancouver*. Laurier Institute, Vancouver, BC.

*Shopping Centers Today* (1991) Report on World Property Performance, Costs, p. 1.; And Offshore Investors See US Markets as Exceptional, p. 2. Vol. 24, No. 7, July.

*Shopping Centers Today* (1992) The World. pp. 100–22, May.

Simper, E. (1987) An expedient end to Town Hall squabbles. *The Australian*, 27 March 1987.

Taylor, M. & Thrift, N. (eds) (1982) *Geography of Multinationals*. Croom Helm, London.

Thrift, N. (1983) *World Cities and the World City Property Market: The case of Southeast Asian investment in Australia*. Working Paper: Australia National University, Research School of Pacific Studies, Department of Human Geography, Canberra.

Vancouver Economic Advisory Commission. Task Force reports on 'Business and Trade Services,' and 'Banking/Finance/Insurance' (various dates, 1984 to 1992), Vancouver Economic Advisory Commission, Vancouver, BC.

Vancouver Planning Department (1989) *Housing Symposium, Collected Papers*. 8 May 1989. Planning Department, City of Vancouver, Vancouver, BC.

Wurtzebach, C.H. & Miles, M.E. (1994) *Modern Real Estate*, 5th edn. John Wiley & Sons, New York.

## Further reading

Compton, E. (1987) *The New World of Commercial Banking*. Lexington Books, Lexington, MA.

Economic Council of Canada (1989) *A New Frontier: Globalisation and Canada's Financial Markets*. Economic Council of Canada, Ottawa, Ontario.

Goldberg, M.A. (1993) The Evolving Pacific Property Market. In: Yeung, Y.M. *Geography and Development in Pacific Asia in the 21st Century.* The Chinese University of Hong Kong Press, Shatin, HK.

Goldberg, M.A. (2001) Airports and Territorial Development: The Case of Vancouver. *Proceedings of the OECD/CEDEX Conference Airports and Territorial Development,* CEDEX, Paris, France, April 2001.

Goldberg, M.A. (2002) Transportation and the Future of the Vancouver Region: A Core Element for a New Canadian Trade and Development Strategy. Working Paper, Faculty of Commerce and Business Administration, University of British Columbia, Vancouver, B.C., January 2002.

# 5

# Facilitation and Constraint: Institutions of Urban Planning in Hong Kong

## *Bo Sin Tang, Sujeet Sharma, Stanley Chi Wai Yeung*

Urban planning is about spatial ordering of the economic and social activities in a city. It is often conceived as a rational and progressive process whereby the governing body, usually representing the local community, implements and regulates changes in the use and appearance of the environment (Cullingworth & Nadin 1997: 104). The origin of urban planning was closely linked to the social movements of the eighteenth and nineteenth centuries, which sought to resolve the urban and environmental problems caused by industrial revolution (Boyer 1983; Hall 1988). This background lent support to public intervention in the land development process. According to Klosterman (1996: 162), urban planning serves four key social functions including promoting the public interest, eliminating negative externalities, improving the information base for decision-making, and redistributing public costs and benefits. Efficiency, equity, orderliness, comprehensiveness and rationality are some key normative principles that guide the discourse of professional planning practices.

Why does our society need urban planning? Different theoretical paradigms provide different justifications. *Pigouvian welfare-economics* argues that land and property markets, if left to operate freely, are prone to all sorts of failures, resulting in an inefficient allocation of resources. Externalities and public goods are the 'market failures' in the urban development context. Pollution, traffic congestion, environmental degradation and loss of amenities are the typical examples of negative externality. The private markets are also said to undersupply or fail to provide the non-marketable public goods such as infrastructure and public open space. The Pigouvian perspective recommends state intervention and provision as the solutions to these problems. Urban planning, in the form of development control and regulatory zoning, is said to be required in restraining individual welfare-maximising behaviour that ultimately leads to negative externalities and social inefficiency. The government is also conceived to be the appropriate provider for supplying the public goods that are collectively consumed (that everyone tends to free-ride and consume without paying).

*Coasian institutional economics*, however, challenges the Pigouvian proposition that government intervention is necessarily efficient (Lai 1994). It argues that state intervention is not costless. These costs, termed as transaction costs, cover the costs of policy formulation, implementation, monitoring and enforcement. It argues that it is entirely possible for these costs to exceed the welfare losses caused by negative externality, which the government intervention seeks to eradicate. A Coasian perspective makes no suggestion that government should step in whenever symptoms of market failure arise, because its intervention can also fail. Thus, whether urban planning is socially more beneficial and efficient in comparison with an unregulated market is a contingent question. The acid test is to compare the transaction costs of the different institutional arrangements and solutions. Indeed, the Coasian perspective argues that high transaction costs and unclear delineation of property rights are the real reasons that prevent market solutions to externality problems. Coase's 'invariance theorem' has demonstrated that, given zero transaction costs, market negotiations and exchanges, free of government intervention, can resolve externality problems irrespective of the initial property right entitlements of the resources being traded.

*Transaction-cost theory* of urban planning examines the various institutional forms of governance for the production of urban built environments (Alexander 1992a,b, 1994, 2001a,b). Following the logic of the Coasian perspective, government planning and development control is a means to reduce transaction costs in the land market. Public land-use planning, broadly speaking, represents government assignment, attenuation, and restrictions of private individual rights over the use of land resources. However, transaction-cost theory suggests that this is only one possible institutional form of governance, which involves hierarchical decision-making, a statutory framework and third-party regulation and enforcement. Urban planning, in other words, is not carried out exclusively by the government. There are other feasible forms of land-use governance which can also reduce transaction costs depending on the attributes of the transactions in the land development process. Indicative planning, contract zoning, private–public partnership and voluntary contractual covenants are examples of the bilateral type of governance structure. Transaction-cost theory therefore rejects the dichotomous contrast between planning and the market (Alexander 1992b) and suggests a blurred boundary between public and private sector planning for land development.

*Public-choice theory* regards urban planning as an exogenous institution to be influenced by the political market (Poulton 1991a,b, 1997; Webster, 1998a,b). It conceives of society as comprising a world of rational actors, who seek to compete, bargain and negotiate with one another with a view to maximising their self-interests. Public policies, such as urban planning, are supplied by the politicians in responding to the voters' demand, often in the interests of the most powerful voter group (or the median voters). Thus Poulton (1997: 81) posits that zoning is 'a municipal service provided in response to private demands, primarily aimed at raising real estate values and consumption benefits linked to neighbourhood communities'. Different community groups have different interests and hence diverse motivations for different styles of planning, as the distribution of social costs and benefits of alternative policies fall unevenly on them. According to this theory, government planning bureaucracy is always motivated to expand in size and administrative power beyond its socially efficient levels. As Pennington (2000: 15) summarises, 'the institutional reality of planning will be characterised by special interest politics and chronic bureaucratisation'.

*Marxian political economy* perspective grounds its analysis of urban planning on power struggles and class conflicts in society (e.g. Harvey 1973; Castells 1977; Dear & Scott 1981; Boyer 1983). Its key argument is that planning, like all institutions in a capitalist society, must systematically serve the ultimate interests of the capitalist class. As a tool of the state, urban planning helps to facilitate capital accumulation, legitimate class exploitation and resolve potential contradictions in the urban built environment. Urban development problems in a market economy are conceived as the 'self-disorganizing tendencies of *privatized* capitalist social and property relations as these appear in urban space' (Dear & Scott 1981: 13). In resolving these problems, urban planners seek to restore 'social harmony', but in so doing, reproduce the unequal and exploitative power relations in the society. Foglesong (1986) argues that urban planning serves the interests of capital by providing an authoritative method of policy formulation and decision-making process that simultaneously preserves the private property rights system and avoids democratic interference on land under majority rule. Others emphasise the regressive, sinister social functions of planning (Flyvberg 1998; Yiftachel 1998). Thus, planning can never be truly reformist under this perspective.

This brief review illustrates that it may not be feasible, nor is it necessary, to give a single explanation for urban planning. Urban planning is a 'subject matter' as well as a 'method', and its scope and function are influenced by changing historical, political, economic and cultural forces of society (Fainstein & Campbell 1996). For instance, urban planning means totally different concepts and processes between capitalist and socialist cities. Thornley (1996) argues that planning, in a market economy, is always linked to the market but their relationship varies in different places and across time. Different urban problems come up at different times and thus no single issue is adequate to explain the logic of planning (Foglesong 1986). Though subscribing to transaction-cost theory, Alexander (2001b: 46) also claims that the rationale of urban planning should be judged by 'its accuracy (does it look like my real world?) and normative utility (what can I do with it?)'.

In the following sections, we will examine the relationship between urban planning and property development, using Hong Kong as an example. Following Simmie (2001: 306), we treat planning as 'the distribution of scarce land uses and property rights to different groups, organizations and social classes producing, working or living in cities'. Urban planning is the 'rules of the game' in managing urban social activities, interactions and changes over space. This social rule certainly affects individual, private land and property interests, as Roweis (1981: 170) considers planning as 'collective action pertinent to decisions concerning the social utilization of urban land'. In this respect, the key questions that often concern property developers are, *inter alia*: What are these rules? How are these rules set? How can these rules be changed?

## Urban planning and development control

Perhaps the best way to illustrate our arguments is to examine the institutions of development control. Land development (as statutorily defined) is always subject to some form of public control, which provides the mechanism of guiding investment, implementing public planning policies and monitoring spatial changes. Development control has long attracted intellectual studies from various angles (Harrison 1972; Underwood 1981; Harrison & Mordey 1987; Pearce 1987; Wakeford 1990; Rowan-Robinson *et al.* 1995; Willis 1995; Gilg & Kelly 1996; Thomas 1997). One of the key emphases lies in the development control decisions, which reflect the degree of facilitation and constraint provided by the planning system on private development initiatives (Bramley *et al.* 1995). Individual landlords and property developers obviously have a stake in the decisions as these directly confer, attenuate or withdraw development rights of their sites. The property industry is generally in favour of having a system of development control although individual parties are also keen to 'insert their interests within policies and practices in place of established assumptions and process' (Healey *et al.* 1988: 10).

The basic goals of urban planning in Hong Kong are to avoid incompatible land uses, to control the urban form and landscape of a city functionally, aesthetically and ideally to have health, social harmony and civic identity. The inability to control changes of use within buildings in Hong Kong has led to many incompatible land uses (Yeh 1990: 6). Compatibility refers to both vertical and horizontal, both within the buildings and outside. All systems for controlling development are designed to control physical development, cope with the problem of uncertainty, resolve conflicts between different stakeholders of society, look for flexibility, and make every decision-maker (in the process) accountable. Yeh (1990) points to the conflicts arising out of the contradictions prevailing between what is specified in the land lease conditions and the statutory zoning plans.

Development control in Hong Kong comprises mainly three separate levels including planning, lease and building controls. Empowered by the Town Planning Ordinance (Chapter 131, Laws of Hong Kong), land-use planning control is exercised by means of zoning embodied in statutory town plans. Statutory zones set out the range of permissible uses on the site and thus have a direct impact on the redevelopment potential of private land lots.

On the other hand, as all land in Hong Kong is leasehold, development control can also be achieved, contractually, through the lease conditions. The government as the ultimate lessor can impose various requirements on lessees. Every site can be subject to a different set of requirements for the lease period, including permitted land use, building form, development intensity and other appropriate development restrictions.

Finally, the Buildings Ordinance (Chapter 123, Laws of Hong Kong) requires that all private building and construction works must obtain prior approvals from the Building Authority. By vetting building plan submissions from private developers, the government can ensure that the proposed development does not contravene any statutory and administrative provisions. Although these three levels of control are enforced by separate government departments, they generally complement each other in implementing prevailing government policies. All these departments report ultimately to government administrators. Thus, development control authority in Hong Kong is fragmented, yet centralised.

Planning is at the forefront of all these controls. This means that private developers have to obtain the necessary planning permissions prior to proceeding to apply for other approvals. The zoning of the subject sites is thus crucial in this respect. Comparatively speaking, the land-use zoning system in Hong Kong is less complicated than in other cities. Every piece of land is designated under a land-use zone. Attached to every zoning is a Schedule of Statutory Notes that shows the types of land use that are always permitted within the zone (Column 1 uses) and the other uses (Column 2 uses) for which prior permission from the Town Planning Board (TPB) must be sought. The TPB is the statutory decision-making body responsible for plan making and planning control in Hong Kong. It is chaired by a senior government administrator and comprises mainly government-appointed part-time, unofficial members, and is serviced by the government's Planning Department.

In the statutory town plans, Column 1 land uses are entirely harmonious with the zoning and are thus permitted as of right on the sites. However, applications for planning permissions are required if private developers intend to develop sites for Column 2 uses. Landowners and property developers therefore know the boundary of property development opportunities for their sites under the respective zoning. This system is intended to strike a balance between public control and market efficiency. It waives the planning approval process if the proposed development is wholly compatible with the zoning. Further, it provides flexibility for private initiatives to seek a possible change in land use when there are market needs, for instance, from housing to commercial development, or from industrial to housing use. Planning controls on development density (in terms of floor area ratios) and built form (through site coverage and building height restrictions) are sometimes stipulated in the Notes.

Statutory zoning has no retrospective effect. In other words, the existing use of buildings or land is permitted to continue without any planning permission until redevelopment or a change of land use takes place. Redevelopment or a change of use may be carried out only if it conforms to the plan or upon receiving planning permission. In Hong Kong, the government source claims that, in considering planning applications, the TPB would 'usually take into account such factors as the planning intention and Government policies, social, economic and environmental impacts of the development on the wider area, traffic and infrastructure implications, and compatibility of land uses' (Planning Department 1995: 27). The term 'usually' reflects the discretion in the decision-making process for development control. In other words, the planning authority would consider a broad range of factors, which are not well defined at the outset and cannot be specified distinctly before its decision. These factors can vary from case to case, since every statutory town plan contains a standard clause stating that every planning application will be judged on its own merits. Theoretically speaking, the planning authority should have taken into account all 'material' considerations. However, what factors are regarded as 'material' and how these factors have been weighted against each other by the decision-makers are rather obscure, because the decisions are made behind closed doors and in the absence of the applicants.

Booth (1996) suggests that, in comparison with the US and the UK, Hong Kong has a 'hybrid' planning control system in regulating property development. It essentially entails a discretionary approval process for private development applications made within a statutory framework of land-use zoning plans. This system is said to lie in between a rigid 'regulatory' zoning institution in the US and a 'discretionary' planning permission system in the UK. To understand the key criteria and process of the planning decisions, we will discuss in the following sections four related issues in connection with the performance and outcomes of the development control system in Hong Kong.

## Certainty vs. flexibility

Property development is inherently a risky and lumpy kind of investment. Market volatility and uncertainty will dampen private development initiatives and ultimately reduce the supply of floor space to the economy (Bramley *et al.* 1995). Urban planning helps to reduce the uncertainties faced by the property industry. On the other hand, planning policies must always be responsive to unforeseeable circumstances over time. Therefore, it is also important for the planners to exercise a certain flexibility in the decision-making process. There is a need to strike a balance between certainty and flexibility in planning for land uses.

Certainty and flexibility are often claimed as the two hallmarks of Hong Kong's hybrid development control system. For example, the consultation document on proposed amendment of the Town Planning Ordinance (Planning, Environment and Lands Branch 1996: 2) defines these two principles as:

> to state clearly the planning intentions and requirements in statutory plans so as to provide a high degree of certainty to land owners, developers and the public at large, but at the same time to allow a reasonable degree of flexibility to cater for changing circumstances and new requirements.

The distinction between Columns 1 and 2 land uses is a typical illustration of this combination. The landowners and property developers enjoy the benefits of both certainty and flexibility conferred by this system. They can be certain of the as-of-rights uses (Column 1 uses) under a particular statutory land-use zone and they have the opportunity to convert their sites, after securing planning approval, to other higher value uses (Column 2 uses). The appropriateness of the land-use zoning of a particular site is surely debatable. Nonetheless, the system provides at least a baseline scenario for application and negotiation for changes.

The Hong Kong development control system has itself gone through a regime change (from colonial to Chinese rule) that made room for much speculation and uncertainty while the planning authorities walked a tightrope in providing both certainty and flexibility from a unique hybrid kind of system. For that matter most criticisms are not directed to the system itself but to the decisions on planning applications. Lai (1997) criticises the arbitrary nature of planning control in Hong Kong by a comparison between planning applications and building applications. He points to the fact that the reasons given by the TPB in rejecting applications are often so vague and general that there is no assured method by which an applicant can revise the original submission in order to get through the approval process. Staley (1994) also comments that the planning application process increases uncertainty in the development process since the public administrators have the discretion over determining the type, pace and pattern of development at district level. Such regulation may result in project delays, and is thus inefficient and costly.[1]

The planning approval process is never mechanical, or straightforward. The property industry obviously faces enormous difficulties when planning decisions do not reflect a discernible line of logic, and when no explicit set of decision-making criteria is spelt out. In the latter respect, planning guidelines, which the TPB does not necessarily have to follow, have been released on some types of development applications. There are obvious benefits for decision-makers in maintaining a certain flexibility in the process, to cover unforeseeable circumstances (Purdue 1977; Harrison & Mordey 1987), although they know that achieving consistency in their decisions is equally important to enhance credibility and legitimacy of the whole system. Property projects are complex and each of them is unique in its development particulars. It is unlikely that either intuitive judgement or mechanistic scrutiny is an accurate reflection of the deliberation process of the decision-makers in considering these applications. Planning decisions fall somewhere between art and science.

Although planning decisions in Hong Kong lie within a shadowy process, it appears that the authority has applied a fairly consistent set of criteria in determining whether planning applications should be approved or rejected. By reviewing past decisions over a long time frame, Tang *et al.* (2000) and

Tang and Choy (2000) have revealed that planning policies for urban office development in Hong Kong have been quite coherent. They attribute this outcome to the strong bureaucratic control of the authority by the government, primarily through appointment of its chairmanship and membership of the TPB, monopoly of planning information and setting of planning agenda (Cuthbert 1991). Coupled with the low relative autonomy of the appointed unofficial members within the TPB, the lack of public participation also helps to hold political struggles at bay and thus enhances consistency.

## Technical vs. political considerations

Another related issue concerns the nature of decision-making criteria. The meaningful question is: On what basis does the TPB approve or reject a particular development proposal? The statement that 'each development case will be judged on its individual merits' does not imply an absence of criteria in the mindset of the decision-makers. So, what are these criteria? They surely vary across space and time. Some planning parameters appear to be more important in determining the outcomes of applications. Davies *et al.* (1986), for instance, identify a long list of 87 planning considerations, which can be grouped into either practical or strategic factors. Harrison (1972: 270), on the other hand, suggests a stronger emphasis on aesthetic matters and spatial solutions. McAuslan (1980) reveals that physical and environmental amenity factors remain the key decision criteria, although there has been a shift towards socio-economic factors. Others underscore factors such as marketability assessment by the builders (Healey *et al.* 1988), and property market conditions (Bramley *et al.* 1995: 134–67).

For analytical purposes, it seems useful to distinguish between two major categories of evaluation criteria: technical and political. Technical considerations refer to the examination of physical, engineering and tangible characteristics of the development proposals. It is often possible to set out the working principles, and in some cases, the exact quantifiable benchmarks, of these technical criteria, in order that decision-makers can compare them with the performance of the development proposals. These technical criteria are commonly found in the guidelines issued by the planning authority to assist applicants in preparing their development applications. In contrast, political criteria refer to a whole range of more subtle, intangible and deeper issues that affect decision-making. These issues are less directly related to the projects in question and more to the social forces associated with power, authority and status in the context. To give a simple example, technical evaluation is primarily concerned with the question: 'What is your development proposal about?' Political evaluation is more interested in issues such as the identity of the applicant and other stakeholders.

Previous studies on the Hong Kong system illustrate several interesting observations in this respect. In examining planning decisions on development applications within the statutory residential zones in Hong Kong over the past 24 years, Lai and Ho (2001) refute the common conception that TPB decisions were particularly in favour of large-scale housing developers. In other studies on urban office development, Tang *et al.* (2000) and Tang and Choy (2000) posit that technical merits of the proposals are only necessary, but not sufficient, conditions in securing success in planning applications. They suggest 'hidden' criteria and argue that the planning guidelines have failed to provide adequate coverage on the decision-making criteria. For instance, market supply, which the authority did not acknowledge as a factor for consideration, was found to have an impact on the ultimate decisions. The rejection reasons stated by the authority were often misleading and tended to disguise the most crucial considerations in rejecting the proposals. Their different methodologies and emphases notwithstanding, these studies stress the crucial influence of government policy on these decisions. The independence of the TPB, as asserted by the government, is suspect.

## Plan vs. market

The next issue is concerned with the relationship between planning and the market. Healey (1992) has identified three different conceptions about such a relationship. First, planning is in opposition to the market because planning is focused on social needs (use value) whereas market emphasises demand (exchange value) of development. Second, planning is said to reflect public interest and is therefore 'above' the market. Third, planning is always supportive of the market because, under capitalism, planning has to facilitate capital accumulation and reproduce the social system. Healey (1992) concludes that, since the private sector is the key player in property development activity in a market economy, the land-use planning system must be 'market-aware' in regulating the development process. Market-aware planning takes different forms depending on the specific institutional characteristics of the context.

Economic and political restructuring of many western cities has in recent years transformed the relationship between plan and market. Economic recessions have widened spatial disparities and heightened inter-urban competition for capital (Duffy 1995; Parkinson 1996). The rising political ideology of the 'New Right' has weakened the traditional welfare, market-critical conceptions of planning (Thornley 1991; Brindley *et al.* 1996). All these forces are said to undermine the traditional assumptions, practices and interests in support of planning (Yiftachel & Alexander 1995). Planning is being used to facilitate economic production, private investment and market profitability. Many cities have turned to property development as the engine of urban regeneration by trading government permissions, relaxing planning restrictions, providing subsidies and granting land to developers (Turok 1992). Urban planning is used to support marketing of the city and promotion of 'mega-projects' in the international context (Berry & Huxley 1992).

However, the extent to which planning has become increasingly oriented to market interests varies across cities. Brindley *et al.* (1996), for instance, have identified six different styles of planning intervention that coexisted under the Thatcher regime in the UK. In other words, urban economic conditions do not necessarily dictate the approach to planning. Market-critical and market-led planning can be found in cities with a buoyant economy, and similarly in marginal and derelict areas. Nonetheless, it is increasingly evident that an over-reliance of urban governments on the property industry has not only reinforced the spatial imbalance of urban development but also resulted in destabilising property markets by increasing development risks and speculative floor space supply (Edwards 1990; Fainstein 1995).

Hong Kong is sometimes exemplified as a free market economy and pro-development. Do planning decisions always follow the market then? The studies on the Hong Kong context have shown a mixed picture. Lai and Ho (2001) reveal that the local development control mechanism for two residential zones was fairly responsive to market conditions in increasing housing supply, and these policies were formulated as a response to rising property prices. In another study, Hui and Ho (2002) detect a dramatic increase in approval rates for applications and reviews for housing development since 1993. They view this leniency as a response to changing market demand as the government controlled the approval rates as well as residential floor area supply to the market. Tang *et al.* (2000) and Tang and Choy (2000) also argue that planning decisions on development applications for urban office development were affected by the prevailing market circumstances. They reveal that the TPB tend to reject the applications, hence restricting the possible supply of future office floor space, when it is evident that the existing supply becomes abundant. Thus, planning is not autonomous of the market, nor is it a technical exercise. Planning control also performs a function in regulating market forces (Schiffer 1991).

Owing to the hybrid planning system, Hong Kong's development control mechanism appears to be heading towards an odd mix of more regulatory plans (for example, the proposed planning certificate) as well as greater discretion to planners that further adds to the debate of plan versus market. When planners have considerable discretion over the granting of use rights, there can be little assurance as to whether the applicants will get what they are due. Under the new framework proposed in the previous Town Planning Bill, discretionary powers over density control and other planning-related provisions would be transferred to the Planning Authority from the Building Authority. The introduction of the proposed planning certificate would also entail a substantive shift in the development approval process from a system that emphasises processing building applications to one that determines the suitability of development for planning purposes. The planning certificate will also give formal control over the development process to planners (Staley 1992). Another type of uncertainty likely to have the most important economic impact is the philosophical shift in planning practice that may take place under the new system of planning. Not only is the current system well known, it is also fundamentally non-interventionist. Since the new system is intended to give planners more discretion over development, less flexibility will be given to developers. To the extent that the new system facilitates more interventionist planning, the current system of property rights will be significantly affected.

Contrary somewhat to the above findings, however, Lai and Ho's (2002) empirical studies suggest that Hong Kong planning permission was market neutral (neither pro-market nor anti-market) towards the container industry. They argue that there was a mismatch between strategic forward planning and local development control decisions: the stated planning policy of permitting and concentrating container-related uses in 'open storage' zones had not been followed. This contradiction between planning and implementation appears to become particularly prominent when the Planning Department has been given increased legal power to influence land use and spatial order (Cuthbert 1995). Planners have become more and more willing to intervene in the development process to direct or influence the pace and pattern of development (Staley 1992). Nevertheless, planning rules are rarely developed within a market framework or context (Staley & Scarlett 1998). This can easily lead to conflicting planning policies and unrealistic expectations of market reaction (Tang & Tang 1999).

## Openness vs. opaqueness

Another important feature of the planning system is concerned with its openness and opaqueness. The attention is focused upon the transparency of the decision-making process and its receptiveness to outside influences. These issues are intimately linked not only to the specific set-up of the planning institution itself but also to the configuration of the urban power structure of the community at large. Society comprises not a homogenous whole but numerous social elites and interest groups competing for their own benefits (Judge *et al.* 1995). In this respect, there is a wide body of literature suggesting that property capital can exert a powerful influence on the planning process (Form 1954; Feagin 1982, 1983; Rydin 1984; Short *et al.* 1986; Logan & Molotch 1987). Nonetheless, this does not imply that property capital, or the wider business interest, can always pursue its own objectives at the expense of other groups. Modern societies, especially those with the institutions of liberal democracy and popular elections, are inherently complex. The process of coalition-building between government and non-government actors and the dynamic of interest group mediation have arguably become crucial aspects of successful urban governance in contemporary cities (Stone 1993, 1998).

Hong Kong has never had open elections to its government. Nonetheless, openness is designated as one of the objectives of the planning system, as stated below:

> Planning is carried out for the public good. It is only fair and logical in an open society that the public should be involved in the planning process. Public involvement provides a sounder basis for planning decisions. Greater public involvement in the plan-making process and planning application system, based on the dissemination of more information for public comments and discussion during various stages of the planning process, should be a guiding principle.
>
> *Comprehensive Review of the Town Planning Ordinance*,
> consultative document (July 1991: 6)

In other words, the decision-making process remains firmly held within the executive and bureaucratic domain in Hong Kong. Openness of the planning system refers simply to solicitation, but not necessarily adoption, of the public views at the appropriate moments to be decided by the planners. The initiative and decision to consult the public lie with the government. As the monopoly landowner in the city, the government can carry out major development projects that have major implications on the economy, the people's livelihoods and its revenue (Ng 1992). Insofar as strategic plan-making is concerned, it appears that the public consultative process is not entirely satisfactory. For instance, Loh (1997) is of the view that as there was no real consultation forum for objection nor access to the decision process for the strategic airport planning in 1989, it was little wonder that such plan received only muted public opposition. At a conference to discuss strategic development in 1997, 69% of the participants considered that there was insufficient input into the present strategic planning process; 65% were in favour of the establishment of a Strategic Planning Advisory Council to offer stronger public input to long-term planning of the territory (Citizen Party 1997). It appears that community development has taken a new turn, and especially after the handover it has become more active, vocal and organised in fighting for their interests. Government officials have to face this new reality (or new constraint) when they choose to continue with the same dose of hubris that influenced many large-scale development proposals in Hong Kong.

The current irony is that planning control practice has no provisions for elaborate public participation. Neither does the Outline Zoning Plan (OZP) or Territorial Development Strategy (TDS) and Sub Regional Plan (SRP). It is also observed that the Town Planning Board relies on explanatory statements in determining planning applications. Since it is expressly declared to be not part of the plan, objection to the statement is not entertained by the Board despite the fact that the statement may contain matters which may adversely affect the interest of government tenants (Chan 1997: 15). This poses a serious threat to 'fairness', one of the basic objectives of the planning system in Hong Kong. Moreover, it is currently not possible for those who want to object to the Explanatory Statement of an OZP where the planning intentions are outlined because the planning intentions are not part of the statutory plan.

In Hong Kong when it comes to the area of planning regulation of private development, public consultation probably becomes a misnomer. The development model in Hong Kong has always been growth centred and economy oriented. The government largely respects the bundle of private development rights conferred by the contractual land leases it signed with the private landlords under the current leasehold system. Lai (1998) describes this as 'planning by contract'. As such, it becomes quite natural that redevelopment is a 'contractual' matter between the lessor and the lessee, and the third party plays a minimal and peripheral role in influencing this process. Statutory planning control provides the avenue, if not further ammunition, for the lessor in negotiating and imposing changes to the terms of development (eventually entering into new leases) with the lessees. Under such circumstances, there is therefore little surprise in witnessing that any attempt to strengthen the statutory rights of the community in public control, through amendment of the Town Planning Ordinance for example, has basically gone astray.

The distinction between statutory and non-statutory (administrative) planning in Hong Kong also becomes comprehensible. Out of the five levels of planning hierarchy ranging from territorial to site-specific levels, only one level, i.e. the land-use zoning plans, has statutory effect.[2] Strategic and administrative plans comprise the upper and lower levels of the hierarchy of plans. Plans at a specific level are supposed to fall within the framework of those above and in turn provide the framework for the plans below (Ling 1997). However, all these plans are often updated at separate time intervals and the connections between these amendments are often loose. Some strategic plans are described as merely statement (Bristow 1988), which represents merely a gathering of existing policies and statements of government organisations, rather than a strategy or even a plan. This nature of strategic documents often generates more confusion than providing a firm direction for development pursuits. Yet the process of public consultation is often held in a most extensive fashion for this administrative planning. In other words, public debates and confrontations are contained within the social spheres that have little immediate and direct bearing on private development rights. Such practices perhaps help to bury the inherent contradictions between the socialised nature of land-use planning and the private property rights system, as elaborated by the Marxian political economy perspective.

## Planning, politics and economy

The institutions of urban planning are embedded within the political, social and economic evolution of any city. To explain Hong Kong's urban planning in its present form, there is a need briefly to review its past development. Furthermore, a study on development control cannot be independent of the wider planning and development framework, which is often claimed as an offshoot of the broad, but widely contested, economic philosophy of laissez-faire.

Urban planning in Hong Kong is described as a western import (Ng 1992) and is overwhelmingly overshadowed by the property development process (Yeh 1990: 14). The statutory cornerstone of urban planning, the Town Planning Ordinance, was enacted in 1939. However, it was not until the 1970s and 1980s that urban planning began to take up some significant importance when the Hong Kong economy diversified and the government took responsibility for carrying out massive infrastructure projects to push for economic and social development (Ng 1992). It was also during the 1970s, when new satellite towns were in the process of development for the purpose of decentralising the urban population and employment, that the function of urban planning was further realised.

From the earliest days of colonial rule, however, the government held an abiding faith in the market to regulate itself. 'I am afraid I do not believe that anybody can have enough knowledge of the past, present and future to estab-lish future priorities', Sir John Cowperthwaite (Finance Secretary between 1961 and 1971) once said (Woronoff 1980: 34). This ideology has become the fundamental principle of the planning and development process in Hong Kong. As a result, the practice of planning had dominance over the theory (Ng 1997). Lack of theorisation has been instrumental in providing meaningful alternatives to the planning process. The main consideration in the earliest comprehensive planning for the whole territory, the Abercombie Report in 1948, was to identify suitable areas for housing, industry and commerce for the anticipated population increase and economic growth (Bristow 1988: 12). Housing and industrial development began to dominate the scene from the 1950s. Most land was made available for the new towns for which urban planning was one of the primary tools. Urban planners prepared plans as the basis for development of land sale and for allocation to different departments (Yeh 1990).

It can be argued that the planning policies in the 1980s and 1990s were formu-lated on the basis of a typical rational approach, which began with problem identification, data collection and its analysis. The process then proceeded with formulation of goals in broad terms followed by identification of more precise objectives that must be achieved to move towards these goals. This hierarchical process can be depicted as a simple linear process or as an itera-tive process whereby goals and objectives were constantly changing over time. The sequential nature of the planning process has often resulted in an over-simplistic or over-straightforward approach to address problems and reach decisions. It is difficult to argue that this simplistic planning process did not exert any influence on the nature of the development control process in Hong Kong. More important, such an approach tended to camouflage the complex political interactions between the relevant powerful actors in the decision-making process. One obvious implication was that the views of the community in evaluating different options were easily marginalised.

Hong Kong has often been held up as a global example of a free market econ-omy (Rabushka 1979). Its development impetus is said to rest upon market initiatives with a clear division of labour between capitalist entrepreneurs and enterprising workers working under a benevolent colonial state that provides the greatest possible economic freedom. The biggest impulse of the colonial state to pursue such a hands-off approach can be traced not to the economy but to its political consideration in maintaining a distance from the ruled. The less the state was involved in the day-to-day interactions with the people, the less the legitimacy of its colonial regime was likely to be criticised. Under this principle, people were expected to manage on their own, market forces would decide their wages and bureaucracy provided a safe retreat. This was obviously not only the policy that the colonial state knew best but the policy that involved the least political risk.

It was not until the end of World War II that fully fledged capitalism became operational in Hong Kong and only in the last couple of decades before the new millennium that economic development of the territory began to take a giant leap. The presence of overseas companies, the rise of local Chinese entrepreneurs and the emergence of an affluent population gave strong impetus to economic growth in Hong Kong. These forces continued to put enormous pressure on the colonial government to provide infrastructure, housing and community facilities to sustain the new economic and social activities. Land, the biggest asset of the government, was increasingly in demand.

Land and property development has long had geopolitical implications in Hong Kong. Politically, following the riots of the late 1960s that triggered a legitimacy crisis, there had been a conscious attempt on the part of the colonial government to adopt a corporatist strategy that involved increasing state intervention and supply of public services. Construction of affordable public housing and implementation of the new town programme were two examples. With economic growth being almost the sole criterion in justifying and legitimising British colonial rule, the government's interventionist strategies were consciously or unconsciously geared towards capitalist accumulation. The colonial bureaucracy took up active functions as the state managers who would intervene whenever the interests of economic accumulation and social stability were in jeopardy (Cheung 1998).

By the 1980s, the then Financial Secretary, Sir Philip Haddon-Cave (1984), admitted the government stance was one of positive non-interventionism rather than laissez-faire, meaning that the government had to respond when industries with social obligations ran into trouble or when an institution needed regulation to prevent inequitable practice. Accordingly, the laissez-faire economic policy continued in the guise of positive non-interventionism as the government prepared new ways to tackle the heightened and increasingly complex economic activities with a territorial development strategy, port and airport strategy and long-term housing policy. Behind the smokescreen of non-interventionism there existed carefully regulated economic activities, administered prices of food, subsidy of social wages and, at times, intervention in the stock market (Schiffer 1983; Castells *et al.* 1990; Cuthbert 1996). It was also during this period that urban planning in Hong

Kong underwent institutional reforms and changes, in substance as well as in form.

Political sovereignty of Hong Kong returned to China in July 1997. Under the 'one country two systems' framework, Hong Kong's capitalist system and ways of life were to remain for another 50 years. No matter how the political changes are downplayed it is obvious that, following the handover, the new Special Administrative Region government would attempt to pursue, as a process of decolonisation, new social and economic blueprints to surpass the achievements of the British colonial administration (Cheung 1998). Evidence of such new policy departures in the new post-colonial state can be found most notably in the areas of housing, education, transport and strategic land development which invariably follow the Pigouvian formula, as evident in planning statements that are replete with references to social benefits and public interest. Urban planning has always formed a crucial part of the state strategy and it is no surprise that it has taken up a heightened role under the new administration. Lai (1997: 15) branded the planning paradigm in the 1950s and 1960s to be determinedly interventionist and raised important questions about whether the social benefits of public interest truly get down to the community. This question is perhaps even more relevant today.

However, in discussing planning control one also needs to pay attention to the details of the institutional environment. Private ownership and control work well in an environment with good supporting institutions of both market and state. Although Hong Kong has one of the most efficient market systems, it lacks the legal and administrative framework for public participation; compensation and other forms of indemnity are still in a nascent state. As the institutional realities are mostly far from perfect, they cannot be expected to function as well in the short run, resulting in higher transaction and opportunity costs. This may typically create the need for a more active control of the system by the government.

It is however agreed that government control over use rights does not have obvious advantages over market ownership and control when it comes to the economic argument, specifically in the long run. This is because the government has both economic interests and political objectives. In some sense having a government with a strong profit motive works well, especially when the private sector has no incentive to act on certain matters. The big difference between the government and the private sector is power: the more power bestowed to planning authorities, the harder it is to make credible commitment and vice versa. This tightrope act is harder to achieve than we perhaps imagine.

## Conclusions

Urban planning, like the private market, is an institution constructed by human society. Institutions comprise both formal and informal rules, norms and practices that influence perception, knowledge, resources and interests of the actors and hence structure the patterns of their interactions in daily life. Such arrangements govern the relationships between the stakeholders in the process of economic and social transactions. In the property development process, urban planning is mostly concerned with the spatial distribution of social activities through the conferment, distribution and attenuation of property rights in the use of land. As a means of state intervention, it affects and structures the relationship between landowners, property developers, government and the community at large in relation to the use of space. An institutional analysis of urban planning must therefore be concerned with (1) how rights are allocated, (2) how rights and claims are assessed and (3) how incentives are designed and enforced.

Different theories put emphasis on different needs for urban planning. Pigouvian welfare-economic theory underscores market failure arguments for state planning intervention. Coasian institutional economics and transaction-cost theory suggest that urban planning is a means to reduce the transaction costs in the land development market and is usually more efficiently undertaken by the private sector rather than the government. Public-choice theory posits urban planning as a service to be provided by politicians in order to satisfy the demand of the voters. The Marxian political economy approach emphasises the political and ideological functions of urban planning in sustaining the exploitative capitalist system. While all these theoretical paradigms provide important yet different insights, we believe that the rationale, arrangement and operations of urban planning are intimately linked to the evolution of history, politics and economy of the society in question.

Even though the institution of urban planning is unique in each place, it is still possible to assess its performance and outcomes in relation to property development. In this chapter, we have briefly discussed four related dimensions of urban planning, using Hong Kong as an example. First, we examined whether the decision-making of the planning institutions enhances certainty in the development process. It is believed that excessive discretion and flexibility to the planners is likely to weaken confidence in property investment. The second related issue is whether the decision-making criteria of the planning authority in regulating property development comprise technical or political factors. Third, we discussed the relationship of urban planning to market trends and property interests. Lastly, the receptiveness and responsiveness of the planning system to outside influences reveal important features about the openness and opaqueness of the planning system. These four dimensions are by no means exhaustive. But we believe they probably provide a useful framework for meaningful questions to be asked when assessing the possible impacts of the institution of urban planning on property development activities.

## Acknowledgement

The authors acknowledge the funding support from the Research Grants Council of the Hong Kong Special Administrative Region, China (Project No. PolyU 5008/01E), which has contributed to the work in this chapter.

## References

Alexander, E.R. (1992a) A transaction cost theory of planning. *Journal of the American Planning Association* **58**(2), 190–200.

Alexander, E.R. (1992b) Why planning vs. markets is an oxymoron: asking the right question. *Planning and Markets*, 1999–2000.

Alexander, E.R. (1994) To plan or not to plan, that is the question: transaction cost theory and its implications for planning. *Environment and Planning B: Planning and Design* **21**, 341–52.

Alexander, E.R. (2001a) Governance and transaction costs in planning systems: a conceptual framework for institutional analysis of land-use planning and development control – the case of Israel. *Environment and Planning B: Planning and Design* **28**(5), 755–76.

Alexander, E.R. (2001b) A transaction-cost theory of land use planning and development control: towards the institutional analysis of public planning. *Town Planning Review* **72**(1), 45–75.

Berry, M. & Huxley, M. (1992) Big build: property capital, the state and urban change in Australia. *International Journal of Urban and Regional Research* **16**(1) 35–59.

Booth, P. (1996) *Controlling Development: Certainty and Discretion in Europe, the USA and Hong Kong.* UCL Press, London.

Boyer, M.C. (1983) *Dreaming the Rational City: the Myth of American City Planning.* MIT Press, Cambridge, MA.

Bramley, G., Bartlett, W. & Lambert, C. (1995) *Planning, the Market and Private Housebuilding.* UCL Press, London.

Brindley, T., Rydin, Y. & Stoker, G. (1996) *Remaking Planning: the Politics of Urban Change.* Routledge, London and New York.

Bristow, R. (1984) *Land-Use Planning in Hong Kong: History, Policies and Procedures.* Oxford University Press, Hong Kong.

Bristow, R. (1988) The Role and Place of Strategic Planning in Hong Kong. *Planning and Development.* Vol. 4, No. 1.

Castells, M., Goh, L. & Kwok R. Y-W (1990) *The Shek Kip Mei Syndrome: Economic Development and Public Housing in Hong Kong and Singapore*. Pion Ltd, London.

Castells, M. (1977) *The Urban Question*. MIT Press, Cambridge, MA.

Chan, A. (1997) Land Use Planning in Hong Kong Beyond 1997: Objectives, Control and Enforcement. *Planning and Development* 13(1).

Cheung, A.B.L. (1998) A new state form after the change of sovereignty and government? – the case of post-1997 Hong Kong. Presented at an *International Conference on the State in the Asia-Pacific Region*, organised by the City University of Hong Kong, 6–7 June 1998, Hong Kong.

Citizen Party (1997) http://www.citizensparty.org/save_our_harbour1.html

*Comprehensive Review of the Town Planning Ordinance*, consultative document. July 1991, Hong Kong Government Printer, Hong Kong.

Cullingworth, J.B. & Nadin, V. (1997) *Town and Country Planning in UK*, Routledge, London.

Cuthbert, A. (1991) For a few dollars more: urban planning and legitimation process in Hong Kong. *International Journal of Regional Research* 15.

Cuthbert, A. (1995) Under the volcano. In: *Postmodern Cities and Spaces* (eds Watson, S. & Gibson, C.), pp. 138–48. Blackwell Publishers, Cambridge, MA.

Davies, H.W.E., Edwards, D. & Rowley, A.R. (1986) The relationship between development plans, development control and appeals. *The Planner* 72(10).

Dear, M. & Scott, A.J. (eds) (1981) *Urbanization and Urban Planning in Capitalist Society*. Methuen, London.

Duffy, H. (1995) *Competitive Cities: Succeeding in The Global Economy*. E & FN Spon, London.

Edwards, M. (1990) What is needed from public policy. In: *Land and Property Development in a Changing Context* (eds Healey, P. & Nabarro, R.), pp. 175–85. Grower, UK.

Fainstein, S. (1995) Urban redevelopment and public policy in London and New York. In: *Managing Cities: the New Urban Context* (eds Healey, P., Cameron, S., Davoudi, S. *et al.*), pp. 127–43. J. Wiley, Chichester and New York.

Fainstein, S.S. & Campbell, S. (eds) (1996) *Readings in Planning Theory*. Blackwell Publishers, Oxford.

Feagin, J.R. (1982) Urban real estate speculation in the United States: implications for social science and urban planning. *International Journal of Urban and Regional Research* 6(1), 35–60.

Feagin, J.R. (1983) *The Urban Real Estate Game: Playing Monopoly with Real Money*. Prentice-Hall, Englewood Cliffs, NJ.

Flyvberg, B. (1998) *Rationality and Power*. University of Chicago Press, Chicago, IL.

Foglesong, R.E. (1986) *Planning the Capitalist City: the Colonial Era to the 1920s*. Princeton University Press, Princeton, NJ.

Form, W.H. (1954) The place of social structure in the determination of land use: some implications for a theory of urban ecology. *Social Forces* 32(4), 317–23.

Gilg, A. & Kelly, M. (1996) The analysis of development control decisions: a position statement and some new insights from recent research in south-west England. *Town Planning Review* **67**(2), 203–28.

Haddon-Cave, P. (1984) [1980] The making of some aspects of public policy in Hong Kong (Introduction to the first edition). In: *The Business Environment in Hong Kong* (ed. D.G. Lethbridge), Oxford University Press, Hong Kong.

Hall, P. (1988) *Cities of Tomorrow: an Intellectual History of Urban Planning and Design in the Twentieth Century*. Basil Blackwell, New York.

Harrison, M.L. (1972) Development control: the influence of political, legal and ideological factors. *Town Planning Review,* **43**(3), 254–74.

Harrison, M.L. & Mordey, R. (eds) (1987) *Planning Control: Philosophies, Prospects, and Practice*. Croom Helm, London/Wolfeboro, NH.

Harvey, D. (1973) *Social Justice and the City*. Edward Arnold, London.

Healey, P. (1992) Development plans and markets. *Planning Practice and Research* **7**(2), 13–21.

Healey, P., McNamara, P., Elson, M. & Doak, A. (1988) *Land Use Planning and the Mediation of Urban Change: the British Planning System in Practice*. Cambridge University Press, Cambridge, New York.

Hui, E.C.M. & Ho, V.S.M. (2002) *Relationship Between the Land Use Planning System, Land Supply and Housing Prices in Hong Kong*. Department of Building and Real Estate, Hong Kong.

Judge, D., Stoker, G. & Wolman, H. (eds) (1995) *Theories of Urban Politics*. Sage Publications, London and Thousand Oaks, CA.

Klosterman, R.E. (1996) Arguments for and against planning. In: *Readings in Planning Theory* (eds S. Campbell & S. Fainstein), pp. 150–168. Blackwell, Malden, MA.

Lai, L.W.C. (1994) The economics of land-use zoning: a literature review and analysis of the work of Coase. *Town Planning Review* **65**(1), 77–98.

Lai, L.W.C. (1997) *Town Planning in Hong Kong: A Critical Review*. City University Press, Hong Kong.

Lai, L.W.C. (1998) The leasehold system as a means of planning by contract: the case of Hong Kong. *Town Planning Review* **69**(3), 249–75.

Lai, L.W.C. & Ho, W.K.O. (2001) A probit analysis of development control: a Hong Kong case study of residential zones. *Urban Studies* **38**(13), 2425–37.

Lai, L.W.C. & Ho, W.K.O. (2002) Planning for open storage of containers in a major international container trade centre: an analysis of Hong Kong development control statistics using probit modeling. *Environment and Planning B: Planning and Design* **29**, 571–87.

Ling, M. (1997) Improving strategic planning process: a practitioner's perspective. *Territorial Development Conference*, Hong Kong.

Logan, J.R. & Molotch, H.L. (1987) *Urban Fortunes: the Political Economy of Place*. University of California Press, Berkeley, CA.

Loh, C. (1997) Improving the strategic planning process: a community perspective. *Territorial Development Conference*, Hong Kong.

Macleod, H. (1992) My six months walking a financial tightrope. *Sunday Morning Post*, 9 February, Hong Kong.

McAuslan, J.W.P. (1980) *The Ideologies of Planning Law*. Pergamon, Oxford.

Ng, Mee Kam (1992) The changing politics of planners in Hong Kong: whither the role of planners. *Working paper 54*, University of Hong Kong.

Ng, Mee Kam (1997) A comparative study of urban planning mechanisms in Hong Kong, Singapore and Taiwan. *Progress in Planning* **51**(1), 1–90.

Parkinson, M. (1996) Twenty-five years of urban policy in Britain – partnership, entrepreneurialism or competition? *Public Money & Management* **16**(3), 7–14.

Pearce, B.J. (1987) Development control and the development process: an introductory review. In: *Planning Control: Philosophies, Prospects and Practices* (eds M.L. Harrison & R. Mordey), pp. 11–31. Croom Helm, London.

Pennington, M. (2000) *Planning and the Political Market: Public Choice and the Politics of Government Failure.* Athlone Press, London.

Planning Department (1995) *Town Planning in Hong Kong: A Quick Reference.* Hong Kong Government Printer, Hong Kong.

Planning, Environment and Lands Branch (1996) *Consultation Paper on Town Planning White Bill.* Hong Kong Government Printer, Hong Kong.

Poulton, M.C. (1991a) The case for a positive theory of planning. Part 1: what is wrong with planning theory? *Environment and Planning B: Planning and Design* **18**(2), 225–32.

Poulton, M.C. (1991b) The case for a positive theory of planning, Part 2: a positive theory of planning. *Environment and Planning B: Planning and Design* **18**(3), 263–75.

Poulton, M.C. (1997) Externalities, transaction costs, public choice and the appeal of zoning: a response to Lai Wai Chung and Sorensen. *Town Planning Review* **68**(1), 81–92.

Purdue, M. (1977) The scope of planning authorities' discretion – or what's material? *Journal of Planning and Environment Law* (August), 490–97.

Rabushka, A. (1979) *Hong Kong: A Study in Economic Freedom.* Chicago University Press, Chicago.

Rowan-Robinson, J., Ross, A. & Walton, W. (1995) Sustainable development and the development control process. *Town Planning Review* **66**(3), 269–86.

Roweis, S.T. (1981) Urban planning in early and late capitalist societies: outline of a theoretical perspective. In: *Urbanization and Urban Planning in Capitalist Society* (eds M. Dear & A.J. Scott), pp. 123–58, Methuen, London.

Rydin, Y. (1984) The struggle for housing land: a case of confused interests. *Policy and Politics* **12**(4), 431–46.

Schiffer, J.R. (1983) *Anatomy of a Laissez-Faire Government: The Hong Kong Growth Model Reconsidered.* Centre of Urban Studies and Urban Planning, University of Hong Kong, Hong Kong.

Schiffer, J.R. (1991) State policy and economic growth: a note on the Hong Kong model. *International Journal of Urban and Regional Research* **15**(2), 180–96.

Short, J.R., Fleming, S. & Witt, S.J.G. (1986) *Housebuilding, Planning and Community Action: the Production and Negotiation of the Built Environment.* Routledge & Kegan Paul, London.

Simmie, J. (2001) Planning, power and conflict. In: *Handbook of Urban Studies* (ed. R. Paddison), pp. 385–401. Sage, London.

Sowell, T. (1980) *Knowledge and Decisions.* Basic Books, New York.

Staley, S.R. (1992) Planning and Development in Hong Kong. *Hong Kong: HKCER Letters*, **16**, Sept 1992.

Staley, S.R. (1994) *Planning rules and Economic Performance*. Chinese University Press, Hong Kong.

Staley, S.R. & Scarlett, L. (1998) Market-oriented planning: principles and tools for the 21st century. *Planning and Markets* (September), **1**(1). (e-journal of University of Southern California: http://www-pam.usc.edu/volume1/index.html).

Stone, C.N. (1993) Urban regimes and the capacity to govern: a political economy approach. *Journal of Urban Affairs* **15**(1), 1–28.

Stone, C.N. (1998) Regime analysis and the study of urban politics: a rejoinder. *Journal of Urban Affairs* **20**(3), 249–60.

Tang, B.S. & Choy, L.H.T. (2000) Modelling planning control decisions. *Cities* **17**, 219–25.

Tang, B.S., Choy, L.H.T. & Wat, J.K.F. (2000) Certainty and discretion in planning control: a case study of office decentralization. *Urban Studies* **37**, 2465–2483.

Tang, B.S. & Tang, R.M.H. (1999) Development control, planning incentive and urban redevelopment: evaluation of a two-tier plot ratio system in Hong Kong. *Land Use Policy* **16**, 33–43.

Thomas, K. (1997) *Development Control: Principles and Practice*. UCL Press, London.

Thornley, A. (1991) *Urban Planning Under Thatcherism: The Challenge of the Market*. Routledge, London.

Thornley, A. (1996) Planning policy and the market. In: *British Planning Policy in Transition: Planning in the Major Years* (ed. M. Tewdwr-Jones), pp. 189–204. UCL Press, London.

Turok, I. (1992) Property-led urban regeneration: panacea or placebo? *Environment and Planning A* **24**(3), 361–79.

Underwood, J. (1981) Development control: a review of research and current issues. *Progress in Planning* **16**(3), 179–242.

Wakeford, R. (1990) *American Development Control: Parallels and Paradoxes From an English Perspective*. HMSO Books, UK.

Webster, C. (1998a) Analytical public-choice planning theory: a response to Poulton. *Town Planning Review* **69**(2), 191–209.

Webster, C.J. (1998b) Public choice, Pigouvian and Coasian planning theory. *Urban Studies* **35**(1), 53–75.

Willis, K.G. (1995) Judging development control decisions. *Urban Studies* **32**(7), 1065–79.

Woronoff, J. (1980) *Capitalist Paradise*, pp. 3–56. Heinemann Asia, Hong Kong.

Yeh, A.G. (1990) Urban planning under the leasehold system. *Working paper 7*, University of Hong Kong.

Yiftachel, O. (1998) Planning and social control: exploring the dark side. *Journal of Planning Literature* **12**(4), 395–406.

Yiftachel, O. & Alexander, I. (1995) The state of metropolitan planning: decline or restructuring. *Environment and Planning C: Government and Policy* **13**(3), 273–96.

# Notes

1  A 1992 study by Staley (1992) shows that, if development were delayed for one year, added costs per project on Hong Kong Island could range from HK$241 million for a 500,000 square foot commercial office building to HK$603 million for a 1 million square foot office building, depending on prevailing interest rates. If all new office space added on Hong Kong Island in 1991 were subject to a one-year delay, the added costs for financing new developments would exceed HK$1 billion. A one-year delay could add between HK$480 per square foot to HK$603 per square foot to the cost of commercial development, depending on prevailing interest rates. Similarly, a one-year delay in the construction of new residential units could add HK$1.1 billion to the cost of developing a 5 million square foot residential estate. Overall, the added costs to residential construction could vary from HK$250 per square foot to HK$300 per square foot, depending on prevailing interest rates.

2  At the highest level of urban planning, the Territorial Development Strategy (TDS) as the policy guidance sets out the optional paths and directions of the territory's planning to meet the long-term social and economic needs of the people. It sets the parameters in terms of broad land use, population and infrastructure distribution within which Sub Regional Plans (SRP) are prepared. This second level includes, for example, Metroplan, and the Development Statements. These in turn provide frameworks for the preparation of the third level of development plans such as the Outline Zoning Plan (OZP) for new towns and other settlements and urban districts. The last two levels include the administrative Outline Development Plans (ODP) and the Layout Plans (LP) to cover the district-wide and site-specific levels of planning.

# 6

# Emerging Institutions in Europe

*Derek C. Nicholls*

## Historical context

In 1951, a group of western European nations signed the Treaty of Paris, establishing the European Coal and Steel Community in the following year. Most of the continent of Europe had been embroiled in two World Wars in the first half of the twentieth century, and then there was a desperate search for peace. Visionary leaders, notably Jean Monet and Robert Schumann of France and Winston Churchill of the United Kingdom, saw the possibility of a continent of nations so closely integrated, so economically interlocked, that war among them would be effectively unthinkable and practically impossible. There was no single clear view of the institutional framework necessary to achieve the goal, just a vague understanding that some national authority might need to be ceded in pursuit of the common good. Liberalising trade was seen as the best approach towards a kind of European unity. The imperative was lasting peace and stability. Sensible, then, to start with a treaty to link together the two industries fundamental to the development of weapons of war with mid-twentieth-century technology – the coal industry providing fuel for the steel industry.

Visions of a kind of European unity are not new. Indeed, for the first few centuries of the first millennium AD, much of the continent was united under the rule of the Roman Empire, with a greater measure of unification than in any other period of history. Since the demise of Rome's dominance, various leaders have sought to emulate the Caesars and establish a pan-European empire. Success has been costly and usually short-lived. Wars have raged across the continent, kingdoms have risen and fallen, nations have been created and extinguished, alliances formed and broken, and boundaries constantly revised. Two thousand years after Julius Caesar came to power Europe was on its knees, exhausted and impoverished by yet another major conflict.

Were the leading European powers prepared to make a fresh start? Were they all prepared to abandon any idea of total dominance over the continent and, instead, voluntarily share some of their power in the pursuit of lasting peace? East of the 'iron curtain' that had descended through central Europe after 1945 and divided the continent, old-style ambition apparently remained. But to the west, a different approach began to emerge, with a search for some kind of unity, not only in defence against the great power of the Soviet Union (notably in linking to the might of the USA in the formation of the North Atlantic Treaty Organization) but also in pursuit of permanent peace among the western nations. The Treaty of Paris was an early signal.

Fifty years on from that modest beginning, how has the European institutional framework developed? The purpose of this chapter is not to give a full assessment of a half-century of European political and economic history, but to focus on land, its ownership, use and regulation. What effect, if any, have institutional changes had upon patterns of land use and the workings of real estate markets in Europe? What kinds of patterns of land-use governance are emerging in the new century? Is the concept of a single European market valid for real estate? What is the likely impact on real estate investment of the introduction of a single currency, already adopted by twelve nations? And what will be the consequences for real estate markets of the intended substantial expansion of the membership of the European Union in 2004 and beyond to embrace most of central Europe?

## Common market

Five years after the Treaty of Paris, six nations took potentially a much bolder step and signed the Treaty of Rome – France, Germany, Italy, Belgium, the Netherlands and Luxembourg. This treaty committed the signatories to work for free trade in the context of a new European Economic Community (EEC) and, crucially, to develop certain other common policies – notably on agriculture which, at that time, was still a major sector of most national economies of the member countries, and even more so of substantial regions in all of them. Regional policy was not included as such, but reduction of regional disparities within the Community and aiding less-favoured regions was mentioned in the Preamble to the treaty, and transport policy was expected to play a significant role towards that end (Williams 1996; Balchin & Sykora 1999).

A rival trade grouping was established – the European Free Trade Association (EFTA) – which had more limited objectives and was more attractive to countries, like the UK, which were nervous about commitments to common policies other than reduction of tariff barriers to trade. The EEC, however, gained momentum and EFTA was not a great success. The six eventually became nine, when the UK, Ireland and Denmark were admitted to membership in 1973. Greece became a member in 1981 and Spain and Portugal joined in 1986.

How would the creation of transnational policies on agriculture, transport and regional development affect land-use patterns and land markets? How far would harmonisation of institutional infrastructure be taken? Would each member's national constitution and distinct legal system provide protection against excessive erosion of national sovereignty or would such fundamental differences be seen more as obstacles to the realisation of the new 'European ideal'? Would the embryonic European Commission in Brussels remain subservient to national governments, or would it gain status and power and even take over in matters of land use and environmental regulation? Would trade really become 'free', and with what effects?

## Single market

After one of many periods of wrangling and apparently little progress, fresh impetus to trade liberalisation and economic cohesion was given by the Single European Act of 1988 (Balchin & Sykora 1999: 22). This treaty set forth the goal of free movement of goods, services, capital and people by 1 January 1993 to achieve a Single European Market. Free movement of goods and capital may have appeared relatively straightforward, though more than 30 years after the Treaty of Rome it was sobering to realise how much more remained to be accomplished, but free movement of services and of people?

What does 'free movement of services' mean? Can a real estate consultant, trained and experienced in, say, Portugal practise in Austria without further qualification or registration? Surely not! How can 'free movement' of real estate services be achieved? Is it more than a matter of adopting common standards, such as the European Valuation Standards painstakingly developed through the European Group of Valuers' Associations (TEGoVA 2003), a collaboration of professional organisations? Common standards are important, but working in accordance with those standards demands knowledge of national and local laws and customs, to say nothing of an ability to communicate with local people. The third report by the European Commission on *Financial Services Priorities and Progress* (European Commission 2002a) noted just how much was still to be achieved in that area and that rapid progress was necessary 'to ensure that the Union does not face a sub-optimal situation in its capital markets and financial services policies'. To the Royal

Institution of Chartered Surveyors (RICS), the conclusion of a 'damning report is that 10 years after its creation the European single market in services is a long way off' (RICS 2002).

The free movement of capital has been achieved in the sense that money may be freely moved from one member country to another. In recent years, advantage has been taken of this by real estate investors. At various times, small waves of investment have moved across frontiers, mostly confined to investment in prime properties. Yet markets remain essentially distinct from one another, and there are few signs of convergence into something which might eventually resemble a 'common' real estate market.

## European Union

After 40 years of growing together, the 1990s saw real tensions developing among the member nations of the EEC. Paradoxically, the immediate cause of tension was the Treaty of Maastricht and the debates leading up to it in 1992. The treaty committed the signatories to closer integration, and henceforward the allies were to be known as the European Union (EU). The change of name masked deepening divisions and, for the first time, member nations fought for, and secured, a right to 'opt out' of unacceptable sections of the treaty. The UK chose not to sign up to the 'social chapter', which dealt with a variety of measures affecting individual rights and social benefits. But, most strikingly, the UK was joined by Denmark in resisting the call to commit to participation in a single currency. The franc, the mark, the lira and the guilder were to be relinquished in a common monetary policy within a decade, but the British government was not prepared to contemplate the surrender of the pound sterling. That was seen as a step too far along the road of European integration, particularly when the UK's painful experience and exit from the European Exchange Rate Mechanism earlier in the same year was still very fresh in the government's mind.

## Community institutions

An assessment of the potential impact of European integration on land-use controls and real estate markets requires at least a brief glimpse of the main institutions which have been created by agreement among the member countries, as the means whereby EU policies and the will of the members can be achieved (European Communities 1999). The EU is not a static organisation: its role and means of operation are under continual review and adjustment, and further reforms are expected following a report by the Convention set up by the Heads of Government in 2002.

*European Council:* The Council of Ministers constitutes the most influential body and is comprised of government ministers from all the member states. Every few months, the Council meets at head-of-state or head-of-government level, but normally meetings are attended by ministers holding particular portfolios, for example, all environment ministers, all agriculture ministers, or all transport ministers. Unanimity is required for all major decisions, thus effectively giving every country a veto. On certain issues, the Council proceeds by qualified majority voting, under which the votes allotted to each country are roughly proportional to its size. The Council initiates new policies (although ideas and proposals may emerge first from other institutions) and it is up to the 'Summit' to give political direction, resolve major disputes and provide impetus for continuing evolution of the Union.

*European Parliament:* While the Council is indirectly elected via elections for national parliaments, the European Parliament has been directly elected since 1979. Voting systems in member countries are designed to secure a greater measure of proportionality in the outcome than is usually achieved by a 'first-past-the-post' system, and the number elected from each country is determined under the Community treaties, broadly in proportion to population but with an increased weighting for the smaller countries. The 626 members serve for five-year terms. The Parliament's powers have been slowly increased and it has three main roles apart from providing an important public forum: (1) limited co-decisions with the Council on certain new legislation; (2) approval (or rejection) of the annual EU budget; and (3) supervision of the executive (including the appointment and dismissal of the Commissioners en bloc).

*European Commission:* The Commission is the EU's main professional staff, headed by 20 Commissioners drawn from the member countries (currently two each from France, Germany, Italy, Spain and the UK and one each from the other ten). The work is organised into Directorates-General (DGs) and other specialised services. Each DG comes under a Commissioner who has the political and operational responsibility for the DG's work. The Commission has three main functions: (1) initiating proposals for legislation to put to the Council and Parliament; (2) monitoring observance of the treaties and launching infringement proceedings where appropriate; and (3) acting as the EU's executive body, for example, in administering budget appropriations. Checking that EU revenue and expenditure comply with relevant legal provisions and accepted accounting principles is the function of the *European Court of Auditors*.

*European Court of Justice:* This court, which sits in Luxembourg, provides the judicial safeguards to ensure that Community law is upheld – both by the Commission and other EU institutions, and by member states. (The *European Court of Human Rights* is a distinct and entirely unrelated organisation. In recent years, that court has delivered important judgments concerning the rights of individuals and companies in relation to planning decisions involving central government acting in a quasi-judicial capacity and as an interested party.)

*European Central Bank:* The Bank acts as the central bank for the *euro-zone* – the area covered by countries which have adopted the euro as their currency. It has the normal central bank functions, including setting the base interest rate common throughout the euro-zone.

*Committee of the Regions:* This committee is a consultative body comprising representatives of regional and local governments in the EU member states. Though lacking executive power, it has some influence on decisions in such matters as regional policy, spatial planning, energy and the environment. The committee, predictably, has taken much interest in pushing the principle of *subsidiarity* – the idea that decisions should be taken at the lowest level consistent with efficiency and effectiveness – in making the case for strengthening the powers of regional and local authorities.

## Single continent?

Following a series of summit meetings at the beginning of the new millennium, the 15 members of the EU decided to admit a number of new members from Central and Eastern Europe. The first ten were expected to join in May 2004 and other applicants were on the waiting list. There is a real prospect that, within ten years or so, most countries of Europe will be members of the Union. What difference will that make? Will it increase real estate investment opportunities? Will the risks associated with investment in, say, the Baltic States or Slovenia change? What new openings will there be for real estate and financial advisers? Will international valuation standards take on greater importance? Can there be a European market – in real estate? Such a possibility is far removed from the tradition of real estate markets as imperfect, fragmented, localised markets.

### Local markets

Traditionally, real estate markets have been driven by local and national needs and demands, in the context of national and local policies, where 'local' may refer to any administrative, geographic or economic area at a sub-national scale. In other words, real estate markets and real estate management took place in the context of a single nation state and a sub-division thereof. International considerations were relevant only in cases of military significance or major export industries.

The national government was the supreme authority for all internal matters and international relations were governed by the concept of paramount national sovereignty – unless, that is, one nation decided to invade the sovereign territory of another. National government took many forms within a diversity of constitutional frameworks; governments displayed a broad spectrum of political colours; some were weak, some were strong.

Regional, provincial and county government took many forms too. In Germany, the *Länder* formed powerful units within a federal structure; French *départements* were a little less powerful; the Dutch had provinces, the English had counties – all these have or had a role in land-use planning. Some, like the German *Länder*, were entrenched in the national constitution; others, like the English counties, were creatures of the whim of national government and could therefore be abolished as easily as they were created. In the last 50 years, England has seen a series of local government reforms, with the boundaries as well as the powers of the counties undergoing significant changes, and some bodies disappearing altogether.

Even greater variety prevailed at the municipal level. Some, like the French, had powerful city mayors; other mayors were largely impotent figureheads. Some mayors had strong political and economic bases; others lacked both. Local government was characterised not only by great variety of political colour and competence, but by variety of technical and professional competence as well.

It was therefore hardly surprising that, at the time of the first tangible moves towards European integration in the 1950s, land-use regulation and real estate markets were essentially local affairs. National governments sometimes spoke of national policy coordination but, with the Netherlands perhaps the main exception, limited coordination appears to have been achieved. Rivalry between cities and districts often militated against solutions to problems straddling administrative boundaries.

## The case of England from 1947

The modern land-use regulation system in England stems from the Town and Country Planning Act of 1947. From nineteenth-century concerns over public health and housing standards there emerged a wider interest in issues of amenity and environmental improvement (though the word 'environment' had barely been discovered in the early twentieth century). Largely permissive legislation gave way in 1947 to the effective nationalisation of all development rights and a formal obligation on local planning authorities to prepare development plans.

The county councils were given the responsibilities of plan preparation and administering development control. No development could take place without planning permission. Sweeping powers of compulsory purchase of 'any land in the interests of the proper planning of the area' provided back-up against recalcitrant landowners and formidable urban redevelopment needs. For a brief period, an attempt was made to collect the 'unearned increment' in land value arising from planning permission, by imposing a development charge on a grant of permission. (Like all other attempts to collect 'betterment' in England, the development charge was abandoned for a combination of practical and political reasons.)

Central government was much involved, even in the absence of a coherent national land-use policy. The Minister of Town and Country Planning's approval was required for all development plans and all compulsory acquisitions, and aggrieved applicants for planning permission to develop had the right of appeal to the Minister. (See Cullingworth & Nadin 2002, chapter 2, for a summary of the history of planning in England; see also Cullingworth 1999.)

During the ensuing half-century, the detailed county development plans gave way to broad-brush 'structure plans' prepared by county councils and much more detailed local plans prepared by the districts. At the beginning of the twenty-first century, those plans are to be abandoned in favour of strategic regional plans on the one hand and local development frameworks on the other. The declared intention is to create a clearer strategy with a more flexible context for swifter decision-making in relation to specific developments. In the absence of elected regional authorities, central government's influence in plan making has tended to grow. But what agency (and with what legitimacy) will straddle local boundaries and devise policies for economic sub-regions?

Development control remains virtually as enacted in 1947, except that applications are now made to city and district councils rather than to the counties. Though there is a strong presumption that the policy of the latest approved development plan will prevail, the local planning authorities retain discretion to take into account any other material consideration when coming to their decision. Compulsory purchase powers remain. Whereas in 1947 it was assumed that those powers would be widely used and that local authorities would be the dominant players in urban redevelopment, 50 years on, under tightening central government control over local government finance, local authorities lack the resources for significant land purchases – other than for immediate release to private developers – and they have been forced to dispose of virtually the whole of any land bank they may have once had.

Over the same period, greater scope for public participation in the planning processes has been created and non-governmental organisations have become more influential in shaping and channelling public opinion. All applications for planning permission are open for comment; major projects usually involve a lengthy public inquiry. At least three opportunities for public representations are provided during the making of any form of development plan, and compulsory purchase procedures include a right for any objector to be heard.

The evolution of England's town and country planning system has taken place under the influence of a sovereign national Parliament and central government. England's entire local government system is a creature of Parliament: Parliament has abolished authorities and tiers of government, as well as created them. Parliament has decided which authorities should be given what powers, the government holds the purse strings and issues policy guidance. Even where the final decision on plan approval rests with the local authority, there are effective ways of ensuring that the national view is fully accommodated.

## English land tenure

Land ownership patterns and systems of land tenure have traditionally varied widely from country to country, even from region to region. In most countries of western Europe, land tenure has ancient roots. The origins of England's freehold ownership lie across the English Channel in France. King William I brought with him in 1066 AD not only an array of nobles and a conquering army but also his feudal system of tenure. The king was the paramount lord, the holder of the fundamental title to all land. Only the king could speak of 'my land'. All other interests in land were derived from the superior title of the king and were dependent upon the terms of a grant from the king. Large tracts of England were granted in exchange for services rendered – retrospectively and prospectively. The types of services and the terms of land grants were very diverse. Until 1290 AD, the holder of one grant could sub-grant an interest in all or part of the land to another and in many instances a long 'feudal ladder' was created. Over time, many services became unimportant, some were commuted to money payments, and many of the middle rungs on the ladder disappeared. The hierarchical feudal system gradually faded until, in 1925, the Law of Property Act established the present position, namely that, while freeholds are still nominally held under the Crown, for all practical purposes, the freeholder is virtually the absolute owner.

The English leasehold grew out of a need to find a way around strict laws governing the payment of interest in the Middle Ages and also from a desire to have a non-feudal interest in land which could be passed on death to someone other than the legal heir. By the beginning of the twentieth century, 90% of England's agricultural land and a similar percentage of houses were occupied under the leasehold system. Building leases offered a tenurial basis for the rapid development of Victorian towns and cities, leases for 99 years being most usual, but local traditions of 75 or other number of years or a lease for 'two lives' were common.

In the second half of the twentieth century, leaseholds again played an important role in urban development in England. This time, comprehensive urban redevelopment took place in the 1950s and 1960s, typically with the local authority acquiring the freehold interest, using its powers of compulsory acquisition, and then granting a long lease to a developer to implement the approved scheme. A common approach to long-term funding was for the developer to sell his interest to a financial institution, which in turn became the landlord of the shopkeepers, residents and office users who actually occupied the premises. In the last quarter of the century, the local authority's role diminished and institutions acquired freeholds of commercial premises or of land for development in the open market.

Occupation leases of commercial premises also developed with distinctive national or regional characteristics. In England, the typical 'institutional' lease emerged as a lease for 25 years, with the tenant responsible for all repairs and insurances, and provision for a review of the rent every five years – provided that any change of rent was upwards. If rental values had fallen since the last review, the rent passing under the lease would not be changed. By contrast, in many European countries, including France, commercial leases have traditionally been much shorter and more flexible, with opportunities to escape from the contract at intervals and without the built-in ratchet for the rent. Under the pressure of the recession in real estate markets in England in the early 1990s, tenants gained more power in the marketplace and many leases have become shorter and more flexible as a result. For many kinds of lease, the perceived bargaining imbalance between landlords and tenants led to Parliamentary intervention to tilt the scales in the direction of the weak, as in the case of rent control and security of tenure for farmers and many householders. Towards the end of the century, however, different market conditions and different political ideology resulted in substantially reduced 'interference'.

In some jurisdictions, the equivalent of the freeholder enjoys a large measure of protection under a national constitution, for example, the United States. In England, Parliament has the authority to prescribe both the circumstances under which a freeholder may be deprived of his freehold and what, if any, compensation shall be paid in return.

In all matters of land use and land ownership, every nation would have regarded itself as in complete control and able to shape patterns of use and tenure to suit national and local goals and circumstances.

## Growing EU influence

Within the European Union, however, recent years have witnessed a notable loss of national independence in matters of land use and environmental protection. Planning systems, policies and practice vary enormously across the EU member states (Nadin *et al.* 1997) but the application of EU Structural Funds to regional and sub-regional development and a succession of European Commission Directives and Regulations in the wake of increasing attention to spatial issues from a transnational perspective will inevitably lead to a certain convergence.

The essential goal of EU Structural Funds is to reduce disparities of per capita gross domestic product (GDP) by providing financial aid for economic and social development of the poorest regions. Most of the funds go to a wide range of projects in areas with less than 75% of the EU average GDP. Bridges, tunnels, dams, new roads, land reclamation projects and urban redevelopment schemes in many parts of the member states testify to the contribution from EU funds towards economic regeneration goals in both urban and rural contexts, and hence to the implementation of national and regional planning policies. Without such aid, for example, Ireland's boom of the late 1990s would have been much more fragile – though a great deal of infrastructure investment is still needed to secure the benefits for the long term. Overall, during the 1990s, the situation in the ten poorest regions in the EU improved from an average of 41% to 51% of the EU mean per capita GDP. To the pursuit of equity has been added a clearer linked objective of improving economic competitiveness of the regions.

The accession of central European countries in 2004 will present a new scale of challenge to reduce regional disparities and it is not surprising that the full rate of contribution from EU Structural Funds will not be immediately available, to prevent exhaustion of funds for poor regions of existing member states.

An offer of funding to facilitate implementation of locally and nationally agreed policy is one thing; an instruction by a supra-national institution to change policy and undertake specific action is quite another. If the European Council approves a new law, it may take effect directly, as a *Regulation*, without the need for any action by national governments, or it may be issued as a *Directive*, which binds the member states to achieving the declared objectives while allowing each state to choose the form and means of implementation. A member state may thus attach a lower priority to a particular measure than most other members may wish, and implementation of a new law across the whole EU often takes many years. All states are guilty of extending the 'transposition gap' between EU decisions and national implementation; some, perhaps, are more guilty than others.

Environmental protection and improvement has formed a major area of EU legislation since the first Environmental Directive (on packaging and labelling of dangerous substances) was issued in 1967. Among the significant improvements resulting from EU initiatives over the ensuing 35 years are reductions in toxic emissions, restrictions on the use of particularly harmful pesticides and an increase in the recycling of waste products (European Commission 2002b). A European Environment Agency was established in 1994 and a number of directives have focused on conservation of flora and fauna. A directive on environmental impact assessment (EIA) in 1985 set the pattern for the incorporation of EIA into national and local planning procedures. Now, for example, all planning applications for major developments in England must be accompanied by an environmental impact statement: without one, the planning authority may not grant permission.

Early in 2003, the European Commission initiated proceedings against the UK government alleging that the government had failed to produce an EIA for a redevelopment scheme in west London (Harvey 2003). The main aim of the Commission in this case seems to be to draw attention to alleged defects in the implementation of the 1985 directive. Perceived failure by local planning authorities and planning inspectors to pay due regard to the need for, and contents of, EIAs has become a common basis for applications by aggrieved parties for judicial review of planning decisions.

In the 1990s, following a lead given by the Organization for Economic Co-operation and Development (OECD), the EU began fine-tuning some of its regional thinking by putting more emphasis on spatial development. The Commission saw a particular need to address 'transnational spatial development strategies' where regional problems straddled national boundaries. It seems likely that consideration of funding for less prosperous areas will involve consideration of aspects of physical planning and sub-regional land-use strategies to a greater extent in future.

In the context of more and more involvement by EU institutions in matters of land use and environmental policy, coupled with a tendency towards centralisation at a national scale in some countries, what scope is there for local initiative? Where and how does the principle of subsidiarity apply? Will real estate markets inevitably follow a similar trend and become less local and more international?

## European Monetary Union

Following agreement in principle in the Treaty of Maastricht, 11 EU countries entered a new European Monetary Union on 1 January 1999. Denmark and the UK had opted out of the commitment in 1992, and Greece was forced to defer joining until she met the prescribed economic and monetary conditions. From the starting date, the exchange rates between the member currencies were permanently locked and the euro was adopted as the single currency for all 11 countries. The European Central Bank was empowered to act for the whole currency zone and notes and coins were issued from 1 January 2002.

Almost from the day of its launch, the euro declined sharply from its starting value of $1.17, reached approximate parity with the dollar by the end of 1999 and sank as low as $0.85 by late 2000, remaining well below parity for a further 18 months. However, 2002 saw a fairly steady recovery, and further rapid improvement in the first half of 2003 resulted in the euro exceeding its launch value against both the dollar and the pound. The euro now seems to have established its place as a global currency and, since the size of the total EU market is comparable to that of the US, the European Central Bank faces pressure to have regard to the impact of its decisions on the global economy, not just to act in the narrower EU interest. Frequently, of course, the expectation will be that those interests are not in conflict. EU economic growth depends not just on internal factors but also on expansion in world markets.

Internally, there may be greater conflicts between the interests of different EU members, or even between different regions of a single member state. Some national or regional economies may be overheating and would benefit from the dampening effect of a higher lending rate, whereas other areas may be in need of a monetary stimulant to get them out of a slowdown. Relinquishing national authority over interest rates as well as over the value of the currency substantially reduces the range of policy tools available to national governments to manage their economies. Many governments appear voluntarily to have placed further restraints on their freedom of action by promising their electorates that taxation will not be increased.

## Implications for real estate markets

How will these fundamental changes affect markets in general and real estate markets in particular?

The most obvious impact is the elimination of currency risk for movements of capital within the euro-zone. An investor from Italy can now purchase an investment in Finland in his own currency, without having to consider possible fluctuations and the need for hedging. The cost associated with changing from one currency to another is also eliminated from the already substantial transaction costs of real estate deals.

Portfolio diversification becomes a more feasible proposition and a spread of direct property investments in different countries within the currency zone may give even better diversifying effects, for there is only limited evidence of reduction of the differences in the characteristics of different local, regional and national markets. Sirmans and Worzala (2003), after a review of research literature on international real estate investment, suggest that: 'For the most part, results [of the studies reviewed] concluded that international real estate did provide diversification benefits and investors should not ignore this asset class when making asset allocation decisions.' Cross-border investments may well increase within a single currency zone.

For consumers, prices become more transparent for comparisons between countries and that is likely to result in downward pressure on prices. That increased transparency may help to lower some of the transaction costs associated with real estate sales and purchases and may eliminate the need for at least one tier of professional advice.

The larger market of the single currency zone compared with any one member country increases the attractiveness of the zone for foreign direct investment. Countries in Europe remaining outside the euro-zone may therefore expect to experience some reduction in their share of foreign investment in future. In the 1990s, around 40% of all inward investment into the EU came to the UK, but warnings that the UK is in danger of losing out if a decision to join the single currency is long delayed probably need to be taken seriously. A stronger euro, accepted as a world currency, is likely to mean sterling becoming rather more volatile, and thus currency risk as well as market size could divert some foreign investment into the euro-zone.

Prior to the introduction of the euro, fears were expressed that financial services in Europe would gravitate towards the single currency zone, and that London's pre-eminence among European finance centres would cease. There appears to be no evidence from the early years of the single currency to support such predictions. London remains the biggest international financial centre in the world. Problems in the early years of the millennium in the office markets in the City of London and in the Isle of Dogs have their origins elsewhere, in a sluggish economic performance rather than a diversion of business.

## Emerging market patterns

There is no doubt that Europe has undergone profound changes over the past 50 years. International laws have joined local laws in forming the legal context for investment decisions. Land-use planning is no longer essentially a matter of local preferences but now features transnational policies and involves processes established by a supra-national institution. There is now a much larger marketplace with a single currency, leading among other things to greater transparency. Information technology in many guises has transformed the acquisition of information about real estate markets, making them slightly less 'imperfect' than before, and could similarly revolutionise conveyancing in the wake of full land registration.

Much more interest is shown by large investors in possibilities for investing in real estate outside their own country. In some cases they may be more risk averse than at home, and move cautiously in unfamiliar territory in pursuit of portfolio diversification. In other cases, entry into a new foreign market may be in search of a higher yield to boost overall portfolio returns and there may well be a willingness to take larger-than-usual risks with a very minor part of the total portfolio. Germans recently investing in Hungarian commercial real estate form a case in point. Is that kind of investment sustainable in the long run? Such investors may well be disposed to 'cut and run' if returns take a dip and meantime local investors, less inclined or less able to take higher risks or to diversify internationally, find the reduced yields in their own market have the effect of pricing investments beyond their reach. Thus the local investors are not well positioned either to share in the full rewards of a boom or to sustain the local market in more difficult times. Greater rather than less market volatility may result.

Real estate performance across European cities seems as diverse as ever. The ATIS REAL Weatheralls (2003) report on the European office market reveals a wide variation in office rental value changes in 2002, from –19% in Madrid to +15% in Leeds. The authors comment: 'There is no single European office market where all centres move in the same direction at the same speed' (p. 4). Nor is there ever likely to be. Residential markets are similarly diverse in performance.

What then is the effect of all the institutional change in Europe? Is there an emerging Continental market? Local market characteristics and conditions in many ways seem as strongly differentiating as ever. On the other hand, more international players are becoming involved in more of the local markets, are making comparisons and then taking investment decisions in the light of a much greater supply of information. Local capital has been joined by international capital in pursuit of supply. Securitisation and a single currency will enable a European market in indirect real estate investments to develop, perhaps rapidly. Local supply of real estate as well as demand is partly determined by global and continental economic trends. But local laws, customs and culture, to say nothing of local demand factors and construction methods, for instance, survive strongly to preserve the essentially local nature of markets in real estate.

## Whither Europe?

The European Union remains in a transitional phase, on the point of a two-thirds increase in membership, with continuing evolution in its internal institutions, and a fierce debate about constitutional change and ultimate goals. Will there be movement towards a more federal structure despite strong protestations from many members? Will nation states become less important if the principle of subsidiarity is taken seriously? Will sub-national units become more significant and Europe become essentially a continent of regions, each with direct access to the European Commission in Brussels and effectively represented in EU decision-making by directly elected members of a much-strengthened European Parliament?

At a more practical level, pressures for harmonisation of corporate taxes, for example, seem likely to increase. Taxes on real estate transactions may well be another target for greater uniformity. The flow of environmental directives will not dry up. Brussels will take an increasing interest in spatial planning. Developing more common ground in such matters across the member states will assist international players in real estate markets in making fair comparisons between investment opportunities in different cities, regions and countries, but such measures will not of themselves create a single market in real estate.

The European Union, even before expansion and how much more after, is made up of a great diversity of peoples and cultures, which will surely prove resistant to any tendencies towards substantial uniformity across the continent. It will take more than a single currency to remove such barriers. But change does happen. How significant are those barriers today compared with a century ago and how important will they be 100 years hence?

A century is a long time in European history. Remembering that the impetus for the creation of the Union in the first place came from a yearning for peace in the aftermath of World War II, there is a more fundamental question that should be asked: When the generation of Europeans which experienced major war has faded away, will their successors have sufficient desire for peace to persuade them to subordinate national or regional interests to the greater good of the continent? Will the EU survive?

# References

ATIS REAL Weatheralls (2003) *European Office Market in Perspective.* ATIS REAL Weatheralls, London.

Balchin, P. & Sykora, L. (1999) *Regional Policy and Planning in Europe.* Routledge, London.

Cullingworth, J.B. (ed.) (1999) *British Planning: Fifty Years of Urban and Regional Policy.* Athlone Press, London.

Cullingworth, J.B. & Nadin, V. (2002) *Town & Country Planning in the UK,* 13th edn. Routledge, London.

European Commission (2002a) *Financial Services Priorities and Progress Third Report.* Brussels, EC.

European Commission (2002b) *Choices for a Greener Future: the European Union and the Environment.* Office for Official Publications of the European Communities, Luxembourg.

European Communities (1999) *Serving the European Union: a citizen's guide to the institutions of the European Union.* Office for Official Publications of the European Communities, Luxembourg.

Harvey, P. (2003) Europe's deep impact, *Property Week*, 23 May 2003, pp. 40–41.

Nadin, V., Cooper, S., Shaw, D., Westlake, T. & Hawkes, P. (1997) *The EU Compendium of Spatial Planning Systems and Policies*. Office for the Official Publications of the European Communities, Luxembourg.

RICS (2002) *Brussels Briefing 09 September 2002*. Royal Institution of Chartered Surveyors. www.rics.org

Sirmans, C.F. & Worzala, E. (2003) International direct real estate investment: a review of the literature. *Urban Studies*, **40**, 1081–114.

TEGoVA (2003) *European Valuation Standards*, 5th edn. The European Group of Valuers Associations, London.

Williams, R.H. (1996) *European Union Spatial Policy and Planning*. Paul Chapman Publishing, London.

Much additional information on the European Union is available on the Internet via the Europa server (http://europa.eu.int).

# 7

# Institutional Aspects of Real Estate Investment and Project Appraisal

## *Eddie Chi Man Hui and Yat Hung Chiang*

This chapter argues that property and capital markets, which are central to the efficient functioning of the operational level in market economies, are becoming more global and integrated. International capital markets and, inherently, the efficiency and transparency of the financial institutions that govern the allocation and distribution of capital, have the capacity to assert great influence on local markets. At the operational level, however, this has not meant greater stability or certainty, often the reverse. Greater transparency produces more information to identify, search and evaluate. At the same time, the parallel development of information and communication technology has dramatically increased the volume and speed of communication, without necessarily improving the quality of decision-making. The net result has profoundly affected the choice of capitalisation rates in real estate investment markets and the discount rate for project appraisal.

Capital markets are more open and riskier than in the past, with exponential growth in issuances of, for example, government and private bonds and derivatives. Moreover, market adjustments may sometimes be triggered by 'irrational exuberance', having little regard to local fundamentals. Subsequent corrections can have damaging consequences on market stability, even on a global scale. This, in turn, has 'knock-on' effects for local property markets, and the risk and return borne by investors. At issue is how investors or real estate developers can properly appraise development projects in the current global market context.

## Institutional aspects

Thorstein Veblen is regarded as the progenitor of American institutional economics (Ekelund & Hebert 1997). In contrast to the rationalistic and utility-maximising assumptions of the classical and neoclassical schools, Veblen theorised about human nature, behaviour, instincts and habits. Rather than the deterministic and sterile orthodox views that suggested otherwise, Veblen's institutional economics maintains that the effects of a single disturbing change can only be analysed subject to two conditions. The first is the concept of causal sequence, and the second the premise that the underlying data will not necessarily remain the same. The various institutions surrounding human behaviour support a set of material circumstances that in turn have a significant impact on the formation of individuals' views about the world. Veblen's technological and ceremonial institutions interact with each other to constitute the mainsprings of constant and inevitable changes in his system.

The institutional economics of the early part of the twentieth century covered a wide range of institutions but lacked the focus that transaction-cost economics has subsequently given the subject over the past 50 years. This chapter focuses on financial institutions. Financial intermediaries and markets play crucial roles in the identification, allocation and pricing of project risks. They function primarily at the operational level by providing matching services between (1) the supply of investment opportunities seeking finance and (2) the demand of investors for such opportunities (Beidleman *et al.* 1991). Beidleman *et al.* (1990) classify project risks under three different phases of a project – the development phase, the construction phase and the operating phase. For international projects, there are additional sources of risk including sovereignty or political *force majeure*, and fiscal policy, particularly the control of capital flows and currency exchange rates.

In addition, every project will be subject to such macroeconomic or systemic risks as industrial growth, inflation, and real and nominal interest rates. An understanding of the roles of relevant institutions would include how and to what extent such risks and uncertainties are induced, influenced and determined by the various institutions. The risk premium, as part and parcel of discount rates, determines the price of undertaking the various risks altogether. In a typical discounted cash flow calculation, the sum of the risk premium and the real interest rate constitutes the discount rate used in discounting the inflation-adjusted cash flows.

## The integration of financial and property markets

The financial value of real estate is a function of cash flow and required return. The supply of space and user demand in the property markets determine cash flow, whilst the supply of investments and investor demand in the capital markets determine the required rate of return or the capitalisation rate. The determination of income or cash flow has attracted more discussion than the determination of capitalisation rates. Consideration of the appropriate discount rate to be employed in the valuation process has been relatively neglected (Roulac 2001). In order to understand real estate cycles, capital flows and investment performance are as relevant as macroeconomic factors and the supply of and demand for space (Roulac 2001).

Discounted cash flow (DCF), through which the internal rate of return (IRR) is derived, has been frequently deployed for financial appraisal of development and infrastructure projects. In a recent survey (Chiang *et al.* 2000), institutional investors in Hong Kong responded that IRR was the most frequently used analytical technique after less quantitatively demanding considerations such as company review, risk and return analyses, and past experience. DCF or IRR calculations require two *ex-ante* inputs – cash flows (in and out) and discount rates. Estimates of cash flows are largely a function of local parameters. Use of a building is subject to local governance institutions such as use zoning, planning, development and building regulations. Consequently, costs and revenues reflect to a large extent the institutional arrangements that result from compliance with local rules of property ownership, use and tenure, and local social and economic structures, that is, local institutions. In contrast, discount rates are driven by and inextricably interwoven with global banking institutions and capital markets. Furthermore, more often than not, net present value or profitability of a project is more sensitive to variations in discount rates than in cash flows.

The interaction of 'space' and capital markets in the context of the residential sector in Hong Kong has been addressed by Renaud *et al.* (1997), applying the DiPasquale and Wheaton (1996) four-quadrant model. The determination of discount or capitalisation rates is subject to the tyranny of international capital markets as they become more globalised and integrated. The conjecture that international property and capital markets are highly integrated can be illustrated by the Asian financial turmoil in 1997. This demonstrated that, in a surprisingly short space of time, the domino collapse of Asian banking and capital markets one after another led to drastic downward adjustments in property prices throughout the region. This led to 'knock-on' defaulting on property mortgages.

Perhaps with the benefit of hindsight, this Asian financial fiasco had indeed been waiting to happen. The economic meltdown was the result of a combination of contributory factors: massive inflow of international capital; crony capitalism; moral hazard; overlending; and speculative property investment and development (Hui *et al.* 1998). The turmoil is only the latest case illustrating that economic crises have always been preceded by major movements of capital into real estate development (Leitner 1994). It was a direct consequence of inherent weaknesses in banking and financial institutions across the Asian region, where the demarcation between private financial intermediaries and government agencies is always blurred if not non-existent. Particularly in China and Japan, the two largest economies in Asia, major overhauls in the structure and operation of the banking sectors have been long overdue.

Many studies have therefore advocated a holistic or Copernican approach, simultaneously considering space and capital markets, to explain real estate performance (Fisher 1992; Roulac 1998). Contrary to rational expectations, studies focusing on the space market only are likely to yield results that are inconclusive (Fisher 1992). Changes in rents and values could, when conditions dictate, be responses to changes in the demand for property as a capital asset, rather than to changes in the fundamental condition of the supply side of the property market (Fisher *et al.* 1993).

Deregulation in the capital markets, abolition of exchange control and securitisation of direct and indirect property investments have contributed to integration of property and capital markets (Coakley 1994). The study and the practice of project appraisals therefore have to take into account institutional factors. Property and infrastructure developments are local business in a global market. Projects are localised but the cost and availability of capital are globalised. There is so much integration and globalisation of capital and property markets that the cost of finance is determined on a global basis.

Over-reliance on banks

Commercial banks in Asia are still the major source of project finance in the private sector. Hui *et al.* (1998) noted that the leverage of development firms is generally higher in Southeast Asian countries than in Hong Kong, where the stock market is mature in terms of volume and liquidity. Some countries have 'policy-sector' banks such as a 'construction' bank or 'agriculture' development bank. For example, the Construction Bank of China is responsible for project finance and construction lending. However, it is also one of the four largest state banks struggling for better performance (Casserley & Gibb 1999).

The case of South Korea demonstrates the importance of (1) recapitalising the banking sector and (2) improving its management of credit risk so that capital is recycled and efficiently reallocated to the most productive users. South Korea exemplifies the importance of banking reform as a prerequisite for economic revival. These principles have not been adopted in Japan, facing a massive burden of non-performing loans (bad debts). Instead, political rather than commercial influences on banking institutions and, hence, lending decisions have resulted in a chronically inefficient allocation of capital. Likewise, as China implements a policy of deregulating financial markets (a consequence of accession to the World Trade Organization), state banks that are technically bankrupt cast a dark shadow over economic reform programmes, especially in the wake of foreign bankers entering these newly opened markets (Chang 2001).

The International Bank for Reconstruction and Development (IBRD; World Bank) and the Asian Development Bank (ADB) operate on global and regional scales, respectively. They are major institutional players, and have financed or helped finance infrastructure and other industrial projects around the world and throughout the Asian region. In particular, the ADB was established to foster economic growth in Asia and the Pacific. From its establishment in 1966 through the end of 1998, it had approved loans aggregating more than US$77 billion (ADB 1999a).

On the other hand, the role of the World Bank is expected to diminish as countries continue to privatise their economies. Indeed, there have been comments that the World Bank, the banking arm of the International Monetary Fund (IMF), has not been performing satisfactorily and should be dissolved. *Fortune* (2000) reports that, by its own reckoning, nearly 60% of World Bank projects are failures. The World Bank has been accused of channelling funds into corrupt hands in some countries. For example, the director of the Jakarta office of the World Bank commented that corruption in the Bank's Indonesia projects was 'so systematic and so well-hidden that it's not easy to get your hands around it' (*Business Week* 2000). Coincidentally, Indonesia was the largest recipient of ordinary operations loans from the Asian Development Bank as at 31 December 1998 (ADB 1999a).

Some Asian banks have earned reputations as being more like a family network of politicians, their relatives and friends engaging in crony pursuits. Loans are extended to firms not because of what they will achieve for the economy but because of who runs them. In many instances, it is not the more promising firms but the failing firms that get the bank loans. In order to reduce reliance on the banking sector, which has not proved to be the most efficient channel for capital allocation, in the longer term there is a need for Asia to channel more of its savings into the stock and bond markets. More portfolio capital will be attracted into the region if the capital markets and the banking sector are mature, well-regulated and information efficient.

Encouraging greater participation in real estate markets by global institutional investors requires the creation and maintenance of capital markets that are perceived to be level playing fields for all market participants. Greater participation of global institutional investors and their analysts across the region will encourage the development and adoption of and adherence to international financial and economic standards, including (1) the advancement of proper corporate governance and (2) legal, accounting and auditing standards. This, in turn, would lead to more transparent markets, reflecting all publicly available information in asset prices, and where risk premiums are efficiently and realistically priced. Establishing such conditions certainly represents a major competitive advantage for any economy wishing to attract direct foreign investment.

## Asian capital markets

Further development of regional capital markets has been strongly advocated so that capital can be allocated in a more effective and efficient manner. A market structure that is institutionally mature and transparent, managed according to international legal and accountancy standards, provides the added confidence for channelling investors' surplus money to the most productive firms and projects. However, across the Asian region, perhaps with the exception of Japan, the debt market is generally not as well developed as the stock market. For example, the absence of a mature debt market in Hong Kong inhibits the qualification of this Special Administrative Region of China to be labelled as a true financial centre (Jao 1997). The stock market of Hong Kong is dominated by property firms, and about half of all bank loans are property related (Chan *et al.* 1998). Yet property developers or investors who do not wish to have their ownership diluted by tapping equity finance still have to resort to overseas sources when seeking long-term and fixed interest rate loans. This calls for the development of a debt market.

### Need for a debt market in Hong Kong

A concerted policy response by OECD member countries and reflationary polices in Asian economies have so far limited the contagion of conditions that generate economic meltdown. Synchronised interest rate cuts and fiscal stimuli across the globe have helped Asian economies recover sooner than expected (ADB 1999b). The rebound of some East Asian countries such as

South Korea, the Philippines, Malaysia, Indonesia and Thailand has been attributed to a combination of boost in domestic demand, intra-regional trade and the inflows of portfolio capital (*The Economist* 2002a). There is, however, gloom over the further recovery of Asian economies. A stock market downturn starting from the US could have catastrophic consequences if the recovery has been based on unrealisable growth in earnings and unsustainable margin debts, particularly in Hong Kong where the currency is pegged to the US dollar. The mitigation of exchange rate risk is gained at the expense of an autonomous monetary policy. Interest rates in Hong Kong closely track those established by the Federal Reserve Bank of the US. Deflation in Hong Kong means that, in international terms, real interest rates in Hong Kong are high.

A mature local debt market denominated in local dollars might buffer Hong Kong from repercussions originating in capital markets elsewhere. This debt market together with further development in the local derivatives market would provide more opportunities for investors to arbitrage and hedge risks. Volatility in discount rates would reflect more local economic fundamentals than any 'irrational exuberance' from overseas. Establishing a clearly defined and regulated debt market should benefit the economy in general and the real estate and construction industry in particular. Indeed the need for a fully fledged debt market was recognised by the Financial Secretary in his 1999 Budget Speech, and again by the Chief Executive in his 2003 Policy Address. The absence of a mature debt market forms the weakest link in local financial markets and undermines any claim to the status of an international financial centre.

A well-developed financial centre would be instrumental in the efficient pricing of risk premiums. The survey by Chiang *et al.* (2000) reported institutional investors' perception that liquidity within the property market would be enhanced by mortgage-backed securities (MBS). MBSs have been launched by the Hong Kong Mortgage Corporation and the Mandatory Provident Fund Scheme (MPFS). Further issuance of MBSs and investment by the MPFS in bonds would advance the development of a local debt market. The development of debt markets in Hong Kong and over Asia could also provide a secure investment vehicle to capitalise on Asians' high rates of saving. This source of funding could contribute to infrastructure investment over the region. At present, many Asian countries such as China have financed the national deficit of the US by buying US Treasury bills. Meanwhile, they borrow from capital markets outside their own Asian region, in competition with other borrowers around the globe. Global demand for cash may drive the cost of borrowing higher than if there were mature Asian capital markets.

Estimates suggest that about half of the incremental investment in infra-structure in Asia would be financed by the private sector (ADB 1999a). Hong Kong could and should capitalise on her well-established institutional framework to develop a debt market to enable both local and overseas firms to borrow money at fixed interest rates. In 1998, the Asian Development Bank issued HK$3 billion multi-tranche public bonds (with one- to three-year maturities) in the domestic bond market of Hong Kong. This was the largest ever fixed-rate bond issue in the Hong Kong dollar debt market (ADB 1998). The success of an initial public offering on such a large scale boosted the development of the Hong Kong debt market.

## Asset securitisation

Securitised assets include mortgage-backed securities, real estate invest-ment funds (REITs) and asset-backed securitisation. They provide long-term finance at fixed interest rates, as well as a matching of maturity that bank lending lacks. The long-term nature of residential mortgages poses a liquidity risk to the banks that rely on largely short-term deposits. One major constraint on direct property investment is lumpiness and illiquidity. Securitisation of properties may alleviate these problems but at the risk of losing some of the traditional characteristics of direct investment in real es-tate. Securitised real estate assets are usually held to maturity because small circulation inhibits the development of secondary markets. Their risk pre-miums, as measured by the spread above the yields of government bonds of the same maturity, represent mostly the interest rate risk. REITs are most de-veloped in the US where there were 182 REITs amounting to US$155 billion as at December 2001 (Yip 2002). This relative success must be seen against a regime of tax rules that provides tax benefits for investing in REITs.

REITs are seen as an alternative vehicle for recapitalisation of the property market. In Asia, real estate investment trusts have been offered in South Korea (K-REITs), Japan (J-REITs) and Singapore (S-REITs). In South Korea, Listed Real Estate Investment Trusts (K-LREITs) were established as a result of the financial difficulties experienced by Real Estate Trust Institutions in the wake of the 1997 Asian financial crisis (Kim *et al.* 2000). REITs are a relatively recent innovation in Japan (six J-REITs have been trading on the Tokyo Stock Exchange for a year). They were introduced to provide an alternative source of funds other than bank loans, for Japanese developers, and to develop deeper and more liquid financial markets (*BusinessWeek* 2002). REITs also provide a mechanism for indebted property companies to divest themselves of their properties and restructure their asset portfolios, as in the case of CapitaLand in Singapore (*AWSJ* 2002a). It may also be the means for the Hong Kong government to divest itself of a HK$20 billion commercial property portfolio, now under the ownership of the Hong Kong Housing Authority (*AWSJ* 2003). On the other hand, they provide apparent investment opportunities for such institutional investors as pension funds and other real estate investment funds from both host and overseas countries (*AWSJ* 2002a).

In China, the institutional framework for a market-based economy is currently evolving but remains in a state of flux, generating substantial uncertainty for international investors. The first property trust launched in China, the New Shanghai International Building Investment Trust, was offered for sale in July 2002 with a yield of 4%, compared with the bank deposit rate of 2% p.a. However, this was more a mortgage agreement than a REIT. The properties were used as collateral whereas investors would receive their 'investment' plus interest only (Yip 2002).

Consideration by the Hong Kong Securities and Futures Commission (SFC) of the introduction of publicly listed REITs in Hong Kong was brought to a head in 2002/3. The large proportion of bank loans finding its way into property development and residential mortgages is conducive to the development of a market for securitised real estate assets (cf. Ong & Sing 2001). Despite scepticism that the establishment of REITs is simply a measure to revive the property market by stimulating demand, a mature REIT market in Hong Kong would increase opportunity for constructing more diversified investment portfolios, enabling unsystemic risks to be further diversified, reducing risk premiums. With increasing integration and globalisation of capital markets, there are more diversification benefits between different assets such as real estate, bonds and equities than between equities across different countries (*AWSJ* 2002b). An increasing trend in constructing multi-asset portfolios is therefore conducive to the development of REITs in Hong Kong.

It is anticipated that in Hong Kong the rental yield component of total property return may increase further although capital gains are expected to decline by comparison with the property boom before 1997. An increase in rental yield is also conducive to the development of the REIT market if investors generally seek more stable streams of rental income. On the other hand, there are at least two constraints on the development of a REIT market in Hong Kong. First, the tax incentive that makes the US REITs attractive investments does not apply to Hong Kong, attributed to a lukewarm reception to the introduction of property funds in Singapore (Ong *et al.* 2000). Second, in Hong Kong, the ownership and management of prime office property is retained by and concentrated in the hands of a small number of property developers and investors. Although precise information is scarce, institutional investors are believed to own a very small portion of the stock of investment-grade real estate, in contrast to comparable situations in the UK or the US. Thus, the attitude of these major developers/investors constitutes an important operational factor in the introduction of REITs in Hong Kong. In the meantime, it is expected that the SFC will relax the restriction that prohibits unit trusts and mutual funds from direct property investment.

Real estate investment trusts are a 'halfway house' between direct investment in real estate and indirect investment through the vehicle of property stocks. The return and risk profile also lies, typically, somewhere between direct and indirect property investment. The successful launch of K-REITs demonstrates that REITs can help to revive oligopolistic property markets by introducing additional funding from institutional investors, offered one more vehicle for property investment.

Increasing risk?

Capital markets are not necessarily as well regulated and closely monitored as the banking sector. The systemic risks are not necessarily reduced. The implications are illustrated by the exploitation of bonds and securitised assets. Issues of government and private bonds amount to off-balance-sheet borrowing for banks. Borrowing in this form might have been so excessive that recent asset inflation in the US, Europe and the Asian region could be largely attributable to margin debts. Capital markets have become so highly geared that sudden and catastrophic market corrections around the globe could be triggered any time.

Securitisation of real estate assets into a share-based investment produces a different risk profile (Chiang & Chan 1995); however, overall systemic market risk is unlikely to diminish. There is a transfer but not reduction of total systemic risk. There is some concern that the banking sector (otherwise considered to have been well regulated) has become too absorbed with securitised assets and other derivatives that are not subject to such close scrutiny as their lending business (*BusinessWeek* 2002). Awareness of this risk issue is essential when determining discount rates in discounted cash flows for project appraisal. It is also essential when Asian economies develop their own capital markets including debt markets. A better understanding would shed more light on how discount rates should be estimated, and on the pitfalls to avoid in formulating new and improving existing financial institutions in Hong Kong and in the region.

## Sources of volatility in discount rates

The feasibility or profitability of a development project is sensitive to discount rates. The importance of incorporating an appropriate discount rate into cash flow equations cannot be more obvious. According to the conventions of theory and practice, there are three basic components of a discount rate: real interest rate, expected inflation rate, and risk premium. As debt and equity markets become established in the Asian region and capital and property markets become more integrated, globalised and information efficient, there is an increase in the volatility of the three components of the discount rate. There is thus a need for those undertaking project appraisals to understand how the 'rules' of financial institutions affect the determination of such rates.

The real interest rate multiplied by the expected rate of inflation gives the nominal interest rate. The nominal interest rate is determined to a large extent by central banks, largely through monetarist policies. Warburton (2000) argues that the central banks have generally been successful in keeping nominal interest rates down. This taming of the money market is, however, too good to be true. It is more a delusion than otherwise, due to the exponential growth of the world bond market which has grown from less than US$1 trillion in 1970 to more than $23 trillion in 1997, having tripled in size since 1986. This explosion of credit creation outside the banking system has been accompanied by an erosion of credit quality, as evidenced by the convergence of bond yields around the globe (Warburton 2000). The proliferation of global bond markets facilitates the financing of national deficits without increasing nominal interest rates. Inflation appears to have been curbed at the expense of rising real interest rates. However, the stability of inflation rates is achieved only at the expense of risk premiums. What is worse, economies in deep recession, such as Japan, could fall into a liquidity trap. A near zero nominal interest rate coupled with deflation means that the real interest rate is relatively high. There is, however, not much room left for monetary policies to manoeuvre as nominal interest rates cannot be negative. A deflationary trend on a global scale could even put the world into an economic gridlock (*The Economist* 2002b).

*The Economist* (2000) estimates that about half of all corporate borrowing in the US over the two years preceding 2000 was used to buy back shares, thus helping to prop up the US stock market. The large volume of margin debts could be detrimental to the stock market if prices start falling. Though it has also been suggested that margin debts were only about 1.5% of the combined market value of the New York Stock Exchange and the Nasdaq markets in February 2000 (*AWSJ* 2000), there was still a discernible effect on the leverage effect of the stock market. If stock market 'bubbles' cannot be solely attributable to the unlimited credit that world bond markets create, they could also result from derivatives markets. Investors could readily leverage themselves through options and financial futures.

Since the 1980s, the banking sectors in the US and the UK have undergone a major overhaul. Following the deregulation in the US and the 'big bang' in the UK, distinctions between the banking and the non-banking sectors in these economies have become blurred. Banks trade in securities and derivatives. Rapid technical advances in financial markets and information technology have diminished the link between credit expansion and money supply, and hence weakened the causal relationship between credit supply and price inflation in advanced economies. Central bankers' latitude to determine interest rates through monetary policies has been largely circumvented by financial markets. The banking sector's prerogative of setting out yield curves is now shared by the financial markets. While the institutional arrangements of banking are being fixed, new problems arise from elsewhere. The relationship between financial markets and financial institutions has always been an evolving one. The observation that the institutions could no longer control the financial markets once they were created gives rise to a striking analogy between this relationship and that of Dr Frankenstein and the creature he created.

Many countries are so indebted and so subjected to the tyranny of global markets that some argue that a global crisis of debt default is waiting to happen. At the end of 1995, the aggregate value of all US bonds and equities amounted to US$14204 billion or 42% of the global total (Warburton 2000). The US economy has been among the most indebted in the world, and the share of new saving held in liquid forms fell from 47% in 1984 to almost zero in 1994. In 1997, the average holding of liquid assets for working households was around US$1000 only (Warburton 2000). The US has never been so involved in the stock market and so highly geared as it is now. When the next bear markets arrive, the adverse repercussions throughout the world will be painful. This analysis suggests that the bull markets in the US and around the globe are probably driven more by excessive borrowing than sustainable economic fundamentals. It also means that recent recovery of many Asian economies could be brought to an abrupt stop. There could be more downside risk than the other way round for project developments in the Asian region.

Hong Kong, being one of the most ostensibly open economies in the world, has been very susceptible to the volatility of global capital markets. In rankings produced by Roulac (2001), Hong Kong ranked second, after Switzerland and above the US and Australia, for 'development rating' and 'degree of economic securitization'. This suggests that Hong Kong has the second most developed stock market in the world, indicating a strong financial sector and great interest to overseas investors. In terms of 'economic reach', Hong Kong ranked fifth, after New York, Tokyo, San Jose and London. These rankings point to the conclusion that Hong Kong is closely connected to the global economy and capital markets. The capitalisation rate is subject to rapid and volatile global movements, which can be expected to become even more volatile as investment all over the world has generally become more 'geared' as a consequence of the proliferation of financial markets, institutions and instruments.

## Reflection

The discussions so far have argued for a global perspective when carrying out financial appraisal for projects. The conclusions are however perhaps more applicable to open economies such as Hong Kong (now a Special Administrative Region of the People's Republic of China) than the less open ones such as mainland China. A comparison of office property investment returns and risks between 1991 and 1997 in four cities of China – Shanghai, Guangzhou, Shenzhen and Hong Kong – shows that the risk of property investment is largely systemic (Tse *et al.* 1999). This is despite the fact that property investment in Hong Kong is, for historical reasons, subject to a set of institutions different from that of the other three cities of China. Modern portfolio theories (MPT) would suggest that risk premiums arising from idiosyncratic institutional factors in Hong Kong or the other three cities can be minimised. However, apparently super-normal returns of property investment in Guangzhou and Shanghai suggest that, contrary to the assumptions of the MPT, the markets are not integrated and efficient; investors do not diversify enough; and unsystemic risks are indeed priced.

For the time being, country- or location-specific institutional factors still command risk premiums in property investments. It is, therefore, expected that local institutions would command no less risk premiums in property developments. Property developers usually undertake projects in their home countries. They do not generally develop portfolios of projects around the region or the globe. The possibility of information asymmetry increases their transaction costs if they develop projects abroad. It is thus logical for property developers to factor location-specific risks into their equations. In addition, due to the extra risk of development lag, there are in general more risk premiums in property development than in property investment. Yet it is fair to say that an appreciation of the impact of the global financial institutions on project appraisal could only improve understanding of what is apparently a local property development or infrastructure project. There is always implicitly an 'international' element in real estate.

## Institutional features of project appraisal

At first sight, the institutional influences on the appraisal of the viability and value of projects may seem obscure. It is essentially concerned with the task of establishing the value of proposed projects at the operational level. The parties to the transaction appear to be free to select their own method of appraisal. However, the choice of method may be constrained by: (1) professional standards applied as operational rules of the game; (2) the requirements of powerful stakeholders such as banks and funding bodies (particularly if they possess governance or constitutional power, for example, the Asian Development Bank); and (3) constitutional rules designed to protect the parties to a transaction from unfair practices. The need to monitor and regulate the consistency, fairness and, sometimes, transparency of the approaches to and methods of appraisal lead to the selection of methods that meet these institutional criteria. These methods tend to favour consistent, settled practice.

### Economic evaluation of projects

Project appraisal can mean both economic analysis and financial analysis in a general sense. An economic analysis assesses 'social' profit by measuring the effects of the project on the fundamental objectives of the whole economy. In contrast, financial analysis is concerned with private profit. Undertaking an economic analysis for a project is usually more complicated, because it relates not only to private elements but also to the social effects that represent costs and benefits to society. To meet the specific purposes of an investment, project appraisal sometimes embraces in greater detail other important techniques and concepts, such as real estate valuation standards, environmental impact analysis and value management.

Project appraisal measures the value of the net benefits flowing from an investment, in the presence of institutions and their influences, i.e. the rules of the game. Financial analysis identifies money profit accruing to the project-operating entity. To break the confined view of assessing merely financial returns, and to consider overall economic advantages or disadvantages, project appraisal is needed for social projects. Economic analysis embraces social elements to measure the 'social' profit, instead of 'money' profit only.

This broad perspective of appraisal methodology reflects the importance of meeting the various objectives of the stakeholders in development projects, bearing in mind that the objectives of constitutional and governance level stakeholders may differ from those of the operational proponents of a project. Although governments attempt to overcome examples of perceived market failure, they also attempt to balance other objectives at the same time, such as maintaining employment and macroeconomic stability. The task of setting public-sector objectives that are simple, clear and unambiguous can be difficult. This helps to explain the difficulty in evaluating efforts to achieve those objectives (Duff 1997). Furthermore, the whole process of evaluation is complicated by a variety of rule regimes operating at different levels in a sophisticated operating environment that includes market forces and other institutional influences. The objectives that government agencies apply to projects within a given institutional environment can be grouped into three categories – economic efficiency, administrative efficiency and equity.

Economic efficiency is about getting the most out of available resources. Its objectives can be further categorised into discrete efficiency criteria based on allocation, production and internal organisation. Administrative efficiency refers to the costs of administering a policy approach. This includes the quality of accountability and decision-making in the use of resources as well as the administrative costs involved in executing a particular approach – for example, the cost of public information materials, the cost of loopholes in the system and the costs of non-take-up benefits. In contrast to the objective of efficiency of allocation, equity objectives involve the wider concept of wealth distribution in a just and equitable way. They are concerned with the distribution of income and wealth within a given institutional framework. To meet these objectives, governments can intervene in transacting behaviour in three broad ways – direct public provision, regulation, and taxes and subsidies. Such intervention may be generated at the constitutional level, is normally administered through the governance level, and its impact is designed to be felt at the operational level.

All countries face the problem of allocating limited resources to satisfy national needs and to achieve national objectives. Especially in some less developed countries, project appraisal enables decision-makers to allocate resources more efficiently and effectively. Efficient allocation does not simply mean achieving different uses of resources within the community. Rather, the ultimate aim is to allow an economy to marshal its resources in the pursuit of more fundamental objectives such as the alleviation of poverty, the promotion of growth, and the reduction of inequalities in income (Squire & van der Tak 1975).

## Approaches to project appraisal with institutional influences

### Enumeration of costs and benefits

Generally, the difference between the social effects of a project and those which are of purely private consequence are known as 'external' or 'spillover' effects. In the absence of rules requiring external effects to be incorporated into project appraisals, the detrimental impacts of these effects are largely omitted or heavily discounted in financial evaluations. In economic appraisals, however, they should be carefully considered. This is assisted by the incorporation of 'shadow prices' into the calculation. Shadow price is a more satisfactory indicator of social benefits and costs than market price. A shadow price is treated as a 'management' or 'planning' price, normally calculated by reference to market indicators. For example, if a project employs a person who has been unemployed, the 'shadow price' is zero or negative because it costs society nothing. Indeed, if unemployment is considered a bad thing, the employment of the person will benefit society by saving social security payments.

### The social rate of discount

Assessing public projects involves some measurement of the community's view of the value of extra consumption (i.e. an increment to the general living standard) in the future as compared with the present. The application of a discount rate implies that the community values benefits and costs according to when they accrue. Depending on whether project resources are obtained from present consumption or investment, the discount rate is based on either the social time preference (STP) rate or the social opportunity cost (SOC) rate of interest. In practice, governments may set their own desirable discount rate, usually at a much lower level than market rates. The Hong Kong SAR government adopts 4% as its discount rate for project appraisal.

Adopting additional risk premiums

Adding a premium to the discount rate to allow for perceived additional risk is widely adopted in project analysis. Arguably, however, this provides little improvement to the appraisal. Not all phenomena associated with a particular project will exhibit the pattern of risk that is implied by raising the discount rate, yet the discount rate will be applied to all aspects of the project. Thus, a minor technical adjustment to the discount rate creates a possible source of error in estimating the individual items in the project appraisal. To reflect particular risk or uncertainty attached to individual items, Walsh and Williams (1975) suggest an approach to evaluation of costs and benefits that employs three key components, namely (1) expected values, (2) sensitivity analysis and (3) decision-theory techniques. Other judgements may be as significant as the discount rate. These include judgements relating to best possible use(s); optimal scale of the project; likely market rents or prices (and/or shadow prices); estimates of development time, project costs, phasing of construction.

Evaluation approaches: institutional change and option pricing

Apart from the Walsh and Williams approach, other project appraisal methods include comparative methods, investment methods, residual methods and 'option pricing'. Although the investment and residual methods incorporate techniques such as discounted cash flow (DCF) and net present value (NPV), they neglect 'economic irreversibility'[1] and 'sequence of building',[2] which are inherent characteristics of a project.

The option pricing method captures 'operating flexibilities' in terms of timing and the scale of development, giving decision-makers an option to review and revise decisions in response to unforeseen market and institutional changes. This flexibility can be expressed as a set of 'real options' that can improve the expected outcome and limit downside risk. It also enables the decision-maker to reap the benefit should the market or institutional aspects turn out to be more favourable or undesirable than expected. The application of option pricing involves a quantitative analytical approach to evaluating complex multi-option projects (Hui 2000). Typically, a project could have four options, namely, (1) to defer, (2) to expand, (3) to contract, (4) to switch use. Appraising the net present value of a project has two components, one with options and the other without. The degree of interaction and additivity among the options is governed by:

- Whether the options are mutually consistent and reinforcing;

- The separation of the time for which they are capable of being exercised;

- Their relative ability to generate and accrue benefits;

- Their sequential order.

Selecting a suitable quantitative model for the options requires judgement on the information gathered about the future. This forecast is normally based on analysis of past experience, which in turn is dependent on the confidence associated with the relationship between historic and future events. A standard binomial contingent claim model can be constructed incorporating market and institutional aspects (e.g. compoundness, discrete cash flows, exogenous competitive arrivals, multiple flexibilities) and capturing option interactions.

## Role of international funding agencies: the World Bank and the Asian Development Bank

The World Bank and the Asian Development Bank exemplify non-governmental organisations with sufficient power to establish 'rules of the game' for implementing their role of financing projects at the operational level. They share similar objectives such as promoting economic growth, poverty reduction, human development, gender equality and environmental protection. Most of the projects that they support are located in developing countries, supporting agricultural development, management of natural resources, provision of social infrastructure, primary industry, provision of transport and communications infrastructure, energy and financial services. Owing to the nature of project finance and international standards, the World Bank and the Asian Development Bank are strong advocates of robust and transparent project appraisal before undertaking any loan commitment.

The following case study illustrates the application of these principles. It demonstrates that large-scale project appraisals are undertaken mainly for the purposes of 'due diligence' on the part of the funding agencies institutionally located at the governance level. However, the data upon which they are based derives from the operational level.

# ChengduNanchong Expressway, Sichuan Province, People's Republic of China (PRC)

**Sector:** Transport and Communications infrastructure

**Project cost:** US$ 667.20 million

**Loan amount:** US$ 250.00 million

**Description and scope:**

(1) Construction of 208 km controlled access toll expressway from Chengdu, the provincial capital, to Nanchong, a major commercial centre, including interchanges with toll facilities, link roads and service and parking areas.

(2) Upgrading 300 km of county and village access roads in Nanchong District.

(3) Procurement of equipment for traffic monitoring and surveillance, toll collection, axle load testing, and road maintenance and inspection.

(4) Land acquisition and resettlement of affected people.

(5) Consulting services for construction supervision and training.

(6) Institutional development to promote improved quality, road safety, and benefit monitoring and evaluation.

**Strategic development objectives:** Economic growth

## *Project brief*

The average per capita gross domestic product (GDP) in Sichuan in 1997 was RMB 4,048 (43% below the national average). This low level is partly attributable to transport bottlenecks on major routes and poor accessibility to population centres in rural areas. Removal of such constraints is a prerequisite for sustainable economic growth and poverty reduction. Within the government's strategic framework for developing the road sector, attention is being given to strengthening access to less-developed communities and disadvantaged areas. The Project area falls into this category. The proposed Project will promote economic and social development by improving road infrastructure in the Chengdu–Nanchong corridor and assist poverty reduction by connecting poor areas in the east and northeast of Sichuan to the economic mainstream.

The main objectives of this project are to support the economic and social development of the eastern part of Sichuan Province by alleviating transport bottlenecks on the existing roads. Through a programme of upgrading of county and village access roads, the project will also help reduce poverty in the designated poverty counties in which the average income per capita is RMB 1,123 (46% below the national average).

### Methodologies for undertaking economic analysis

Taking into account the expected social benefits and costs of this project, it is expected to generate an economic internal rate of return of 24.9%, compared with a financial internal rate of return of 8.3%. The economic analysis generally follows the approaches and procedures described. However, attention should be paid to the following.

The economic benefits are based on forecasts of the impact that the Project is expected to have on (1) the reduction of poverty and (2) enhancement of transport services. The benefits actually achieved will be monitored by the collection and analysis of socioeconomic data. This will require (1) the cooperation of relevant government agencies, NGOs and local enterprises and (2) frequent consultations with target groups (local government agencies, village associations, individuals, representatives of relevant organisations and industry). Specific mechanisms are required for:

- Monitoring and reporting the outcome of resettlement measures.

- Independent participatory rural appraisal (PRA) of project impacts in poor counties. This must include training in PRA methodology for four local appraisers.

More specifically, this project needs an environmental impact assessment (EIA), to include an environmental monitoring programme and mitigation measures designed to minimise adverse environmental impacts.

### Expected major social benefits

Lowering the cost of road transport and alleviating traffic congestion will help to improve the capacity of the current infrastructure in order to accelerate economic and social development in designated poverty areas in eastern Sichuan Province. Local residents will benefit from improved access to markets and social services. Other expected, measurable benefits include savings in journey times, in vehicle operating costs, and reduced accident costs. The primary beneficiaries of the Project will be the residents of the towns and villages along the route.

### Expected major social costs

The value of village areas and farmlands surrendered to the government. Permanent removal of some villages and temporary disruption in others resulting from the construction works.

## Conclusion

This chapter attempts to illustrate that settled practice at the operational level can have an influence on the appraisal of investments based on direct investment in land and buildings or real estate-related projects that is as profound as the rules of common law, statute or public administration. The effect increases in proportion to the size and distinctiveness of the investment or project. Transactions are the point at which all other extrinsic risks attributable to the institutional framework 'come home to roost'. The ways in which these risks are evaluated, precisely or imprecisely, have a direct impact on the computation of the value of the transaction.

It also argues that in establishing capitalisation rates, the operational level is heavily influenced by global capital flows. Furthermore, it demonstrates that in the case of international funding for large-scale projects, methods of analysis are largely determined by the financial stakeholders such as the World Bank and the Asian Development Bank. In other words, in cases where large-scale investments and projects must follow established procedures of settled practice, the apparent freedom to determine the financial terms and methods of appraisal for those investments and projects is highly constrained by a variety of influences acting as rules of practice.

# References

ADB (Asian Development Bank) (1998) *Annual Report 1998*. Asian Development Bank.

ADB (Asian Development Bank) (1999a) *Information Statement*. Asian Development Bank.

ADB (Asian Development Bank) (1999b) *Asian Development Outlook 1999 Update*. Asian Development Bank.

*AWSJ* (2000) Don't Squeeze the Margin. *Asian Wall Street Journal*, 17 April 2000.

*AWSJ* (2002a) CapitaLand Offers Singapore REIT. *Asian Wall Street Journal*, 2 July 2002.

*AWSJ* (2002b) Global Slump Sparks Diversification Debate. *Asian Wall Street Journal*, 14 October 2002.

*AWSJ* (2003) Government May Form First Hong Kong REIT. *Asian Wall Street Journal*, 16 January 2003.

Beidleman, C.R., Fletcher, D. & Veshosky, D. (1990) On allocating risk: the essence of project finance. *Sloan Management Review*, Spring, 47–55.

Beidleman, C.R., Fletcher, D. & Veshosky, D. (1991) Using project finance to help manage project risks. *Project Management Journal* **XXII**(2), 33–7.

*BusinessWeek* (2000) 17 April 2000, pp. 16–17.

*BusinessWeek* (2002) 29 October 2002, p. 70.

Casserley, D. & Gibb, G. (1999) *Banking in Asia: the End of Entitlement*. J. Wiley & Sons, Singapore and New York.

Chan, M.W., Chiang, Y.H. & Choy, L.H.T. (1998) Real estate finance. In: *Real Estate Development in Hong Kong* (eds T.N.T. Poon & E.H.W. Chan), pp. 134–53. PACE Publishing Limited, Hong Kong.

Chang, G.G. (2001) *The Coming Collapse of China*. Random House, New York.

Chiang, Y.H. & Chan, M.W. (1995) Property investment in a portfolio context: the potential of mortgage backed securities for institutional investors in Hong Kong. *International Journal for Housing Science and its Applications* **19**(4), 277–88.

Chiang, Y.H., Tang, B.S. & Yue, Cheryl S.M. (2000) Role of property in institutional investment: a Hong Kong survey. *Proceedings of the International Symposium on Urban Development towards the New Millennium*, 4–7 January 2000, Harbin, China. pp. 220–32.

Coakley, J. (1994) The integration of property and financial markets. *Environment and Planning A* **26**, 697–713.

DiPasquale, D. & Wheaton, W. (1996) *Urban Economics and Real Estate Markets*. Prentice-Hall, Englewood Cliffs, NJ.

Duff, L. (1997) *The Economics of Governments and Markets*. Addison, London.

Ekelund Jr., R.B. & Hebert, R.F. (1997) *A History of Economic Theory and Method*. McGraw-Hill, New York.

Fisher, J.D. (1992) Integrating research on markets for space and capital. *Journal of American Real Estate and Urban Economics Association* **20**(1), 161–80.

Fisher, J.D., Hudson-Wilson, S. & Wurtzebach, C.H. (1993) Equilibrium in commercial real estate markets: linking space and capital markets. *The Journal of Portfolio Management*, Summer 1993, 101–107.

*Fortune* (2000) 15 May 2000. p. 97.

Hui, C.M. (2000) Option pricing for real estate. *Real Estate Tech,* Abstracted by Chung, S. Jan 2000.

Hui, C.M., Chiang, Y.H. & Tang, B.S. (1998) Asian real estate markets: boom and oversupply. *Journal of Financial Management of Property and Construction* **2**(3), 63–75.

Jao, Y.C. (1997) *Hong Kong as an International Financial Centre: Evolution, Prospects and Policies.* City University of Hong Kong Press, Hong Kong.

Kim, J., Lee, S.Y. & McGeorge, D. (2000) A study of real estate trust institutions in Korea. *Journal of Construction Research* **1**(1).

Leitner, H. (1994) Capital markets, the development industry, and urban office market dynamics: rethinking building cycles. *Environment and Planning A* **26**, 779–802.

Ong, S.E. & Sing, T.F. (2001) Valuation and development of real estate capital markets. *International Valuation Forum Bangkok,* 2–4 October 2001.

Ong, S.E., Ooi, J. & Sing, T.F. (2000) Asset securitization in Singapore: a tale of three vehicles. *Real Estate Finance,* Summer, pp. 47–56.

Renaud, B., Pretorius, F. & Pasadilla, B. (1997) *Market at Work: Dynamics of the Residential Real Estate Market in Hong Kong.* Hong Kong University Press, Hong Kong.

Roulac, S.E. (1998) Property and Ptolemy, Copernicus and commerce: toward a strategic perspective for global property involvements. *Journal of Property Valuation & Investment* **16**(5), 431–46.

Roulac, S.E. (2001) *Stephen Roulac on Place and Property Strategy.* Property Press, San Francisco and Hong Kong.

Squire, L. & van der Tak, G.H. (1975) *Economic Analysis of Projects (A World Bank Research Publication).* Baltimore, Johns Hopkins University Press, Maryland.

*The Economist* (2000) 22 Apr 2000. p. 80.

*The Economist* (2002a) 12 Oct 2002. p. 12.

*The Economist* (2002b) 12 Oct 2002. pp. 71–2.

Tse, R.Y.C., Chiang, Y.H. & Raftery, J. (1999) Office property returns in Shanghai, Guangzhou, and Shenzhen. *Journal of Real Estate Literature* **7**, 197–208.

Walsh, H.G. & Williams, A. (1975) *Current Issues in Cost-benefit Analysis (Civil Service College Occasional Papers).* Her Majesty's Stationery Office, London.

Warburton, P. (2000) *Debt and Delusion.* Penguin Books, Harmondsworth.

Yip, J. (2002) Changing gear. *Surveying, The Newsletter of the Hong Kong Institute of Surveyors,* Sept, pp. 20–23.

# Further reading

Barnes, R.J. (1971) *Economics Analysis: An Introduction.* Butterworths, London.

Field, B.C. (1994) *Environmental Economics: An Introduction.* McGraw-Hill Book Co, Singapore.

Johansson, P.-O. (1987) *The Economic Theory and Measurement of Environmental Benefits.* Cambridge University Press, London.

Johansson, P.-O. (1991) *An Introduction to Modern Welfare Economics*. Cambridge University Press, London.

Picciotto, R. & Wiesner, E. (1998) *Evaluation and Development: the Institutional Dimension*. Transaction Publishers, Rutgers University, New Jersey.

RICS (Royal Institution of Chartered Surveyors) (1994) *Economic Cycles and Property Cycles*. Royal Institution of Chartered Surveyors.

Seabrooke, W. & Kent, P.S (2000) *Institutions of Real Estate*. Study guide for MSc International Real Estate, Hong Kong Polytechnic University.

Silberberg, E. (1995) *Principles of Microeconomics*. Prentice-Hall, New Jersey.

Tang, S.L. (1997) *Economic Feasibility of Projects* (revised edition). McGraw-Hill, Hong Kong.

World Bank (1998) *Assessing Aid: What Works, What Doesn't and Why (A World Bank Policy Research Report)*. Oxford University Press, New York.

Zerbe, R.O. & Dively, D.D. (1994) *Benefit-Cost Analysis in Theory and Practice*. HarperCollins, New York.

## Websites

World Bank (http://www.worldbank.org).
Asian Development Bank (http://www.adb.org).

## Notes

1 Once a project is undertaken, it will generally last for some time and be used for some particular purpose. Multiple ownership and zoning laws further increase irreversibility.

2 Investment decisions are made before a project is completed, or commissioned. In between commencement and completion, new information and circumstances may arise, rendering earlier decisions redundant.

# Part 3

## Institutional Aspects of National Real Estate Markets

# Introduction

The overall purpose of the chapters grouped into this section of the book is to illustrate quite profound national differences in the nature and characteristics of real estate markets at the operational level. This illustrates important difficulties associated with global investment in real estate.

There is no standard content format for the chapters; each has something different to say. The chapters provide powerful contrasts between the sophistication of real estate investment in sovereignties that are institutionally mature (i.e. the rule regimes of the constitutional and governance levels are stable and robust) and those that are institutionally immature and in a state of flux. In the former, transactions at the operational level 'mesh' closely with the rules of the constitutional and governance zones and with the informal rules of powerful players at the operational level such as pension funds. In such an institutional environment, transactions can be highly sensitive to relatively detailed changes in rule regimes such as a shift in the rules relating to the taxation of transactions. In institutionally immature real estate markets, the rules of the game are evolving rapidly, generating great uncertainty at the operational level.

Chapter 8 provides a stimulating review of the role of US pension funds in the US investment market. Coming from one of the biggest institutional investors in US real estate, it illustrates how the fortunes of real estate investment ebb and flow at the operational level in response to apparently minor shifts in the rules of the game. This is complemented by chapter 9, which adopts a broader view of the US real estate market and addresses the paradoxical dislocation between space markets and the capital markets.

Chapter 10 reviews the nature and characteristics of the investment market for real estate in the United Kingdom, with a focus on England. The investment market for prime investment-grade real estate in London and the provinces is dominated by financial institutions such as insurance companies and pension funds. These are professional investors: in addition to safe, long-term investments, they seek tax-efficient vehicles for their investments. The chapter explains why and how the rules of the game militate against REITs (popular in other countries such as the US and Australia) and addresses the new popularity of limited partnerships as an alternative investment vehicle.

Chapter 11 demonstrates how the peculiarities of the Canadian federal system link with the geographically and economically discrete characteristics of the Canadian provinces to produce distinctive real estate markets. It explains the institutional and economic independence of the provinces (1) from each other and (2) from the federal government. This creates distinctiveness in (1) the rules of the game from province to province and (2) key markets within the respective provinces. This chapter also mentions the issue of native title.

Japan represents another sovereignty that is institutionally mature and this maturity extends down to the operational level. The market for real estate in Japan has distinctive features, such as an institutionalised lack of transparency, that effectively deter foreign real estate investment. Chapter 12 addresses a variety of issues that illustrate this distinctiveness and contribute to the difficulties faced by foreign investors in Japanese real estate markets. They include the system of tenure, tax burdens, the government-determined land value system, the banking system and the link between non-performing loans and real estate investment.

Developers and investors are tempted by the perceived potential of real estate investment in mainland China (the subject of chapter 13). Despite the country's economic expansion, this is an economy in transition from central planning to market-based principles. This evolution is not uniform across all sectors of the economy or geographically within sectors. This is demonstrated by the evolution of markets for real estate. In the introduction of real estate markets, the primary concern of the Beijing government has been the development of residential property markets. This emphasis is reflected in the chapter.

# 8

# US Pension Funds and Real Estate: Still Crazy After All These Years

## *Bernard Winograd*

As the extent of the fallout from the technology meltdown in the stock market became clearer in 2001, many institutional investors revisited Old Economy ideas, including the real estate industry. Institutional interest in investing in property dates from the 1970s but faded from the top of many fund agendas after the industry's poor investment experience and liquidity crisis in the late 1980s and early 1990s. Since 2001, as the search for 'safe harbour' investments and income vehicles has taken on new urgency, many investors who have spent little time on the industry in recent years are revisiting the issue of whether real estate belongs in their portfolio, and, if so, what role it should play.

As this review proceeds, it is important to learn from history. Today's real estate industry differs in important ways from the industry that pension fund fiduciaries first considered 30 years ago. So also is its capital market different and, as a consequence, the investment vehicles available. Yet some of the fundamentals remain the same, and much of the original logic for institutional investment in the asset class has held up remarkably well over time through a number of different market cycles.

The purpose of this chapter is not to go into the argument for having real estate in a multi-asset portfolio in detail. There is an abundance of literature available on this subject for those seeking a detailed treatment. Instead, the intent of this piece is to provide a concise history of the institutional investment community's love/hate relationship with the real estate industry to date, for those who want it and those who need it – even if they do not know they do. In the course of revisiting where this relationship has been, it may become clearer where it goes from here, which is likely to be a future with interesting opportunities but, inevitably, not without risks.

# In the beginning...

Long before institutional investors showed up, the US real estate industry had matured and developed many of the fundamental attributes that still characterise it today. Although very little data was collected prior to the arrival of institutional investors, it is clear that the valuation of real estate over time has tended to be a remarkably stable consequence of its cash flow. Put another way, capitalisation rates for most investment properties have varied around a relatively narrow band. Now that we have more than three decades of valuation data from institutional investing at our disposal, it becomes clear that the long-term expected return from unleveraged real estate is in the high single digits, intermediate between the expected returns from stocks and bonds.

However, the industry also has a long and storied history of financial engineering and continues to create many different ways to take the income from properties and use it to support sometimes dizzying capital structures. These in turn have created much of the volatility, both good and bad, that investors have experienced in real estate investing. Strip these elaborate capital structures away, concentrate on the hard assets, and what you have is typically an investment with reasonably predictable cash flows and reasonably predictable and stable capital values.

In addition, the source of value creation in the industry has always been and remains development – building or rebuilding, positioning or repositioning, and leasing or re-leasing. Once built and leased, the industry refers to properties as being stabilised and with good reason. More often than not, value fluctuates very little for such stabilised properties, gradually rising if market rents rise and eventually – and usually gradually – declining when obsolescence of one kind or another sets in. But if a property is under development or able to be re-leased at a higher value if redeveloped, the returns to capital involved in that relatively short phase of a property's life can be significantly higher. Leveraged, they can be higher still. Of course, this is also the point in the life of a property when things can go dramatically wrong for an investor, given the risks of development, especially if compounded by leverage. Most institutional investors in real estate tried to avoid these risks and returns, at least initially, and instead focused on stable, leased, income-producing property; but that gets us ahead of the story.

One other long-standing characteristic of the industry is a long history of boom and bust. Capital availability has tended to drive development. This is rooted in the unusual environment for the industry in the US, which has relatively loose governmental controls over land use, an almost inexhaustible supply of undeveloped land (yes, really), and a capital market that has been willing to make debt financing available to individual real estate developers to an extent almost unimaginable in other parts of the developed world. The result has been a market where the availability of financing always triggers development, as there is no shortage of opportunities or developers competing for it. The history of the real estate capital market in the past 30 years can in many ways be viewed as a gradual effort by capital providers to learn when and how to discipline development. But while the future may be different as a result of increasing sophistication among capital providers, it has traditionally been an industry where capital availability has driven activity levels, resulting in periods of excess capital creating too much supply, leading to falling rents and rising vacancies, leading in turn to a withdrawal of capital until absorption of excess space creates the conditions to start the cycle all over again.

This landscape of entrepreneurial developers and institutional capital providers had a new entrant in the 1970s, the US pension fund industry. Several factors combined to entice this new group of players to consider real estate investing. Then as now, there was a search for investment vehicles that would do better than the stock market, which went through its worst two-year period since the Great Depression, losing more than 40% of its value in the two years 1973–74. Bond investing was even less rewarding, as unanticipated inflation created huge losses in most fixed income portfolios. This same inflation fed returns in real estate, as hard assets of all kinds rose sharply in nominal value.

At the same time, the stage had been set for consideration of new approaches to pension fund investing, as the passage of the Employee Retirement Income Security Act (ERISA) encouraged fiduciaries to diversify their portfolios. Modern portfolio theory was used to create an academically grounded way to think about asset allocation, a gospel spread by a new breed of consultants to the pension fund industry who researched investment ideas and managers and recommended asset allocation strategies. In this environment, real estate showed well. While data was scarce, that which existed suggested that real estate returns had a low correlation with stocks and bonds, and could add to risk-adjusted returns when incorporated into a multi-asset class portfolio. Arguments were also made that real estate represented a relatively large share of the 'investable' universe (much larger then than now, given the relatively smaller stock and bond markets of the time) that should not be ignored. Its ability to act as a hedge against inflation was demonstrated dramatically in the 1970s, and its returns were very strong relative to financial instruments.

As a result, pension fund money began to chase real estate returns. But the investment community quickly ran up against an unfamiliar problem, finding it difficult to know how to invest. Most real estate practitioners had mud on their shoes, as the industry puts it, and were not reassuring to investors more accustomed to the white-shoe world of stocks and bonds. Sensing a business opportunity, the first real estate investment advisory firms were formed aimed at the pension fund market. Large institutions like Prudential, which formed the first commingled real estate fund vehicle for pension funds, the Prudential Property Investment Separate Account (PRISA), in 1970, found themselves competing with an alphabet soup of new firms that combined academic refugees and real estate practitioners. Both channelled money from the pension fund market to the real estate market, surrounded by a nimbus of academic studies designed to justify the decisions to ERISA-sensitised fiduciaries and their consultants.

In the 1980s, the number of real estate advisers grew from 15 to 70. Consultants arrived who specialised in allocating money, among them some not affiliated with general investment consultants. Asset allocation recommendations often suggested putting up to 20% of a fund's assets into real estate. The primary investment vehicle when the decade began was the commingled fund, but partnerships and other closed-end vehicles became part of the landscape by the end of the decade. The early investment experience was good, and the diversification benefits were real, which led more and more funds to participate, and those that got in early generally added to their allocations. The National Council of Real Estate Investment Fiduciaries (NCREIF) was created, and the NCREIF index began to be used as a benchmark for measurement of the performance of the pension fund real estate assets that it included.

With the benefit of hindsight, it is very clear that capital was piling into the industry in the late 1980s at unsustainable rates, not just from the pension funds but also from the savings and loans organisations (S&Ls). But, as is usually the case when greed overwhelms fear, the warning signs were ignored and the problems downplayed. The repeal of special tax incentives in 1986 was seen as a positive that removed a competing source of capital with an 'unfair' tax advantage. Questions about the effect on the investment environment of overly aggressive lending practices of the soon-to-be-defunct S&Ls were rarely raised. It was a spectacular bubble, and the real estate industry was generally delighted to have the pension funds along for the ride.

# The end of innocence

The outcome was a classic real estate down cycle, which pension funds got to experience for the first time with money at risk. Their capital and that of the S&Ls led to an unprecedented building boom, nearly doubling the amount of office space in the US. When demand for property collapsed in the recession of the early 1990s, vacancy rates on office properties in many markets soared to over 20%. When the dust settled, absorption rates for vacant space were so low that some speculated that the US had built enough office space to last for decades. As a result of its investments in junk bonds and lending practices to real estate, the S&L industry went through a massive restructuring led by the newly created government Resolution Trust Corporation (RTC). The RTC took over hundreds of failed savings and loans and set to work liquidating their assets in a market where there was no liquidity. All of the other traditional sources of capital for the industry fled the market as insurance companies and banks originated less in new real estate loans than anyone could remember. For an industry that always needs capital to roll over substantial annual maturities of debt, this environment created a liquidity crisis of historic proportions.

For pension funds, this problem had a specific incarnation. The commingled open-end funds that had been the workhorse of the institutional real estate investment stable promised investors the right to redeem positions on a quarterly basis at appraised value, but only to the extent of available cash. This mechanism broke down when a disproportionately large fraction of the investment group wanted out at the same time, especially when the portfolios themselves often had properties and investments simultaneously demanding capital. Queues of investors waiting to withdraw capital became common, and investor faith in the open-end commingled fund as a vehicle was badly shaken.

Investors were also feeling betrayed by the advisers they had hired. Few alarms were sounded in advance of the collapse in values, and the funds concluded that their interests were not well aligned with those of their advisers. The fee structure in the industry had been patterned after the usual structure for stocks and bonds – so many basis points for each dollar of assets. As a result, advisers' incentives were to keep assets under management, and to maximise reported values – a source of moral hazard in a private asset class where reported values were more subjectively determined than in public markets with daily mark-to-market pricing.

In response, many investors came to believe that partnership structures in which fees were driven primarily by realised gains were a better format to create alignment of interest with their real estate advisers. Others decided that the right solution was to retain as much control as possible over the investment process themselves, and to use their consultants to help decide when to sell. These investors migrated to the single client account format, giving less discretion to investment managers than in commingled funds or partnerships.

The disillusion with the existing cohort of investment advisers had another consequence. New players entered the market as sponsors of opportunity funds, many of them affiliated with Wall Street real estate investment banking departments that previously had not been in competition for pension fund real estate assets. The investment opportunities created by the resale of the S&L assets were substantial, and required familiarity with the pricing of securitised investment vehicles. This was a relatively new field for the real estate industry, largely created as a result of the actions of the Resolution Trust Corporation, and the Wall Street houses were well suited to it. Structuring their investment vehicles as highly leveraged closed-end limited partnerships, the opportunity funds had a simple investment strategy: buy as much as they could, leverage it as much as they could, and wait for markets to recover. They projected that they could earn substantial returns on the equity invested, 20% and more, and they backed up their views with substantial co-investment commitments by the sponsoring firms and the investment principals.

This was a winning formula for fund raising. The co-investment idea became part of the conventional wisdom among institutional investors at this time, along with back-end loaded fee structures and limited life vehicles, all ideas associated with the opportunity funds. These structural features were argued to be the best way to avoid a repeat of the debacle of the 1980s because they would improve the alignment of interest between investors and their managers. For the industry, there was an unexpected consequence: by the end of the 1990s, virtually every major owner-operated real estate investment adviser sold itself to a financial institution, in part motivated by the need to deal with client demands for increasingly substantial co-investment. And the pressure was intensified by the investment success enjoyed by the opportunity funds, as the public markets became an unexpected source of capital and liquidity for real estate and the economy gathered steam in the mid-1990s.

## The cavalry arrives

While the total amount of capital deployed by the opportunity funds has never been reliably measured, it was clearly not enough by itself to deal with the needs of the real estate industry. In a testimony to the resilience and depth of the US capital markets, the gap was soon filled by the first large-scale influx of capital from public sources to the real estate industry. This took the form of two innovations, commercial mortgage-backed securities (CMBS) debt financing and REITs as an equity source. Neither was an entirely new idea, but both were to increase their roles to a scale that had not been seen before. In each case, a few key innovations were catalysts for unleashing huge amounts of new capital for the real estate industry.

REITs had been around since the 1960s. They were originally conceived as a sort of mutual fund for real estate, a commingled vehicle that could be sold to public shareholders that would allow individual investors to invest in diversified pools of mortgages or equity properties or both. They enjoy exemptions from taxes similar to those afforded mutual funds, in that they are not themselves taxpayers, but pass their tax attributes through to their individual investors. In return, they must pass certain tests generally designed to limit their activities to real estate investing. Originally, the rules restricted them from engaging in any business activities, and required them to contract with third parties to manage their assets.

This formulation soon led to no end of trouble, as people with low standards of fiduciary conduct formed equity REITs, put difficult or troubled properties into them at less than arm's length pricing, and proceeded to charge outrageous fees to manage the resulting mess. At the same time, mortgage REITs had a spectacular rise in assets in the 1970s, until they found themselves collectively over-extended with assets that were not matched with liabilities of similar duration, at which point they suffered severe drops in value and liquidity. These experiences caused most investors to swear off REITs as an investment vehicle, and left the industry as a tiny niche of the real estate capital markets with less than $10 billion in assets as the 1990s began.

The few REITs that had done well through this period, along with a group of loyal investors who believed that the public markets would some day be recognised as a legitimate way to invest in the real estate industry, procured changes to the original REIT regulatory framework designed to address these problems. REITs increasingly were allowed to be self-administered, meaning that third-party arrangements for management were less common. In combination, the leading investors in the group supported more activist management of REITs as operating companies, pushed for improved corporate governance and enabled REITs to evolve into fully fledged real estate operating companies.

Nevertheless, it was the creation of the UPREIT structure (or umbrella partnership REIT) that marked the turning point in the relative importance of the REIT as an investment vehicle. Traditionally, large private developers of real estate had avoided REITs for tax reasons. Partnerships were the preferred method of owning property, as they allowed individuals in the real estate business to shelter huge amounts of income by passing through the depreciation to their personal tax returns. Contributing their properties to a REIT in order to become a public corporation was a taxable event that triggered so much depreciation recapture as to be economically prohibitive. Thus, the largest pools of quality real estate were essentially cut off from using the public markets for equity by a moat of tax consequences.

The UPREIT solved this problem by admitting a REIT into existing real estate partnerships as a partner, and then selling REIT shares to the public to raise capital to recapitalise the partnership. The trick was to design the structure so that the REIT investor had the same economic experience as the rest of the partners (other than taxes), and to convince investors that it was okay to buy stock in a real estate company that owned partnership interests in properties rather than owning properties itself.

This feat of financial creativity was first achieved by Taubman Centers in its 1992 IPO, and was quickly imitated in a flood of other UPREIT IPOs (Fig. 8.1)

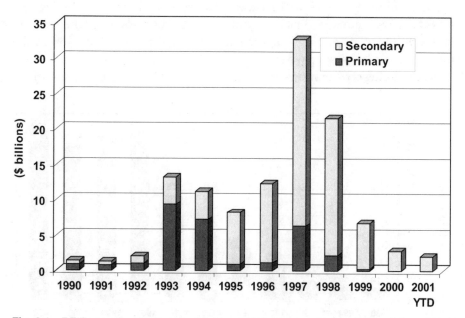

**Fig. 8.1**   REIT security offerings (to 30 June 2001). *Source: National Association of Real Estate Investment Trusts (NAREIT).*

that brought new capital into the industry. About 70% of the capital raised in the REIT sector in the years immediately following was raised by UPREITs, and the attention that was paid to the sector by investment bankers looking for a share of the action made it possible for other REITs to raise fresh capital as well. Within five years, the market capitalisation of the REITs had ballooned from less than $10 billion to over $125 billion (Fig. 8.2).

Obviously, one of the contributors to this success was the dramatic improvement in the fundamentals of the real estate industry in the mid-1990s. As the economy picked up steam, vacancies began to fall and rents began to increase. REITs that issued shares and bought properties generally prospered, as the returns from these investments exceeded the costs of the capital employed to buy them. Many argued that REITs were growth stocks, extrapolating this unusual period into the future, and REITs began to trade at large premiums to the value of their assets. (Ultimately, reality set in as rents stabilised and investment returns reverted to the mean. Growth stock investors fled the sector, causing share prices to tumble, and instead focused their capital on inflating the size of the technology stock bubble.)

In the same time period, the other public market source of new liquidity was the dramatic growth in commercial mortgage-backed securities as a source of long-term debt financing. CMBS issuance began to escalate sharply in 1996 (Fig. 8.3). The growth of this market was a direct consequence of the activities of the Resolution Trust Corporation in working out the seized assets of the S&L industry. The government effectively pioneered the creation of a technology for pricing pools of real estate assets, one that allowed the rating agencies to pick up where they left off in the rating of single assets and to begin issuing credit ratings for pools of mortgages. As a result, institutions

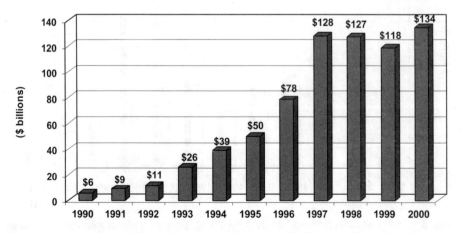

**Fig. 8.2**  Equity REIT market capitalisation (to 30 June 2000). *Source: NAREIT.*

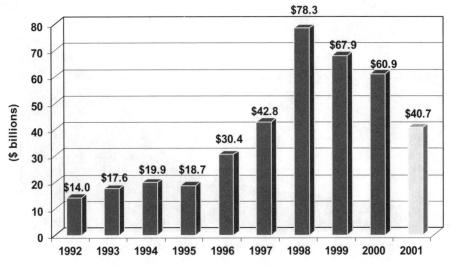

**Fig. 8.3**   Annual CMBS issuance (to 30 June 2001). *Source: Commercial Mortgage Alert.*

that needed obligations with high credit ratings to invest became sources of capital for commercial mortgages on a much larger scale than before.

Up to that point, insurance companies had been virtually the only buyers of long-term mortgage debt, with an annual capacity of approximately $20–$25 billion a year. Rated CMBS paper eliminated a number of obstacles that had stood in the way of other institutional buyers: the complexities of servicing a mortgage, the lack of a secondary market, the problems of measuring risk of default without employing a sophisticated and large real estate organisation, and the uncertainties of cash flows that resulted from all these problems. Now, buying the topmost credit tranches of a CMBS issue allowed even the most risk-averse lenders to participate in lending to the real estate industry. Annual CMBS issuance quickly became a multiple of the lending done by the insurance companies, and CMBS outstanding grew in a mirror image of the growth of REIT market capitalisation (Fig. 8.4).

The consequences to the real estate capital markets of these twin sources of public market capital were profound. Liquidity increased significantly. The complexity and range of investment vehicles available to investors in the industry multiplied. Public market volatility introduced new kinds of liquidity risk to real estate investing. In late 1998, the real estate market was fundamentally sound, yet the disruptions in public capital markets triggered by the implosion of Long Term Capital Management and the Russian bond default caused liquidity to the industry to dry up virtually overnight. As lending spreads widened in sympathy with the rest of the market, asset values probably dropped 15–20% in a single quarter, to the amazement of

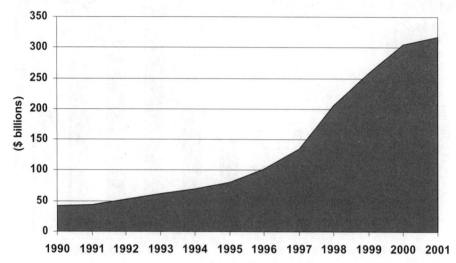

**Fig. 8.4**   Principal outstanding – all CMBS (to 31 March 2001). *Source: Federal Reserve Board.*

long-time industry participants who saw nothing wrong with the real estate market and who appreciated for the first time that using public markets as a capital source had drawbacks as well as rewards.

From a longer-term perspective, however, an increasing number of observers began to be convinced that the effect of the public markets was likely to promote a less volatile real estate cycle, one likely to have fewer, shorter and shallower corrections than in the private capital market era. Although some predicted this result, the way in which it eventually occurred was largely unanticipated. Many who had hoped for this result had predicted that public markets would discipline capital more effectively by punishing REITs that built in the face of evidence that supply was exceeding demand. But REITs have not become large enough relative to the scale of the industry (see Fig. 8.5) for their capital programmes to determine the extent of over-building, at least not yet.

Instead, it was the transparency the public markets created that began to have the most important effect. Thanks to the public disclosures of the REITs and the credit analysis of the rating agencies, there was an explosion of information about how real estate of various kinds was faring in the US property markets. Increasingly, it became less likely that lending decisions would pass the scrutiny of investment committees if REIT analyst reports said there was evidence of overbuilding in a market. After the liquidity crisis of 1998, CMBS buyers of the lowest rated tranches also found that they could require the elimination of troublesome loans from a pool proposed for

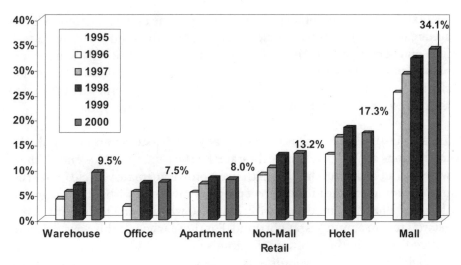

**Fig. 8.5**  Public market commercial real estate penetration. *Source: Prudential Real Estate Investors.*

sale, making the CMBS market another agent of discipline. Increasingly sophisticated reports on trends in default rates provided by the rating agencies enhanced the market's understanding of risks and further facilitated these decisions.

As a consequence, the real estate industry experienced an unusual period of equilibrium that began after the liquidity crisis of late 1998 and continued at least into early 2001. Supply and demand stayed in rough balance, leading to sustained low levels of vacancies without a rush of overbuilding. Such a two-year-plus period of stability was virtually unprecedented in the industry. Industry veterans were puzzled, like sailors encountering an unfamiliar and prolonged period without prevailing winds or storms. The most plausible explanation for this unusual state of affairs was that transparency had begun to create permanent changes in the volatility of the market. It was the most material change in the environment, and seemed the logical choice as an explanation.

## The pension funds react

For US institutional investors, the changes in the real estate industry in the 1990s were disorienting. After all, the original idea of real estate investing had been justified by modern portfolio theory analysis of the benefits of adding unleveraged, income-producing real estate to a multi-asset portfolio, aiming for a low volatility return series somewhere between stocks and bonds. In that

context, how did one think appropriately about the proper reaction to leveraged real estate investment vehicles like opportunity funds, with little cash
flow and very high objectives for total return? Or about REITs, which were
pass-through vehicles for tax purposes but clearly were otherwise common
stocks devoted to real estate? Or about CMBS and other forms of exposure to
the real estate industry through debt instead of equity investing?

These questions led to the collapse of any consensus about how and why
institutions should invest in real estate. By the time the 1990s ended, there
were still advocates of the notion that the only legitimate vehicle for real estate investing was the kind of direct property investing without leverage that
the asset allocation models usually assumed when trying to determine real
estate's role in a multi-asset portfolio. For those who felt this way, opinions
differed as to whether commingled funds or direct ownership of properties
through single client accounts was the best approach. But there were also
pension funds that had foresworn direct investing in real estate, and whose
exposure to the industry came entirely through a portfolio of REITs. More
common still, there were enthusiasts for investing in real estate exclusively
for return, who felt that it should be classified with other alternative investments such as private equity, and who purchased only to the extent its
returns were competitive with other unquoted investments. Most of these
investors were almost exclusively invested in opportunity funds.

This diversity of practice did not arrive overnight, or without a great deal of
impassioned debate about the relative merits of these ideas. Indeed, much of
the 1990s was consumed by what might be called 'vehicle wars', in which advocates of the merits of one investment vehicle or another generally were reluctant to concede that there were redeeming virtues in any of the alternatives.

For example, the advocates of using REITs as a means to achieve exposure to
the real estate industry argued that REITs combined the appeal of liquidity
with the virtue of being subject to the customary shareholder discipline of
the US public capital markets and the accompanying laws regarding fiduciary responsibility to shareholders, plus a welcome alignment of interest with
management through stock ownership. Opponents argued that the degree of
correlation between REIT returns and stock market returns was unaccept-
ably high, that they were just stocks, maybe a distinct industry, but hardly
one that justified a separate asset class designation and allocation. Advocates
retorted that the apparent differences in correlation were a measurement effect, caused solely by the daily mark-to-market pricing of REITs, and that the
advocates of private real estate investing were – deliberately or unknowingly
– making an argument for asset class treatment that was little more than an
artefact of a flawed and backward-looking appraisal process that created an

illusory degree of non-correlation with other investments. In the genteel world of institutional investing, this was pretty heated rhetoric.

The arguments about opportunity funds were no less forgiving. To their advocates, the back-end loaded incentive fees and limited life of these vehicles eliminated the drawbacks of appraisals because fund sponsors were paid primarily on realised returns. The use of leverage was seen as little more than a recognition of the realities of the real estate capital markets, whose focus on debt as the primary means of finance was a natural result of the availability of financing for assets with such low volatility in their cash flows. To their detractors, opportunity funds were vehicles that often did little more than invest in property that investors could have bought for themselves with lower fees. The sceptics also argued that the use of leverage was inappropriate for an institutional investor, given how expensive real estate debt was relative to other forms of financing that the funds could also have used. The initial success of the funds in the early part of the decade was written off as little more than good timing, not real estate skill. Finally, later in the decade, the lack of transparency in reported information was increasingly questioned as returns fell off and some significant problems reluctantly surfaced at a few of the funds.

The debate about the merits of commingled funds versus separate accounts also increased in intensity as the limitations of the separate account structure became more apparent over time. While greater control was unquestionably left in the hands of pension funds and their consultants, it became clear that one of the consequences was that it was often harder to reach target allocations, as the resulting investment approval process often proved unwieldy, or, worse, subject to political manipulation. As the decade went by, many increasingly questioned whether the increased control had resulted in better performance than would have been achieved by simply remaining in commingled funds. Data was hard to come by, but it was clear that the answer to this question depended on the relative quality of the decision-making at the fund versus that in the remaining commingled funds, rather than because there was a systematic benefit from asserting control. Still others raised concerns about the potential lack of accountability for separate accounts, since the client ultimately was responsible for choosing the assets, even if the fund manager retained control over the asset management.

The question of the role of real estate fixed-income vehicles generated still more complexity. Advocates of the redundantly titled 'four quadrants' thesis argued that a real estate investment programme needed exposure to debt and to equity, each a combination of privately and publicly issued. Few found this construct compelling enough to rewrite their investment guidelines accordingly, but the debate about how to take fixed-income investing into account gained currency as the low interest rate environment at the end of the decade prompted a renewed interest in real estate's income-generating characteristics among increasingly mature pension plans in need of cash flow to pay rising benefit outflows without disrupting asset allocations.

As the 1990s ended, the intensity of all of these debates tended to die down, as it became apparent that there was not one 'right answer'. Instead, each point of view had its advocates, and funds used whichever their particular circumstances made congenial. Thus, larger funds with in-house real estate staffs and substantial portfolios unsurprisingly tended to focus on single client accounts as their principal vehicle. Those whose boards focused on asset allocation as the primary driver of investment policy tended to like real estate for its diversification benefits. Those who had more aggressive investment objectives tended to focus most of their cash flow in opportunity funds. Those who preferred not to spend too much time on the asset class either dropped it – its total capitalisation, always hard to estimate, became increasingly dwarfed by the mushrooming stock and bond markets of the 1990s, making it easier to ignore – or used REITs to achieve their exposure to the industry.

These reactions in the pension fund industry were symptomatic of the issues confronting every institutional investor in real estate during the decade. The complexity of the capital market increased dramatically, and along with it the complexity of investing in the asset class. There were all these new vehicles for users of capital to master, REITs and CMBS being the most obvious. And, in the way that markets evolve, the private markets began to react to the price information being made available in the public arena. So it became imperative to understand what was going on in public markets even if your investment vehicle of choice was exclusively private. The demands for sophistication made on providers of investment advice, both managers and consultants, escalated in geometric fashion.

At the same time, as more and more real estate companies came into existence, financing preferences shifted even among the real estate entrepreneurs who wished to run private companies. Project financing lost market share to corporate finance, the capitalisation of an investment vehicle through which multiple deals could be done. The skills of structuring private equity investing were increasingly necessary in order to structure such investments. And, once again, even for those who were not interested in making such investments, it became important to understand what this new capital market looked like in order to compete effectively with it. In this world, relationships and joint ventures became more important, and the cultivation, evaluation and monitoring of partners became an increasingly important part of the institutional real estate investors' toolkit.

# Where do we go from here?

The year 2000 provided almost ideal ammunition for the advocates of a continued role for real estate in institutional portfolios. For most funds which had the exposure, real estate was their top performing asset class. REITs substantially outperformed the broader market for the year, with the NAREIT index up almost 27% while the S&P 500 lost a little more than 9%. Yet the old wariness remained. Those investors who had had poor experiences with real estate at the beginning of the 1990s remained sceptical that the market had changed its stripes and was now a safer place to invest. In fact, a good deal had changed, but it was critical to understand what was different and what remained the same in order to think appropriately about the role of real estate in institutional portfolios going forward.

To summarise the changes:

- Real estate capital markets have become more transparent, and less isolated from the broader capital markets. Accordingly, overbuilding should tend to be corrected more quickly, dampening the boom and bust cycle.

- Even so, new linkages to the broader market have introduced new sources of volatility. Yet it has also become possible for the market to experience longer periods of equilibrium than in the past.

- The greater diversity of capital sources has made the process of assessing the markets for investments more complex.

- A greater diversity in practice and in the rationale for investing in real estate has taken hold among institutional investors.

- Among those who provided investment management services, the days of the owner-operator have passed. The most successful of the institutionally backed survivors have accumulated far more data about the market, and experience in using it to construct portfolios, than had been possible in the industry's beginning.

Arguably, all of these developments made the industry more accessible than ever before. Yet some of the things that initially had deterred investors remain unchanged.

- The industry remains highly fragmented. While there are a few medium-sized companies, much of the industry's assets are in the hands of entrepreneurs whose ability and willingness to work within the constraints of fiduciary capital is questionable.

- The debt markets remain an important source of capital for the industry. This has made it hard for institutional investors desiring exposure to the attributes of real estate assets to work with individuals who want to minimise their personal capital and maximise their use of leverage. Likewise, debt remains a competitor for investment opportunities, and there are periods in which property owners will prefer refinancing to a sale, limiting the depth of the market.

- The liquidity of the market has been enhanced by public sources of capital, but it is by no means assured, as the events of the third quarter of 1998 demonstrated.

- Issues of measurement, performance reporting and benchmarking remain difficult. Disclosures by most opportunity funds are not consistent, appraisals are routinely used as a measure of performance despite the scepticism they attract, and the most commonly used benchmark for institutional assets, published by NCREIF, is a relatively small sample of the real estate investment universe, and perhaps not a representative one.

Notwithstanding these issues, some of the original arguments for investing in real estate have stood the test of time very well. The return correlations between real estate and stocks and bonds have followed no discernible course over the past decade, as Fig. 8.6 makes clear. Correlations have peaked from time to time, but in a negative direction as often as a positive one. Essentially,

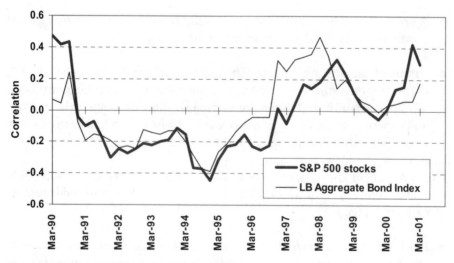

**Fig. 8.6**  20-Quarter trailing correlation with NCREIF index total return. *Sources: NCREIF, Ibbotson Associates.*

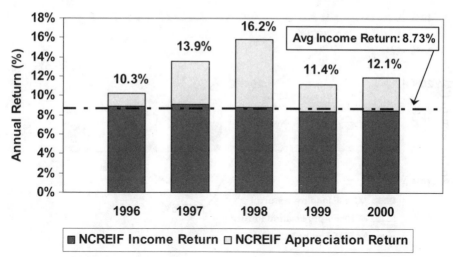

**Fig. 8.7**    NCREIF property index returns, 1996–2000. *Sources: NCREIF, Datastream.*

the expectation that correlations of private measures of real estate return will provide diversification to the portfolio looks as strong as ever.

It is also fair to say that the income returns associated with real estate have been very stable. As Fig. 8.7 indicates, virtually all of the volatility associated with real estate returns from 1996 to 2000 has been associated with appreciation. Income has averaged 8.7%, never more than 9% and never less than 8.5%. While the income measure employed in NCREIF is not the same thing as dividends on stocks or coupons on bonds, it is a fair measure of the income of properties before capital spending. For institutional investors looking for income, the asset class remains attractive.

Even for those who wish to use REITs in place of real estate, the diversification benefits also look appealing. Superimposing REIT returns from 1996 to 2000 over Fig. 8.7, as illustrated in Fig. 8.8, makes it clear that REIT returns are a lot more volatile than the reported results of private real estate. But, as Fig. 8.9 shows, this volatility is not the whole story. The correlation of REIT returns with other stocks has been going down, even as the REITs become a more meaningful part of the market. This is occurring during a period when other ideas that have been used to diversify equity portfolios, like international investing, have shown increasing correlations with the broad market.

In sum, for those institutional investors taking a fresh look at real estate, there are good reasons to consider using it. Some of the reasons for including it are old standards that decades of experience have only made more convincing. Diversification is one. Having a source of income with equity upside is another.

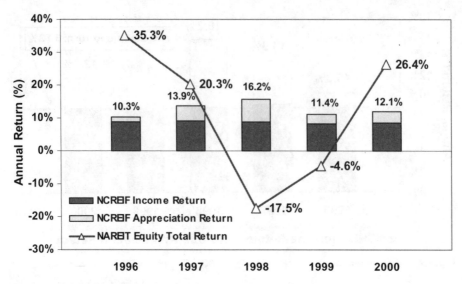

**Fig. 8.8**  NAREIT equity REIT index vs. NCREIF property index returns. *Sources: NAREIT, NCREIF, Ibbotson Associates.*

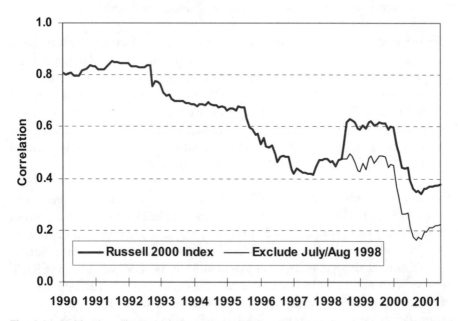

**Fig. 8.9**  60-Month trailing correlation with NAREIT equity total return. *Sources: NCREIF, Ibbotson Associates.*

Other reasons are newer. The range of vehicles available has multiplied as the real estate capital market has become more complex, giving investors more choice about how to use it. While risks remain, manager selection is an opportunity to add greater value than in public markets, as the spread between top and bottom quartile performance is greater in private asset classes than in the more efficient public markets.

Given the ambivalence that the institutional investor community has displayed about real estate over the years, the odds are that the debate will continue about its proper role despite these appealing qualities. As with many private market investment vehicles, the effort required to understand it and invest in it wisely is considerable, and real estate will always seem hard to evaluate for those with backgrounds in the stock and bond world. But for those who make the effort, there are rewards.

# 9

# Real Estate Markets in the United States

## *Mark J. Eppli and Charles C. Tu*

The real estate market in the United States (and elsewhere for that matter) is best described in terms of the space and the capital markets. The intersection of the space and capital markets is where the real estate market emerges. Jeff Fisher describes the real estate market as 'two distinct but interrelated real estate markets: the market for tenant space and the market for investment capital' (Fisher 1992).[1] Historically, real estate markets in the US – both space and capital markets – were local. When a new space need was revealed, local developers would get several wealthy investors together in a limited partnership to provide the equity and a local bank and/or life insurance company would fund the debt.

The real estate space markets, i.e. the supply of and demand for tenant space, determine a property's income stream. Stated another way, the property income stream is a function of the local space market and the quality and location of the subject property. The portfolio of lease contracts for the subject property quantifies the duration, amount and quality of the tenant income stream. In short, property income is dependent on what occurs locally or how strong the 'main street' real estate market is in a particular city for a particular real estate property type.

Capital to fund the space markets was provided by private capital sources until the early to mid 1990s. Since then, capital for real estate has come from both private and public sources. The real estate capital markets in the US are most often described using a 'four quadrants' approach: private debt, private equity, public debt and public equity. The primary difference between private and public sources of real estate capital is whether the capital source is publicly traded. The most common sources of private debt are banks and life insurance companies, and the most common sources of private equity are limited partnerships (or limited liability corporations) and pension funds.

While banks and life insurance companies may be publicly traded, if the mortgage debt they issue is *not* publicly traded, the debt is considered *private* debt.

Public sources of capital came of age in the 1990s. Public capital, both debt and equity, is raised in public auction markets, usually organised stock and bond markets in New York, with proceeds from issuing these public securities used to fund real estate investments. Commercial mortgage-backed securities are the primary source of publicly traded debt. CMBS are fixed-income investments that are collateralised by pools of commercial mortgages that are rated and sold in the bond markets. Approximately $1 billion in commercial mortgages, usually 110–150 loans, are pooled in each deal to diversify property-specific, market-specific and property-type risk. The mortgage pools are then carved into investment interests (tranches) based on credit rating agency recommendations.[2] Real estate investment trusts are the most common form of publicly traded equity in the US. Similar to 'property trusts' elsewhere in the world, REITs are akin to real estate mutual funds, where REITs usually invest in real estate on behalf of investors who purchase shares of REIT stock.

After a general discussion on the space markets, the capital markets, and how these two markets interrelate to create a singular real estate market, the remainder of this chapter focuses on the current state of the US real estate market. Presently, throughout the US almost all of the space markets are overbuilt or significantly overbuilt. With overbuilt markets one would expect that less capital would be flowing into the real estate asset class and that there would be increased risk premiums to account for the additional return volatility of investing in real estate with weak space market fundamentals. However, capital from all four quadrants of the capital markets is currently flowing into almost all property types and, in most metropolitan areas, at or near all-time highs. Furthermore, risk premiums across both debt and equity real estate investments are falling.

This presents a paradox. In the face of weak to very weak space market fundamentals, capital is flowing into US real estate at high levels with low risk premiums. To understand this paradox, we forward three possible explanations for the space market/capital market disconnection:

(1)  Capital is chasing the best risk-adjusted return;

(2)  Real estate is now perceived as a viable portfolio investment alternative; and

(3) Real estate markets have become more informationally efficient and liquid.

Over time the US and international capital markets have created a series of bubbles that have ultimately proven to be unsustainable. The first possible explanation for the real estate market disconnection is that real estate is Wall Street's current investment 'flavour of the day' and therefore the size of capital flows and risk premiums on US real estate are unsustainable and will ultimately burst with risk premiums, capital flows and property values reversing current trends. This flavour-of-the-day argument suggests that the current space/capital market disconnection is cyclical.

The other two explanations argue that there is no disconnection; rather we are undergoing a structural change in how real estate is perceived and valued. The first structural change argues that real estate provides portfolio diversification benefits. With stock equity investments having fallen in each of the past three years and with the S&P 500 index (an index of large capitalisation stocks) off a cumulative 35–45% since all-time highs were reached in early 2000, investors recognise the importance of diversification and start considering alternative investment vehicles to protect their investment corpus. Real estate may be a viable long-term investment diversification vehicle. As investors understand the diversification benefits of greater portfolio allocations to real estate, they may be willing to accept lower risk-adjusted returns on real estate to lower portfolio volatility.

The other structural change argument is based in the advance of the information age and the public trading of real estate debt and equity since the early 1990s. Greater transaction transparency, real estate information and market liquidity may have reduced risk perceptions of the real estate asset class, creating a one-time structural pricing adjustment. This increased information and market transparency may also have reduced the perceived liquidity premium for private investments in real estate as well.

We now conceptually discuss the interrelation between the space and capital markets, followed by an overview of the US space markets. The section after that will present the four quadrants of the real estate capital markets, which brings us to the discussion of the possible explanations of the disconnection between the space and capital markets.

# The interrelation between the space and capital markets

## Conceptual foundation

The most common form of property valuation in the US applies a capitalisation rate to the income stream of a property. In this valuation approach, the property's net operating income (NOI) is divided by the capitalisation rate to derive value:

$$\text{Value} = \frac{\text{Net Operating Income}}{\text{Capitalisation Rate}} \qquad (1)$$

The property capitalisation rate is largely a function of the perceived risk of the property cash flows relative to other investment opportunities. If the perceived risk per unit of return of investing in real estate is lower than investing in other financial and non-financial assets (i.e. real estate investment has higher risk-adjusted return), investors acquire more real estate, driving down property capitalisation rates as property prices are bid up. Property prices continue to increase to the point where the risk-adjusted return matches that of the market for other investments. Conversely, if the risk-adjusted return for real estate investment is inadequate, capital will flow away from the sector, reducing the price of real estate, until risk-adjusted rates of return increase to the point where returns are appropriate for the perceived risks. In short, Wall Street or the capital market participants chase risk-adjusted return across investment alternatives.

On the other hand, the property income stream is solely dependent on what is occurring in the local space market, or 'main street'. The quality of a particular property is a function of its location in the space market where important property-specific linkages include labour, leisure, and other markets. The quality of this location is priced in the tenant market in the form of net rents or property NOI. As a result, the interrelation of real estate space and capital markets can be thought of as occurring at the intersection of Main Street and Wall Street in the following way:

$$\text{Value} = \frac{\text{Main Street}}{\text{Wall Street}} \qquad (2)$$

The real estate market can also be viewed as the intersection of two academic disciplines. Urban economists model local real estate markets, where property value is a function of the proximity to city amenities and the quality of site-specific property attributes. On the other hand, property returns are established in the capital markets, where financial economists guide market participants to determine when, if, and at what rate capital flows into real estate or other asset classes. Similar to equation 2, real estate lies at the intersection of these separate academic disciplines:

$$Value = \frac{Urban\ Economics}{Financial\ Economics} \qquad (3)$$

In sum, as space market fundamentals strengthen, allowing landlords to secure long-term leases with high rents and viable businesses, the perceived investment risk of a property declines and prospective investors are willing to pay a higher price, or accept a lower capitalisation rate for real estate. Alternatively, as space markets weaken and the rents and viability of tenants in a building are less secure, property values decline as the risk premium embedded in the capitalisation rate increases. All else being equal, the risk premiums of income-producing real estate move in the same direction as the perceived risks of the space markets. Alternatively, property values move in the opposite direction to property risk premiums and capitalisation rates.

## Market foundations

The intersection of the space and capital markets is where real estate value emerges. Currently, the value of institutional investment in commercial real estate in the US is $2.9 trillion, with approximately 63% ($1.834 trillion) of that investment in real estate debt (see Fig. 9.1). Private sources of debt, which include banks and life insurance companies, account for $1.3

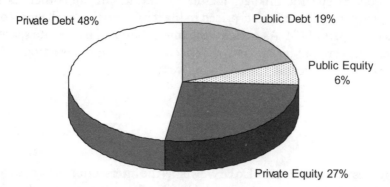

**Fig. 9.1**   US institutional real estate (as of 30 June 2002). *Source: Invesco, Institutional Real Estate, Inc. and Roulac Capital Flows.*

trillion of that debt. The other $534 billion in commercial real estate debt is attributable to loans that have been securitised or sold on Wall Street in the form of CMBS or are multi-family loans securitised by federally related pools (Fannie Mae and Freddie Mac). The remaining investment of approximately $900 billion is invested in equity real estate, of which $173 billion is invested in public equity (REITs) and $735 billion is invested in private real estate investment vehicles such as pension funds, foreign investment and private individual accounts.

The primary measure of equity return in real estate, the capitalisation rates, have generally maintained a tight band between 9% and 11%, as reported by the American Council of Life Insurers (see Fig. 9.2).[3] However, the uncertainties of the US financial markets in the late 1970s and early 1980s pulled real estate capitalisation rates well outside their 38-year range.[4] As can be seen in Fig. 9.2, capitalisation rates are currently approaching record lows, a record that goes back to 1965 when the data were first collected.

The broadest measure of demand for the space markets is GDP growth. If GDP growth rates do not exceed labour productivity growth rates, few, if any, new jobs are created. New employment fills US office and industrial space, and the salaries from these new jobs fund retail purchases and fuel housing demand. As can be seen in Fig. 9.3, US GDP growth has averaged 3.0% since 1986, with the GDP growth averaging 1.6% for the period 2001 Q1 to 2003 Q1.

The macroeconomics of a geographic area determines the strength of the regional space markets. Space markets in the US are rarely in equilibrium, rather they pass through equilibrium on their way to being overbuilt with space or undersupplied with space, often following the path of GDP. The

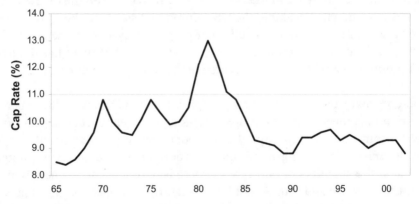

**Fig. 9.2** Property capitalisation rates. *Source: Jerry Crute, Associate Director, Investment Research, ACLI.*

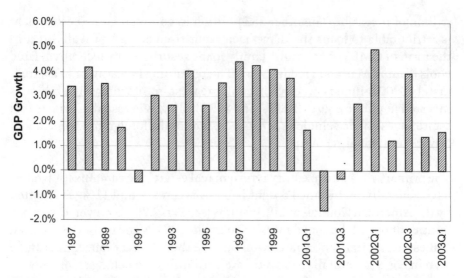

**Fig. 9.3**    Real growth in US gross domestic product (1987–2003 Q1). *Source: Federal Reserve.*

demand for and supply of real estate in narrow space markets is not fluid, rather the space markets are lumpy, with large additions to the market coming in the form of periodic additions of new buildings or, alternatively, the razing of an economically obsolete building. Similarly, the demand for space is seldom fluid for individual space users. While employers often hire additional staff one person at a time (where each additional white-collar employee occupies approximately 150–200 square feet of office space) they contract for space intermittently, adding or shedding space as needed, often at lease termination.

In addition to being described in terms of a location in space (or within a city or metropolitan area), space markets can be described based on the type of space provided. Generally speaking, the US commercial space markets are categorised into four to five distinctly different property types: office, retail, multi-family, industrial and hotel.[5] Each of these space market types has different risk profiles even when they are located in the same geographical area.

There are many reasons why the supply of and demand for space differs across location and property type. First, space market producers, i.e. developers, often specialise in one type of space production. For instance, office and multi-family developers seldom develop retail, and retail developers seldom develop hotels. As such, the suppliers of one type of space (say office) usually supply only that type of space and thus do not have a significant impact on the supply of other space types. Second, demand for space differs by market. For instance, the number of white-collar employees per thousand new employees differs among cities as the amount of office space demanded per new employee in a manufacturing-based city (say Milwaukee, Wisconsin) may differ dramatically from that of a financial hub (say New York City). Third, the amount of space for each new employee may differ based on the type of job created. For example, in Washington, DC, there are many law firms and the amount and quality of space needed per attorney is much greater than the space needed for an employee at a regional call centre (i.e. phone-in centre that addresses consumer service needs). Fourth, not all space is created equal. Attorneys are often located in central business districts (CBD) where law firms often pay premium rents for premium space and quality locations; conversely, call centres are often located in the fringe suburbs where land and space are less expensive. Finally, the type of space and days of the week that the space is needed differ across potential hotel and retail locations. For instance, a tourist destination or airport hub city would clearly demand more hotel space than other similarly sized cities, and the hotel clientele varies by the day of the week and month of the year.

Overall, the supply of space and demand for space may differ, possibly dramatically, among and even within cities. Our review of the space markets largely ignores the difference within and among different space markets; that is a separate and complex discussion. Instead, we briefly discuss each property type individually, addressing several broad space-market demand drivers, changes in the stock of space, property vacancy rates and rental growth rates.[6]

## Space markets in the United States

The quality and stability of a property income stream is determined by the strength of the space market and the relative position of a property within its space market. The strength of the space markets is made explicit in all lease contracts by the rental rate, lease term, rent escalations, among other lease characteristics. In short, site-specific and market attributes determine the size and volatility of a property income stream, i.e. NOI. The quality of a space market is demonstrated by its ability to constrain new supply and grow new demand. For instance, in a market area where there are few limitations on new space in terms of municipal limitations (i.e. legal limitations) or land supply limitations (i.e. physical limitations), the risk of new supply is high.[7] Alternatively, in a market with a core of high-growth companies and desirable amenities, demand for space is likely to remain strong.

For space markets to grow, new employment must occur, and for new employment to occur, economic growth (GDP) must outpace the rate of productivity increase. Since 1993 the average increase in worker productivity was 2.2%; however, during the 20 years before 1993 the average increase in the productivity of US non-farm workers was a mere 1.3%. If GDP growth simply equals unit productivity improvement, there will be little, if any, job growth. On average in the US, for each additional 100 jobs approximately 20 (i.e. 20%) are in detached office space (i.e. detached from manufacturing facilities and not in build-to-suit facilities) and each additional office employee uses between 150 and 200 square feet of space.

In the five-year period ending in December 2002, the US labour market grew by approximately 6.3 million jobs, of which approximately 1.26 million (20%) are estimated to require detached office space (see Fig. 9.4). If the average employee uses 150 square feet of space, approximately 189 million square feet (150 square feet × 1.26 million) of space should have been absorbed in detached office buildings. REIS Reports reveal in Fig. 9.5 that approximately 187 million square feet of office space was absorbed over the period 1998 to 2002.[8] While there are time lags between when jobs are created and space is demanded (alternatively, when jobs are lost and space is vacated), the 618 million square feet of space absorbed since the beginning of 1990 occurred in conjunction with a labour market expansion of 21,909,000 jobs. Again, assuming 20% of the work force each occupies 150 square feet of space, approximately 657 million square feet of space should have been absorbed during that 13-year period, closely matching actual net absorption of 618 million square feet.[9]

The nationwide overbuilding of the office markets in the late 1980s and early 1990s sent vacancy rates above 15% for more than a decade (see Fig. 9.6). As expected, these high vacancy rates left effective office rent growth rates flat to negative for the duration of that period.[10] However, as market vacancy

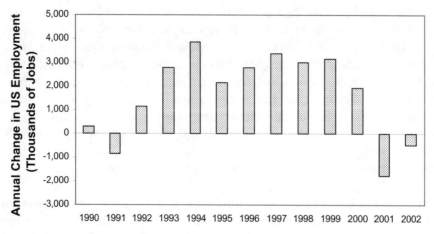

**Fig. 9.4**    US employment growth. *Source: Federal Reserve.*

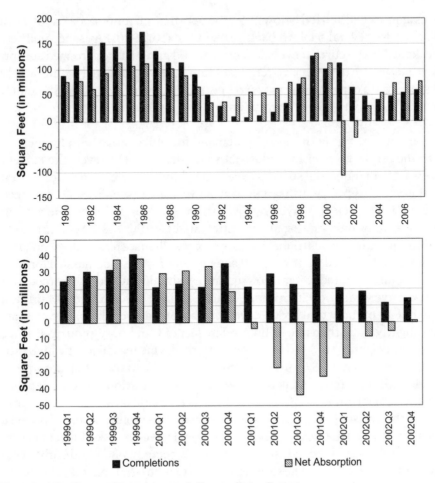

**Fig. 9.5**    US office supply and demand. *Source: Reiss Reports.*

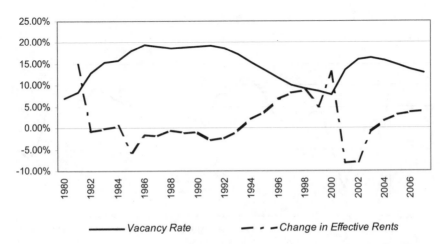

**Fig. 9.6**    Office vacancy rates and changes in effective rent (1980–2007). *Source: Reis Reports.*

rates approached and fell below 10%, the net effect on rents saw a rise of more than 5% for several back-to-back years in the late 1990s. As space markets weakened in the current cycle, effective rental growth rates dropped abruptly. In summary, net effective rent levels are inversely affected by the supply of space. With expected vacancy rates currently hovering around 15%, rental growth is likely to be low to negative in the near term.

As employment growth fuels the demand for office space, employment is also the primary driver for industrial space demand. However, the current oversupply of industrial space is expected to have a slower rate of absorption as the rate of capacity utilisation is at 20-year lows (see Fig. 9.7). The need to lease new space is delayed by low utilisation rates and therefore a lag in the take-up of industrial space is anticipated (see Fig. 9.8). Approximately 40–50 square feet of additional industrial or warehouse space is demanded for each new job created. Assuming 40 square feet of space is demanded for each new job, an estimated 283 million square feet should have been absorbed over the past five years and 986 million square feet since 1990. In fact, 243 million square feet of industrial space have been absorbed over the past five years and slightly more than one billion square feet of warehouse/industrial space since the beginning of 1990 have been absorbed. One reason for the high estimated absorption of 283 million square feet relative to the actual absorption of 243 million square feet is that low capacity utilisation rates are depressing the demand for new space. After a brief economic downturn in the early 1990s, the oversupply of excess industrial space was rapidly absorbed because capacity utilisation rates were relatively high. However, given current capacity utilisation rates, the industrial market is expected to slowly absorb excess space in the mid-2000s. The slow absorption of industrial space is reflected in the negative to low expected changes in effective rents in Fig. 9.9.

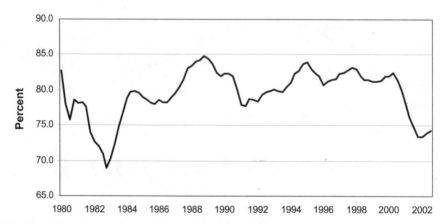

**Fig. 9.7**   US capacity utilisation: total industry. *Source: Reis Reports.*

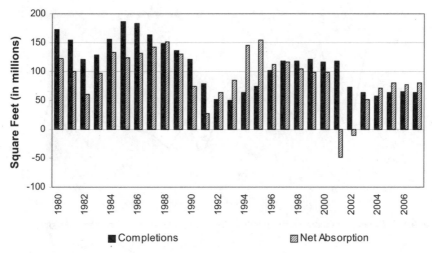

**Fig. 9.8**  US industrial space supply and demand. *Source: Reis Reports.*

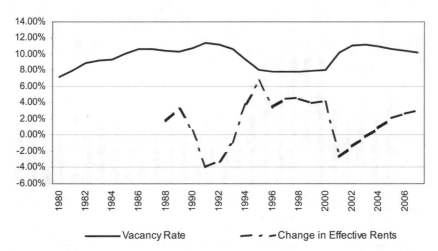

**Fig. 9.9**  Industrial space vacancy rates and changes in effective rent (1980–2007). *Source: Reis Reports.*

The space absorption metrics for retail and apartments are similar to those for office and industrial. As one might expect, changes in personal or disposable income and consumer sentiment directly affect retail spending and thus the demand for retail space. As per capita income has continued to grow over the last 20 years (Fig. 9.10), retail has maintained positive absorption rates (Fig. 9.11), thus keeping effective rents growing (Fig. 9.12).

Changes in the population characteristics of the US, specifically the creation of 'young adult households', have resulted in an increase in demand for housing units (see Table 9.1). A second demand driver for housing units is immigration, although population growth from immigration in the US is focused

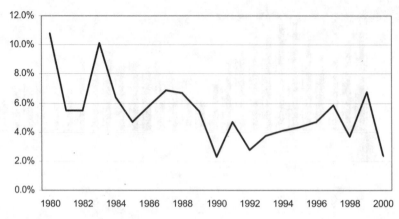

**Fig. 9.10**  Per capita income growth in the US. *Source: Bureau of Economic Analysis.*

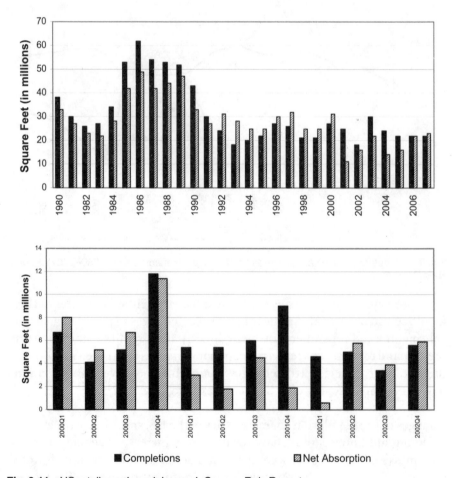

**Fig. 9.11**  US retail supply and demand. *Source: Reis Reports.*

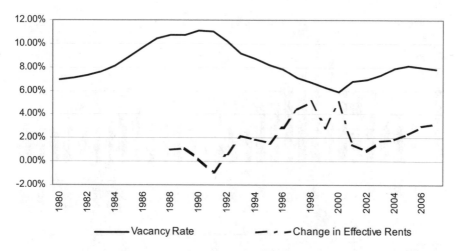

**Fig. 9.12**  Retail space vacancy rates and changes in effective rent (1980–2007). *Source: Reis Reports.*

**Table 9.1**  Population characteristic of the US.

| Group characteristic | Born | Approximate age on 1 Jan 2003 | Population in age cohort (000) | Population change from previous cohort |
|---|---|---|---|---|
| Young generation Y | Post-1986 | 7–16 | 39,689 | 2.88% |
| Old generation Y | 1977–1985 | 17–26 | 38,587 | 3.76% |
| Generation X | 1965–1976 | 27–36 | 37,189 | 17.01% |
| Young baby boom | 1955–1964 | 37–46 | 44,813 | 18.91% |
| Old baby boom | 1946–1954 | 47–56 | 37,685 | |

*Source: Census Bureau.*

on a limited number of markets, namely in the states of California, Florida, Texas, New York and Illinois. However, due to a variety of factors, home-ownership rates in the US have soared from 64–65% in the mid-1990s to a record high of 68%.[11] This increase in the rate of home ownership has reduced the demand for rental units by more than three million units.[12] While REIS Reports are expecting a relatively quick absorption of existing apartments, a continuing drop in mortgage interest rates may slow the absorption of apartments as US households continue their migration to owner-occupied units, further depressing effective rents for apartments (see Figs 9.13 and 9.14).

A list of potential demand drivers that captures all the subtleties of specific space markets would be long: this chapter covers just a few. Numerous local and national firms estimate space absorption, rental rates and rent growth rates; however, without broad income growth and general gains in employment there is likely to be little, if any, space absorbed across all of the property types.

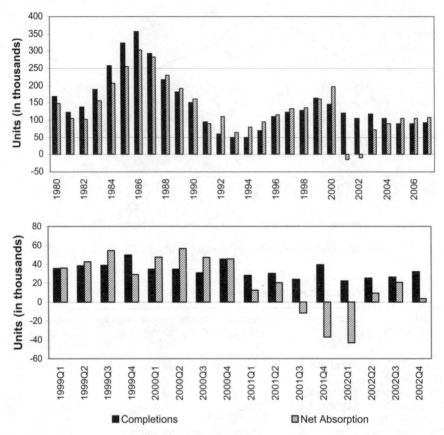

**Fig. 9.13**   US apartment supply and demand. *Source: Reis Reports.*

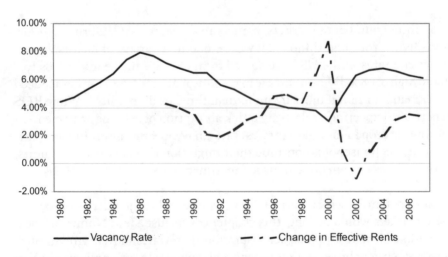

**Fig. 9.14**   Apartment space vacancy rates and changes in effective rent (1980–2007). *Source: Reis Reports.*

# Capital markets in the United States

## *The debt market for real estate capital*

Arguably, nowhere else in the world do borrowers have as many different sources of capital as developers and owners in the US. Debt funds are available during construction and when property income has stabilised, furthermore, debt sources are both public and private (see Fig. 9.15 for the net flow of capital into real estate debt from private and public sources). Funds borrowed during construction (construction loans) are largely the domain of local, regional, and national banks and savings and loans (S&L). Most construction loans are adjustable rate and usually have a two- to four-year term. The term often extends 6–18 months beyond the completion of construction, until the property income is stabilised. Life insurance companies and others also provide construction financing, albeit less frequently. Currently, CMBS do not supply the market with construction loan financing; this market is serviced exclusively with private sources of capital. Most construction loans are recourse or partial recourse loans.[13]

Permanent loans are offered to property owners upon income stabilisation. Most permanent loans from life insurance companies and CMBS issuers are non-recourse loans; however, permanent loans issued by banks may or may not be recourse. Property income is usually considered stabilised when occupancy rates reach 90–95% and a minimum debt service coverage ratio is met. Most permanent loans are fixed-rate, 10-year loans with a 30-year amortisation schedule. Permanent loans usually require minimum occupancy rates, minimum debt service coverage rates and maximum loan-to-value ratios. Generally speaking, property income (NOI) must be 1.2–1.6 times higher than annual debt service. In other words, for each dollar of debt service, property net income must be $1.20–1.60, depending on the perceived risk of the property type and property market. In general, apartments are considered the lowest risk collateral and require 1.2–1.3 coverage rates; alternatively, hotel loans are on the risky end of the property-type risk spectrum. Debt service coverage ratios are considered the primary default risk metric during the term of the loan.

Maximum loan-to-value ratios are generally 60–85% of property value or property cost. As the name of the ratio suggests, this principal preservation ratio measures the amount of collateral per dollar loaned. The loan-to-construction cost ratio is used for construction loans and a loan-to-value ratio is then applied when the property is built and occupied and the income stream is in place to value the asset. In short, property development and ownership in the US is heavily debt financed. Again, the property types with the highest

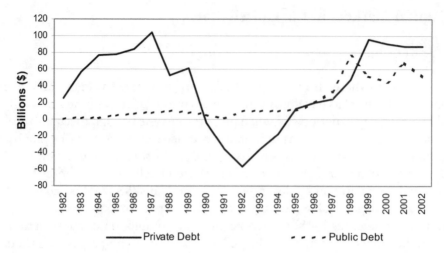

**Fig. 9.15**   Public and private debt capital flows into commercial real estate in the US. *Source: Federal Reserve.*

maximum loan-to-value ratios (i.e. the least risky) are apartments, with hotels considered the most risky and thus maintaining the lowest maximum
loan-to-value ratios. Virtually all sources of public and private debt finance
permanent loans, albeit with varying loan terms and maturities.

Private sources of real estate debt

Debt capital flows into real estate have varied dramatically over the years.
Prior to the mid-1990s, private debt was the dominant source of capital. As can
be seen in Fig. 9.15, 1987 was the high-water mark for the private debt market
with over $100 billion in capital flowing into real estate. This oversupply of
capital pushed real estate development to unsustainable levels, leaving all
segments of the property markets other than the multi-family market significantly overbuilt in virtually all cities in the US. However, this dominant
source of capital largely departed from the market in the early to mid-1990s: in
1992 $57 billion of private real estate debt flowed out of real estate and during
the period 1990–1994 $152 billion flowed out of real estate, precipitating the
worst downturn in the field since the Great Depression in the 1930s.

Figure 9.16 reveals net flows of capital into real estate from the major sources
of private debt. There are several very important things to note in the figure. First, commercial banks are the dominant source of private debt. Banks
provide the majority of construction loan financing but more recently have
been sizeable players in the permanent and mini-perm (three- to seven-year
permanent loan terms) market as well.[14] Furthermore, banks were the only

source of private debt that 'stayed in the market' during the real estate down-turn in the late 1980s/early 1990s, where they were a positive source of debt capital for almost the whole period of the downturn in the market.

Due to Federal financial institution deregulation in 1979 and 1980, S&Ls be-came commercial real estate lenders on a large scale for the first time. This new source of debt capital to real estate developers and owners helped to fuel some of the overbuilding. Of the many different sources of private capital, none was more volatile than the S&L. Freshly deregulated, these formerly staid institu-tions that largely supplied single-family mortgages to home owners could now operate across state borders, became publicly traded, and provided commercial real estate developers with a new source of capital. However, as quickly as they entered the commercial real estate debt markets they departed (see Fig. 9.16). For several years in the early 1980s S&L were second only to banks in the amount of new capital they provided to the real estate industry. However, by the late 1980s and early 1990s they had largely left the market and have not since returned in a meaningful way. A sizeable number of S&Ls were declared bankrupt in the late 1980s/early 1990s. Federal agencies gained control of these organisations and forced the liquidation of the often non-performing and under-performing loans at significant discounts to original loan amounts.

Somewhat paralleling the savings and loan industry experience were the life insurance companies. It should be noted, however, that while life insurance companies are not increasing the amount of real estate debt, they are signifi-cant private market debt players as they continue to replace maturing loans that were made 10 years earlier. It is also worth noting that life insurance

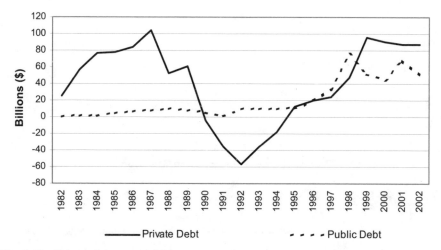

**Fig. 9.16** Private debt capital flows into commercial real estate in the US. *Source: Federal Reserve.*

companies generally lend on the top quality properties and are generally considered more 'conservative' in their underwriting methods than CMBS pools. As such, most life insurance companies did not fail like many of the S&Ls that made commercial loans. Many life insurance companies now fulfil some of their real estate investment needs by purchasing A, BBB, and BB tranches of CMBS issuances. Finally, pension funds are not a sizeable source of debt capital to the commercial real estate markets.

Public sources of real estate debt

The exodus of several of the private debt players from the debt markets in the late 1980s/early 1990s left a void for new players to fill. As the Federal government rationalised failed S&Ls, it quickly realised that the sheer magnitude of the loans acquired from these thrift institutions required a new means of disposing of non-performing and under-performing loans. Some of these loans were sold as mortgage pools on Wall Street to investors and groups of investors, thus creating the public debt market. The data blip in CMBS loans in Fig. 9.17 in the early 1990s largely comes from the sale of Federal pools of failed S&L commercial mortgages that were securitised.

The big story in commercial real estate lending over the past decade has been the emergence of commercial mortgage-backed securities as a viable and ongoing source of capital. CMBS lenders generally lend on C+ to A− grade assets, a market that both banks and insurance companies did not fill well. These loans, originated by banks, life insurance companies, investment

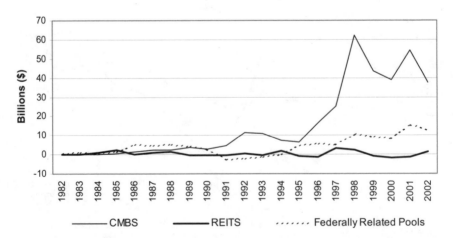

**Fig. 9.17**  Public debt capital flows into commercial real estate in the US. *Source: Federal Reserve.*

banks and credit companies are combined into pools of about $1 billion in size. The pools are property type and geographically diversified but have loan terms that are fairly homogeneous. These pools of commercial loans are then rated by third-party debt-rating agencies that determine the size of the different credit tranches. Over the most recent nine-month period, credit tranching for CMBS issuances was as in Table 9.2.

A bit of interpretation may be helpful. To receive an AAA rating, the investment tranche must meet the rating agency guidelines of an AAA-rated corporate bond. In other words, some portion of a pool of commercial mortgages is considered to be of a quality similar to AAA-rated corporate debt, and some portion of the pool is similar to AA corporate debt rates, and so on. Subordination levels reveal the portion of the CMBS issue that is rated at the different levels lower than the current credit tranche. For instance, the AAA tranche has an 18.08% subordination level, which means that 18.08% of the pool is rated lower than AAA. Alternatively, approximately 82% (100% less 18.08%) of the pool is considered AAA, with the remaining 18.08% of the pool considered lower quality. Similarly, 3.46% (18.08% less 14.62%) of the pool is rated AA, with 14.62% of the pool rated lower or subordinate to the AA tranche. In short, ratings agencies determine what portion of a pool of commercial mortgages is considered to be of adequate quality to be considered for each of the investment tranches.

After several years 'learning' the market with the sale of performing and non-performing loans that were Federal government acquired loans from failed thrifts, the CMBS market has taken off in earnest in the past five years with an average of $47 billion net flow of funds into domestic CMBS each year (see Fig. 9.17). Also worthy of note is the flow of capital from federally related pools, which are Fannie Mae and Freddie Mac funding multi-family debt. Both Fannie Mae and Freddie Mac are publicly traded on the New York

**Table 9.2** Credit tranching for CMBS issuances (recent nine-month period).

| Credit tranche | Subordination level |
| --- | --- |
| AAA | 18.08% |
| AA | 14.62% |
| A | 10.94% |
| BBB | 7.34% |
| BB | 3.67% |
| B | 1.96% |

The credit tranching information was obtained from page 16 of the Fitch CMBS presale or rating summary of 'Credit Suisse First Boston Mortgage Securities Corporation: Series 2003-C3', obtained online at www.fitchratings.com on 14 June 2003. Once this issue is sold on the open market, Fitch will no longer keep this information online. However, historically, Fitch has a continual flow of newly rated transactions that is posted on its website.

Stock Exchange; however, they were both formerly chartered by the Federal government. As such, the debt issued by these two organisations maintains the implicit guarantee of the US government. Therefore, Fannie Mae and Freddie Mac often are able to quote loan originators a lower risk spread than most CMBS pools.

During several years in the late 1990s, capital flows from public sources were larger than the private sources of debt capital. However, the most important issue regarding the rise of publicly traded CMBS debt securities is that a new source of capital for real estate emerged, creating greater liquidity and competition for debt capital.

## The equity market for real estate capital

Equity investment in commercial real estate has largely followed the path of the debt markets. After several years of large growth in capital flows into private equity investment in commercial real estate in the early 1980s, private sources of equity departed the markets in the early 1990s (see Fig. 9.18). With the traditional private equity sources on the sidelines, the public market stepped in, in the form of real estate investment trusts (REITs). These property trust-like investment vehicles rapidly ascended in importance, with $60 billion and $73 billion in new investment in real estate in 1997 and 1998 respectively. Since then, private equity sources have returned as active participants in the equity real estate markets and REITs have largely maintained modest new capital flows into equity real estate investments.

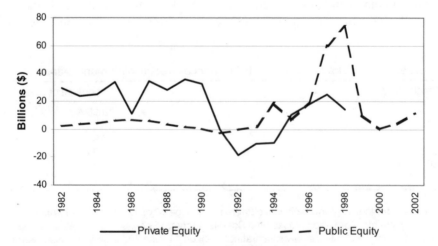

**Fig. 9.18**   Public and private equity capital flows into commercial real estate in the US. *Source: Federal Reserve.*

Private sources of real estate equity

Historically, equity investment in commercial real estate was the domain of private investors. As local private investors and investment companies were most familiar with the demand for and supply of space in their own markets, they were best prepared to capitalise on market needs. However, beginning in the 1980s, national pension funds began to compete with local private investors. Throughout the 1980s and 1990s pension funds continued to invest in commercial real estate, with positive capital flows into this asset class during the entire two-decade period (see Fig. 9.19). While cumulative investments by pension funds in real estate stagnated in the 1990s as property values declined in the first half of the decade, investment continued. Pension investment in equity real estate is tracked using the NCREIF (National Council of Real Estate Investment Fiduciaries) property index. Recently, pension funds have stepped up their investment in and allocation to real estate (see Fig. 9.20). Pension funds generally invest in the four core property types: office, retail, industrial and multi-family. (See Fig. 9.21 for a breakdown of pension investment in equity real estate by property type.)

Another active participant in the private real estate equity markets are private investors. Private investors are usually small groups of investors that create a limited partnership or limited liability corporation with the explicit objective of investing in commercial real estate. Private investment in commercial real estate has, at times, been the dominant source of equity capital for this asset class. It has, however, been volatile over the past two

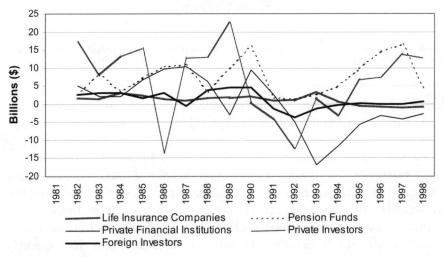

**Fig. 9.19**  Private equity capital flows into commercial real estate in the US. *Source: Federal Reserve.*

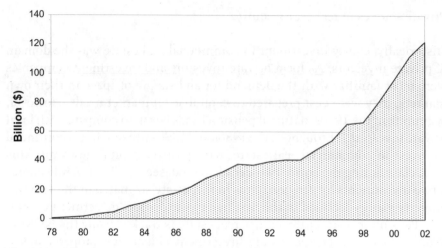

**Fig. 9.20**  Private pension fund direct investment in real estate. *Source: Invesco and NCREIF.*

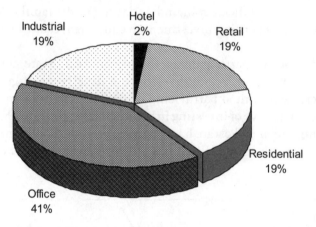

**Fig. 9.21**  Private pension fund direct investment in real estate by property type. *Source: Invesco and NCREIF.*

decades. Like pension funds, private investors are active equity participants in the current real estate market (see Fig. 9.19).

Three other private investors round out the many different investment entities in real estate. Foreign direct investment in US real estate has varied over the years, with the Japanese being significant players in the 1980s and the Dutch and Germans pouring investment capital into real estate more recently. Private financial institutions, such as General Electric Capital and similar entities, came into the equity real estate market in the 1980s, subsequently departed and have not returned. Finally, life insurance companies have maintained a modest role in equity investment in commercial real estate. Overall, private sources of equity capital, which were active participants in the 1980s real estate boom, largely left the markets in the early 1990s and more recently have become active participants in the real estate investment markets.

Public sources of equity real estate capital

The flow of public equity capital into commercial real estate is solely attributable to REITs. Fully 91 % of REIT investments are made in commercial real estate equity investments. Due to a dearth of private equity capital during the early to mid-1990s, REITs re-entered the market and became a viable investment vehicle for the first time. While REITs have been a congressionally approved means of publicly holding real estate since the early 1960s, arguably they were under-utilised as an investment vehicle until 1993 when the UPREIT (umbrella partnership REIT) structure was created. The UPREIT structure allowed private real estate partnerships to transfer the ownership of their partnership interests to an operating partnership controlled by the UPREIT. This was very appealing to US private investors in limited partnerships as this transfer could be completed without triggering Federal income taxes. During the early to mid-1990s, UPREITs were one of the few sources of equity capital in a market undergoing extremely thin trading volumes.

As UPREITs acquired partnership interests, they bought out some limited partners and paid off some debt obligations through money raised on Wall Street in REIT offerings. The growth in REIT capital flows was tremendous in the late 1990s; however, the growth became a trickle in the years that followed. For a variety of reasons, the promise of this new source of public capital did not live up to expectations (see Fig. 9.22).[15] The flow of capital into REITs remained positive throughout the 1990s but the share value of REITs fell for several years as the investment sector fell out of favour on Wall Street (see Fig. 9.23). REITs generally have a broader appetite for real estate than pension funds, often venturing outside traditional areas of real estate investment. Figure 9.24 reveals that REIT investments include healthcare facilities and self-storage investments, and the 'other' category includes golf courses and privately run prisons.

Another form of public ownership was master limited partnerships. For a short period in the mid-1980s, real estate limited partnerships were rolled up into larger master limited partnerships and then publicly traded on the organised stock exchanges. While successful for a short period of time, the Federal government quickly recognised that these rollups of limited partnerships cannot be partnerships and be publicly traded as corporations, putting an end to this potential upstart publicly traded security. In summary, public

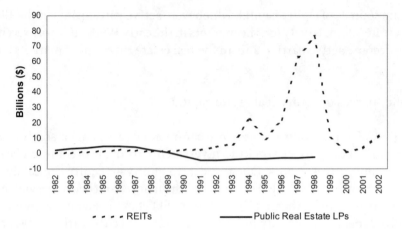

**Fig. 9.22**    Public equity capital flows into commercial real estate in the US. *Source: Federal Reserve.*

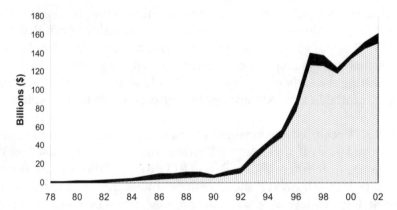

**Fig. 9.23**    REIT investment in commercial real estate. *Source: Invesco and NAREIT.*

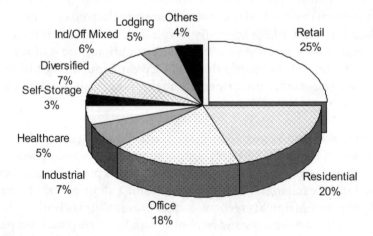

**Fig. 9.24**    REIT investment in commercial real estate by property type. *Source: Invesco and NAREIT.*

equity investment in real estate was embraced by Wall Street in the late 1990s; however, since then a more modest, albeit constant, flow of capital continues to come from REITs.

## The space market/capital market disconnection

As previously mentioned, US real estate markets are currently experiencing weak to very weak market fundamentals, however; capital is flowing into US real estate from all four capital market sectors. To understand this paradox of weak market fundamental and strong capital flows, three possible explanations are offered:

(1)  Capital is chasing the best risk-adjusted return;

(2)  Real estate is now perceived as a viable portfolio investment option; and

(3)  Real estate markets have become more informationally efficient and liquid.

The first explanation is a cyclical one where the size of capital flows into US commercial real estate are unsustainable and will eventually burst with risk premiums, capital flows and ultimately property values reversing current trends.

The other two arguments are structural ones where we suggest that commercial real estate investment is undergoing a structural change in how it is perceived and valued. The first structural change discussion argues for a portfolio diversification value premium for real estate. The second is based on information efficiencies and the public trading of real estate debt and equity since the early 1990s. Increased transaction and market transparency may have reduced risk perceptions of investing in the real estate asset class, creating a one-time structural pricing premium.

*Wall Street chases risk-adjusted yield and commercial real estate is 'flavour of the day'*

Both domestically (in the US) and internationally the financial markets have seen a number of bubbles in the past 10 years. Is the commercial real estate market in the US currently in the middle of yet another cycle that is unsustainable and will shortly burst? The following discussion provides relevant information on the possibility that current US real estate market values are unsustainable.

A quick review of space and capital market fundamentals is appropriate here. Across all real estate property types, with the possible exception of retail, property vacancy rates approach or exceed 10% and in some cases exceed 15%. Furthermore, macroeconomic fundamentals are expected to be weak for the foreseeable future (i.e. the next 12–24 months). That said, excess space is expected to be absorbed more slowly than in past economic recoveries and effective rental rate increases are expected to be weak to modest. While the US space markets are overbuilt and expected to remain overbuilt for some time, capital flows into the asset class continue at near-record highs across all four of the capital market quadrants. Are debt and equity, public and private, real estate investors all chasing the same deals, unsustainably driving down expected returns and driving up real estate asset prices?

To assess the possibility of an asset bubble in commercial real estate, we focus on expected risk premiums for both debt and equity investments in real estate and review several of the underlying metrics for these risk premium measures. We largely ignore expected inflation and real rates of return on US financial assets as all investments require these two components of return.[16] We begin with a discussion of risk premiums on commercial real estate debt risk.

The best source of commercial real estate debt risk premiums comes from the CMBS market. CMBS risk spreads across all investment grade tranches; those rated BBB– or higher have tightened over the past three years. A three-year horizon is relevant because real estate space markets and absorption rates began to weaken after the technology bubble burst and employment rates turned negative in early 2000 (see Fig. 9.25).[17] Before that time, few if any market participants expected the sharp weakening that was to follow. While investment grade risk spreads have tightened on CMBS issuances, high-yield risk spreads have largely remained stable. However, approximately 95% of CMBS tranches are rated BBB– or better, which suggests a significant reduction in the weighted average risk spreads on mortgages originated for placement in CMBS pools.

As Fig. 9.26 reveals, the risk spreads on CMBS tranches have fallen relative to corporate bonds as well. In 1999, AAA-rated CMBS were trading at risk spreads similar to A-rated corporate debt. In the past, CMBS debt traded at a premium to corporate debt as CMBS carried a 'new security' risk premium, and the liquidity of CMBS investments was weak during the capital market events of the Fall of 1998, when CMBS transaction volume dramatically declined. With that said, since 1999 CMBS risk spreads have fallen relative to corporate spreads and now A-rated corporate debt no longer trades at a premium to AAA CMBS debt.

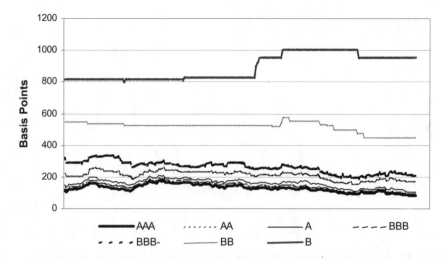

**Fig. 9.25**   CMBS spreads over 10-Year US Treasuries (May 1999–May 2003). *Source: Prudential Mortgage Capital Company.*

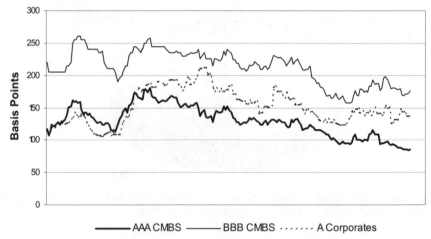

**Fig. 9.26**   CMBS and corporate spreads over US Treasuries (May 1999–May 2003). *Source: Prudential Mortgage Capital Company.*

One possible reason for the reduction in the commercial mortgage risk premiums is the low level of commercial mortgage delinquency rates. Both the American Council of Life Insurers (ACLI) and CMBS report delinquency rates that are low to very low given property market fundamentals. ACLI data reveals that delinquency rates over the past several years are at record lows (see Fig. 9.27), and while CMBS 60-day delinquency rates have ticked up, they too are relatively low (see Fig. 9.28).[18] For example, a sizeable body of literature suggests that approximately 30–40% of delinquent loans default and of the loans that default, the loss rate is approximately 35%. Table 9.3 presumes that delinquency rates may rise to 2.0–5.0% over the next couple

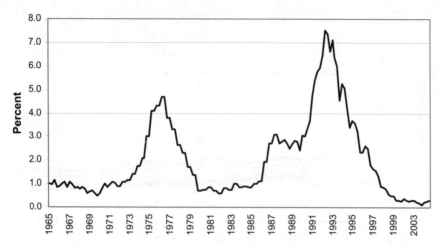

**Fig. 9.27**  Insurance company commercial mortgage delinquency rates. *Source: ACLI and Morgan Stanley.*

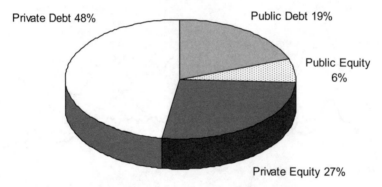

**Fig. 9.28**  CMBS 60-day delinquency rates (November 1999–November 2002). *Source: Invesco, Institutional Real Estate, Inc. and Roulac Capital Flows.*

**Table 9.3**  Pricing credit risk.

| Delinquency rate | 2.0% | 3.0% | 5.0% |
|---|---|---|---|
| % of delinquent loans that default | 30.0% | 30.0% | 40.0% |
| Default rate | 0.6% | 0.9% | 2.0% |
| Loss rate on defaulted loans | 35.0% | 35.0% | 50.0% |
| Expected loss | 0.21% | 0.32% | 1.00% |

of years: even when applying reasonable to stiff default and loss rates, the expected loss is a relatively low 0.21–1.00%, with loss rates expected to stay at the lower end of that range.

Reflecting the relatively low delinquency/default/loss risk expectations, the debt rating agencies have downgraded only one CMBS tranche for every four that they upgraded over the past four years (see Fig. 9.29).[19] However, early reports in 2003 reveal that downgrades are slightly outpacing upgrades for the CMBS markets. Rating changes are reported by the three bond rating agencies (Fitch, Moody's, and Standard & Poor's) based on the probability of a bond or CMBS tranche defaulting. Furthermore, and importantly as a negative sign for CMBS, when reviewing CMBS ratings actions by cohort year (i.e. year of issuance) recent CMBS issuances have more downgrades than upgrades (see Fig. 9.30). Overall, the rating agencies have also eased their underwriting standards or perceived risk of CMBS pools have become safer as the subordination levels have also fallen slightly over the past several years.

Risk premiums for equity real estate investment have also tightened over the past several years, as capitalisation rates continue to fall (see Fig. 9.31). Presuming that the real rate of return portion of a capitalisation rate remains relatively stable over time, the risk premiums across all the real estate property types are falling as capitalisation rates are either approaching or below 9.0%. However, as capitalisation rates have fallen over the past several years investment returns on real estate still either outpace or are competitive with other investment asset classes over one, three, five, and ten-year investment horizons and have outpaced other investment yields (see Figs 9.32 and 9.33).

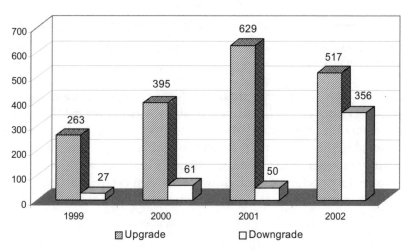

**Fig. 9.29**   Historical CMBS credit rating actions. *Source: Morgan Stanley, Fitch, Moody's and S&P.*

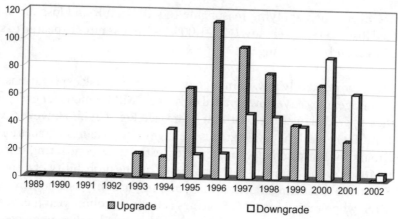

**Fig. 9.30**    2002 CMBS rating changes by cohort year. *Source: Morgan Stanley, Fitch, Moody's and S&P.*

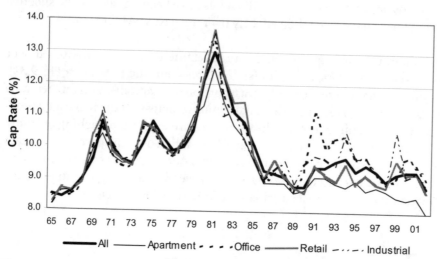

**Fig. 9.31**    Capitalisation rates by property type. *Source: Jerry Crute, Associate Director, Investment Research, ACLI.*

In summary, investment risk premiums for real estate debt and equity are approaching either record lows or cyclical lows. However, while these risk premiums are low, real estate still provides some of the highest cash flow yields found in the capital markets and total investment returns are either competitive or superior to other asset classes. Therefore, while we are reaching or exceeding cyclical capital flow norms, real estate still appears to be attractive relative to other investment options.

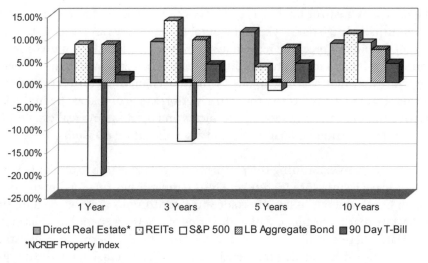

□ Direct Real Estate*   □ REITs   □ S&P 500   ▨ LB Aggregate Bond   ■ 90 Day T-Bill

*NCREIF Property Index

**Fig. 9.32**   Investment returns for one, three, five and ten-year holding periods (30 September 2002). *Source: Invesco, Ibbotson and Associates, NCREIF.*

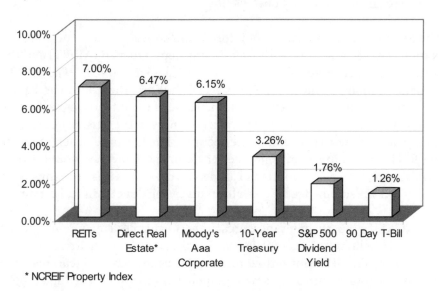

* NCREIF Property Index

**Fig. 9.33**   Investment cash flow yields. *Source: Invesco, S&P, Moody's, Ibbotson and Associates, and NCREIF.*

## *Is real estate the alternative investment vehicle that we have all been looking for?*

According to the modern portfolio theory (MPT)[20] an efficient portfolio is one that has the lowest risk for a given expected return or one with the highest expected return at a given level of risk. Therefore, the impact of real estate on a portfolio depends on the interaction of its returns with those of other asset classes. Many institutional investors have the perception that real estate has low returns and high risk.[21] This unfavourable characteristic of real estate (even if true) should not preclude real estate from being included in an investment portfolio as long as it can provide diversification benefits, which may explain why real estate may have undergone a structural change in return expectations. In this section we investigate the return performance of real estate in the US relative to other major investment vehicles and discuss how real estate may play a role in portfolio management and asset allocation decisions.

The first task in examining the performance of real estate is to identify the proper ways to measure its return. Unlike most other financial markets in which homogeneous assets are traded in a continuous auction system, the real estate market is one in which the price of a heterogeneous asset is often negotiated between the buyer and seller directly. Furthermore, real estate properties are not traded as frequently as financial assets. Due to the unique circumstances, the price level of real estate (as an asset class) cannot be easily measured and is not readily observable.

The two most popular sources of information on real estate returns are the National Association of Real Estate Investment Trusts (NAREIT) and the National Council of Real Estate Investment Fiduciaries (NCREIF). NAREIT compiles a monthly index for equity REITs.[22] While the price of an equity REIT reflects investor perceptions of the value of the underlying real estate assets, investors may also value the effectiveness of the trustee or management team in their valuation of the security. Furthermore, when purchasing REIT shares, investors enjoy better liquidity than they would if they acquired and managed commercial properties directly. Thus, investing in an equity REIT is somewhat different from investing directly in real estate.

The NCREIF property index measures the performance of income-producing properties held by tax-exempt institutional investors.[23] Quarterly returns are reported since 1978 for various property types and geographical areas, and include the total return and its two components – income return and capital return. The data incorporated in the NCREIF index is voluntarily contributed by members of the NCREIF, and the reported property values are based on appraised value (except for the properties that are sold during the quarter). The index employed in this chapter covers all property types and markets, and thus represents a well-diversified portfolio of commercial real estate.

Let's first compare the long-term performance of real estate investment (based on both the NAREIT and the NCREIF indexes) to that of other asset classes, including large-cap stocks, small-cap stocks, government bonds, corporate bonds and risk-free securities. Table 9.4 describes the indexes representing these asset classes.

**Table 9.4**   Asset class definitions.

| Asset class | Index |
|---|---|
| Public real estate | NAREIT equity index |
| Private real estate | NCREIF property index |
| Large-cap stocks | S&P 500 |
| Small-cap stocks | Russell 2000 |
| Government bonds | Lehman Brothers government bond index |
| Corporate bonds | Lehman Brothers credit index |
| Risk-free securities | US 1-year Treasury constant maturity index |

Figure 9.34 shows the cumulative total return of $1 invested in different asset classes for the period from 1978 to 2002.[24] Over this 25-year period, equity REITs outperformed all other asset classes with $1 growing to nearly $21. Figure 9.34 reveals that, before 1997, REIT returns closely resembled stocks; in recent years, however, REIT returns have started to move differently from stocks. In contrast to the strong performance of REITs, $1 invested in private real estate would return only slightly higher than $8 during this period.

When making portfolio selection decisions, investors consider not only how much return the investment provides but also how risky it is. As investors are generally risk averse (i.e. dislike risk), they require higher return on a riskier investment as compensation for taking the extra risk. The riskiness of the investment is often measured by the standard deviation of its returns. Table 9.5 compares the mean and standard deviation of quarterly returns of different asset classes over the same time period and several sub-periods.

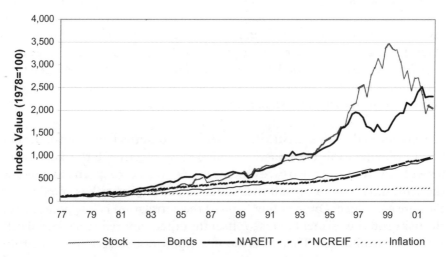

**Fig. 9.34**   Cumulative investment returns for selected indices (1978–2003). *Source: Ibbotson Associates.*

**Table 9.5**   Quarterly returns and volatilities (%).

| | Large-cap stocks | Small-cap stocks | Government bonds | Corporate bonds | NAREIT | NCREIF | T-Bills | Inflation |
|---|---|---|---|---|---|---|---|---|
| *1978–2002* | | | | | | | | |
| Mean | 3.42 | 3.51 | 2.32 | 2.4 | 3.41 | 2.28 | 1.85 | 1.08 |
| SD | 8.07 | 11.14 | 3.37 | 4.55 | 6.83 | 1.71 | 0.81 | 0.9 |
| *1978–1982* | | | | | | | | |
| Mean | 3.62 | 6.67 | 2.43 | 2.03 | 4.74 | 3.81 | 2.96 | 2.29 |
| SD | 7.72 | 12.36 | 5.32 | 8.41 | 7.43 | 1.34 | 0.68 | 1.13 |
| *1983–1987* | | | | | | | | |
| Mean | 4.34 | 2.86 | 2.87 | 3.32 | 4.11 | 2.62 | 2.14 | 0.84 |
| SD | 9.62 | 12.56 | 3.33 | 4.26 | 6.27 | 0.98 | 0.47 | 0.5 |
| *1988–1992* | | | | | | | | |
| Mean | 3.93 | 4.13 | 2.55 | 2.77 | 2.68 | 0.46 | 1.73 | 1.04 |
| SD | 6.06 | 10.77 | 2.53 | 2.38 | 6.87 | 2.02 | 0.45 | 0.48 |
| *1993–1997* | | | | | | | | |
| Mean | 4.81 | 4.03 | 1.82 | 2.09 | 4.49 | 1.91 | 1.3 | 0.64 |
| SD | 4.57 | 5.93 | 2.52 | 2.92 | 6.88 | 1.15 | 0.27 | 0.36 |
| *1998–2002* | | | | | | | | |
| Mean | 0.41 | 0.49 | 1.92 | 1.79 | 1.02 | 2.58 | 1.11 | 0.58 |
| SD | 10.81 | 13.1 | 2.49 | 1.76 | 6.6 | 0.92 | 0.38 | 0.55 |

While standard deviation is the most common measure of risk when making comparison among investments, it may not be the most appropriate measure when the riskiness of an investment is assessed in a portfolio context. Investors also consider the extent to which the acquisition of additional investment may affect the risk and return of the portfolio. The interaction of returns may cause the risk of the portfolio to be less than the average risk of individual investments. When investors add real estate to an existing portfolio, it is important to understand how the acquisition of real estate may affect the return and risk of the entire portfolio.

Correlation is the key statistic that provides a numerical measure of the extent to which returns of two assets tend to move together. If the correlation between the returns of two investments is close to one, they tend to move in the same direction; as a result the reduction in portfolio risk is small when they are combined. On the other hand, if the correlation is low or negative, the risk of one investment tends to offset the other, thus reducing the volatility of the portfolio risk. Therefore, the idea in portfolio selection is to identify assets with low correlation with the existing portfolio so that inclusion of the asset can improve the efficiency of the portfolio.[25]

For example, consider two investments with the following characteristics: investment S has an expected rate of return of 12% and standard deviation of 17%; investment B has an expected return of 8% and standard deviation of 7%. A portfolio that consists of 50% S and 50% B will have an expected return of 10% but the portfolio standard deviation depends on the correlation between S and B. If they are perfectly positively correlated (correlation coefficient, $r$, is equal to 1), then the standard deviation equals 12%; if the correlation coefficient is 0.5, the portfolio standard deviation is reduced to 10.7%; and if they are independent (i.e. $r = 0$), the portfolio standard deviation is only 9.2%. Figure 9.35 shows the results of combining these two investments given different correlation.

As shown in Fig. 9.35, combining investments with low correlation creates diversification benefits, that is, lower risk at a given level of expected return. Whether real estate represents a good diversifier depends on its correlation with other asset classes. Table 9.6 presents the correlation matrix of the asset classes examined in this chapter.

The data in Table 9.6 reveal two interesting points. First, while large-cap stocks are highly correlated with small-cap stocks (0.8773) and government bonds are highly correlated with corporate bonds (0.9298), the correlation between the two measures of real estate investment returns is negative during the entire sample period (–0.0137). This raises a question: which measure is more representative for the returns of real estate investment? Geltner and Rodriguez (1998) argue that the low correlation is caused by data problems.

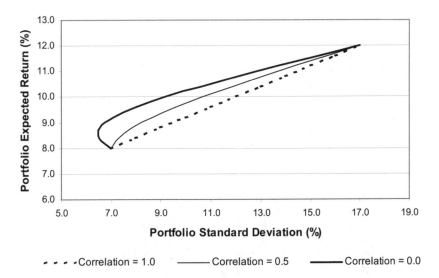

**Fig. 9.35**   Example of investment efficient frontier.

**Table 9.6**  Investment correlations.

| | Large-cap stocks | Small-cap stocks | Government bonds | Corporate bonds | NAREIT | NCREIF | T-Bills | Inflation |
|---|---|---|---|---|---|---|---|---|
| *1978–2002* | | | | | | | | |
| Large-cap stocks | 1 | 0.8773 | 0.1694 | 0.3445 | 0.603 | −0.0309 | 0.0114 | −0.1992 |
| Small-cap stocks | | 1 | 0.0699 | 0.2062 | 0.6915 | −0.0516 | 0.0246 | −0.0319 |
| Government bonds | | | 1 | 0.9298 | 0.2584 | −0.1078 | 0.1643 | −0.2201 |
| Corporate bonds | | | | 1 | 0.3959 | −0.1721 | 0.0753 | −0.3047 |
| NAREIT | | | | | 1 | −0.0137 | 0.0007 | −0.1271 |
| NCREIF | | | | | | 1 | 0.4716 | 0.3498 |
| T-Bills | | | | | | | 1 | 0.5217 |
| Inflation | | | | | | | | 1 |
| *1998–2002* | | | | | | | | |
| Large-cap stocks | 1 | 0.8816 | −0.7712 | −0.6494 | 0.2083 | 0.2608 | 0.1038 | −0.2629 |
| Small-cap stocks | | 1 | −0.7865 | −0.6601 | 0.5161 | −0.0072 | 0.0275 | −0.1627 |
| Government bonds | | | 1 | 0.854 | −0.3652 | 0.0402 | 0.0337 | 0.0453 |
| Corporate bonds | | | | 1 | −0.3199 | −0.0389 | −0.0967 | −0.0901 |
| NAREIT | | | | | 1 | −0.2357 | 0.0287 | 0.136 |
| NCREIF | | | | | | 1 | 0.7573 | 0.1862 |
| T-Bills | | | | | | | 1 | 0.3322 |
| Inflation | | | | | | | | 1 |

First, because of infrequent trading in property markets, return data for NCREIF has been based mainly on appraised value. This causes smoothing of the returns over time. In contrast, the NAREIT index is based on transaction prices and thus not smoothed. However, the volatility of REIT prices also reflects the leverage utilised by the trusts. Geltner and Rodriguez show that when the NCREIF index is unsmoothed and the NAREIT index is unlevered, the two indexes display overall similar movement patterns, although public real estate generally leads private real estate by about one or two years.

Second, over the entire sample period, 1978–2002, direct real estate investment represented a much better diversifier than investment in equity REITs, as indicated by the low correlation between the NCREIF index and other investments and the high correlation between NAREIT and others. However, as some researchers have pointed out, the characteristics of REIT returns have changed substantially in recent years (e.g. Ghosh *et al.* 1996). If we consider the five-year rolling correlation between the return of REITs and that of large-cap stocks and government bonds, the correlation has dropped significantly since the late 1990s (see Fig. 9.36). As a result, real estate investment via REITs can now offer great diversification benefits for investors seeking more efficient portfolios. Figure 9.37 compares portfolios consisting of only large-cap stocks and government bonds with those consisting of stocks, bonds and REITs. Thanks to low REIT correlations with stocks and bonds, inclusion of public real estate significantly improves the efficiency of portfolios.

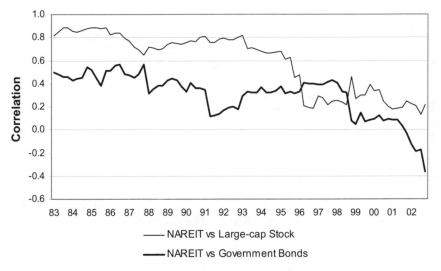

**Fig. 9.36**   Five-year rolling correlations.

*Informationally efficient and liquid enough to reduce expected returns?*

The Internet has changed everything. In the case of commercial real estate there may be some truth to that statement. Over the past five to seven years, real estate, much like other narrowly traded auction markets based on privately held information, has been undergoing an information transformation from private to public. Although the information may not always be free, the sources of information are known and relevant information can be purchased. One only needs to access www.google.com to see the vast field of searches available at the click of a mouse. Similarly, www.ebay.com has changed the way we sell items that historically had a limited market. While commercial real estate has not been directly affected by either of these web pages, they both reveal how the search for information has changed and how prices for the most exotic of items can be determined using a world-wide auction. Furthermore, the public markets for real estate debt and equity have similarly forced a level of transparency previously unheard of in real estate.

While it is illegal to make stock trades using insider information, inside information historically was the essence of most real estate deals. Local players had local knowledge and maintained a clear advantage when investing in commercial real estate. While we do not pretend to be information transfer experts, we feel that the combined effects of the Internet and publicly traded securities has permanently affected the private world of real estate, levelling the playing field for those not holding inside information.

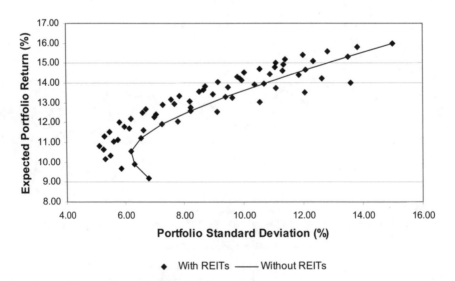

**Fig. 9.37**   Stock-efficient frontier with and without REITs.

## Summary

Investment in US commercial real estate is at a crossroads. Historically, the intersection of Main Street and Wall Street determined the value of commercial real estate. Using historic metrics, the location of that intersection has moved. Maybe the disconnection between the space markets and capital markets is cyclical and the commercial real estate markets will follow the path of other asset bubbles and burst, with property values falling and capital flows reversing current trends. Alternatively, a structural shift in real estate returns may be under way. If real estate is now valued for its portfolio diversification benefits, why have market participants waited so long to price real estate as part of a portfolio's assets? Did it take several other bubble markets for the investing public to finally heed the advice of Markowitz? Alternatively, maybe a game that was perfectly suited for insiders has become more transparent, levelling the investment playing field for all.

## References

DiPasquale, D. & Wheaton, W. (1992) The Market for Real Estate Assets and Space: A Conceptual Framework. *Journal of the American Real Estate and Urban Economics Association* **20**, 181–90.

Eppli, M.J. (1993) The Theory, Assumptions, and Limitations of Direct Capitalization. *Appraisal Journal* July, 419–25.

Fisher, J.D. (1992) Integrating Research on Markets for Space and Capital. *Journal of the American Real Estate and Urban Economics Association* **20**, 161–80.

Geltner, D. & Rodriguez, J.V. (1998) Public and Private Real Estate. In *Real Estate Investment Trusts* (eds R.T. Carrigan & J. Parson). McGraw-Hill, New York.

Ghosh, C., Miles, M. & Sirmans, C.F. (1996) Are REITs Stocks? *Real Estate Finance*, pp. 46–53.

Markowitz, H. (1952) Portfolio Selection. *Journal of Finance* **7**, 77–91.

Worzala, E.M., Zietz, E.N. & Sirmans, G.S. (1999) What's Wrong with Real Estate? *The Real Estate Finance Journal* pp. 14–16.

## Notes

1 Another insightful conceptual discussion of the space and capital markets in the US is provided by DiPasquale and Wheaton (1992).

2 The three companies that rate US CMBS debt tranches are Moody's, Fitch, and Standard & Poors.

3 It should be noted that the ACLI capitalisation rates are reported by the life insurance companies that lend on real estate. Generally speaking, these capitalisation rates are 50–150 basis points higher than what most equity investors report on similar deals.

4 The spike in property capitalisation rates in the late 1970s and early 1980s was not expected. While inflation premiums hit cyclical highs at that time, property income growth rates are not embedded in property capitalisation rates. Capitalisation rates include a property risk premium and a real rate of return only. For more detailed discussion of capitalisation rates see Eppli (1993).

5 In the US, multi-family apartments are usually included in the commercial real estate markets as they provide a stream of rental income like other property types. However, condominiums and single-family residential are excluded from a discussion of the commercial real estate markets as they are 'owner-occupied' and therefore not included in the 'investment real estate' realm.

6 The supply of and demand for space in different geographic markets is analysed by a variety of national, regional and local firms. Several of the larger space market information providers include Reis Reports, Torto-Wheaton Research, and PPR (Property and Portfolio Research). Furthermore, most commercial real estate brokers and appraisers (valuers) maintain space market data for their locale.

7 Generally speaking, growth in rental income is a function of the growth in the cost of developing new space. In a market unconstrained by municipal zoning and the physical availability of land, property income streams can grow only as fast as the growth in land costs and construction costs. Limited land and strict municipal land-use regulations often increase the cost and risks associated with new development, which is forced onto irregular infill sites where municipal approvals are uncertain. Higher development costs and difficult municipal approval processes often limit the development of new space until a point where the costs and risks associated with new development are met by higher rents, which increases property rents across the entire market.

8 'Absorption' in this context refers to net absorption (i.e. net space leased in a market after subtracting the amount of space vacated).

9 The REIS data does not include build-to-suit or owner-occupied buildings.

10 Effective rents are the economic rents that landlords effectively receive during the lease term and include the effect of free rent.

11 The increase in home-ownership rates can largely be attributed to mortgage market events. First, long-term fixed-rate mortgage interest rates are currently the lowest they have been in 45 years, making home ownership more affordable. Second, credit scoring has become an efficient and transparent means of predicting mortgage default, which reduces the uncertainty surrounding the mortgage lending decision. Finally, new sub-prime mortgage lending instruments have opened the mortgage markets to many who previously were precluded from the market due to relatively minor credit history problems.

12 There are approximately 110 million households in the US. If home-ownership rates increase by three points, approximately 3.3 million apartment units will become available, all else being equal.

13 Recourse loans hold the borrower personally responsible for the repayment of the loan. Non-recourse loans do not hold the borrower responsible for the loan. Non-recourse loans only use the property being borrowed against as collateral.

14 Banks and life insurance companies also originate loans that are sold for the CMBS markets. These loans are not considered private debt (i.e. debt that is held in whole-loan form on the balance sheets of banks and life insurance companies).

15 REITs fell on hard times for several unrelated reasons. First, in May 1998 the US Treasury limited the growth of REITs by clearly delineating 'rental income' and thus the types of passive investments that REITs can make in real estate. Second, the New York Federal Reserve issued a warning about the rapid expansion of this industry in the Fall of 1998. Finally, some of the 'hype' surrounding the income growth and expense efficiencies that REITs could obtain through the real estate 'platform' was not realised.

16 While the risk-free rate of return is commonly expressed as the short-term US Treasury interest rate, we use the long-term Treasury rate as almost all real estate investments are long-term and are priced from long-term Treasury bonds.

17 CMBS risk spreads reached their low point just before the capital markets bubble in the Summer/Fall of 1998. At that time Asian contagion was under way, Russia defaulted on its debt, and Long Term Capital Management received a Wall Street bailout. Since those events, risk premiums on debt have increased and stayed higher than pre-1998 spreads.

18 The reason total CMBS delinquency is higher than the three property types reported is that delinquency rates on the other 'non-core' assets are higher. Specifically, hotel delinquency rates exceed those of the core property types.

19 Fig. 9.29 presents only rating changes; most CMBS and corporate debt ratings do not change year-on-year.

20 The modern portfolio theory is based on the seminal work by Harry Markowitz (1952).

21 See results of a survey of portfolio fund managers for pension funds and life insurance companies conducted by Worzala *et al.* (1999).

22 More information about the NAREIT indexes can be found on the association's website at: http://www.nareit.org.

23 For more information about the NCREIF index, log on to http://www.ncreif.org.

24 The NAREIT data began in 1972 while the NCREIF data began in 1978. The cumulative total returns are based on a $1 investment at the beginning of 1978 with quarterly price changes and reinvestment of dividend or interest.

25 While the risk of the portfolio is lower than the average risk of individual investments, the expected return is the weighted-average return of the investments. Therefore, combining investments with low correlation reduces portfolio risk without sacrificing returns.

# 10

# Real Estate Markets in the United Kingdom

*Andrew Baum*

## UK real estate: the asset class

In 2000, directly owned real estate accounted for some 7% of the value of the institutional investment market throughout the world (an estimate made by, among others, Prudential, a US insurance and financial services group). This represents a sum of over US$1,250 billion. According to Henderson Global Investors (2000) European property constitutes around 30% of this global market, and the UK (with an estimated $175 billion or £110 billion) constitutes around one-third of all European institutional real estate and around 12% of the global property market. This represents the third largest market after the US ($380 billion, or 30%) and Japan ($217 billion, or 17%). These are broad estimates and open to much interpretation, but they confirm that the UK is a leading real estate market in international terms and the flagship for the European region.

The London Business School has estimated the total value of all commercial property in the UK, including private investments, owner-occupied and government property and overseas ownerships, to exceed £250 billion. (This is broadly the universe from which the institutional estimate of £110 billion should be drawn.) The value of all residential property exceeds £1,000 billion. While the quoted property sector represents less than 2% of the market capitalisation of the London Stock Exchange, the institutional investor places much more importance on commercial property.

The importance of the UK market in terms of its size is supported by the institutional and structured nature of the UK market. The professional organisation of property services is probably most recognised in the UK, through the history and power of the Royal Institution of Chartered Surveyors and the global expansion of partnerships such as Jones Lang Wootton (now Jones Lang LaSalle) and Richard Ellis (now part of the Insignia group). In addition, the collection and analysis of ownership data is at its most developed in the UK, partly through the work of the Investment Property Databank, now an expanding global business. Finally, the City of London is the world's leading fund management centre (Baum & Lizieri 2000), and this naturally adds to the importance of London as a centre for property investment and the services associated with it.

## Real estate allocations in the UK

UK real estate has been one of three major asset classes which UK insurance companies and pension funds like to invest in, usually directly and less usually through property shares. The cult of the equity has dominated western investment strategy in the 1980s and 1990s to the extent that equities now dominate most institutional portfolios, especially in the US, the UK and Hong Kong. On the other hand, in Germany and some other continental European countries, bonds have always been the largest component of the mixed asset portfolio. In either case, property has been treated as the third asset class.

UK institutions held over 20% of their investments in real estate in 1980. The average is now around 7%. There are two reasons for the decline. First, the returns on property relative to equities were low in the 1980s, so that the allocations to equities have increased as a result of the unmatchable growth in the capital values of equity portfolios. Second, the positive performance characteristics of property, traditionally seen as reasonable return, low risk and a good diversifier, have been challenged.

The experience of property investors in the early 1990s was enough to persuade many of them that it was time to abandon the asset class. Several property companies became bankrupt; many banks developed severe shortfalls in their loan books through exposure to property loans; many householders found they owed more than they had borrowed by developing negative equity; and it became acutely apparent that the liquidity of property was not the same as the liquidity of equities and bonds. Perhaps property owners did not reduce their asking prices quickly enough; certainly it takes longer and costs more to sell property.

Because of this, the investment market in the late 1990s pondered hard over the potential for global securitisation of real estate. Property companies in the UK are neither sufficiently tax-efficient nor appropriately regulated to provide a securitised real estate product capable of being offered to institutional and retail markets. But over the period 1990–98, real estate investment trusts in the USA and authorised property trusts in Australia each saw explosive growth in markets where the legal and regulatory framework permits privately held real estate assets to be transferred into tax-efficient public vehicles. The UK and other markets seemed to be poised for a similar revolution. For reasons discussed below, this did not happen; instead the number of private real estate vehicles boomed. This is discussed further below.

## Real estate investment: the rationale

Real estate may be acquired for many purposes other than investment. For businesses, property is a factor of production; for human beings, it provides food and shelter; for investors, it provides a stream of income. Broadly speaking, a distinction may be made between property owned for occupation (although there may be a simultaneous investment function performed by that property) and property owned for investment per se.

Real estate in the UK owned as an investment may be either freehold, connoting effective superior ownership, or leasehold, connoting an inferior form of ownership subject to a superior landlord. The superior landlord may itself be either a leaseholder or a freeholder. In a period of inflation a freehold property investment may be expected to show a profit on resale. Obsolescence may contribute to a declining (although difficult to measure) building component value, so that refurbishment or redevelopment may be necessary to maintain performance, but the general trend of value is normally expected to be upward.

Property is differentiated from other assets by four main factors. First, it is a physical asset, requiring maintenance and suffering obsolescence. Second, its income delivery is governed by lease contracts. Third, its supply side is inelastic and is regulated by both central and local government policy. Finally, it is not traded in a centralised market, and as every property is unique, it is valued consequently without the benefit of direct reference to quoted trading prices for identical properties.

### Depreciation

The problem of building depreciation or obsolescence of freehold buildings should not, as has usually been the case in the property world, be understated. Poorly designed buildings located in low land value areas will produce a more rapid fall-off in performance than carefully restored and refurbished buildings in, say, the City of London. Not to distinguish between these vastly different investment types is very dangerous.

The lease contract

The income produced by a property investment is in the form of rent, which will normally be received at regular intervals, quarterly in advance being typical in the UK. Against the rent received must be set operating expenses to the extent that those operating expenses cannot be recovered from tenants. Operating expenses are incurred both frequently (management, service provision) and infrequently (repairs).

The payment of rent is governed by the provisions of the lease. The UK has begun to move away from the previously standard 25-year lease, which appears to favour UK landlords and to suggest their peculiar strength in the market.

The UK lease of commercial property usually fixes rents for five-year intervals with upward-only reviews, while continental European leases often have rents indexed annually. Longer North American leases may have rents tied to the rate of inflation or, more often, for retail tenants, to the tenant's turnover; this is rare in the UK. The rental pattern in the typical prime UK investment property is therefore stepped upwards (in a period of inflation or growth) at five-yearly intervals.

Rents at each review point are renegotiated in line with the open market rent. It is arguable that market rents (ERVs; estimated rental values) reflect the fixed nature of the review period and are higher than annually reviewable rents would be. Similarly, longer review periods will attract even higher rents.

In summary, the investment provides a varying income depending on rental values, which are themselves a product of the demand for use of that type of property and the supply of alternatives. Fluctuation in the rental income is reduced by a long lease and fixed level of rent between reviews; upward-only reviews will produce, at worst, a minimum level of income, assuming no tenant default.

The UK government has recently begun to question the validity of the upward-only rent review (discussed later in this chapter). Several commentators are convinced that it will disappear in the near future. Owners are increasingly able to understand the financial implications of varying rent terms, and will as a result be more willing to grant break clauses, two-way reviews and other variations from the standard lease in return for an appropriate adjustment to the rent paid. Equally, the option value which is provided by the upward-only rent review will be recognised by a second group of owners.

### Planning and supply

Unlike equities, the supply of property is regulated to some extent by central government. Unlike gilts, the spatial nature of property as an asset means that local government also has a say in the supply side. Unlike both, supply is inelastic in response to economic conditions. This has several effects, most important of which is the exaggeration of the well-known property cycle and the occasional boom and bust.

The mid- to late-1980s is a case in point. A change in central government policy towards a pro-development stance coupled with available finance and positive demand-side factors encouraged investors and developers to create more buildings, especially in the Central London office market. The lead time from conception to completion of a large office building can be three years or more. Between 1986 and 1990 the economy moved from boom to recession, and in 1990 the pipeline of office supply was at an all-time high. The result was a severe crash in rents, from £60 per sq ft to £25 per sq ft in the City.

## The sectors: principal characteristics

Commercial property risk and return characteristics vary from property to property and from sector to sector. What follows is a brief description of the qualities of the major UK sectors.

### Shop units

There are over 500,000 shops in the UK and thousands of shopping parades. There are about 500 locations which attract a reasonable spread of multiple retailers. However, there are only 100–200 'prime' retail locations, typically with at least 100 shops each and minimum catchment populations of 50,000 plus. High-street shop unit values typically range from £100,000 to £5 million and offer the potential for effective diversification.

As single tenant investments they are straightforward to manage. They depreciate very little, as much of the value resides in the land. Supply is restricted by the importance of the location, so owners are protected from competition in many cases. Nonetheless, smaller high streets have suffered in recent years as shoppers have sought greater shopping choice and convenience in out-of-town retail warehouses and shopping centres.

## Retail warehouses and parks

Highly popular with the price-conscious, time-poor, car-borne shopper in the 1990s, retail warehouses were the best performing sector for investors through most of the 1990s. Planning limitations usually restrict sales to bulk goods (DIY, furniture, carpets, white goods).

Single units have lost popularity at the expense of retail parks, typically of 75,000–150,000 sq ft (£10–30 million capital value). The few retail parks combining areas of 200,000 sq ft and more with open A1 (unrestricted retail) planning consents can become open-air shopping centres and command much higher rents. Rents in Fosse Park, Leicestershire, the most notable example, are now 10 times the rate of stand-alone DIY units in many locations.

Good parking and highway access are vital. Recent poor performance may be explained by excessive buying pressure though the mid-1990s and general doubts about the retail sector in the midst of the e-commerce revolution. However, out-of-town retail planning consents have become increasingly difficult to obtain, supporting investor interest.

## Shopping centres

About 600 shopping centres have been built since the 1960s. They are mostly in town centres, typically providing 20–60 additional retail units. In-town shopping centre values range between £20 million and £100 million.

The earlier shopping centres were often open to the elements. The later ones are in the main covered and climate controlled. A new generation of 1 million sq ft centres such as Metro Centre (Gateshead, outside Newcastle), Lakeside (M25 east of London, north of the Thames), Bluewater Park (M25 east of London, south of the Thames), Merry Hill (Birmingham) and Meadowhall (Sheffield), all on the edge of town, have all been successful and command values of £500 million–£1,000 million. All have excellent road communications, creating enormous shopping catchment populations of one million plus.

Refurbishment, depreciation and service charges for common parts are big issues for shopping centre owners and their tenants. Specialist managers are necessary to manage the shopping mix and to extract full value from the centre; each centre is a major business in its own right. Because lot sizes can be as high as £1 billion, diversification is a challenge, although limited partnerships have recently taken a greater share of the market and offer some divisibility.

## Offices and business parks

Traditional town centre offices have been the worst performing UK property sector over 30 years. There is an enormous range of lot sizes. Outside London, only the biggest and best buildings are worth more than £20 million. In Central London, there is a reasonably active market for lots of £100 million plus.

Depreciation and obsolescence have badly affected performance as occupiers' needs have changed and flexibility of layout and services has become the key issue. Many of the earlier buildings have been incapable of providing air-conditioning and raised floors for computer cabling.

Some business parks have begun to command higher rents than town centre offices; time has yet to tell how robust this sector will be, but a movement towards the much higher levels of out-of-town or suburban offices common in the US is clearly under way.

## Industrials and distribution warehouses

Traditional industrial estates have historically performed best late in the cycle: strong performance following strong retail performance was a typical pattern for the 1970s–1990s. Many older industrial buildings have shown surprising resilience to obsolescence and are still lettable several decades after construction. The perceived value of the industrial sector has increased with greater recognition of the lower risk to total returns associated with higher initial income.

About 300 'high bay' distribution warehouses have been built since the end of the 1980s. They typically have floorplates of 100,000–300,000 sq ft and eaves heights of 12–25 m. They have attracted industrial investors because they offer reasonably large lot sizes (typically £5 million–£25 million), new highly specified buildings and tenants with good covenant strength. Distribution warehouses have generally failed to produce competitive total returns as low initial yields have combined with low levels of rental growth. Rents have been held down by just-in-time delivery methods and the resulting collapse in inventory levels; a ready supply of land outside the South East; and the willingness of developers to work on narrow profit margins due in part to the abundance of pre-lets. This attitude is partly explained by the lack of speculative risk and the short period for which capital has been deployed.

## Leisure schemes

Leisure parks, normally anchored by a multi-screen cinema, a themed restaurant, a fast-food restaurant and a mixture of bowling, discotheque and other facilities, became a popular investment in the 1990s. However, there are still less than 50 complete leisure parks and the schemes have been dominated by a handful of developers.

Many funds have sought an exposure to the sector through co-investment vehicles and others are planned. Overall, however, the size of the sector makes it relatively unimportant.

## Residential

UK allocations to this sector are tiny but growing. Traditionally excluded from the institutional market due to legislative risks and small lot sizes, residential property is now the subject of around 10 specialist vehicles for institutional investment (OPC 2002). Returns have been high in recent years but falling.

# The vehicles available for property investment

While many larger investors choose to invest by assembling portfolios of buildings (segregated portfolios) or by appointing managers to do the same (separate accounts), smaller investors may choose indirect investment in property through the purchase of property shares or by participating in pooled property vehicles.

Several problems are associated with property investment. These include illiquidity, the bias of pension fund minimum solvency requirements against relatively illiquid assets, poor comparative returns during the 1980s and 1990s, and a lack of trust in property return indices.

In addition, while institutional property investment in the UK has traditionally been effected through the segregated or separate account, through which an insurance company or pension fund will invest in property assets which it owns 100%, the scale of investment required to achieve diversification is a tremendous barrier to entry. Due to a shift in attitude towards real estate and improvements in market liquidity, and to the diversification efficiencies which result, indirect property investment vehicles have increased in popularity in recent years.

An apparently obvious solution is the use of liquid traded property vehicles in place of the direct asset. Many countries have their own unique vehicles, such as the Australian listed property trust and the US real estate investment trust (REIT). These vehicles may have the primary objective of reducing tax, of achieving liquidity or of aligning the interests of the investors and the managers. They may exist to permit co-mingling of investors, or may be special-purpose vehicles for the use of one investor acting alone. Their use has multiplied in recent years as a result of the continued search for liquidity and the success of REITs, the increase in cross-border investment activity, often more attractive in a co-mingled format, and the generally more punitive impact of tax on foreign investors (but see College of Estate Management 2000).

The success of the REIT in the US has prompted many investors and managers to encourage the creation of a similar quoted, tax-transparent product in the UK. Unfortunately, the UK government has made it clear that it regards such a development as tax negative.

In addition, investing in property shares has tended to deliver performance which is linked to the performance of the stock market and fails to provide the diversification advantages of property. Recent work by ABN-AMRO also suggests that returns have been very similar as for direct property investment, but for much greater risk. Hence, this means of investing in property has become less popular in recent years.

Attention has instead focused on a variety of other legal structures which are capable of providing a means for investment in domestic or international real estate. Private property vehicles (PPVs) include limited partnerships

(LPs) and to a lesser extent property unit trusts (PUTs), private corporate vehicles, offshore corporate structures and some others.

In addition, much work is being expended in the development of new vehicles to provide this solution, such as offshore property unit trusts and property index certificates. The future appears to hold much promise in particular for the limited partnership and property unit trust, both onshore and offshore.

## Property company shares

Securitisation may result in the longer-term possibility that real estate investment becomes either venture capital in its riskier form or an industry sector in its developed form. The UK has been no exception in its development of securitised and other indirect forms of property ownership. The packaging of listed securities into funds which provide exposure to a country's property sector, or to a region or a sector, gathered pace in the late 1990s. The growth of property share benchmarks such as those provided by Salomon Smith Barney and Global Property Research and the development of global and regional property share funds (Jupiter, Henderson, ABN-AMRO) were signs of a maturing market.

However, for the supply of property share funds to grow requires growth in the number and size of listed property companies. In 2000, market pressure in the UK was operating in the opposite direction, as large discounts of share price to net asset value made it more attractive to take property companies private and exploit the property values in other ownership formats whose performance is unlinked to the stock market.

Over the longest time series available, property companies have outperformed direct property investment by around 1.5% each year. Both have significantly underperformed the UK equity market.

The volatility of property company shares has, however, been much higher than that of the direct property market. On an annual basis, the standard deviation of returns has been only 12% on direct property compared with 37% on property company shares.

In addition, the performance of property company shares has not mirrored that of direct property. The correlation of return between direct property and property company shares has been only 20% compared with a correlation between property company shares and the UK equity market of 60%.

In other words, UK property company shares look like equities, and a poor substitute for direct UK property.

These relationships are not fixed: the result of any analysis is subject to the time period used. For example, the relationship between property company shares and the UK equity market was very strong in the 1970s, while the relationship between property company shares and the direct property market has been stronger since 1980. This has been the defining variable which has seriously damaged the property company sector as a home for long-term institutional property investment. Meanwhile, the PPV market has boomed, led by the limited partnership.

## Limited partnerships

Conceived by the Limited Partnership Act of 1907, this vehicle has been in common usage in other investment markets and industries, but has only been regularly heard of in the UK property market since the 1990s. The limited partnership enables a pool of investors to invest together in one or more assets. The number of partners was limited to 20 but is now unlimited. While at least one, the general partner, must have unlimited liability, the other partners may be limited. The investment is, therefore, passive and, importantly, the investment itself is tax transparent.

It is common practice that limited partnerships have a predetermined lifespan, usually varying between six and ten years. There is a statement of intent, when the partnerships are established, that at the end of the period the partnership will be wound up and the assets disposed of, although this need not be the case if the partners vote to extend the vehicle life.

Limited partnerships can be complex in their management structures, but a simplified description of a typical structure is as follows. A general partner (GP) will usually be created by the originator of the concept and/or will act as lead investor. The GP may be a special purpose company owned by more than one lead investor, and will have unlimited liability. The GP will usually appoint an operator, required by the Financial Services Act of 1986 to be an FSA regulated body, which will be responsible for a defined set of administrative functions.

In establishing the pool of capital required, the GP may appoint a promoter to raise capital from limited partners (LPs); in some cases, the promoter may be the originator of the concept and seek a GP to act as lead investors. LPs will contribute capital and may form an advisory board, but cannot be seen to be making decisions without losing their limited liability status. In rare examples, LPs may contribute non-executives to the GP.

The GP will also appoint an investment manager or an asset manager; in turn, the investment or asset manager may appoint a property manager. The relationships of promoter, operator, GP and asset manager can be subtly or obviously connected: in some cases, the same financial services group will provide all of these functions.

The limited partnership structure is regulated but simpler to operate than the unit trust (see below). It has recently been successful in attracting investors, usually into specialist or single property investments. Limited partnerships are tax-neutral or tax-transparent vehicles, meaning that the vehicle itself does not attract taxation, and partners are treated exactly as if they owned the assets of the limited partnership directly. This creates an enormous advantage for the vehicle, which has become increasingly popular in the UK as a vehicle for co-mingled property ownership.

Although the legislation for limited partnerships has been in existence since the passing of the Limited Partnership Act of 1907, conspicuously few were established as a vehicle for property prior to 1997. Following a model established by Dusco for the UK Prime Limited Partnership in 1992, there has been a proliferation in their number to the extent that they are now a well-established and significant part of the UK investment market. Over £12 billion was invested in limited partnerships in the 1997–2002 period alone. The ownership of Bluewater Park, for example, a £1 billion shopping centre developed by LendLease, was converted to a limited partnership in 1998 and partnership shares sold to investors.

The main disadvantages are limited liquidity, with stakes tradable only on a matched bargain basis, and limited ownership spread. Limited partnership shares may become tradable on secondary market platforms, in which case this vehicle may become enormously popular and a true revolution in UK property ownership would then be set in train, similar to the REIT revolution in the US. Figure 10.1 illustrates the growth of this market.

Oxford Property Consultants offers the leading database of these vehicles and lists 95 current vehicles, with a mean number of investors of 2.3, a median number of investors of 3, 45 managers and 101 investors. It should also be stated that there are many more limited partnerships, most of which are not collective investment schemes as such but convenient ways of sharing property ownership (joint ventures).

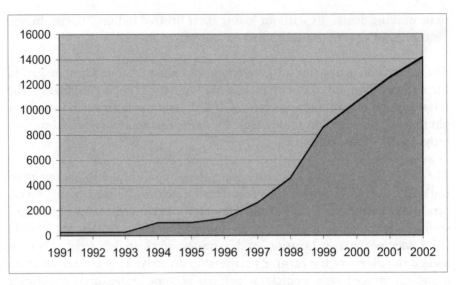

**Fig. 10.1**    The UK LP market (£bn, gross asset values). *Source: Oxford Property Consultants (2002).*

The gross asset value of all the limited partnerships presently equates to approximately £14 billion. There is almost £4 billion of gross asset value in the top 10 funds (see Table 10.1).

Limited partnerships do not appear to favour particular types of property over others, but a key theme is that in many cases a fund will often be sharply focused on a single specialist property type. Examples include Airport Hotels Partnership, Apreit V Nursing Homes and MWB's leisure funds. Some are more similar to property unit trusts, diversified partnerships including Lionbrook Property Partnership, and the Threadneedle Tandem Property Fund.

**Table 10.1**    The 10 largest UK limited partnerships.

| Limited partnership | Gross asset value (£m) |
| --- | --- |
| UBS Triton Property Fund | 587 |
| Industrial Property Investment Fund | 461 |
| LendLease Retail Partnership | 458 |
| Ashtenne Industrial Fund | 350 |
| Matrix Portfolio No 1 LP | 350 |
| Mall Limited Partnership | 330 |
| Junction Limited Partnership | 328 |
| Basingstoke Investment Partnership | 300 |
| Bedfont Lakes Limited Partnership | 300 |
| UK Prime Limited Partnership | 300 |

*Source: Oxford Property Consultants (2002).*

The lifespan of limited partnership vehicles appears in many cases to be between five and ten years; however, many have the built-in option of being extended for additional periods. An extension is usually possible only where there is a majority vote of 75% or more by the partners. Recent performance appears to have been better than the IPD universe. Specialist funds in the universe include LPs, and specialist funds have outperformed each year for the last four years. DTZ suggests that three-quarters of insurance companies and a third of pension funds have invested in real estate through limited partnerships.

> Typically, the proportion of property assets held in LPs was 6%, although the range varies markedly. It is well known that a number of institutions including Equitable Life and Barclays Property Investment (now Aberdeen) hold more than a quarter of their property assets in LPs.

DTZ (2002)

## Property unit trusts

Many smaller professional investors use what are known as collective investment schemes or co-mingled funds. Typically managed by fund managers, these are pooled funds that allow smaller insurance companies and pension funds to achieve diversification without the high fixed costs and illiquidity of holding direct property. The main type of pooled fund is the property unit trust (PUT).

Property unit trusts are the main vehicle used by pension funds to gain access to diversified portfolios of UK real estate, in a form which allows replication of direct market performance characteristics. They are unlisted, the unit prices are determined by valuations, and liquidity is limited to a small amount of secondary market trading activity and the guarantee that managers will buy and sell units, albeit at spreads which replicate the cost of buying and selling direct property.

Property unit trusts are usually tax-exempt and unauthorised (marketable only to pension funds) and, in some cases, offshore funds. Balanced PUTs generally hold a wide mix of property assets, by type and location. Specialist property unit trusts focus upon particular types of property, or on particular geographic regions. Participating PUTs are members of the Association of Property Unit Trusts (APUT) and are bound by its voluntary code of conduct.

Unauthorised property unit trusts (UPUTs) are tax-free for qualifying pension funds. While they have to invest in domestic property to protect this status, they can be established offshore to appeal to international investors. In addition, specialist unit trusts are increasingly being established. Leicester's Fosse Park, the highest rent out-of-town retail park in the UK, is held in an offshore property unit trust vehicle for the benefit of a mix of domestic and international investors.

The investment performance of property unit trusts has been similar to that of direct property. For example, between 1979 and 1994 (see Table 10.2) the total return on direct property was 11.1% each year. The total return on property unit trusts compared favourably at 11.8%, and their risk had been slightly lower. The absence of large Central London offices from most unit trusts in the early 1990s, when these assets severely underperformed the market, explains a large part of this. The correlation between property unit trusts and the direct property market over this period was higher than 90%.

There is a small secondary market dealing with the transfer of units on a matched bargain basis, so that the liquidity of the property unit trust market may be a little better than the liquidity of direct, but liquidity is still limited by three factors. First, the current property unit trust market is worth only around £5 billion, 5% of the direct institutional market. Second, property unit trust managers typically trade only on a quarterly basis. Third, property units are ultimately as illiquid as the underlying asset.

The open-ended nature of property unit trusts means that investors can deal directly with the manager rather than with each other through a secondary market. This can be problematic in rising and falling markets. Flows of capital into and out of the vehicle can create greater difficulties for the manager than rising and falling share or unit prices would create for the managers of a closed-ended vehicle such as a property company.

**Table 10.2**   Total return and standard deviation: direct property and property unit trusts, 1979–94 (%).

|                      | Return | Risk |
| -------------------- | ------ | ---- |
| Direct property      | 11.1   | 9.8  |
| Property unit trusts | 11.8   | 8.3  |

*Source: IPD/Watson Wyatt Worldwide.*

Particular difficulties were evidenced in 1990–93, when net sales of units led to forced sales of property, damaging the performance of some unit trusts. This in turn led to more investors wishing to exit, forcing further sales of units and then forced sales of properties in a vicious downward spiral.

In strong markets, intense performance pressure can be placed on managers by net inflows of cash. Managers are forced into a position where they wish to invest quickly, but only in attractively priced assets.

Despite the problems caused by the open-ended structure, property unit trusts remain popular. In general they behave like direct property. Liquidity is not significantly better than for direct property, but property unit trusts are ideal for small funds due primarily to the professional management and diversification benefits of a pooled vehicle.

Property unit trusts can be complex. A supervisory board may be appointed to represent what is usually a larger pool of investors (the LendLease Retail Partnership, the LP with the largest number of investors, has 19 investors; The Schroder Exempt Property Unit Trust, the largest PUT, has over 600). The supervisory board will appoint a trustee to operate the fund, and an investment manager to buy and sell assets and act as issuer and redeemer of units. The promoter or originator of a property unit trust will usually be the investment manager, who will then appoint the supervisory board and effectively appoint the trustee; but there have been recent examples of supervisory boards terminating their investment manager's contract and appointing a new manager. This is different from the limited partnership model. The general partner, which cannot be removed, appoints the asset manager, often a connected company.

The unauthorised property unit trust market has been in existence since the 1960s and at present contains 40 trusts. Roughly 75% are based onshore in the UK, with the remaining 10 being offshore trusts (located principally in Jersey) for taxation benefits. The onshore-based UPUT market has a current market capitalisation of £6.8 billion, in comparison to the offshore market, which is less than one-third the size at £2.1 billion. The onshore UPUT market also contains a combination of funds ranging from those that special-ise in one particular form of real estate like the Electricity Supply Pension Scheme UK Forestry Fund, to those which have a more balanced portfolio of commercial property like the Schroder Exempt Property Unit Trust, with a gross asset value of £1.2 billion. The offshore UPUT market on the other hand contains a much greater proportion of funds specialising in one particular area of real estate like the Chiswick Park Unit Trust, Deutsche Bank's UK Industrial fund or the Schroder Retail Park Unit Trust.

The Financial Services (Regulated Schemes) Regulations 1991 led to the authorisation of unit trusts as property funds. The authorised property unit trusts (APUTs) were designed primarily for retail investors, giving them a medium whereby they could invest in units of a collective property fund offering a relatively good degree of tax transparency. The structure has had very limited impact, evidenced by there being only two present in the market today. The Norwich and Liberty funds have a combined value approaching £400 million.

## Managed funds

Managed funds are the insurance companies' equivalent of the pension funds' property unit trust. They are usually managed by insurance-based fund managers. Their performance is tracked in regular reports issued by HSBC and APUT. There are presently 36 UK managed funds, which have a total combined capital value of £114.5 billion (OPC 2002).

## Property investment trusts

Investment trusts are generally restricted regarding the proportion of their assets that can be held in property. As a result, despite industry demands for the liquidity that a quoted vehicle provides, this has not been a popular format for holding property. There are presently only three property investment trusts (PITs) in existence in the UK: TR Property, Wigmore and Trust of Property Shares. The TR Property Investment Trust is a rare example of a large property investment trust, with a market capitalisation of over £300 million.

Property investment trusts are listed investment trust companies which specialise in property investment, primarily by holding portfolios of listed property shares. Property investment trusts have the ability to invest directly in property, but direct investment is restricted in order to retain the investment trust status of the fund for tax purposes.

## Property index certificates

Property index certificates, launched by Barclays in the mid-1990s, are derivative investments whose buyers are provided with synthetic returns matching the annual return on the IPD annual index. As in the gilt or bond market, the buyer pays a capital sum which is either par value or a price representing a premium or discount to par depending on demand in the market. The issuer provides a quarterly-in-arrear income based on (but not exactly the same as) the IPD annual income return, and following expiry the par value is repaid together with a large proportion, but not all, of the capital appreciation in the IPD index.

While performance is directly linked to the capital performance of the IPD annual universe, under normal circumstances property index certificates lock in marginal underperformance of the IPD annual index due to the management costs charged. Correlation with the direct market is nonetheless very high, and in a multi-asset or international context these instruments provide the pure diversification benefits of UK property. However, liquidity is low due to the small size of market and the lack of a true secondary market.

## Special-purpose corporate vehicles and cross-border structures

For a variety of reasons connected with financing, accounting and tax, many corporate vehicles have been created as special-purpose vehicles for holding property assets off balance sheet. In addition, some property funds have been created in offshore corporate form, but usually for the purpose of holding overseas assets in a tax-efficient way. Examples of offshore structures include Delaware Limited Liability Partnerships and Limited Liability Companies, Luxembourg SOCARPIs, and others.

The company is a popular format for the ownership of both domestic and international property. Its prime advantage is to allow complete flexibility in the size and quantity of the number of investors in the vehicle; in addition, it introduces the possibility of liquidity if the vehicle is offered in the public markets. In the UK, however, tax is paid on the capital gains made by UK companies and on the profits made by these companies. In addition, tax is paid by shareholders on the dividends distributed by companies, so the conversion of freehold ownership into a corporate structure introduces an extra layer of tax (College of Estate Management 2000). This is more of a problem for taxpayers, typically overseas owners or private individuals and corporates, than it is for institutional investors. However, international institutions may be caught in this net.

**Table 10.3**  After-tax returns on equity.

| | |
|---|---|
| Property cost | £2,000,000 |
| Loan | £1,500,000 |
| Tax on profits/gains | 35% |
| Interest rate | 7.00% |
| Growth | 2.50% |
| Gross running yield | 7.50% |
| Gross total return | 10.00% |
| Return on equity after tax | 12.35% |

The most common means of addressing this disadvantage is to reduce double income tax as far as possible by minimising profits and dividends. This is most commonly achieved by introducing borrowing, so that the interest charge will be set against rental income to reduce annual profit. This may have the added advantage, depending on the relationship between interest rates and running yields, of introducing a positive leverage or gearing effect, so that returns to equity after tax may exceed total returns on the vehicle as a whole after tax and even in some cases before tax (see Table 10.3).

A second means of reducing income tax is to introduce equity in the form of debt. This can be achieved by issuing investors with loan notes instead of, or alongside, share certificates. Tax on interest received may then be treated differently.

Established offshore, corporate vehicles can be highly tax-efficient and hence attract international investors. Companies set up in the Channel Islands, for example, can sell property free of all UK capital gains tax. For this reason and others, the UK is seen to some extent as a tax haven for international investors.

Opportunity (private equity) funds

These are special-purpose vehicles, usually in a corporate format and often involving complicated cross-border structures. They are always closed ended, and usually limited life co-mingled funds. This type of investment vehicle was commonly used for domestic investment in the US in the 1980s. For many reasons the format became largely discredited, but the access provided to difficult markets for foreign investors, tax efficiency and a lack of alternatives have all helped to overcome resistance to the vehicle.

This is now a popular medium for international property investment. Over 60% of the value of the European private vehicle market is US opportunity fund money (OPC 2003). The returns advertised are high, usually in excess of 15% on equity. It can be purpose-made and therefore tax-effective for certain investor domiciles and types. Gearing is common, at levels up to 60–80%, both for performance and tax purposes. The fund manager often has an investment alongside clients and includes a performance element in the fee charged.

This vehicle has carried much of US 1990s investment in markets such as Poland, Thailand and China. While there are many flaws in this investment format – the limited life format and its lack of liquidity being two – its main advantage is that it clearly accesses the diversification potential of private real estate.

Much European property investment utilises this type of vehicle (OPC 2003). It raises some interesting questions. A UK life fund may typically consider this type of vehicle in allocating cash to international property investment. Its decision may be based on the returns available after tax on equity, compared with the gross returns available in their domestic market. Its domestic investments are unlikely to be geared, and the false comparison of similar returns on low-risk domestic investment and high-risk, highly geared or levered international investment may be tempting.

Fee structures in such corporate vehicles, modelled on US private equity (venture capital) funds, typically attempt to align the interests of investor and manager by rewarding the manager on a performance basis. The manager may typically charge a base fee calculated as a percentage of the value of the assets managed, and additionally take a proportion (say 20%) of the total return over a minimum hurdle (say 15%).

Real estate investment trusts

The US real estate investment trust (REIT) is a tax-transparent, quoted vehicle which is forced to distribute the majority of its earnings and to limit its gearing. This provides the features sought by many investors as the ideal property vehicle, providing pure property performance features in a liquid form. Its growth in the 1990s from a total market capitalisation of around $8 billion to something over $175 billion demonstrates this view.

This appears at first sight to be the perfect liquid property vehicle, but the UK government has made it clear that it is unlikely to be given the required tax status in the UK as it is regarded by the government as tax negative for government.

## Commercial property owners

Insurance companies, pension funds and other investing institutions hold over £90 billion, or around four times the aggregate value of the quoted property sector, in commercial property as part of their investment portfolios – typically 3–10% of their total assets. They have gained importance over recent decades at the expense of the traditional property owner. Recently, high net worth individuals and the so-called retail investor have been added to the list of buyers of property investment products.

### Decline of traditional owners

The structure of ownership (or, more accurately, control) of UK commercial property has been changing in both obvious and subtle ways over the last 25 years.

First, the combined forces of privatisation and globalisation have had their intended and inevitable impact. The traditional owners – the great private landed estates, such as the Church, the Crown, the Oxbridge Colleges, central and local government – have, as a whole, lost relative influence, while overseas owners have increased their presence. To take an example, the overseas ownership of City of London office buildings increased from around 3–5% to 20–25% over the period from 1972 to 1998 (Baum & Lizieri 2000), while the proportion owned by the City Corporation and the Worshipful Companies fell markedly.

Second, there has been a less apparent shift in management away from the insurance companies and pension funds which were so dominant in 1980, when property made up as much as 22% and 12% respectively of their total assets, towards fund managers and property companies (the distinctions between which are becoming increasingly blurred). Through the 1980s the institutional investor dominated the higher levels of the industry, controlling the larger transaction business and (in collaboration with chartered surveying businesses) driving best practice and forming industry lobbies such as the Investment Property Forum. In the 1990s the effects of privatisation and outsourcing reached down to the institutions. There has recently been a restructuring of their investment and property divisions, with the result that the power base now lies within specialist fund management operations, which may themselves be owned by what used to be insurance companies and are now financial services groups.

## Property companies

Property companies have been successful at surviving two severe challenges to their existence, in 1973–75 and in 1991–93. In both property recessions many famous property companies became insolvent and disappeared. The extremely strong performance of the stock market in the 1980s and again since 1993, coupled with a growing demand for liquid (easily traded) property investment vehicles, has provided some support to the albeit poorly performing share prices of the survivors. However, the weighting of property companies as a proportion of the stock market has declined significantly since 1989 and suffered greatly again in the technology boom of the late 1990s. Nonetheless, the property company sector includes well over 100 companies and the largest UK property owner of all, Land Securities, is a FTSE 100 company.

## Overseas owners

Over the last 15 years the UK, alongside the US, has been one of the few countries capable of attracting a wide range of overseas property investors. Most have been particularly attracted to the City office market, home to more international banks than anywhere else in the world. The City property stock was almost wholly domestically owned until the 'Big Bang' in the mid-1980s, after which successive waves of Japanese, American and German capital have taken levels of overseas ownership from 2% to something approaching 25% (Baum & Lizieri 2000). London is a major international property market, and the financial services output of the City accounts for some 5% of UK GDP; the importance of the City property market alone to the national economy is substantial.

The category of overseas owners includes property companies, US-based REITs, insurance companies, pension funds, German open-ended funds and others. They are almost certain to continue their recent expansion into the UK commercial property market. The more committed participants in recent years have included:

- German open-ended investment funds (e.g. CGI, DESPA, DEGI and DIFA);

- German insurance companies and pension funds;

- Pension funds and property companies from the Netherlands (e.g. ABP, PGGM, Rodamco and Wereldhave);

- Sovereign investors such as the Abu Dhabi Investment Authority and the Government of Singapore Investment Corporation;

- US-based funds looking for international diversification and/or higher returns at the riskier or development ends of the UK market (e.g. Blackstone and Security Capital).

The historic compartmentalisation of real estate into domestic property markets is unlikely to continue for long. The City of London office market provides an excellent example (Baum & Lizieri 2000).

### Family offices, high net worth individuals and the retail market

Family offices (the self-administered family trust money manager for extremely wealthy families), high net worth investors and the 'man and woman in the street' are increasingly committed to property as an investment. Many recent vehicles have been launched with these capital sources in mind. Continued inventiveness is pushing these structures closer to the listed tax-exempt format, but not yet in a standard manner. There is an element of circularity here as Bill Gates becomes the new Duke of Westminster, traditional owner of serious amounts of private property, and professional footballers club together to buy London office buildings.

## Property fund managers and advisers

### Institutional fund managers

The ownership and management of institutional investment property is becoming increasingly concentrated, and the last two years have seen a major shake-up of insurance companies which invest in property. Consolidation has occurred due to rationalisation in financial services provision and the resulting economies of scale available to fund management groups. Most institutions with less than £200 million of property have effectively closed down their direct property activities and either sold the portfolio or outsourced the responsibility to another fund manager.

In large institutions, for managerial and regulatory reasons there has been an increasing tendency to separate fund management as a business in its own right, even where the resulting business manages assets solely or mainly for the parent or sister company's own policy holders. Increasingly, insurance-based fund management businesses are responsible for a variety of funds (a life fund, their own group pension fund, a unit-linked fund and one or two limited partnerships). Examples of the largest insurance-based players include Aberdeen, Henderson Global Investors, Morley, AXA, Prudential Property Investment Managers, Threadneedle and Scottish Widows.

Here are two typical examples. Prudential started life as an insurance company. It formed an investment management business (Prudential Portfolio Managers) in the 1980s, which soon absorbed the property management business. Prudential is now a financial services group that owns a bank (Egg), other financial services providers (Scottish Amicable, M&G), a fund manager (now called Prudential M&G) and a property investment management business. Prudential Property Investment Managers now manages over £11 billion of commercial property assets in the UK.

Henderson Global Investors was established in 1932 as Henderson Administration to administer the estate of Alexander Henderson, later Lord Farringdon. It was sufficiently successful to take on external business, and by the early 1970s gained a stock-market listing as an investment manager. Meanwhile, Australian Mutual Provident, an Australian insurance company, had grown its own UK insurance business (AMP UK), acquired two UK insurers (Pearl and London Life) and formed a joint venture with Virgin to create a UK-based financial services provider (Virgin Direct). A fund management subsidiary (AMP Asset Management, or AMPAM) was formed; the assets of AMP UK, Pearl, London Life and Virgin Direct were managed by AMPAM; AMP then acquired Henderson Investors. Now the AMP Group, a financial services organisation, owns several insurance companies, a pension provider (NPI), part of a retail financial services brand and a global fund manager. If property service providers wish to do business with Pearl, they need to contact Henderson Global Investors, which now manages in excess of £4 billion of UK and international property funds from London.

Changes such as this have also affected pension funds. For example, Hermes, a fund management company owned by the British Telecom Pension Scheme, manages the assets of both the Post Office and British Telecom pension schemes, which include more than £4 billion of commercial UK property. Towards the end of 2000 Hermes also took over management of the former Hill Samuel Property Unit Trust, now the Hermes Property Unit Trust.

## Property companies

The poor performance of property companies in the 1990s left the majority trading at a discount to net asset value in early 2000. The result was the taking private of several large companies, including MEPC, and a drive to diversify activity out of asset accumulation towards an income-based business whose valuation might be less punitive. Pressure grew to add more fee income through asset management without extending the capital invested: this naturally led to property companies seeing the promotion of LPs as an attractive alternative to value-destructive equity-raising. Hence a group of property companies has entered the fund management business through the LP explosion.

## Property consultants

Lawyers, auditors and tax advisers, investment consultants and actuaries and lenders form the backroom community which orchestrates the UK property investment market. Many chartered surveyors and property consultants have been pushed out of property investment management and into support functions – asset and property management, valuation, research, facilities management and brokerage.

The chartered surveying partnership went through significant change in the 1980s and 1990s: financial services regulations forced the separation of some corporate finance arms in the late 1980s, and globalisation and resulting transfers of ownership from partnerships to multinational corporations created more flexible and multi-faceted property consultancies in the mid to late 1990s. Naturally, these businesses (largely excluded from direct involvement in the corporate finance activities of the public quoted property sector) have also taken part in the PPV market, especially in capital raising and promotion.

These developments have produced a proliferation of vehicles, a more complex industry structure and a confusion of ownership and management. The traditional UK property service providers, the chartered surveying partnerships, have been severely challenged by these changes. While (prior to the recent explosion of Internet-based property listing services) there has been no serious threat to the transaction-based business of the traditional surveyor/agent, investment management is another story.

First, fund managers have access to large sums of capital for business development or for co-investment in large blocks of property alongside clients, which traditional partnerships cannot do. Second, the Financial Services Act of 1986 imposed discipline on the securities businesses of financial services groups. While the regulations do not apply to property, they nonetheless suggest the possibility of unmanaged conflicts of interest among the traditional service providers, which may earn the majority of their fees from transaction business while acting as investment managers.

Even so, many of these businesses have been successful in maintaining their own fund management operations by creating their own 'Chinese walls' (Jones Lang LaSalle, for example, now being a top three property fund manager by assets under management, separately branded as LaSalle Investment Management). Some now have access to significant capital, but this has been at the cost of their independence. An epidemic of takeovers in the mid-1990s resulted in the sale or merger of many of the most respected chartered surveyors to or with US-based real estate businesses. As examples, Jones Lang Wootton merged with LaSalle, Richard Ellis and St Quintin were sold to Insignia, Hillier Parker was sold to Coldwell Banker, and Healey and Baker was sold to Cushman and Wakefield.

## Professional organisations

The 1980s and 1990s saw rapid growth in the number of non-profit organisations seeking to represent the interests of owners, managers and funds within the ever-changing UK and European property industries. The changes have been driven by shifts in focus away from national towards international, and away from industry-wide groupings towards specialist groupings.

Formerly dominant within the UK property industry, the Royal Institution of Chartered Surveyors (RICS), representing 80,000 professionally qualified service providers, and the British Property Federation (BPF), representing property owners, have been joined by several other UK and European interest groups.

Loosely associated with the RICS, the Investment Property Forum has grown from its origins in the late 1980s as a lobby group to an education provider with over 1,000 members, specialising broadly in finance, investment and fund management. It was joined recently by the Property Valuation Forum (PVF). The Society of Property Researchers (SPR) exists to represent members of what is essentially a brand new profession employed within chartered surveying businesses, independent specialist research houses and fund managers.

The Office Agents Society, the Shop Agents Society, the Out-of-Town Retail Agents Society, and the Industrial Agents Society are forums for those involved in the marketing and selling of commercial space to occupiers. The British Council for Offices (BCO) and the British Council for Shopping Centres (BCSC) bring together professional advisers with the developers, owners, managers and occupiers of these specialist high-value market sectors.

The European Property Federation (EPF) brings together major owners throughout Europe while INREV, created in 2002, brings together investors in non-listed real estate vehicles. The Urban Land Institute (ULI), a US-based organisation covering all aspects of property development from planning and design to finance and investment, has committed resources to ULI Europe. The European Real Estate Society (ERES), based on the American Real Estate Society, brings together academics, researchers and consultants for a major annual conference. The European Public Real Estate Association, EPRA, was formed in 1999 to promote and encourage the development of the European quoted property sector.

## The role of government

The role of government as a regulator of and participant in the UK property market is a key one. The principal legislative and regulatory issues of current concern to the UK property industry include the usual taxation and control regimes applied to all industries – corporation tax, capital gains tax, health and safety law, employment law, accounting standards, and so on – but also include regulation concerned with the land-use planning system, construction law, and landlord and tenant matters, not to mention the UK government's attitude to the single European currency and the development of pan-European legal and financial structures.

### Securitisation

The UK property industry recently had high hopes that the government had accepted the principle of securitisation and would discuss with the industry how best to introduce a new REIT-type vehicle. However, securitisation is off the agenda until the next Parliament at the earliest, as the issue is seen to be likely to reduce the government's tax intake.

## Planning

Current government initiatives are concerned mainly with the links between the land-use planning system and transport and regeneration, and making the land-use planning system function efficiently and effectively. Since 1997, new policy guidance has been published on a wide range of issues including Housing (PPG 3); Regions (PPG 11); Development Plans (PPG 13); and Transport (PPG 12). In addition, there has been a plethora of advice on operating the planning system (appeals, costs, etc.) and the *Report of the Urban Task Force*, followed by the *Urban White Paper* in November 2000.

## Stamp duty

Stamp duty on residential transactions raised £2,160 million in 2000/2001; by contrast in 1992/93 the total was only £280 million. With the increase in house prices and the failure to raise thresholds, stamp duty has proved to be a valuable way of raising additional revenues. Commercial property has been caught in this net. At first sight, it would appear that this is a relatively painless additional form of revenue and certainly does not attract the same degree of political criticism as increases in income taxation or VAT. Nevertheless, stamp duty potentially distorts the efficient working of the market to the detriment of the industry and its customers. The industry's competitiveness is damaged by charging capital invested in the property sector 4% stamp duty while capital invested in the equities sector is charged 0.5%.

## Monetary union

The UK government position on monetary union is complicated. It appears committed to entry, but also to sticking by the outcome of a future referendum which appears unlikely to confirm the government position.

EMU membership, when it comes, seems likely to have one significant beneficial effect on UK property investment and for UK investors. It will eliminate currency risk for cross-border European investors, and reduce currency concerns for global investors with pan-European strategies. It may at the same time reduce the scope for hedging economic cycles through diversifying investments across different immobile property markets.

Equally important are the consequences of the harmonisation directives which will inevitably accompany the creation of the single market. Clear contenders for imposed EU-wide regulation are: VAT regimes (already under active consideration); valuation methods; and transactional taxes.

### The Commercial Leases Code

Following lobbying by tenants concentrated in the retail sector, the UK government wants to encourage more choice and flexibility in the commercial property market and to promote a better understanding of property matters, particularly among small business occupiers. In particular, the industry is focusing on the long lease with upward-only rent reviews as a possible restraint of trade. This led to the publication of the 2002 Commercial Leases Code.

The principal requirement of the Code is that landlords should offer flexible and alternative terms for consideration by a prospective tenant and for both parties to ensure that they have obtained professional advice before committing themselves to a lease and fully understand the basis on which the lease is issued.

In assessing flexibility and alternative terms, landlords are encouraged to reflect on the terms that they are prepared to accept and tenants are required to ensure that such terms truly represent the circumstances upon which they are prepared to be bound during the course of the lease. Where alternative terms are offered, rents will differ accordingly.

The market has already moved forward considerably from the days when the standard 25-year lease term was adopted by both landlords and tenants, regardless of the circumstances. Nonetheless, the government is hoping to encourage more leases of short duration. Break clauses are an effective compromise.

The code also recommends that rents should generally be at open market levels and that, wherever possible, alternatives such as upwards and downwards rent reviews should be adopted as opposed to upward-only reviews. It is accepted by the Code that the rent agreed at the commencement of the lease should be the base rent below which a review will not fall. Otherwise the Code strongly promotes the adoption of rent review arrangements which identify the true market rental level at the rent review date.

## Conclusion

While the performance of UK property in the past 25 years has not matched that of equities, it has sufficient advantages in terms of liability matching to continue to be a popular investment class in future. Recent strong perform-ance has now placed property at the top of the performance table over one, two, three, five and ten years.

Forces of change will continue to challenge our perceptions of the place and importance of property. Globalisation is damaging the ability of domestic markets to remain insular. Securitisation is a response to global investors placing more emphasis on the liquidity and divisibility of investments. In tandem with this, more unquoted pooled vehicles will be provided to enable global investors to diversify more effectively.

Technological revolution continues at a pace, with e-commerce creating changes in the way we shop, work and distribute goods. Corporate restruc-turing in the property sector is inevitable, with more emphasis on service provision (characterised by such new concepts as serviced offices and indus-tries such as facilities management), leading to shorter and more flexible UK leases.

The nature of UK property as an asset will change in response to these funda-mental drivers, but its place in the investment world seems assured. At the same time, the role of the institutions which own and manage this key asset is guaranteed to continue to change in response to global economic drivers.

# References

Ackrill, A., Barkham, R. & Baum, A. (1992) *The Performance of UK Property Companies.* Department of Land Management, University of Reading.

Baum, A. (1999) Changing styles in international real estate investment. *Australian Land Economics Review* **5**(2), 3–12.

Baum, A. (ed.) (2000) *Freeman's Guide to the Property Industry.* Freeman Publishing, London.

Baum, A. (2002) *Commercial Property Investment.* Estates Gazette, London.

Baum, A. & Lizieri, C. (1999) Who owns the City of London? *Real Estate Finance*, Spring, 87–100.

Baum, A. & Lizieri, C. (2000) *Space Race: the Contribution of Property Markets to the Competitiveness of London and Frankfurt.* Department of Land Management, University of Reading.

Baum, A. & Schofield, A. (1991) Property as a global asset. In: *Investment, Procurement and Performance in Construction* (eds P. Venmore-Rowland, P. Brandon & T. Mole). E & FN Spon, London.

College of Estate Management (2000) *Destination UK: International Property Investment and the Role of Taxation.* CEM, Reading.

D'Arcy, E., Keogh, G. & Roulac, S. (1999) The internationalisation of US and UK real estate service providers: competing for a global badge of quality. Paper presented to *European Real Estate Society, Sixth European Conference*. Athens, Greece.

DTZ Debenham Tie Leung (1999) *Special Report – Overseas Investment in UK Commercial Property*. DTZ Debenham Tie Leung, London.

DTZ Debenham Tie Leung (2002) *Money into Property*, 27th edn. DTZ Debenham Tie Leung, London.

Economist Intelligence Unit (1997) *Global Direct Investment and the Importance of Real Estate*. Royal Institution of Chartered Surveyors, London.

Eichholtz, P. & Lie, R. (1999) *Property Capital Flows: Moving the Frontiers*. The Hague, ING Bank/ING Real Estate.

Henderson Global Investors (2000) *The Case for Global Property Investment*. HGI, London.

Investment Property Databank (1999) *The UK Property Cycle: a History from 1921 to 1997*. Royal Institution of Chartered Surveyors, London.

Investment Property Forum (1995) *The Pensions Act 1995 and Property Investment*. City University, London.

OPC (2001) *Limited Partnerships: Examining the Current Market*. Oxford Property Consultants, Reading.

OPC (2002) Private Property UK database.

OPC (2003) *European Private Property Vehicles: The Emerging Property Market*. Oxford Property Consultants, Reading.

RICS (2002) The Commercial Leases Code: www.commercialleasecodeew.co.uk Royal Institution of Chartered Surveyors.

Scott, P. (1998) *The Property Masters*. E & FN Spon, London.

University of Reading & DTZ Debenham Thorpe (1995) *The Chartered Surveyor as Management Consultant: an Emerging Market*. Royal Institution of Chartered Surveyors, London.

# 11

# Real Estate Markets in Canada

## C. Tsuriel Somerville

Despite Canada's small number of urban centres, trying to generalise to a 'Canadian' real estate market is challenging. The country's political and economic institutions accentuate clear regional differences. Relative to other countries with federal systems, Canadian provinces are especially powerful. The economies of British Columbia (Vancouver), Alberta (Calgary and Edmonton), Ontario (Ottawa and Toronto) and Quebec (Montreal) are driven by very different factors. For British Columbia, these are forestry and resource extraction, tourism, and trade with Asia. For Alberta, it is oil and gas drilling and exploration. Key sectors in Ontario are motor and car parts manufacturing, high technology and finance. And in Quebec it is diversified manufacturing and forestry. High technology is also a presence in Vancouver and Calgary but in different areas. This chapter focuses on the institutional framework in the four principal Canadian real estate markets, Calgary, Montreal, Toronto and Vancouver.

Canada is a nation of immigrants and continues to have one of the highest levels of per capita immigration in the world.[1] This has resulted in a tremendous ethnic diversity and has helped to encourage considerable foreign ownership of real estate and development activity. Foreign ownership of larger Class A downtown properties ranges from a high of nearly 17% of all square footage in Vancouver, to 12% in Calgary, almost 6% in Toronto and over 7% in Montreal. The development of the former Expo lands on the south side of Vancouver's downtown peninsula was initiated by investors from Hong Kong led by Li Ka-Shing. Compared to other G7 nations the Canadian market is small, but it does have advantages in openness, transparency, and stable legal and political environment.

Though regional issues are extremely important in Canada, there are important national similarities. A simplistic but accurate characterisation of

English Canada, that is, Canada excluding Quebec, is an overlay of American individualism on an English legal and social tradition. Canadians have a more communitarian approach to social issues and greater suspicion of wealth than one would find in the US. Cultural themes, urbanisation and degree of government presence in the economy do vary, but these are dominated by shared values, especially across the major business centres.

The important exception is Quebec, whose social, legal and cultural traditions are markedly different from those in the rest of Canada. French speakers in Canada are concentrated overwhelmingly in Quebec. Over 90% of Canadians who speak French in the home live in Quebec and represent 82.8% of Quebec residents. This can be compared to 2.9% in Ontario. Quebec has a strong, though mostly non-violent, separatist movement. The root of this movement is the 'quiet Revolution' of the 1960s that recast French-Canadian nationalism as Québécois nationalism. This movement reached its zenith in 1995, when a referendum endorsing separation came within one percentage point of passing. The effect of the separatist movement has been to strengthen French language and cultural institutions in Quebec. The election of the Parti Québécois in 1976 on a platform of sovereignty for Quebec and with an aggressive programme to preserve French by downgrading English has resulted in Toronto replacing Montreal as Canada's primary business and financial centre.

This chapter presents a number of the central issues that affect real estate investment and development in Canada. Following this introduction, the first section describes the allocation of law-making and governance powers over real estate between the federal, provincial, and local governments. The second section examines property rights in Canada (a constitutional issue with important operational implications), with a major emphasis on issues connected to aboriginal land claims. The third section addresses land use and development regulation. The fourth section provides an overview of Canadian real estate markets. It includes a brief description of the historical performance of residential and non-residential real estate in the four principal metropolitan area real estate markets – Calgary, Montreal, Toronto and Vancouver. It also discusses the changes in the patterns of ownership, between REITs and public corporations, and the growing share of real estate held by pension funds. The fifth section addresses real estate financing and marketing.

## Government institutions and real estate

*Canadian federalism: provinces vs. federal government*

Canada adopts a federal system of government based on provinces and 'territories' and largely on a common-law legal system. Unlike most countries with federal systems, the provincial governments are extremely strong. Provinces are autonomous from the federal government in those areas where the Constitution grants them authority. Territories are technically subordinate to the federal government, but have gained province-like powers over time. Separation of powers between the national and provincial levels of government was drawn up in the Confederation Settlement (also known as the British North American Act) in 1867 that created Canada as an independent nation. Section 92 lists 16 specific enumerated powers that are given to the provinces, including power over property and civil law. Fights between the provincial and federal government over power, jurisdiction and revenues have been a constant feature of the Canadian federal system. While the Confederation Settlement indicates that all powers not granted to the provinces are by default in the sphere of federal jurisdiction, the courts have tended, over time, to reduce and restrict non-emergency federal power in these areas of dispute. Thus, for most areas related to real estate development, there is no explicit federal role.

The federal government through the legislative actions of Parliament does retain powers to regulate the use of land pursuant to a limited number of federal purposes. Thus, land adjacent to or near airports and harbours is subject to federal action to ensure the proper operation of these facilities. Properties adjacent to Crown lands, and property owned by the federal government, can also be subject to federal influence or action.[2]

The primary area of dispute between the federal and provincial governments over control with relevance to real estate development is environmental policy. In the absence of explicit references to the environment in the Confederation Settlement, provinces have assumed primary responsibility through their control over natural resources and municipal institutions. At the same time the federal government is also active in environmental policy and regulation. Court rulings in the mid-1980s gave the federal government more legal authority to regulate the environment at the expense of the provinces.[3] The primary basis for federal intervention has been its powers and oversight granted for matters concerning sea coasts and fisheries. The Fisheries Act gives the federal government clear powers to regulate activities that affect fish habitat in water frequented by fish anywhere in Canada. Any development that will lead to the release or runoff into waterways of deleterious substances that can harm fish is subject to regulation under the Fisheries Act by Fisheries and Oceans Canada. For development this is a particularly critical issue in British Columbia, where the federal government has regulated and restricted new development within fixed distances of salmon-bearing creeks, streams and rivers, because of the negative effects on salmon habitat.

## Allocation of powers: provincial vs. municipal governments

In contrast to the US, municipal governments in Canada are quite weak. All municipal and regional government powers are granted by provincial legislation. With a few notable exceptions, provinces have not passed home-rule amendments to give municipal and regional governments independent and equal legal standing as is the case in the US. Without constitutional protections for their status or explicit charters, the independence and scope of powers available to municipalities and regional governments are entirely a function of provincial government permission and, perhaps more critically, subject to change with the political regimes at the provincial level. Conditions and issues in the relationships between provincial and metropolitan governments in Alberta, British Columbia and Ontario that have a bearing on real estate, and particularly on real estate development, are presented below.

Alberta enjoys a relatively high degree of harmony in the relationship between the provincial and the lower level governments. The reasons stand out. First, all levels of government in the province have been led by right of centre governments for a considerable period of time. Second, the two largest cities, Calgary and Edmonton, include a much higher percentage of their metropolitan area's population than in other Canadian cities.[4] Consequently, there is relative philosophical harmony and the political interests of the provincial and principal local governments have been fairly consistent.

Municipal governments in Alberta are extremely weak. Although they have wide-ranging powers granted to them in the Alberta Municipal Government Act, this same act limits municipal funding to the property tax, which is market value based. In particular, the Act makes it illegal for communities to impose levies on developers. Land-use planning powers are delegated to the municipalities, but the province retains the power to overrule municipalities regarding 'environmentally sensitive' sites, a power which they have been wielding with greater frequency. The constraints on municipal finance have ensured that the province is a major player in the discussion over infrastructure provision.

In contrast to Alberta, Ontario exhibits considerable tensions between the various levels of government. Local governments in Ontario have considerably more independence in levying by-laws and imposing fees on development than do local governments in Alberta. The Ontario provincial government has tended to take a hands-off approach, except in areas of 'provincial interest'. However, the provincial-level Ontario Municipal Board (OMB) acts as a constant constraint on municipal independence.[5] Members of the OMB are appointed by the provincial government, but the board's operations are independent of cabinet and any provincial ministries. The OMB acts as an appeals court for any individual citizens, public bodies or corporations which wish to appeal the decision of public authorities such as local or regional councils, land division committees, boards of variance (committees of adjustment), or the provincial Minister of Municipal Affairs and Housing. Among the areas of jurisdiction for the OMB are official plans, zoning by-laws, subdivision plans, variances and development charges. In hearing appeals, the board acts much like a court with testimony under oath and the allowance for legal representation.

The practical effect of the OMB is to constrain the ability of jurisdictions to block development maliciously or extract unreasonable concessions from developers. The OMB tends to be more consistent with general planning principles and less willing to listen to local citizen groups and the environmental lobby than local politicians have been. It is quite easy for developers to appeal to the OMB. Since the mid-1990s, local government has been under an obligation to reach a decision regarding development applications within 90 days. If they do not reach a decision, developers can immediately appeal to the OMB. The practical effect is that in areas where development has tended to encounter stiff resistance from local groups opposed to redevelopment, such as in the City of Toronto, developers will simultaneously submit a redevelopment application to the city and an appeal to the OMB.

The Ontario provincial government has been quite aggressive at forcing amalgamations of municipalities and school districts in the name of achieving scale economies. Between 1996 and 2001 the Ontario government managed to reduce the number of municipalities from 815 to 590. The most dramatic example is the 1 January 1998 amalgamation of Municipal Toronto and five surrounding suburban jurisdictions to form the new City of Toronto. The move was both politically motivated, and an attempt to solve the problem of conflict between a regional body, Metropolitan Toronto, and its constituent jurisdictions.[6] These had grown in intensity following the introduction in 1988 of elections for seats on the Metropolitan Toronto (Metro) council. However, this amalgamation has not solved the most pressing regional issues of infrastructure capacity and congestion as most of the economic growth is occurring in those parts of the Greater Toronto Area (GTA) outside of the new City of Toronto.

The provincial government in Quebec is extremely strong and actively interventionist both in local governance and the economy. This reflects a statist tradition that has long been present in Quebec. It cleaves more to a European model of government intervention than one observes elsewhere in the US and the rest of Canada. For instance, the government has frequently put pressure on the largest provincial public employee pension fund, the Caisse, to use its assets to insure Quebec-based ownership of business institutions in the province.

In real estate, public monies are used to fund development. For example, in an effort to turn Montreal into a high-tech centre, the province announced the development of the 3.2m sq ft E-Commerce Place. They also offered $C1.5 billion ($US1.0 billion) in tax credits over 10 years to induce firms to move into the development.[7] This explicitly crowded out private investment, stopping construction of the first private downtown office tower to be built in 10 years. A second provincial project, the 1.5m sq ft Cite du Multimedia (Multimedia City), is the renovation and redevelopment of an old factory and warehouse district. It has been extremely successful and has not generated as much criticism from the development community, though it has siphoned away tenants from other locations. Emblematic of the interventionist approach in Quebec, in Toronto and Vancouver this type of development was all done by private developers without the use of public monies. Finally, the provincial government has interfered at the local level. Against much opposition, the Quebec provincial government forced a 2002 merger of the 28 municipalities on the Island of Montreal to form a new larger City of Montreal. A chief objective for the separatist Parti Québécois in power was to reduce the power of smaller communities with English-speaking majorities by diluting them in a larger majority French city.

As in other Canadian provinces, the government in British Columbia has wide-reaching powers and abilities to dictate to municipal governments. No city has home rule, though the charter granting municipal powers to Vancouver is broader and farther reaching than the Municipal Act, which governs all other jurisdictions in the province. The current Liberal Government, which is right of centre, has proposed legislation to expand the powers and independence of municipalities in the province. The proposed 'Community Charter' would fundamentally alter the allocation of powers and responsibilities between province and municipalities.[8] Municipalities in British Columbia would come much closer to the US model of local government independence, though there would remain clear spheres of distinct provincial and municipal jurisdiction. While the current Municipal Act limits areas of municipal jurisdiction to areas explicitly set out in the act, a list which includes land-use regulation and zoning, the proposed Community Charter would reverse this, granting municipal governments powers in all areas *except* those identified in the charter. Effectively, local governments would gain greater scope for action and raising revenues, without being subject to provincial oversight and review. More critically, the proposed Charter includes an explicit statement that the powers of local government must be interpreted broadly. Currently, all by-laws are subject to provincial veto.

The real estate development community, through its lobbying arm, the Urban Development Institute (UDI), has argued that this change will increase the ability of local and neighbourhood groups to thwart measures that are in the best interests of the entire community. UDI's concern is that in the absence of legal provisions for compensation, downloading powers to lower level governments will result in more violations of developer rights. In response, supporters, such as the British Columbia Association of Municipal Governments, contend that because the bill leaves land-use regulatory rights unchanged, the Community Charter should not adversely affect real estate development interests.

## Property rights

Property rights in most of Canada are derived from English common law as part of the English settlement of Canada.[9] In Quebec, civil law is based on the French Civil Code that held upon English conquest of French lands in Canada. Canadian landholding rights are in the form of estates held of the Crown with the most common holding being a fee-simple estate. Typically, urban properties are governed by a provincial charter but some have federal charter, in which case the property may be exempt from certain provincial levies and charges.

Property owners in Canada do not have the same protection as owners in the US against government actions that reduce or eliminate the economic value of the land. In the US, the Fifth Amendment to the US Constitution, the 'takings clause', states '...nor shall private property be taken for public use, without just compensation'. The US courts have ruled that this applies to temporary or permanent complete loss of economic value, but not to diminution of value in a legitimate act of state power. In Canada, there is no overarching constitutional protection to prevent legislatures from passing statutes that reduce or eliminate a landowner's economic value without compensation. There is a tension between the power of the legislature to legislate and the general principle of no unjust expropriation.

Recently, the Supreme Court of Canada made clear that expropriation without compensation is possible. The constraint is that 'encroachments on the enjoyment of property should be interpreted rigorously and strictly ... that the legislature express himself extremely clearly where there is any intention to expropriate or confiscate without compensation'.[10] Other cases have made clear that at the same time the courts can give tremendous leeway to government in making decisions on property rights.[11] There are legislative controls in place to ensure compensation. For example, in British Columbia the Local Government Act, the enabling legislation for municipal governments, requires that local governments, except Vancouver, have funds available in the current budget to compensate landowners at market value if they act to remove all economic value. However, as a statute, this can be overcome by any succeeding statute. In total, property rights are weaker in Canada than they are in the US.

## Aboriginal land claims

A large area of uncertainty over title involves ownership and use right claims by Canada's aboriginal population. From the perspective of Canadian law, the introduction of English and French law by European settlement did not replace the pre-existing property rights of aboriginal communities. Rather it overlays them. Only a 'legitimate act' of power can remove those rights. This was typically done by treaty, where aboriginal title was extinguished in exchange for a set of guarantees, usually for use of natural resources and hunting and fishing grounds. These rights could also be extinguished by a legislative act, in which case the Crown would then act as a trustee for the land.[12] Critically, from a legal perspective, recognition of aboriginal title does not require an act of government, as it already exists. However, it does not typically include the same package of rights found in English property law. As a practical matter, outside of British Columbia and Crown lands, issues of aboriginal title principally bear on aboriginal use rights for forestry and fishing.[13]

In British Columbia, title has not been resolved on land held by the Crown because it is the only province where treaties were not signed. In the absence of treaties, aboriginal title remains in force and is protected under Section 35 of the Constitution Act, 1982: 'Existing aboriginal and treaty rights of the aboriginal peoples of Canada are hereby recognised and affirmed.' The scope of the problem is extremely broad. Overlapping claims by First Nations groups mean that more than 100% of British Columbia's land mass is in dispute. One site held by the federal government in Vancouver is claimed by three different bands. The courts have directed the provincial and federal governments and the First Nation groups to negotiate treaties to resolve issues of title.

The British Columbia Treaty Commission (BCTC) was established in 1992 to oversee and shepherd the three party negotiation process.[14] Since then, 53 First Nations representing 122 Indian Act bands and approximately two-thirds of the aboriginal people in British Columbia have started the process. However, the process has been slow. Despite 10 years and millions of dollars, only one First Nation (Sechelt Indian Band) has even progressed to the fifth and last stage. The only treaty signed and put into place by mid-2002 was with Nisga nation, and this was done outside the formal BCTC process. Even in the absence of signed treaties, the potential for court action by aboriginal groups over land-use decisions made on land in dispute will affect provincial government decisions. The current government in British Columbia has developed a new policy that requires government officials to '"accommodate" First Nations, through negotiations, side deals, or other forms of agreement' on 'all decisions ... that are likely to affect aboriginal interests'.[15] The effect of this policy may be to allow First Nations groups in British Columbia a de facto veto over provincial government land-use decisions.

The unresolved treaties and native land claims have the potential to negatively affect investments, especially in rural areas where most land is owned by the crown, and title is unresolved. The uncertainty manifests itself in a number of ways. First, the outcome of the treaty process may render existing leases of crown land (a category that includes many resort developments) void or with reduced rights. Second, even those with clear fee-simple title may face problems if their property use depends on access that crosses, or their infrastructure is located on, land in dispute. For instance, access to the Sun Peaks ski resort outside Penticton in the south-central part of the province has been blockaded, on several occasions, by members of the Secwepemc (or Shuswap) nation in a dispute over land traversed by the ski resort's access road. A third area of concern applies even to land with clear and secure title. The one treaty negotiated and signed to date with the Nisga nation created a new level of government with the power to regulate land use, but one where non-Nisga have strictly reduced political rights.

## Land-use regulation

### General conditions and processes

The Canadian provinces have different philosophies about land-use regulation and restrictions on development. As well, within any province, there can be large differences across jurisdictions, from those that welcome development to those that make it extremely hard to engage in any significant redevelopment. This section examines a number of important issues in Alberta, Ontario and British Columbia that characterise the regulatory environment for real estate development.

Development applications in most cities in Canada follow a similar process and deal with the same types of institutions, constraints and procedures. What vary are the details, flexibility and participants, and the disposition to accepting development. There are two steps, the development approval and the building approval. The first is an application process for the concept, the second for a particular building. Any development is expected to be consistent with the various community and official plans that describe the city's objectives for development and vision of its future. The relationship between the vision outlined in these plans and what development is actually allowed will be specific to every city. Development plans are submitted to a specific department that then guides them through a review process. In Calgary this is the Corporate Planning Applications Group (CPAG).[16] Comments are solicited from any city agency or department affected by the plan, and developers are expected to comply with these comments. Typically, a mechanism exists to solicit public input, though the importance of these hearings varies. When a proposed development is inconsistent with existing zoning and the various city plans, the process becomes much more problematic. Prior to the standard development application process, the developer must apply for a re-zoning or variance. This involves many of the same stages, but with greater opportunity for public and political input. It is here in particular that 'pro' and 'anti' development environments are most evident.

One area of variation across Canada is the difference in the explicit monetary cost of the various government fees and charges tied to development. All locations charge fees to defer the costs of processing applications, though the amount varies. For instance, the cost for a major re-zoning application in Vancouver is over C$700,000.[17] Development cost charges, called impact fees in the US, are levied to pay for off-site infrastructure and public facilities. While these charges are prohibited in Alberta, they are aggressively used elsewhere. Municipal and regional charges in the Toronto area can easily exceed $20,000 per single-family house and for parkland dedication and school construction in addition to infrastructure. In British Columbia, local governments are also aggressive in their use of development cost charges, though total fees and development cost charges tend to be below $20,000 per single-family unit.

## Sustainable growth

An area of uncertainty for land-use regulation is how the issue of sustainable growth will play out. This is a topic that is on the agenda of all of the provinces, though they take different approaches. In Alberta the primary issue of concern is the relationship between growth and infrastructure provision. Calgary's fast growth, the metropolitan area (CMA), grew 10% between 1998 and 2002 compared with 3.7% for the other 19 largest CMAs, has made congestion a priority item. Unlike other areas in Canada, the government response has not been to limit growth, confine it to certain areas, or try to enforce higher densities, but to form a joint provincial/municipal task force to figure out mechanisms for financing and providing infrastructure to meet the increase in demand that comes with growth.

The interest in sustainable development in Ontario has taken on a different form. In February 2001 the provincial government established the Smart Growth Secretariat.[18] The secretariat is charged with (1) developing recommendations to promote and manage growth and (2) incorporating the views of all levels of government and public and private stakeholders. To date the government has divided the province into five zones and charged panels in each zone with developing an agenda with strategies for addressing solid waste, gridlock and growth management. However, it is not clear whether there will be any binding recommendations. Unlike Alberta, in Ontario there will clearly be provincial and regional level strategies for growth management at some point in the future. The prospect for provincial action is real, as the current right-of-centre government has shown a willingness to intervene and impose policy on development in areas of provincial interest. The most recent example is its imposition of a development freeze, using provincial legislation to override municipal decisions in defining the areas open and closed to development in the Oak Ridges Moraine.[19]

Sustainable growth in British Columbia has been delegated to the province's regional governments. Like most Canadian provinces, British Columbia has been fairly aggressive in creating regional government bodies. British Columbia first established regional districts in 1965 and there are now 29 regional districts in British Columbia, covering virtually the entire province. In rural areas they do have effective land-use powers, but all decisions also require the agreement of the affected provincial ministries, particularly those with responsibility for highways, environment, forestry and agriculture. In the Vancouver area, the regional government is the Greater Vancouver Regional District (GVRD), a partnership of the 21 municipalities and one electoral area that make up the metropolitan area of Greater Vancouver. In addition to its role as the supplier of services that are regional rather than local in nature, including the regional park system, drinking water and sewage treatment, the GVRD is involved in land use planning. The oversight of public transportation and major arterials are under the responsibility of a separate regional authority, 'Translink'.

The GVRD adopted the Liveable Region Strategic Plan (LRSP) in 1996. The objective of the LRSP was to encourage higher-density development in a number of centres to protect green space and promote transit use. The provincial Growth Strategies Act requires municipalities in the GVRD to submit regional context plans, demonstrating how they will comply with the goals of the LRSP. Any proposed development that is not in compliance with this plan, and thus the city's objectives under the LRSP, must be approved by the GVRD board, which is made up of mayors and city councillors from the member municipalities. In November 2002, the GVRD for the first time used powers granted to it by this provincial legislation to reject a development proposal already approved by a city on the grounds that it was in conflict with the municipality's regional context plan.[20]

## Specific provincial issues

Government regulation of development in Alberta is much weaker and governments are more 'pro-development' than elsewhere in Canada. The consensus view of developers is that the process is more straightforward and less fraught with uncertainty in Calgary and Alberta than in other provinces. Thus, in the spring of 1999, the Urban Development Institute Alberta (UDI), representing the real estate industry, initiated discussions with the Alberta Urban Municipalities Association (AUMA), representing local government, to develop a set of guidelines to address regulation and development levies. This resulted in a set of guiding principles for development regulation to be submitted to the Alberta Minister of Municipal Affairs.[21] The guidelines recognise that 'municipalities and developers have a shared responsibility for defining and addressing the existing and future needs of the community'. While municipalities have flexibility to address community objectives, the principles state that 'policies should be applied equitably and fairly to all within that community', that participation in financing infrastructure should be shared on an 'equitable basis' by 'all beneficiaries of development', and that there be full disclosure of the allocation of costs. It is hard to identify explicitly the direct effect of the agreement. However, it does indicate that in Alberta, municipalities and the real estate community have been able to work together to address a set of issues that typically result in consensus between developers and local government.

Alberta provincial regulation is relatively structured and organised. Projects move along a process where the power of individual bureaucrats has relatively limited scope. As in Ontario, developers can appeal and have the case reviewed on its merits. Local and provincial governments have strict timelines for reaching decisions, and failure to reach a decision in the allotted 90 days is grounds for appeal. Alberta land-use laws grant developers more certainty, so that there is more communication and consistency across departments and ministries. Once a development permit has been granted, a developer faces little regulatory uncertainty or risk. Contrast this with British Columbia, where departments act independently, there are no limits on how long government officials can take to make a decision, and the opportunities for appeal are circumscribed.

The City of Toronto has undertaken a number of new approaches to encourage the redevelopment of older industrial areas. This has taken the form of replacing old zoning categories with more flexible zoning for non-residential areas ripe for redevelopment. For example, the downtown shoulder areas of King/Parliament and King/Spladina were re-zoned to remove restrictions on density and non-nuisance uses. In its place, the city retained controls on design, setbacks and community integration, where each project was evaluated on its own merits. Active redevelopment has followed. The 1998 municipal amalgamation has resulted in the need for a new Official Plan for the newly enlarged city. The objective of the new plan is to continue this approach, designating 25% of the city along certain corridors and in redevelopment areas as locations with fewer hurdles and constraints on redevelopment and more flexibility for developers.[22] Despite this official openness, community groups in Toronto fight against most development quite aggressively.

Land use is strongly regulated in British Columbia. Bureaucrats have considerable latitude and flexibility in making decisions on allowable land uses, re-zoning, subdivision plans, building and development permits. While land-use decisions are the jurisdiction of municipal governments and the regional districts in areas without municipalities, the province has asserted its interests in a number of ways. Through the Agricultural Land Reserve (ALR) and Forest Land Reserve (FLR) considerable tracts of land have been designated off-limits to all development.[23] Lands in the ALR include most of the farmland in the Vancouver metropolitan area, lands suitable for resorts in the valleys of the province's interior, and farmland surrounding the fast-growing cities in the Okanagan region such as Kelowna.[24] One single-family dwelling per land registry parcel is permitted within the ALR, and land cannot be subdivided. In addition, one secondary suite within a single-family dwelling and one manufactured home up to 9 m in width, for use by the owner's immediate family, are also permitted, unless otherwise prohibited by a local government by-law. Additional permanent dwellings may be permitted if they are required for full-time, legitimate, bone fide farm operations.

Environmental regulation by the province in British Columbia has been especially strict. This has mainly targeted the preservation of streams and waterways that serve as fish habitat, especially for salmon. In 1997 the province passed the Fish Protection Act, which was subsequently strengthened in a January 2001 amendment. These statutes effectively prohibit development up to 50 m from the top of a bank or ravine bordering a stream. The stream does not even need to have flowing water all of the year. While the election in May 2001 of a right-of-centre government was likely to weaken this, British Columbia remains a location with strict environmental regulations on development.

## Canadian real estate markets

While Canada is a physically large country, the population is not only highly urbanised but concentrated in a small number of cities. Collectively in 2001 the four cities of Calgary, Montreal, Toronto and Vancouver claimed approximately 35% of Canada's population of 31 million.[25] Nearly 80% of the office space in the nine investment real estate markets in Canada in 2001 was found in these four cities, and of this, half (40% of the total) was in Toronto. These four cities also dominated the market for industrial properties: they had an 87% share of industrial space, with Toronto accounting for over half of this with a 47% share of the total amount of space.

### *Market description and performance*

Table 11.1 summarises mid-2001 conditions in Canadian class A office markets. In both Ottawa and Vancouver, growth in demand has been much stronger outside the downtown core. This reflects the importance of the high-tech sector in these markets.[26] The downtown cores are relatively more important in Calgary, Edmonton and Montreal. As in other cities in North America, suburban vacancy rates tend to be higher. Data for industrial space in 2001 is shown in Table 11.2. Industrial activity has been strong across the country, except in Ottawa, where the tech sector has tended to use office

**Table 11.1**   Canadian office markets, 2001.

| City | CBD/downtown, class A | | | Suburban/non-CBD, class A | | |
| | Inventory | 5-yr avg absorption | Vacancy rate | Inventory | 5-yr avg absorption | Vacancy rate |
| --- | --- | --- | --- | --- | --- | --- |
| Calgary | 20,614,000 | 486,000 | 5.5 | 3,676,000 | 341,000 | 9.2 |
| Edmonton | 8,345,000 | 85,000 | 14.0 | 2,629,000 | 142,000 | 7.3 |
| Montreal | 19,535,000 | 523,000 | 2.5 | 6,961,000 | 434,000 | 8.3 |
| Ottawa | 7,730,000 | 140,000 | 2.2 | 10,898,000 | 556,000 | 6.4 |
| Toronto | 34,520,000 | 1,294,000 | 4.2 | 37,348,000 | 1,436,000 | 10.0 |
| Vancouver | 14,462,000 | 110,000 | 5.4 | 6,278,000 | 723,000 | 8.0 |

*Source: Penreal Capital.*

Vacancy rate is as of June 2001.

**Table 11.2**   Canadian industrial markets, 2001.

| City | Inventory | 5-yr avg absorption | Absorption as percent of stock | Vacancy |
| --- | --- | --- | --- | --- |
| Calgary | 75,968,000 | 2,286,000 | 3.0 | 3.2 |
| Edmonton | 67,750,000 | 1,804,000 | 2.7 | 4.1 |
| Montreal | 262,600,000 | 4,267,000 | 1.6 | 4.0 |
| Ottawa | 23,379,000 | 360,000 | 1.5 | 2.6 |
| Toronto | 656,971,000 | 9,997,000 | 1.5 | 4.4 |
| Vancouver | 151,450,000 | 3,061,000 | 2.0 | 3.0 |

*Source: Penreal Capital.*

Vacancy rate is as of June 2001.

space. However, the strength of the oil economy in Alberta shows up in the notably higher absorption rates in Calgary and Edmonton.

The cities differ dramatically in their employment growth, with growth highest in the west. Between 1987 and 2001 total employment in Calgary and Vancouver grew nearly 55% and 46%, respectively.[27] This is significantly higher than the growth rates of 14% and 26% achieved in Montreal and Toronto. Table 11.3 breaks down the composition of employment by sector. Several things are most notable. First, the importance of the oil industry means that the employment share of primary industries in Calgary is nearly seven times greater than in the other cities. The two larger, older cities in central Canada have twice the employment share in manufacturing than do the two faster-growing western cities. Vancouver has a relatively larger share of employment in commercial and non-commercial services.

Both the residential and non-residential real estate markets in Calgary show the effects of the city's dependence on the oil industry.[28] As Fig. 11.1 shows, real housing prices and housing starts fell dramatically (35% and 80% re-

**Table 11.3**    Employment by sector, 2001 Q4.

| Sector | Calgary | Montreal | Toronto | Vancouver |
|---|---|---|---|---|
| *Goods-producing industries* | *24.8%* | *23.7%* | *24.3%* | *15.3%* |
| Primary and utilities industries | 7.5% | 0.5% | 0.6% | 1.1% |
| Manufacturing | 8.8% | 18.7% | 17.3% | 8.8% |
| Construction | 7.5% | 3.6% | 5.7% | 4.8% |
| Utilities | 1.1% | 1.0% | 0.7% | 0.5% |
| *Services* | *75.2%* | *76.3%* | *75.7%* | *84.7%* |
| Transportation, storage and communication | 6.6% | 5.0% | 5.0% | 6.0% |
| Wholesale and retail trade | 15.7% | 16.2% | 16.3% | 17.0% |
| Finance, insurance and real estate | 5.8% | 6.5% | 8.9% | 6.7% |
| Commercial services | 30.9% | 26.9% | 29.7% | 34.1% |
| Non-commercial services | 13.1% | 16.9% | 12.6% | 17.1% |
| Public administration and defence | 3.1% | 4.7% | 3.3% | 4.0% |

*Source: Conference Board of Canada.*

spectively) following the collapse of oil prices in the early 1980s. Housing starts accelerated in the mid-1990s and the market remained Canada's fastest growing through 2001. Since 1996 real house prices are up over 20%, with starts nearly doubling since 1995. Still, neither real prices nor starts have approached their 1981 peak.

Conditions in the Calgary office market are shown in Fig. 11.2. The market was weak through the late 1980s and early 1990s with high vacancy and relatively little absorption. Growth in absorption in the mid-1990s with the recovery of the oil market and the emergence of Calgary as a home for

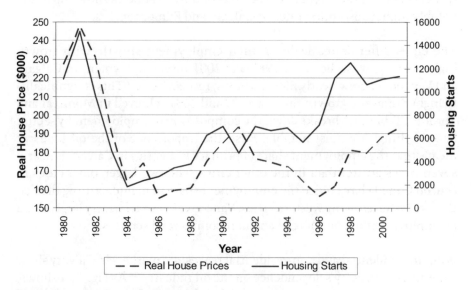

**Fig. 11.1**    Housing market, Calgary.

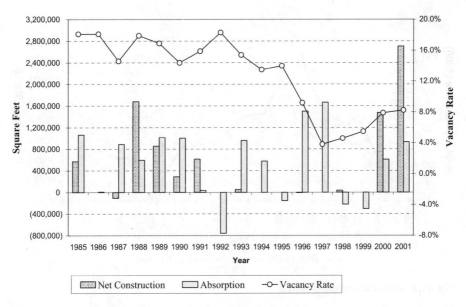

**Fig. 11.2**   Calgary office market. *Source: Colliers Research.*

corporate headquarters such as Canadian Pacific, which moved from Montreal to Calgary instead of Toronto, led to dramatic declines in vacancy and
substantive new construction in 2000 and 2001. With a smaller technology
sector and one geared to oil exploration, Calgary has survived the technology
meltdown better than Ottawa and Vancouver.

Real estate markets in Montreal declined for 10 years from the mid-1980s
through the mid-1990s. Housing starts and real house prices shown in
Fig. 11.3 indicate that conditions only began to improve in 1995, but this
improvement has been modest at best. Current housing starts in Montreal
are similar to those in Calgary, a city one quarter the size. Conditions in
Montreal's commercial real estate market (Fig. 11.4) were so bad as to have
three consecutive years of negative absorption. While absorption has picked
up, private construction activity remains quite low. Part of this is because
two government mega-projects, E-Commerce Place and Multimedia City,
have both taken growth and cannibalised existing buildings.

Like Montreal, Toronto suffered a sharp downturn in the real estate market
in the early 1990s. As Fig. 11.5 shows, housing starts plunged over 50%
while real house prices fell 35%. However, the strong North American car
market in the late 1980s revitalised Ontario's economy and brought a 147%
increase in starts, though even after a climb of 15%, real house prices remain
close to 25% below their 1990 peak. The consequences of the late 1980s orgy

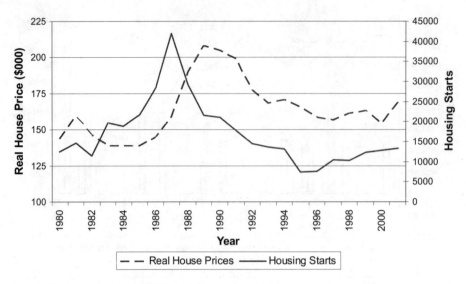

**Fig. 11.3**  Housing market, Montreal.

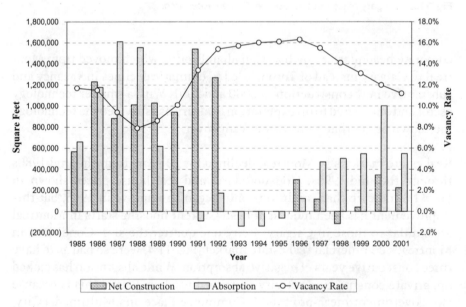

**Fig. 11.4**  Montreal office market.

of overbuilding in Toronto are shown in Fig. 11.6, where the office vacancy rate topped 20% in 1994. The legacy of this crash was so great that there was no new construction in Toronto's downtown until 2002. Real estate markets have basically recovered. However, except for the technology peak in 2000, absorption from 1990 to 2001 was below the levels of the late 1980s.

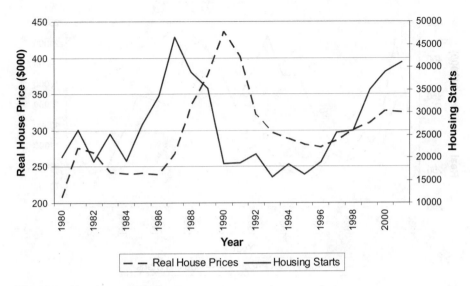

**Fig. 11.5** Housing market, Toronto.

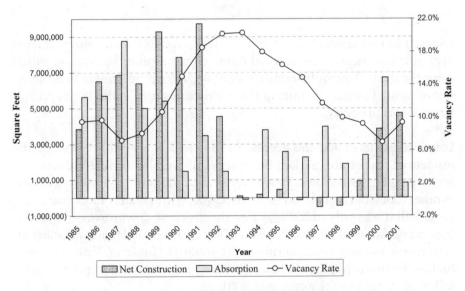

**Fig. 11.6** Greater Toronto office market. *Source: Colliers Research.*

Vancouver's real estate market has been atypical for Canada. First, driven by internal migration and international immigration, the residential market reached its peak in the early 1990s when other markets were suffering (see Fig. 11.7). Residential markets then began a long slide, reaching their nadir in 1999, when growth was strong in both Alberta and Ontario. This slide had two causes: negative real per capita growth of the provincial economy

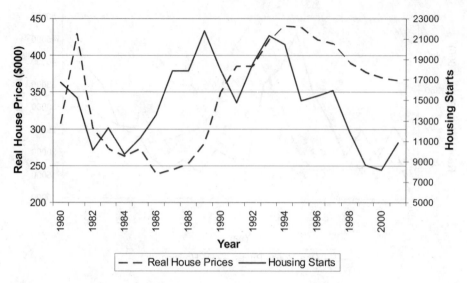

**Fig. 11.7**   Housing market, Vancouver.

under its left wing government and the 'leaky condo' crisis.[29] Rot problems kept new buyers away from wood-frame condominium structures, which comprise the bulk of multi-family, owner-occupied properties in Vancouver, and prevented owners of units in those structures from selling without suffering losses in equity.

Low interest rates and the decline in the stock market have revived the residential real estate market, but it remains well below historic levels of activity. As Fig. 11.8 shows, Vancouver's office market did not suffer as much as other Canadian markets in the early 1990s, with vacancy rates peaking at 13%. Still it was only in 2002–03 that the first new downtown office buildings in a decade were being completed. During this period there was substantial growth and new construction in the suburbs. However, Vancouver was hit hard by the technology bubble: extremely high rate of absorption in 2000 followed by negative absorption in 2001–02.

## Public vs. private real estate in Canada

Compared to the US, the securitisation of real estate equity in Canada has proceeded quite slowly. And in some ways it has moved in the opposite direction. In the last five years, real estate investment trusts (REITs) have grown in number and capitalisation, but do not yet approach the market share of REITs in the US. At the same time, the largest Canadian pension funds have

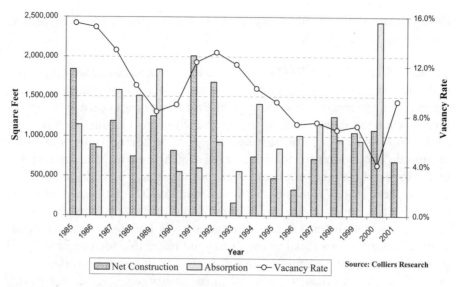

**Fig. 11.8** Greater Vancouver office market. *Source: Colliers Research.*

taken a dominant role in the holding of class A office and industrial properties. Their acquisitions have actually reduced the size of the public real estate market.

For a variety of reasons REITs as a form of securitised real estate have developed slowly in Canada. The term 'REIT' and the institution originated in the US in 1960 with the amendments to the Internal Revenue Code that created this vehicle. By the 1980s the number of REITS in the US exceeded 100, and by 1994 there were over 200 REITs. In contrast, the first Canadian REIT was not formed until 1993, and the third REIT was not created until 1996. Canadian REITs emerged out of problems with existing liquid real estate vehicles. Until the early 1990s investors could acquire shares in open-ended real estate funds, so there was not an explicit need for another liquid vehicle for investing in real estate.

In the early 1990s the sharp downturn in property markets caused these funds severe financial distress. When returns turned negative investors redeemed their shares. As open-end funds in illiquid assets, redemption prices were based on appraised values, which lagged behind the falling market. The funds faced additional problems in meeting these redemptions because of the difficulty in selling real estate assets in a market where liquidity had disappeared. In May 1994, the Department of Finance announced amendments to the Income Tax Act that allowed a real estate investment trust to qualify as a closed-end trust and a mutual trust. The first four Canadian

REITs – RealFund, Canadian (CREIT), RioCan and Summit – were all former open-ended mutual funds.

Canadian REITs, like US REITs, have substantial tax advantages over public real estate corporations for holding existing properties. Subject to certain restrictions, the income distributed to unit-holders is not taxed at the trust level; certain tax shelter features associated with depreciation flow through to the unit holders; and the trust can designate certain portions of income as capital gains, which are currently taxed at 50% of earned and interest income. In exchange for these advantages they face many restrictions similar to those faced by REITs in the US. A minimum of 80% of assets must be in property, cash, bonds or mortgages situated in Canada. A minimum of 95% of the trust's income must derive from these assets, and the trust must make required distributions equal to the maximum of taxable income or 85% of pre-depreciation net income. Among the many other restrictions two stand out.[30] First, the trust has only a very limited ability to engage in real estate development. Second, the REIT will lose many of its tax benefits if at any time 50% or more of the units are owned by non-residents. The latter limits their place in the international real estate market.

A number of factors has limited the success of REITs in Canada, particularly among institutional investors. First, because they are organised under the legislation for income trusts, REITs do not have the complete veil of corporate liability. Unit-holders can be held liable at law for damages resulting from environmental problems. Second, the small size of many REITs makes them illiquid for larger investors, as any sales of shares would depress unit prices. As of October 2002 there were 15 REITs with Canadian properties trading on the Toronto Stock Exchange (TSE) with a market capitalisation of C$8.7 billion (US$5.4 billion). The largest, RioCan REIT, has a market capitalisation of close to C$2 billion, but it is more than twice the size of both the second and third largest REITs. Though the number of Canadian REITs is not dramatically different from the number in the US, relative to the size of the economy, Canadian REITs are on average four-tenths the size of US REITs. Particularly striking is how small REITs are compared with public real estate corporations. The three largest of these corporations have a larger combined market capitalisation than for all of the REITs combined.[31] These problems mean that, for many institutional investors, REITs can be inferior to direct investments in real estate.

The effect of a small REIT sector shows up in Table 11.4, which presents ownership shares in office markets for different classes of investors. The size of the pension fund share relative to that of publicly traded real estate is striking. Combining REITs and public corporations gives shares ranging

**Table 11.4**  Office market ownership shares (percentage of building square feet owned).

| Ownership class | Vancouver | Calgary | Toronto | Montreal |
|---|---|---|---|---|
| *All classes* | | | | |
| Pension fund | 34.8% | 32.8% | 30.8% | 27.4% |
| REIT | 1.8% | 5.3% | 5.0% | 2.4% |
| Public | 3.2% | 8.7% | 5.7% | 0.7% |
| Private | 15.0% | 18.4% | 18.8% | 27.1% |
| Financial inst. | 9.7% | 10.8% | 8.7% | 8.3% |
| Other owners | 27.0% | 19.4% | 20.5% | 22.4% |
| Total unaccounted for | 8.4% | 4.6% | 10.5% | 11.6% |
| *Class A* | | | | |
| Pension fund | 39.9% | 40.2% | 44.0% | 45.5% |
| REIT | 0.8% | 4.7% | 5.7% | 0.5% |
| Public | 3.9% | 10.0% | 6.7% | 0.9% |
| Private | 11.6% | 12.3% | 13.6% | 15.4% |
| Financial inst. | 10.9% | 11.0% | 7.8% | 11.6% |
| Other owners | 25.9% | 20.6% | 14.4% | 13.3% |
| Total unaccounted for | 7.0% | 1.1% | 7.7% | 12.9% |

*Source: Bank of Canada.*

from 3.1% to 14% for all classes and 1.4% to 14.7% for class A buildings. In comparison, the market share for pension funds is 2.3 to 8.8 times as high for all classes and 2.7 to 32.5 times as high for class A properties. Pension funds also hold 40% of the regional shopping centres across Canada, with a 54% share by rentable area. Overall, in 2001 Canadian pension funds held C$30.3 billion in real estate assets, more than three times the market capitalisation of REITs, more than double the same measure for all public real estate corporations, and 33% higher than the two combined. As well, they accounted for 45% of the C$6.9 billion invested in Canadian commercial real estate. In comparison, in the US for all real estate, pension funds had a 21% share, as compared with REITs' 18% share.

The real estate holdings of pension funds have been concentrated in the largest funds. Of the $30.3 billion, 87% is held by the largest funds, even though they hold 52% of total pension fund assets. Over the last three years the largest funds have acquired and taken private some of the largest public real estate corporations in Canada: Ontario Teachers', Canada's largest pension fund, took Cadillac Fairview private in 2000; the second largest pension fund, the Caisse de depot et placement du Quebec (the Caisse), purchased and took private Ivanhoe and Cambridge Shopping Centres in 1999; and in 2001, Ontario Municipal Employees Retirement System (OMERS), Canada's third largest pension fund, acquired all of the shares of Oxford Properties and took it private. As a result, the universe of publicly traded real estate has declined while the share held by pension funds, particularly of trophy properties, has risen. As major portfolios of real estate assets have come up for sale, the pension funds have acquired the assets.[32] This concentration has become particularly acute in some markets. As of 2002, four pension funds own 45% of the class A office square footage in downtown Vancouver.[33]

## Real estate finance

The financing of real estate in Canada has changed greatly over the last two decades. The combination of the financial difficulties incurred by financial institutions such as the trusts and insurance companies in the wake of the real estate meltdown in the mid- to late 1980s, and changes in Canadian banking law, have served to greatly increase the importance of commercial banks in the supply of residential mortgages, term financing of commercial real estate, and the provision of acquisition, development and construction financing. Comparing Canada with the US, several differences relevant to real estate lending immediately stand out. First, Canada has always had national branch banking and lending; second, the historical importance of real estate lending by non-banks; finally, the comparatively low degree of securitisation of real estate debt in Canada. This section presents an overview of the supply of credit to real estate, with a focus on these three aspects.

The primary suppliers of credit in Canada have been the chartered banks, trust and loan companies, the cooperative credit movement (credit unions or *caisses populaires*), life insurance companies and securities dealers. The chartered banks differ first in that they are exclusively chartered by the federal government, as opposed to the trusts and life insurance companies which can have either, and the credit unions which are chartered exclusively by provincial governments.[34] Historically, the chartered banks focused on commercial lending, while the trusts were the primary suppliers of residential mortgage credit. Their small national share hides the major role the credit unions play in British Columbia and Saskatchewan and the *caisses populaires* in Quebec. Mortgage credit has been one of their traditional lines of business.

The role of the commercial banks in mortgage lending has grown dramatically in recent years. Until 1954 the commercial banks were effectively excluded from residential mortgage lending. The amendments to the Bank Act in that year allowed them to make mortgage loans insured under the National Housing Act, insurance now provided by the crown corporation the Canada Mortgage and Housing Corporation (CMHC). The 1967 amendments permitted banks to make conventional uninsured mortgage loans. From a market share of 10% in 1970, banks' share of residential mortgages

**Table 11.5** Mortgages outstanding ($m).

| Year | Chartered banks | Credit unions | Life insurance companies | Trusts & mortgage loan companies |
|------|-----------------|---------------|--------------------------|----------------------------------|
| *Residential* | | | | |
| 1984 | 34,956 | 16,770 | 10,159 | 32,425 |
| 1985 | 40,899 | 18,381 | 10,626 | 35,881 |
| 1990 | 102,660 | 31,994 | 16,339 | 72,084 |
| 1995 | 184,499 | 47,057 | 20,742 | 40,029 |
| 2000 | 269,323 | 56,619 | 16,640 | 4,976 |
| 2001 | 295,341 | 62,232 | 16,425 | 5,401 |
| Share 1984 | 37.1% | 17.8% | 10.8% | 34.4% |
| Share 2001 | 77.8% | 16.4% | 4.3% | 1.4% |
| *Non-residential* | | | | |
| 1984 | 3,079 | 3,403 | 10,255 | 6,329 |
| 1985 | 3,525 | 3,388 | 11,920 | 7,235 |
| 1990 | 7,505 | 2,863 | 29,176 | 15,610 |
| 1995 | 13,012 | 7,265 | 27,476 | 4,005 |
| 2000 | 15,811 | 9,170 | 22,674 | 529 |
| 2001 | 15,898 | 10,253 | 22,516 | 511 |
| Share 1984 | 13.3% | 14.8% | 44.5% | 27.4% |
| Share 2001 | 32.3% | 20.8% | 45.8% | 1.0% |

*Source: Bank of Canada.*

has grown steadily. As Table 11.5 shows, by 1984 the banks had become important suppliers of mortgage credit. They are currently the dominant providers, following their acquisition of most of the major trust companies in the early 1990s, many of which had suffered greatly from the downturn in commercial real estate in the late 1980s and early 1990s.

## Securitisation of residential and commercial mortgage debt

In comparison to the US, the securitisation of real estate debt has lagged tremendously. At the end of 2001, of the US$6.194 billion in outstanding residential mortgage debt in the US, US$3,462 billion or almost 56% was held and securitised by the government-sponsored enterprises (GSEs) Fannie Mae, Freddie Mac and Ginnie Mae, and private mortgage securitisers (the latter have an 18% share). In sharp contrast, in 2001 in Canada only C$34.7 billion of the C$460 billion in outstanding residential mortgage debt, or 7.5%, was securitised. One reason is that until parliament allowed CMHC to guarantee timely payment in 1985, there was no possibility of securitisation by a government-affiliated agency. More critically, compared to the US there has been little demand or supply-side pressure for these securities. National banks, trusts and life insurance companies already have a geographically diversified portfolio, so they do not need to sell mortgages to achieve balance.

Since the 1960s the deposit-taking lenders have done a good job of matching their mortgage and deposit terms, so they have not faced disintermediation risks. Deposit insurance only covers deposits with terms of no more than five years and financial regulations in Canada for conventional mortgages allow the prohibition on pre-payment for the first five years of a mortgage. Thus, most mortgages in Canada have a term of five years or less. Competition for mortgages is quite aggressive and they are perceived as a desirable asset to hold. Consequently, more loans remain in a lender's portfolio. On the demand side, CMHC, the crown corporation that is the securitising agency, can only work with National Housing Act-insured loans (42% of new loans in 1999), which reduces the size of the market.

The Canadian commercial mortgage-backed securities (CMBS) market has also lagged behind that in the US. In the US, CMBS rose from US$5 billion in 1990 to US$74 billion in 2001. Since 1996, CMBS in the US has been the largest single source of permanent commercial mortgage financing. In Canada, the first issue was not even brought to market until 1998. Total new issues in Canada in 2001 were C$1.6 billion, less than 2% of the US total, and well below the 10% rule for Canadian markets as a percentage of those in the US. The two primary issuers of CMBS in Canada have been Merrill Lynch Canada and CDP Mortgages, an arm of the Caisse de Depot. Since the banks have preferred to keep mortgages in their own portfolios and they own most of the major investment banking firms, there has been less impetus for this market to develop. MCAP financial is bringing the first development loan CMS to market in 2004.

## Development financing

The growing importance of banks as a source of financing also holds for development lending. Data on construction financing in the Vancouver area by Somerville (2002) finds that between 1985 and 1997 the banks dramatically increased their share of construction loans from 24% to 56%. As with national term financing, this growth came principally at the expense of the trusts, many of which were absorbed by the schedule I banks. Figure 11.9 shows this change over time. One important difference here is that, although most bank loans are by national lenders, a substantial portion of the growth in activity is because of lending by the Hong Kong & Shanghai Banking Corporation (HSBC) following its purchase of the Bank of British Columbia. The growing role of HSBC, whose Canadian unit's home office is in Vancouver, is most evident in data on market share by lender home office location. Ontario-based lenders, which include nearly all of the national banks, increased their shares through 1992. But with the downturn in their home market,

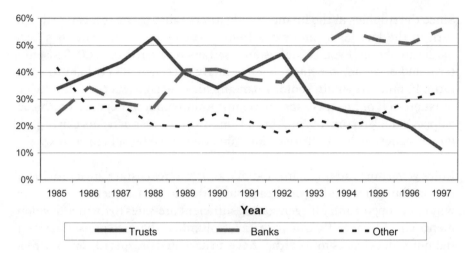

**Fig. 11.9**  Strata construction loan shares by type of lender.

there was a sharp drop in their British Columbia market share in 1992 and 1993. At the same time, British Columbia-based lenders, especially HSBC and to a lesser extent the province's largest credit union, VanCity, started to increase their loan activity. British Columbia-based lender share increased through 1997.

Analysis of lending flows into the Vancouver strata (condominium) market finds that bank capital flows across the country in response to market conditions. As the Vancouver market improved relative to a lender's home market, banks increased their lending in Vancouver. The number of senior and junior loans made in the Vancouver metropolitan area falls as market conditions in a lender's home housing market rises relative to the Vancouver market. This pattern holds true for market share as well. This research provides evidence that suggests that Canada's lending market allows capital to flow effectively, but that there is clear segmentation within the market by class of lender into loan size, types and clientele.

The statistical analysis of mortgage characteristics raises some provocative results that demonstrate quite strongly that there are qualitative differences across lender types. First, irrespective of housing market conditions, national banks are more likely to make senior loans. Schedule I banks charge a premium in the spread over prime for their loans relative to other lenders. Local lenders make smaller loans, and appear to provide capital to smaller, less well-capitalised builders.

Since the troubles in the financial industry because of the real estate downturn in the late 1980s and early 1990s, development financing has been
harder to obtain. Even as real estate markets recovered in 2000–02, senior
term and development financing has rarely exceeded a 75% loan to value
ratio. In order to obtain senior financing for new construction, developers
must pre-sell or pre-lease space; the minimum amount depends on the developer's track record. In Alberta and Ontario, pre-sales deposits can be used
for construction, but in British Columbia they must be held in escrow.

Rules governing the financing and marketing of real estate are a provincial
responsibility. Depending on the province, developers can face a very narrow
window of opportunity for generating sufficient pre-sales to finance development. This is especially true in British Columbia where, to pre-sell residential units, developers must either have an accepted prospectus or have filed
a disclosure statement with the Office of the Superintendent of Real Estate
(SRE). The former is a much more strenuous requirement and takes longer
to be accepted, such that it effectively precludes pre-sales. Amendments to
the Real Estate Act in 1985 that allowed a disclosure statement in lieu of a
prospectus are what allowed pre-sales to become possible. However, if the
SRE does not like the prospectus or believes the development is 'risky' it
will require that a prospectus be accepted and place a halt order on all sales
activity. Critically for development finance, both the disclosure statement
and prospectus require that financing and building permits be in place prior
to sales.[35]

Developers face a challenge in that they need pre-sales to obtain financing,
but cannot file a disclosure statement and receive deposits without financing in place. To break this deadlock, developers have several options. First,
even without a disclosure statement they can engage in market testing, but
they explicitly are not allowed to enter into contracts, receive deposits, list
a specific price or give prospective purchasers 'the impression they have the
right of first refusal or have actually purchased a lot'. Second, Policy Statement no. 5 by the SRE allows pre-sales prior to the issuance of a building
permit, if it will be issued within six months and a number of other restrictions. Third, the SRE's Policy Statement no. 6 creates a six-month window
where developers can pre-sell and take deposits of up to 10% of the price
prior to a commitment of financing. However, once the financing commitment is obtained and the final disclosure statement is filed and delivered to
purchasers, they have seven days in which they can cancel their contract and
receive all monies in return with applicable interest. Effectively, developers
have six months after getting through most of the regulatory process to sell
enough units to obtain financing.

# Conclusion

The adage by the late US Speaker of the House of Representatives, Tip O'Neil, that all politics are local applies equally well to real estate. In Canada, it is not just that market conditions can be highly localised. Rather the intersection of Canada's high degree of provincial autonomy and local regulation of land use means that, while it is one country, local institutional knowledge is critical. Although the shared legal traditions and the federal framework allow capital, developers and investors to seamlessly cross provincial boundaries, much must be relearned in each jurisdiction, especially for real estate development. With Quebec even these similarities are complicated by differences arising from language, cultural and legal traditions.

# References

Brooks, S.M. & Laing, C.A.M. (2002) *The Canadian REIT Guide*. Canadian Institute of Public and Private Real Estate Companies, Toronto, ON.

Broughton, T. (2001) Exploring Pension Funds' Growing Involvement in Real Estate. *Benefits and Pensions Monitor*, Oct.

Chipman, J.G. (1996) *The Planning Act in Transition: A Step by Step Guide to the Statutory and Regulatory Changes*. Canada Law Books, Toronto, ON.

Dyck, R. (2000) *Canadian Politics: Critical Approaches*. Nelson Thomson Learning, Scarborough, ON.

Freedman, C. (1998) *The Canadian Banking System*. Bank of Canada Discussion Paper.

Rothblatt, D.N. (1994) North American Metropolitan Planning. *Journal of the American Planning Association* **60**(4), 501–21.

Somerville, C.T. (2002) Does the Lender Matter? Lender Type and Home Office Location and Real Estate Development Lending. *Canadian Journal of Administrative Sciences* **19**(4), 321–32.

Superintendent of Real Estate, British Columbia Financial Institutions Commission (periodic) *Guide to Disclosure Statements*.

Webb, K. (1997) Gorillas in Closets? Federal-Provincial Fisheries Act Pollution Control Enforcement. In: *Managing the Environmental Union: Intergovernmental Relations and Environmental Policy in Canada* (eds P.C. Fafard & K. Harrison). Institute of Intergovernmental Relations, Queen's University, Kingston, ON.

Winfield, M.S. (2002) Environmental Policy and Federalism. In: *Canadian Federalism: Performance, Effectiveness, and Legitimacy* (eds H. Bakvis, & G. Skogstad). Oxford University Press Canada, Don Mills, ON.

Ziff, B.H. (1996) *Principles of Property Law*. Carswell, Scarborough, ON.

# Notes

1 During 2001–02, over 255,000 individuals immigrated to Canada, representing 0.81% of the July 2002 estimated population of 31,413,990. In comparison, the US accepted 849,807 immigrants, approximately 0.3% of the population.

2 Crown lands include all national parks, defence establishments, 99% of the land in the Yukon, Northwest Territories and Nunavut, and many sites in the Ottawa area.

3 *R. v. Crown Zellerbach* (1988) and *Friends of the Oldham River Society* v. *Canada* (1992).

4 The cities of Calgary and Edmonton have population shares of the metropolitan areas (CMAs) of 92% and 71% respectively. This compares to 53%, 30% and 27% in Toronto, Montreal and Vancouver, respectively.

5 http://www.omb.gov.on.ca/.

6 The five suburban jurisdictions were themselves products of earlier mergers. Other important Canadian amalgamations took place in Ottawa and Halifax.

7 Subsequent to the 2001 technology meltdown and following substantial criticism from the local development community, the project has been cut in half and the e-commerce tax credit extended to the entire downtown area.

8 Detailed information is available from the British Columbia Ministry of Community, Aboriginal, and Women's Services, http://mcaws.gov.bc.ca/charter

9 This section draws heavily from Ziff (1996).

10 *Pacific National Investments Ltd.* v. *Victoria (City) 2000.*

11 In *Shell Canada Products* v. *Vancouver (City), 1964*, the British Columbia Court of Appeal ruled that 'the courts, in interpreting the scope of powers of municipal authorities, ought to take a more generous and deferential approach ... and should confine themselves to rectifying clear excesses of authority...'.

12 Two recent Supreme Court cases bear on this. First, in *Delgamuukw* v. *British Columbia, 1993*, the Court ruled that aboriginal land-use rights are not eliminated if the primary purpose of a state action is the transfer of land to non-aboriginals. In *R* v. *Sparrow, 1990*, the Supreme Court of Canada ruled that government must provide a legitimate public policy justification for any reduction of aboriginal rights.

13 Crown lands constitute most rural non-agricultural land in Canada, especially in the territories.

14 British Columbia Treaty Commission: http://www.bctreaty.net/

15 Palmer, Vaughn 'Natives Get a Veto on Government Decisions', *Vancouver Sun.* 1 November 2002. www.vancouversun.com

16 Information on the details of the process for the City of Vancouver and the City of Toronto are available from http://www.city.vancouver.bc.ca/commsvcs/developmentservices and http://www.city.toronto.on.ca/planning/planning_app.htm respectively.

17  Most of the areas of Vancouver not zoned for single-family residential uses are for a comprehensive development district. These are effectively site-specific zoning. Use, density and design are not proscribed in advance, but all applications must go through an arduous review process.

18  http://www.smartgrowth.gov.on.ca

19  The Oak Ridges Moraine is a ridge of sandy hills 160 km in length, of which 65% lies within the Greater Toronto Area. Provincial legislation halted all development, planning and zoning activity in the area while the province developed a plan to identify areas for preservation, conservation and development. The final plan limits development in 90% of the Moraine and even areas targeted for development put conservation and protection requirements on development.

20  By a vote of 55–52 the GVRD board rejected a plan to build high-density residential buildings in Richmond on land designated for agricultural and industrial uses.

21  AUMA/UDI/AAMD&C Development Levies Task Force. See position and policy papers of the Alberta Urban Municipalities Association (AUMA) http://munilink.net

22  See http://www.city.toronto.on.ca/torontoplan for details on the new Official Plan. The areas targeted for less constrained and more flexible redevelopment are mixed use, employment, regeneration (brownfield) and institutional areas.

23  The ALR was established in 1973 through the Agricultural Land Commission Act and includes 4.7m ha, about 5% of the province, but about 50% of the non-mountainous land. It is administered by the Agricultural Land Commission (http://www.alc.gov.bc.ca).

24  Approximately 38% of the land in the City of Richmond, due south of the City of Vancouver, is in the ALR. The city of Surrey has a population of nearly 350,000 and has been one of the fastest-growing cities in Canada, yet approximately half of the city's land mass lies in the ALR. These percentages are higher for undeveloped land.

25  The metropolitan areas had 2001 populations as follows: Toronto 4,682,897, Montreal 3,426,350, Vancouver 1,986,965, and Calgary 951,395.

26  With the collapse of the technology bubble, vacancy rates increased dramatically in these suburban markets in the period following the date of the table.

27  Employment data is from The Conference Board of Canada. The raw data comes from Statistics Canada reports.

28  Housing start numbers are those published by CMHC (Canadian Mortgage and Housing Corporation). Real house prices are calculations based on the results of the Royal LePage Survey of Canadian House Prices http://www.royallepage.ca/calculators/nptc/index.asp

29  Buildings suffered building envelope failure caused by rot when water penetrated the structures but was not able to evaporate. The costs of cleaning up the problem range as high as $1 billion. To date the problem has affected wood-frame multi-family structures, typically 3–4 stories in height. There is a growing concern that high-rise concrete structures are also vulnerable, and will be dramatically more expensive to repair. The Barrett Commission reported on this problem: http://www.hpo.bc.ca/Overview/index.htm#The Barrett Commission . This is also

an issue in New Zealand; see the Hunn report http://www.bia.govt.nz/publicat/
pdf/bia-report-17-9-02.pdf.

30  Other restrictions are: a size test for single investments, limits on their holdings
of foreign property, exclusion from most joint ventures, and REITs can only invest
in mortgages that meet certain criteria (maximum 75% LTV and minimum 1.2
debt service coverage ratio).

31  On 21 October 2002, Brookfield Properties, Fairmount Hotels and Resorts, and
Four Seasons had a combined market capitalisation of C$8.9 billion. However,
most other public real estate corporations are the size of or smaller than the
average REIT. The total for all public real estate corporations was C$14.1 billion.
This compared with C$8.6 billion for REITs.

32  Between 1999 and 2001, three of the largest Canadian banks, CIBC, Royal Bank,
and Toronto-Dominion, sold C$2.8 billion of real estate, principally downtown
office towers, to major pension funds.

33  Ontario Teachers' (Cadillac-Fairview), the Caisse (Bentall), OMERS (Oxford) and
the British Columbia Super Annuation Fund (source: private Colliers International
report).

34  The Credit Union Central of Canada (CUCC), which is a national organisation
providing administrative, technical and financial support services to member
credit unions, is governed by federal legislation.

35  These must be filed with the Superintendent of Real Estate.  A disclosure
statement must include descriptive details about the developer, development,
legal interests of the developer, list of existing and proposed encumbrances on
the property, outstanding litigation against the development or developer, an
indication of government development approval, and a filing commitment.

# 12

# Real Estate Markets in Japan

## *Yu Ichiro Kawaguchi*

The rules of the game applying to real estate markets in Japan are closely tied to structural characteristics of the Japanese economy. In particular, informal rules peculiar to the country create inertia and make change difficult. In order that the Japanese economic system may escape from its financial crisis and fully address the problem of non-performing loans, new international standards of practice, referred to as 'full dress' rules, have been introduced (mainly from the US). Nevertheless, local informal rules still apply, maintaining inertia and inhibiting the change needed to give full compliance to international standards. Indeed, the double standard creates conflicts between both sets of rules. For example, an attempt has been made to introduce US/UK-style leasehold agreements (*Teiki-Shakuya* rental contract) to replace the traditional Japanese *Futsu-Shakuya* agreement. However, the effectiveness of the rules introduced from abroad is undermined because they are not properly enforced and do not function well.

In Japan, land represents a high percentage of the total value of real estate, and the design life of buildings is relatively short. Thus depreciation expenses and repair costs tend to be substantially lower than in other countries, including the US. Land prices in Japan have fallen continuously for 10 years or more. One reason for this is the substantial burden of bad loans produced by the collapse of the bubble economy of the early 1990s. The Japanese government introduced US-style real estate liquidation policies in order to resolve non-performing loans. However, far from reducing bad loans, conversely, they continued to increase.

In order to understand the Japanese real estate system, we have to understand not only the mechanism of the market but also the 'rules of the game'. This chapter describes the formal rules (the constitutional rules relating to property rights and contracts) and the informal rules (the norms and customs) relating to real estate in Japan. The real estate system consists of three distinct yet related markets for (1) rentable space, (2) ownership of real estate assets and (3) capital. The broad operating principles for each of these markets are outlined below. A major factor throughout these markets is the system of taxation, which can be particularly onerous.

## The Japanese rental market

The market for space (accommodation) is predominantly a rental market. For example, an outline investigation of the prices of 'fixed assets, etc.', undertaken in 2000 under the auspices of the Ministry of Public Management, Home Affairs, Posts and Telecommunications, indicated that in a metropolitan area comprising four cities and prefectures, of the total stock of office space (20,961 ha), approximately 50% (10,980 ha) was leased. Moreover, according to Mitsui Fudosan Co. Ltd. (real estate-related statistics collection no. 23), in 1999, the national stock of retail store space was approximately 13,388 ha. The average annual increase in supply of office property was approximately 700 ha, of which approximately 70% was rented. In 2001, the average vacancy rate stood at about 6% of the total stock.

Three key features of the Japanese rental market are:

- The *Futsu-Shakuya* rental system (a formal, legal rule regime);

- The *Hosho-Kin* (guarantee money) system (an informal rule regime);

- The taxation of income from rented property.

### *The* Futsu-Shakuya *rental system*

The rental rules for residential and non-residential buildings are exactly the same under Japanese law. There are two kinds of lease contract, *Futsu-Shakuya* and *Teiki-Shakuya*. However, the *Futsu-Shakuya* contract is by far the most widely used rental agreement, applying to 99% of rental property in Japan. The *Teiki-Shakuya* rental contract was only introduced in March 2000. This innovation is similar to a leasehold tenancy in US/UK, in which the agreement terminates at the expiration of the period set by the contract, unless the terms of the contract are modified by agreement between landlord and tenant. As of November 2001, there are only two recorded cases of buildings in which all tenants have agreed to adopt the *Teiki-Shakuya* contract.

Under a *Futsu-Shakuya* contract, a landlord may not resume possession of the property without 'just reason'. This normally means that the landlord needs to resume possession of the property for his or her own occupation. In theory, the tenant's right to exclusive possession and quiet enjoyment of the property can continue indefinitely. A *Futsu-Shakuya* treaty provides the tenant with very strong security of tenure. On the other hand, the landlord may be saddled with the risk of an unsuitable or undesirable tenant.

Key features of the *Futsu-Shakuya* treaty are:

- A tenant may quit without penalty at any time, provided he or she announces their intention to leave six months in advance of quitting;

- The lease contract has a renewable term of two years;

- At the request of the tenant, the contract will be updated almost automatically.

For the majority of rental property in Japan, the rules include provision for automatic renewal of a lease contract subject to an escape option for the tenant.

The circumstances in which a landlord can resume possession of a house or building are limited and apply only if the accommodation is required for the personal use of the landlord and greater hardship would be caused by not allowing the landlord to resume possession. If 'just reason' cannot be demonstrated, then a tenant can use a space in perpetuity. This rule can be susceptible to significant abuse, for example, the space may be occupied by a Japanese Mafiosi (*Yakuza*) without contravening the lease contract rules, provided he is not using the space for illegal purposes.

When the tenant quits, it is the custom (confirmed by judicial precedent) for the landlord to pay for the cost of removal. In the event of disagreement, the cost is decided at the discretion of a court. The normal level of charge ranges from 300,000 yen to about 10 million yen but may reach 100m yen or more in areas of high land prices. The sum of money may be paid to a variety of recipients, ranging from the tenant to the *Yakuza*.

The rent stated in a *Futsu-Shakuya* agreement is normally a flat rent, which may be reviewed when the contract is renewed (i.e. at two-yearly intervals). In the case of retail stores, percentage rents are widely used, often as a hybrid lease under which the tenant and landlord share the operating expenses of the building and a proportion of the rent is based on the turnover of the business. Information concerning the level of contract rents is scarce in Japan: it is very difficult for persons other than owner and tenant to obtain information about current rental levels being achieved in the market. Brokers cannot disclose an actual rent because of the rules relating to confidentiality of information. The author's estimate of the annual total rent attributable to Tokyo's 23 Wards, in June 2001, was of the order of 5 trillion yen.

## Shiki-Kin *and* Hosho-Kin *(guarantee money) systems*

Under the *Futsu-Shakuya* rental contract, in addition to the rent, a tenant normally pays to the landlord a security deposit (*Shiki-Kin*) or an advanced guarantee (*Hosho-Kin*).

### Shiki-Kin

At the time of moving in, the tenant must pay the landlord a deposit of between three and six months' rent as security against the possibility of the rent falling into arrears. If the tenant defaults in paying the rent, the rental arrears are deducted from the deposit held by the landlord. Moreover, if the tenant allows the building to become damaged or neglected, the cost of maintenance and repair are also deducted from the deposit held by the landlord. When a rental contract terminates, the residual deposit remaining with the landlord is returned to the tenant.

### Hosho-Kin

*Hosho-Kin* is more than a simple guarantee; it normally applies to new developments where the tenant is acquiring property on the basis of the plans, before the building is completed. It refers to the right of a landlord to borrow (at zero interest) part of the construction cost of the building from a prospective tenant who will take possession when the building construction is completed. This arrangement saves the developer (landlord) the cost of bank borrowing. In the case of a shopping centre, for example, 'guarantee money' typically accounts for about 30% of construction financing. The tenant of a store chain may contribute 'guarantee money' equivalent to 40 to 50 times the monthly rent, in order to secure the right to open a shop. When a rental contract terminates, the *Hosho-Kin* payment is returned to the tenant but not immediately; the landlord normally benefits from a grace period of between five and ten years.

*Taxation of income from rented property*

Japanese corporate investors and non-resident corporate investors having permanent establishments (e.g. a branch office) in Japan are subject to tax on their net rental income from real estate. Net rental income is the gross rent payable less management expenses, depreciation, interest and other expenses, determined on an accrual basis. This rental income is combined with other taxable income and the total is subject to corporate tax at a rate of 30%, as well as local enterprise and residents' taxes. Therefore, the aggregate effective tax rate is approximately 40%. Foreign corporations having no permanent establishment in Japan are subject to 30% corporate tax on net rental income. Ostensibly, they are also separately subject to a 15–20% withholding tax. However, this can be mitigated to 5–15% by the tax code and may be credited against the corporate tax liability. Similar liabilities accrue to non-resident individuals having no permanent establishment in Japan.

Japan real estate investment trusts (J-REITs) are not taxed if they distribute at least 90% of their taxable income to shareholders. Special laws enable other special entities, such as a *Tokutei Mokuteki Kaisha* (special-purpose company, SPC or TMK), to claim dividends distributed to their investors as an allowable expenditure against their tax liabilities. This includes the expense of making the dividend payment. Buildings may be depreciated at rates prescribed by ministerial ordinance using the straight-line method, while either the declining balance or the straight-line method may be used for fixtures, plant and equipment.

## The market for ownership of real estate assets

One of the most notable features of the real property market in Japan is that non-income-producing properties, including vacant land, serve as primary investment outlets. Although there are no official statistics on commercial real estate sale transactions in Japan, Yamakata (1999) estimates that, with the exception of 1998, between fiscal years 1993 and 1999 the annual number of real estate transactions undertaken by companies listed on the Tokyo Stock Exchange was approximately 200. (In 1998 there were 571 transactions.) On the other hand, during the same period approximately 350,000 transactions per annum involving sales of land were recorded in the Tokyo Metropolitan Area. (This figure represents approximately 20% of the number of land sale transactions for the country as a whole.)

The total value of land assets in Japan is estimated to be 1,616 trillion yen, of which the land assets of the Tokyo region (four cities and prefectures) account for 561 trillion yen (National Economic Accounts of Japan 1998). Using an income approach, the market value of income-producing properties in the Tokyo region may be estimated at about 100–200 trillion yen. From this total, the real estate investment portfolio of life insurance companies is estimated to be worth just 9.15 trillion yen (Ministry of Land, Infrastructure and Transport 1998). By comparison, the scale of institutional investment in real estate in the US is equivalent to about 450 trillion yen. Moreover, the investment value of the income-producing properties owned by eleven major real estate companies is 2 trillion yen (Mitsui Fudosan Co. Ltd 2000: 176). The same eleven real estate companies hold non-income-producing land worth 3.3 trillion yen. In other words, even for these eleven major companies, the book value of their ownership of vacant land is greater than the investment value of their income-producing properties.

In Japan, few institutional investors or other professional investors choose to invest in income-producing real estate. The number of major transactions involving income-producing properties has, traditionally, been very small. However, driven by interest from US investors, this situation is changing. In order to understand some of the intricacies contributing to this state of affairs, it is necessary to know about rules relating to (1) 'hidden assets' or 'unrealised capital gains', (2) real estate taxes and (3) the official declared land price system.

## Unrealised capital gains and hidden assets

Under conditions of economic growth, there is a strong correlation between GDP and land prices in Japan, illustrated in Fig. 12.1 (indexed to 1955 values). For the growth period 1955–90, the coefficient of determination for the index of urban land prices and nominal GDP is 97.9%. As long as economic growth continued, land prices went on rising. On the other hand, market players possess only imperfect knowledge about the future direction of the market. (Most forecasting models are constructed entirely with hindsight.) Most players are largely unaware of (1) the intrinsic structure of the real estate market, particularly the economic fundamentals that drive it or the institutional structure that determines the rules of the game, and (2) the influence of extrinsic factors that affect the way the game is played. They have a subjective model of market behaviour, based largely on their own experience. This tends to rely heavily on the assumption that the future will resemble the past and the outcome of the game will, therefore, not deviate substantially from previous outcomes.

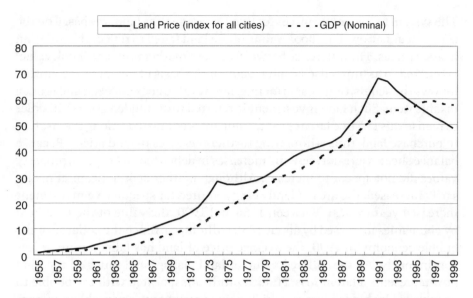

**Fig. 12.1**   Land price and GDP in Japan (1955 = 1.0). *Source (land price): Japan Real Estate Research Institute.*

If the subjective game model is constantly adjusted and updated by players' observation of the facts over a period of time, their actions are reinforced. Moreover, their subjective game model is also used as the basis for selecting further action. For example, over a period of 20 years (1955–75), the coefficient of determination for land price in relation to GDP was 98.9%. For the subsequent ten years (from 1976 to 1985) it fell slightly to 95%. Despite knowing that this result is imperfect, investors nevertheless incorporate into their subjective game model the view that 'land prices rise', thus establishing a shared or collective anticipation about the market. The danger of placing strong reliance on the infallibility of this view is that it turns into a myth. With the benefit of hindsight, the 1980s view that 'land prices surely rise' is now seen as a myth. This became evident when investment in vacant land failed to achieve the results that were expected, giving rise to a search for a new subjective model that is capable of balancing expected and actual results. This has been the state of the real estate market in Japan since 1992.

The rapid increase in economic growth between 1988 and 1997 resulted in increased divergence between GDP and the corresponding average land price. For the period 1986–95, the coefficient of determination for the regression model of land price and nominal GDP fell to 75%. During this period the government eased financial regulations and companies sought and were offered loan facilities from the banks in return for equity in real estate, stimulating a land price bubble.

The system for recording prices for fixed assets such as land was based on the cost of acquisition. The 'book value' of the land failed to reflect the inflation in asset prices. The difference between current market price and 'book value' is referred to as 'unrealised capital gain'. If the basis of business accounting follows the acquisition-cost principle, latent value does not exist and is not a taxable item. Such land investment is referred to as 'hidden assets'. In order to realise this tax-free latent profit, companies competed among themselves to purchase land, thus stimulating further increases in land prices. Because balance sheets were not showing increases in debt or equity capital, property values did not appear to increase. Although neither debt nor capital necessarily increased, the area of land being acquired for speculative investment increased year by year. Between 1986 and 1990, the value of the land held by companies increased by about 1380 trillion yen. Since the collapse of the bubble economy in 1990, the average price of land has fallen, more or less continuously. As the inflated value of land disappeared much of the land now represents a latent loss. Hidden profits disappeared with the bubble to be replaced by hidden losses, which now contribute to the problem of non-performing loans in Japan.

## Real property taxes

### Capital gains resulting from the sale of real property

When real estate is sold and gains from the transfer of property are realised, the gain is treated as income and an individual becomes liable to income tax and a resident tax, or, in the case of a corporation, corporation tax and a resident tax. In some cases, moreover, there may be a liability to other levies such as documentary stamp tax and registration licence tax, irrespective of the existence of gains from the transfer of property.

Under the Japanese tax code, there is no distinction between capital gains and net operating income for corporate tax purposes. The capital gain derived from the sale of real property by a Japanese company is combined with other taxable income and the total is subject to corporate tax at a rate of 30%. Local enterprise and residents' taxes are separately charged as an additional item. As a result, the aggregate effective tax rate is approximately 40%. A foreign company having a permanent establishment in Japan is treated in the same way as a Japanese company for tax purposes. Capital gains realised on the transfer of real estate located in Japan, by a foreign corporate investor without a permanent establishment in Japan, are exempt from the local enterprise and residents' taxes but subject to the 30% standard rate.

As a result of the destabilising effects of economic bubbles in land markets and in order to control land speculation, an additional tax on short-term capital gains realised on the sale of land, land rights and shares in Japanese landholding companies was introduced as a political measure. The tax rate was 15% for land held for two years or less, 10% for land held for five years or less, and 5% for land held for more than five years. The holding period is calculated from its acquisition date to 1 January of the year in which a taxable transfer of the real estate takes place, rather than to the actual date of disposal. However, this speculation tax was suspended for land sold between 1 January 1998 and 31 December 2003. (An additional tax of 15% levied on capital gains accruing from the transfer of super-short-term possession has been abolished with effect from 31 December 1997.)

A withholding (of income) tax of 10% is levied, in principle, on the proceeds of sale earned by foreign corporations that sell Japanese real property. This does not apply to the sale of a residence to an individual for personal use or the use of relatives, where the purchase price is less than 100 million yen. The withholding tax may be credited against the 30% normal national tax by filing a tax return.

Taxes on holding real property

The following taxes apply to the holding of real estate assets.

- A *Land Value Tax*, intended to reduce the profitability of holding land without using it, is imposed on domestic, undeveloped land held by an individual or corporation on 1 January of the relevant tax year. The tax is based on the assessed value of land (as prescribed by the Land Value Tax Law) less an exemption of up to 1.5 billion yen. The rate of tax varies and currently is suspended.

- *Fixed Assets Tax* and *a City Planning Tax*, with standard rates of 1.4% and 0.3%, respectively, are levied on a taxable value determined by the local tax authority. In some cases, since this value can be higher than open market value, the tax burden of these two taxes may reduce a lease profit by half.

- A *Special Land Holding Tax*, aimed at stabilising land prices by controlling speculative trading in 'bare' land and promoting a stable supply of land for housing, is imposed on possession or acquisition of the land beyond a fixed scale. This tax is levied at a rate of 1.4%, based on the purchase price of the property. Other fixed assets tax can be credited against this tax.

- Business Office Tax is a local tax applicable in 69 designated cities such as Tokyo (special ward). This tax is based on floor space and levied at a rate of 600 yen per square metre of floor space used for business purposes, and 0.25% of the annual payroll. The business office tax does not apply to corporations with floor space of 1000 square metres or less, or with fewer than 100 employees.

### Taxes on the purchase of real property

The size of the tax burden on the purchase of real estate is substantial, possibly exceeding the first year's profit from the property. An illustrative calculation produced by the Ministry of Land, Infrastructure and Transport demonstrates the combined impact of registration licence tax and real estate acquisition tax on the purchase of a 30-storey office building in central Tokyo, with a floor area of 100,000 square metres. If the acquisition price is 100 billion yen against expected net revenue of about 4700 million yen, the aggregate tax imposed on the acquisition transaction is approximately 5200 million yen.

- *Registration Tax* is levied when title changes are registered (for example, on the acquisition of real property). The rate of tax is 5% levied on the appraised value of the property. For transactions registered between 1 April 1996 and 31 March 2003, the tax is levied on one-third of the assessed value attributable to the land, but not on buildings or improvements. (A fixed-asset tax base can be used as an appraised value.)

- *Real Estate Acquisition Tax* is a local tax payable by individuals or corporations on the acquisition of real estate. In general, the amount payable is 4% of the assessed value of the real property acquired, regardless of whether consideration is paid for the property. The tax is reduced to 3% for the acquisition of residential properties acquired up until 30 June 2004. Usually, the price on which the amount of tax is based is an official assessment. When no such 'benchmark' value has been assessed, the local prefecture governor determines the base value.

- A 5% *Consumption Tax* is imposed on the trading of buildings but not bare land. The amount payable can be offset against consumption tax received from customers.

## Official declared land price system

On behalf of the Japanese government, the Ministry of Land, Infrastructure and Transport determines an official assessed value of land, *Kouji-Chika*. (A similar system is employed in South Korea and Taiwan.) The Ministry of Land appraises 31,000 monitored sites in January each year. Local governments also appraise a further 28,120 monitored sites, annually, to interpolate the government official land prices. Before 1994, official land prices took little or no account of the profit derived from real estate. In 1994 the government introduced an income approach into the appraisal of official land prices.

The official land price is considered to be the benchmark standard in the following circumstances:

(1) General land dealings: the assessed value of land is used instead of fair market value in relevant calculations.

(2) Appraisal calculations undertaken by real estate appraisers: Japanese real estate appraisers must use official land prices as comparables in financial appraisals of land.

(3) Establishing the standard value of public common ground, etc., in the event of acquisition.

(4) Calculating inheritance tax or fixed property tax liabilities. For the purposes of calculating inheritance tax, the value of land transferred as a result of an inheritance should be calculated at about 80% of the official land price. For the purposes of calculating property taxes, the value of land should be calculated at about 70% of the official land price.

Real estate appraisers and brokers are forbidden by law from indicating actual market prices, which must be kept confidential. Similar restrictions apply to government organisations and private enterprises. The government restricts any indication of market price, other than its own official land price. Consequently, it is very difficult to get to know or analyse the market price of real estate in Japan, though some companies sell real estate market data.

A declared land value is neither a market price nor a fair price. It is an artificial price declared by the government. These artificial prices have greatly distorted the real estate market in Japan. Market prices reflect a variety of information about a market. The official assessed value of land reflects not only market information but also an intention of the government. Because these two factors cannot be disaggregated, the official assessed value is a misleading basis for making accurate market judgements.

One of the aims of government policy relating to the property market is to minimise fluctuations in the price of land. Therefore, when land prices are rising, investors would be justified in suspecting that government estimates determining official land prices would be lower than the market price. Conversely, when land prices are falling, government estimates for determining official land prices are likely to be slightly higher than prevailing market prices.

In order to have a clear picture of the land market in Japan, investors must understand the gap between the official land prices and true land prices. A number of overseas investors and foreign companies do understand the anomaly between actual and official property prices and have been active participants in the real estate market in Japan. Since 1998, the list of overseas investors includes Morgan Stanley, Goldman Sachs, Pacific Century Group, Loan Star Opportunity Fund, Credit Suisse First Boston and Secured Capital. For example, since the collapse of the bubble economy in 1991, the assessed value of land has fallen continuously although, in fact, the market price has not fallen continuously over this period. For example, since 1997, in the Chuo, Chiyoda, Minato and Shinjuku wards of central Tokyo, where prime, relatively new and large office buildings are concentrated, office prices have increased. The true return on investment (yield) for central Tokyo prime office space is of the order of 5–6%, but using official price data would produce a distorted picture.

In general, official land prices are likely to be higher than market prices in residential areas. For example, in 1992/93 Daikyo, Japan's largest condominium builder, completed and offered for sale approximately 1,200 condominium units (mostly studio apartments) at an average price of 30 million yen. The units remained unsold until purchased by Morgan Stanley in 1998 at a 66% discount (a reported contract price of 12 billion yen). The units were turned into rental units, producing an annual 6–7% return on investment (JETRO 1998). Using the official land price to calculate the return on investment would have the effect of reducing the apparent yield to about 4%.

## Capital markets

Since World War II, banks have played a prominent role in the Japanese financial system. According to Allen and Gale (2000: Table 3.1), the ratio of assets of Japanese banks to GDP is of the order of 150%, three times the corresponding figure for banks in the US (53% in 1993) and many times greater than the UK (0.259%). On the other hand, the ratio of equity market capitalisation to GDP in Japan is 71%, compared with 82% for the US and 140% for the UK.

## 'Main bank' system for development funding

A 'main bank' refers to the bank with the greatest loan exposure to any given company. This 'main bank' plays a major role in monitoring the company and its governance. According to an investigation undertaken in 1987 into 110,000 companies with an annual turnover of 1 billion yen or more, virtually every company in Japan, irrespective of size, has a main bank. There is no formal definition of a main bank but according to Allen and Gale (2000) the term refers to the long-term relationship that exists between a bank and its client companies. It includes the holding of debt and equity by the bank, and the active intervention of the bank should its client become financially distressed.

Aoki and Patrick (1994) identify the main characteristics of the Japanese 'main bank' system as follows.

(1) A main bank deals with the main payment and settlement of accounts on behalf of a company. During the period 1977–91, a main bank would typically offer 20% of the total debt to a client company and about 40% of loans through a local city bank.

(2) A main bank is the major stockholder of a company. Although the bank is restricted to direct ownership of 5% of the company's stock, it is able to exert the power of ownership indirectly through ownership of other non-finance companies that are, themselves, owners of the stock of the company in question. This is cross-shareholding between companies.

(3) In the event of a domestic corporate bond issue, a main bank becomes a commissioned bank, and, for overseas issues, it becomes a book runner. The main bank purchases the greater portion of the corporate bonds issued by the company.

(4) The main bank also provides additional managerial services such as information about market opportunities, new enterprises, mergers and acquisitions, and human resource management.

Historically, the Japanese government adopted a post-war policy based on the structure of corporate governance existing at the time, aimed at corporate

reconstruction and economic revival. The structure of corporate governance designed to promote growth was established during the first half of the
1950s. This policy was achieved by focusing and channelling investment
through a growth-minded main bank and encouraging the commitment of
employees to long-term growth by a 'lifetime employment' system.

The company was put under the management of a bank as a matter of fact
by corporate accounting emergency measures and the company reconstruction fixing method. In supplying new money for reconstruction, the Bank of
Japan recommended syndicated loans under the management of the main
bank. Moreover, the government aimed at reconstruction of the company
by encouraging the transfer of the previous responsibility of stockholders to
the main bank, the managers and the employees.

By the mid-1960s, in order to join the OECD, the Japanese government
needed to relax its regulation of the financial system. By the 1980s, financial
markets had become more important as the restriction on issuing bonds
was relaxed. At the same time, main bank relationships came under heavy
strain and the system began to break down, as large firms were able to rely
increasingly on financial markets to raise funds (Allen and Gale 2000: 42).
Government and main banks, however, still have a great influence in Japanese capital markets.

One might imagine that the main banks would welcome the fact that their
subsidiary developers could show on their balance sheets increases in the
value of their real estate holdings, in order to justify increasing financial
support to them to expand their market share of real estate development.
Developers needed stable, low-cost financing over a long period of time in
order to fund their expansion and, under the main bank system, developers
were able to obtain low-cost funding for potentially high-risk real estate
development projects. Banks are forbidden from pursuing real estate business as a subsidiary business activity but, during the period of land price
escalation, they provided mortgage finance secured on the collateral of land.
In this way, the interdependence of a main bank system and market share
expansion was strengthened.

The fall in land values associated with economic recession has continued,
more or less, since 1990. Main banks are now left holding many non-performing loans caused by the fall in the value of their collateral assets. Consequently, the relation between a main bank and developers is gradually
becoming weaker. Many developers have tried to by-pass the banks by seeking funds directly from investors. Nevertheless, the main bank system still
has substantial influence.

*Recourse debt*

Corporate finance in Japan relied heavily on the use of land as security for corporate funding. Most of this debt finance has a recourse note, meaning that in the event of a default resulting in foreclosure on the security for the loan, if the liquidation value of the property is insufficient to satisfy the debt, the lender has the right to pursue other assets of the borrower to recover the debt. If default occurs, the lender can obtain a court order judgment for the amount of the deficiency. Land was widely used as the main security for recourse loans employed in corporate finance in Japan. This is not real estate finance but mainstream corporate finance.

Thus, a recourse debt does not limit the lender's remedy to the value of the property serving as collateral. However, it is contrary to the spirit of the Japanese 'main bank' system for a main bank to engage in active intervention to recover debts, should its client become financially distressed. This means that the recourse debt system may be inconsistent with the main bank system in the event of a default. A 'main bank' lender is faced with a dilemma: it has the right to pursue other assets of the borrower but, at the same time, an obligation to save the client.

In 2000, the loan balance from banks to real estate businesses was 60,300 billion yen, in the form of corporate (mostly recourse) loans. In 1998, the balance of the collateral value of real estate was 118,200 billion yen. Of course, a housing loan is also a recourse loan and such loans amount to 180,300 billion yen (1999).

Corporate-style loans used real estate as collateral but with little meaningful reference to real estate underwriting criteria. It is fair to say that there was no real estate-based lending market in commercial properties before the period 1998–99. In the past, Japanese banks made corporate-style loans to industrial and real estate companies, secured by real estate but with recourse. However, since 1999, non-recourse loans have expanded the scale of the real estate debt market in Japan.

## Conclusion

The rules of the game for old-style real estate investment in Japan are shifting to the rules of a new game. Here, the method by which a game is repeated is also a rule. And, as mentioned above, a 'self-sustaining system of shared beliefs' remains a 'rule' of market behaviour. The old game consisted largely of investing in vacant land, funded by a recourse loan from the main bank based on the official land price system.

Most investors chose to adopt the equilibrium strategy of investing in a vacant lot by observing the continuous rise in land prices over about 40 years. Investment in vacant lots was the manifestation of the shared belief that the market will always continue as it has done in the past. The vacant lot investment game became the rule as outcomes repeatedly reinforced and fuelled expectations. This is an example of a game created by local, informal rules. However, as a result of the collapse of the bubble economy, investment in vacant lots produced huge bad loans. Moreover, since the land price fell continuously from 1992 to 2002, vacant lot investments were no longer an equilibrium strategy for the investor. A self-restraint-rule called vacant lot investment will collapse.

More recently a new game has replaced the old one. The new game consists of investing in income-producing buildings funded by a non-recourse loan from the investor based on the real estate return index. This new game was introduced into Japan in about 1997 by overseas investors, especially the investment banks from the US. They showed that it was possible to exceed their hurdle rate (10% to 20%) by investing in real estate despite falling land prices. Japanese investors also began to emulate the US investment banks, thus gradually helping to establish the new game.

The new equilibrium strategy of investing in income-producing buildings is being created as a response to new economic fundamentals. However, it has not yet reached the stage of acceptability to a broad spectrum of investors. This may be explained by simple inertia. The informal rules of the main bank system, which has, for so long, supported vacant lot investment, have not collapsed completely. Moreover, the official assessed-value-of-land system of the government still remains solemnly as a formal rule.

For a while, two informal rule systems for investment in the real estate market will exist in Japan. The old informal rules and the rules of a new game are mutually opposed to each other. It is essential to analyse the Japanese real estate system to gain a firm grasp of the current situation.

# References

Allen, F. & Gale, D. (2000) *Comparing Financial Systems*. MIT Press, Cambridge MA and London.

Aoki, M. & Patrick, H. (eds) (1994) *The Japanese Main Bank System: its relevance for developing and transforming economies*. Oxford University Press, Oxford.

The Japan External Trade Organization (JETRO) (1998) Overseas companies bullish on Japanese real estate. *Focus Japan*, May 1998 (http://www.dec.ctu.edu.vn/ebooks/jetro/).

Ministry of Land, Infrastructure and Transport (1998) *White Paper on Land Policy in Japan*. Ministry of Land, Infrastructure and Transport, Japan.

Mitsui Fudosan Co. Ltd (2000) *Real Estate Related Statistics Collection 23*.

National Expenditure Division, Department of National Accounts, Economic and Social Research Institute, Cabinet Office (1998) *Annual Report on National Accounts of Japan*.

Yamakata, T. (1999) *Trends in the Tokyo Investment Real Estate Market*. NRI Research Institute, No. 135.

# 3

# Real Estate Markets in Mainland China

## Chang Chun Feng and Stanley Chi Wai Yeung

### Market structure

In China, the 'real estate market' encompasses transactions involving a greater variety of property rights and interests (occupation, tenure, right to generate income and right of disposition) than is common in other real estate markets. A transaction involving a transfer of tenure of the land also includes the transfer of all rights and obligations as stipulated in the lease for the remaining period of the tenure. In general, the markets are classified according to the time sequence in the 'occupation cycle' of buildings. On this basis, markets can be divided into different categories according to the type of user and the types of management. Relying on the time sequence of the real estate entering into the use market, real estate markets can be classified as the primary market, the secondary market and the tertiary market. Thus, the 'primary' market normally refers to new development; the 'secondary' market normally refers to transfers of newly completed buildings to the first user or occupier; and the 'tertiary' market refers to transfers from one user to another. In practice, the secondary real estate market always refers to the selling or renting of newly completed housing units by developers to the first occupiers (users).

Until the 1980s there was no market mechanism for the transfer of real estate. Land was either owned by the State or held in collective ownership by village communities. As a general rule, urban land became state-owned. Nevertheless, since the 1980s many cities in China have expanded rapidly and collectively owned land has been absorbed into urban development. Collectively owned land is transferred to State ownership when urban development takes place. Against this background, the primary real estate market refers to the market in which the government, as the owner of state-owned land, leases land to investors, developers or end-users for a certain period of time. Investors or users are required to pay a land premium based on the value of the land according to the types of use and the duration of the tenure, which is determined by the types of use. Thus, a 'lease' of land for residential use is normally granted for 70 years; for industrial use 50 years; for education, science and technology, culture, hygiene and physical training 50 years; for commerce, tourism and entertainment 40 years; for other uses 50 years. It should be noted that the term 'lease' normally has a narrower definition than that used elsewhere: it normally refers simply to the grant of use rights. Thus, for example, a 'lease' for the development of a site does not necessarily grant immediate vacant possession to the developer.

Issues relating to the real estate markets in mainland China are dominated by the need to provide the population with comfortable and affordable housing. This chapter focuses, therefore, on the evolution of housing markets in mainland China. For all types of property, the economic reforms of recent years have meant that it is now possible to trade real estate, whereas prior to 1980 this was not possible. However, the 'market' for most forms of real estate and the related markets for real estate finance are institutionally immature. The focus on the development of housing markets illustrates some of the issues facing the commercialisation of real estate in mainland China.

Sales of new housing units occur within the primary housing market. Confusingly, transactions involving the transfer of possession from one 'owner' to another (referred to elsewhere as the second-hand market) is also referred to in mainland China as a tertiary real estate market. This refers to the market under which the ownership of a housing unit is transferred between users after the new housing unit has been sold by the developer in the private market. Housing units traded in the tertiary market include housing units that have already been sold or leased; commodity housing (open to all); 'economic housing' units (open to qualified purchasers); state-owned housing (previously provided for employees of 'work units' of State enterprises).

## The reform of urban land-use policy

Before 1980, state-owned land was allocated by the government to users (mostly state enterprises). No land-use fee was charged but transfer of land tenure or use rights was not permitted. On 26 July 1980, the State Council issued the *Provisional Policy on the Use of Land by Joint Venture Enterprises*, which stated that 'a land use fee should be charged upon all lands used by joint venture companies, including newly expropriated land and land already used by enterprises'. A local Chinese joint venture partner could use the land-use fee as capital investment. Under the new policy, land-use rights and land ownership right began to separate and a new land tenure system began to operate in mainland China.

In 1982, the city of Shenzhen (granted special status by the National Government as a Special Economic Zone) began to operate the *Provisional Policy of the Land Management of Shenzhen Special Economic Zone* and became the first city in mainland China to levy urban land-use fees. The policy set out different levels of fee from ¥1 to ¥21 per square metre per year, based on the differential ground-rent theory, according to location. The total land-use fee collected over the year was about ¥10m.

(*Note:* The national currency for mainland China is the yuan (¥), also referred to as the renminbi (RMB). Officially it is a non-convertible currency, though it is convertible into the Hong Kong dollar, which is pegged to the US$. ¥8 is approximately equivalent to US$1.)

Later in 1984, Fushun City in Liaoning Province also started to levy land-use fees on urban land. There were four levels of fee ranging from ¥0.2 to ¥0.6 per square metre per year. The total fee collected for the whole year was about ¥20 million. In the same year, Guangzhou City also began to impose land-use fees on Economic and Technology Development Areas, on land use for new projects and on land use involving foreign investors. Soon the whole country was affected by this trend. By 1988, a total of 100 cities in mainland China had adopted a land-use fee system.

On 27 September 1988, the State Council promulgated the *Provisional Ordinance of the Urban Land Use Tax of the People's Republic of China*, and from November 1988 began to levy urban land-use tax throughout the whole country. The urban land tax policy was designed 'to promote a more appropriate use of urban land and improve the efficiency and management of urban land'. Table 13.1 shows the rates of tax.

**Table 13.1**   Rates of urban land-use tax.

| Size of city by population | Urban land-use tax (¥ m² per year) |
| --- | --- |
| Metropolis (> 10m) | 0.5–10 |
| Medium size city (3–10m) | 0.4–8 |
| Small city (500,000–3m) | 0.3–6 |
| County; town; mines | 0.2–4 |

According to this Provisional Ordinance, the land-use tax replaced the previous land-use fee charged on local enterprises. However, the land-use fee was still to be levied on joint venture enterprises. Generally speaking, there were several advantages in introducing the land-use fee system in the cities:

- The urban land-use reform established and enhanced the sense that urban land should be paid for, not allocated free to users, and should be used more rationally and more economically.

- It also helped to enhance the management and control over the use of land.

- Land users had a financial incentive to use the land more efficiently. As a result, many of the old state enterprises in major cities returned land, which had been put aside for their use for many years, to the local government.

- The reform increased the fiscal income of the local governments, thus assuaging the shortage of funds for construction.

Between 1988 and 1991, the urban land-use tax of the whole country amounted to ¥8850 billion.

The recognition of the economic value of land took a further step forward in 1987. Although the government would not sell its ownership rights, by distinguishing and separating use rights from ownership rights the government was able to sell a form of tenure that permitted the user to transfer or 'lease' the land to other enterprises or individuals or use the land for mortgage finance. Based on the land tenure system in Hong Kong, in 1987 Shenzhen Special Economic Zone became the first city in China to introduce the policy of selling 'leases' in government-owned land to enterprises.

By 1988, several cities, including Fuzhou, Haikou, Guangzhou, Shanghai and Tianjing, had introduced similar land sale practice. At first, there was a legal problem concerning the sale of state land. The Constitution of China clearly stated that no firms or persons could seize, purchase or sell, rent or transfer the land into other illegal forms. Similar restrictions were stated in the Land Management Law of China. Thus, the policy of land renting or transfer of the tenure with reward conflicted with the Constitution and the Land Management Law of China. In order to establish the legal foundation for selling tenure, many cities amended the local ordinances, for example:

- *Ordinance of Tenure Transference with Reward in Shanghai* (amended 29 November 1987).

- *Land Management Ordinance of Shenzhen Special Economic Zone* (passed by the Standing Committee of People's Congress Council of Guangdong on 29 December 1987).

- *Land Management Ordinance of Hainan* (amended 13 February 1988).

- *Ordinance of the Tenure Transference of Haikou* (amended 14 February 1988).

- *Ordinance of the Government-owned Tenure Transference of Xiamen* (amended 14 June 1988).

- Similarly, Tianjing introduced the *Management Ordinance of the Tenure Transference with Reward for the Development Area of Economic and Technology of Tianjing.*

All these local laws prescribed the transference of the tenure of government-owned land in detail. These ordinances were regarded as the legal foundation for the sale of government-owned land.

In 1988, the first meeting of the seventh People's Congress amended the Constitution (part 10, item 4) to remove the proscription that 'land should not be rented', replacing it with 'No firms or persons may seize, purchase or sell, rent and transfer the land in any illegal forms. But land-use rights may be transferred according to the ordinances.' The fifth meeting of the standing committee of the same People's Congress made the corresponding amendment to the land management law. The amended land management law prescribed that:

> No firms or persons may seize, purchase or sell, rent and transfer the land in any illegal forms. ... The right of use for government-owned and collectively owned land may be transferred according to law. The ordinance for the transference of the tenure will be formulated by the State Council.

In 1990, the State Council introduced the *Provisional Ordinance on the Sale and Transfer of the Tenure of the Urban Land of the People's Republic of China*. This clearly prescribed control of the sale, transfer, leasing, mortgage and termination of land-use rights. Subsequently, individual provinces, municipalities directly under the central government (such as Chongqing), together with the autonomous regions, formulated and introduced details for the operation of the Provisional Ordinance.

## Reform of the urban housing system

By 1978, most Chinese families were still living in rather crowded conditions but were required to pay only a nominal rent. Housing was regarded as a kind of social welfare and was the responsibility of the State (directly) or indirectly through the responsibility of state-owned enterprises to house their workers. The problem with such a housing welfare system was the heavy financial burden that it imposed on the State and state-owned enterprises. A major conference on housing construction in Chinese cities acted as a catalyst for urban housing reform, which began in 1978. Since then urban housing reform in China has seen the introduction of a wide range of policy initiatives including selling houses at heavily discounted prices; raising rents with the support of a rent subsidy; developing housing provident funds; and direct housing subsidies in cash. The following examples highlight major types of housing reform policies implemented in large cities in China.

### Sale of state-owned housing at discount rate

In 1982, the central government formulated a policy for selling state houses with the support of a subsidy called 'the double-three system', under which state-owned housing was sold to workers at a price level based on the cost of the housing only. The cost was divided equally between the purchaser, the government and the enterprise employing the purchaser. Changzhou, Zhengzhou, Siping and Shangshi were the first cities to try the new system. As soon as it was put into practice, the system gained wide public support. In 1984, a second group consisting of 82 cities in 23 provinces including Beijing, Tianjing and Shanghai also adopted the new system. The policy emphasised that the price of the houses should be affordable to most of the employees. By the end of 1985, 1604 cities and 300 towns in 27 provinces, municipalities directly under the central government and autonomous regions, had sold houses to individuals with subsidy. During these years the total amount of housing sold to individuals added up to approximately 11 million square metres. Soon, demand exceeded supply.

We can see from this reform that there were a large number of employees with a keen demand to purchase their own housing at an affordable price. On the other hand, it also revealed a shortage of funding for new housing development. There was much state-owned housing that was old and run down for which the rent levels were extremely low. Furthermore, because employees needed to pay only one-third of the price, the burden on city governments and state enterprises was extremely heavy. As a result, in 1985, the government terminated such arrangements.

The most common practice adopted for the sale of state-owned housing was the sale at a discount according to length of employment/service as stated in *Decision Concerning the Deepening of the Reform of Urban Housing Systems* announced by the State Council (Document No. [1994] 43 of the State Council of the PRC). That is to say, enterprises should sell state-owned housing units to employees at a discount that reflected his or her length of service. In addition, state enterprises could purchase housing units in the open market and re-sell the units to their employees. The prices should be set according to the level laid down by the Housing Reform Office. The difference between the market price and re-selling price would be subsidised by the enterprises. In most major cities, the amount of subsidy is substantial.

The policy of selling state-owned houses at a discounted price is the most prevalent form of housing reform in cities all over the country. The policy has the following advantages:

- The subsidy is only distributed among the employees who purchase the houses;

- Enterprises do not have to break the old housing allocation pattern;

- Enterprises are not required to find additional money;

- The procedure is relatively simple;

- It makes some contribution to the problem of housing low-income individuals and families.

The policy helps employees to make the transition from receiving housing at negligible cost to paying for their own housing. However, the policy has some disadvantages:

- Families labelled as 'one family, two systems', with one family member working in a foreign corporation receiving a high salary while other members worked in a state-owned corporation, could still receive the full benefit of subsidised state-owned housing;

- Employees who were able to get the houses received the full benefit of the discount and hence subsidy. Conversely, those who were unable to obtain housing could not benefit from the subsidised discount;

- The policy does not follow the principle of distribution according to work and might induce corruption;

- The amount of subsidy is too large: often, after discounting according to the length of service, the employee may need to pay only 10% of the market price for a new flat. The effect of the discount is magnified in large cities such as Beijing with high housing prices. This policy actually led to an unjustified drain on public resources;

- The policy only encouraged the sale of old, state-owned houses; it could not promote the sale of newly constructed houses.

## Review of the low rent system

In 1987, government policy started to address the reform of the rent system for residential accommodation. The first three cities to follow the policy were Yantai (August 1987), Tangshan (October 1987) and Bangbu (January 1988). The first stage of the reform focused on the system of low rents for residential accommodation. The rent for state-owned accommodation was raised by 13–18 times, from a very low base (from ¥0.1 m$^2$) to over ¥1.00 m$^2$. The rental level should be 70% to 80% of the total operating cost for the property (i.e. maintenance, management, depreciation, interest and tax of the property). Rent increases could be introduced incrementally and could be offset by subsidy payments to tenants. The subsidy was based on the employee's average basic salary, the average size of the housing unit and the percentage of rent increase. The total amount of the subsidy should not exceed 25% of the employee's basic salary (State Council document No. [1988] 11). For any district, the total income generated from rent increases should be equal to the total housing subsidy.

This policy introduced a readjustment of the relationship between the employee, the work unit and the government in housing provision. The notion that 'one needs to pay more for more space', and that this would be reflected by increasing rent, represents an important change in the institutional arrangements associated with the introduction of market principles into the housing allocation system. Second, the policy helped to readjust the economic interests between work units. Work units with ample housing stocks became better off since the extra rent received was more than the extra wages they needed to pay out. Conversely, work units with small housing stocks became worse off because the liability for extra wages exceeded the extra rent they received. Lastly, it improved the management of the existing housing stock. The increase in rental income supported the maintenance of existing dwellings and in some circumstances enabled extra funds to be accumulated for the construction of new housing. It also established the foundation for the commercialisation of housing.

## The Housing Provident Fund of Shanghai

Shanghai was the first city in China to successfully set up a provident fund for housing and this scheme has become the model for housing provident fund (HPF) development in other cities in China. This has become a mandatory policy and is easy to manage. Individual employees are required to contribute 5% of their wages to the fund; the work units contribute a further 5%. The HPF can be used only for housing and is used to provide loans to employees (1) to purchase flats, (2) to construct new housing units, and (3) for maintenance or repair of their existing flats. The HPF provides loans to work units for the development of new housing projects, and also provides retirement benefits: when employees retire, they have the right to withdraw their remaining fund together with the accumulated interest.

The development of the HPF is compatible with other housing reform policies including increasing rents, providing subsidies and selling of state-owned housing at a discount. All these policies are designed to encourage employees to purchase and take responsibility for their own housing. Housing management committees are responsible for the operation of the combined programme of housing reform. HPF management centres are separately responsible for management of the housing provident funds, which accumulate in individual deposit accounts. The HPF centre is responsible for collecting, managing and using the fund. By 1995, the centre had collected ¥7718 billion. (In 1995 alone, it collected about ¥3000 billion.) By 2000, the accumulated sum was sufficient to develop new housing projects to cover the immediate needs of middle-income and low-income employees in Shanghai.

However, the HPF has some limitations. For work units in a poor financial situation, the employers and employees might find difficulty in consistently making full and proper contributions. The interest rate for borrowing and saving under the fund is normally low. Those who use the fund benefit from the low interest rate while those who do not suffer from a low return for their savings. Non-users subsidise the users and this may not be fair. Moreover the way of keeping individual accounts under the fund is not as convenient as giving a simple housing allowance as part of the employees' salary or direct cash subsidies.

## Housing allowance scheme

In the late 1990s, the role of the State as the major supplier of housing began to diminish and the role of the market became increasingly important. A housing allowance scheme was introduced in major cities such as Guangzhou and Shenzhen to encourage workers to purchase or rent their own accommodation in the private housing market. By this time, a significant percentage of the existing stock of state-owned housing had already been sold to workers. The housing allowance scheme would serve new employees, who would no longer be provided with quarters, and help to develop a financial base for private housing development. The allowance was to be allocated to specific categories of employees as part of their salary. When the allowance was paid, the work unit was no longer responsible for providing quarters for the employee.

In Guangzhou, employees who, by October 1997, had not purchased their own flats by means of the scheme for the sale of state-owned housing, and were living in quarters below the official standard, became eligible for the housing allowance. Eligibility is also based on the seniority and rank of the employee. The guidelines for the allocation of the allowance are based on prices and size of flats. The actual level of allowance in practice will vary according to the affordability of the work units and the employees. The price of the flats to be purchased under the housing allowance scheme should be ¥3500 per square metre and the size of flat based on 25 square metres per person. The maximum total allowance is limited to 80% of the purchase price, paid as a monthly allowance up to a maximum period of 25 years.

Housing reform was introduced in Shenzhen in 1988 with the general objective of transferring the responsibility of provision from the government and state enterprises to workers themselves by (1) transforming welfare benefits in kind to monetary payments and (2) encouraging workers to purchase their own flats. By the late 1990s, the Shenzhen government decided to promote a 'dual-track, three categories and multi-pricing' policy. Under the 'dual-track' policy, the local government is only responsible for building 'welfare housing' whereas private developers are responsible for the development of 'commodity housing'. 'Three categories' refers to housing demand from (1) civil servants, (2) staff of state-owned enterprises and (3) private sector workers. Civil servants will be provided with welfare or low-profit housing by the local government. Workers of the state-owned enterprises will be provided with 'welfare housing'. Private sector workers must purchase 'commodity housing' through the private housing market. Under the 'multi-pricing' system, housing prices are set at different levels according to the affordability of different social groups. The price of welfare housing is set according to the construction cost without any profit. The price of low-profit housing is set at a level slightly higher than the construction cost, to allow a minimum level of profit. There is no restriction on the price of commodity housing, which should be determined by the market.

## Relationship between the real estate industry and national economic development

After the introduction of the economic reforms of the 1980s and the 'open door' policy, the real estate and construction industries have been at the core of national economic development. In the 1990s, the national government designated the housing sector as the main area for promoting economic growth and domestic consumption. In 1998, total investment in residential property represented about 7.98% of national GDP. The housing sector accounted for 0.71% of a total economic growth of 8.9%. The relationship between the real estate industry and the national economy is illustrated in Table 13.2. This indicates that investment in the real estate industry, especially the increase in investment in the residential market, was in line with the increase in the average living area of urban residents and the increase in housing completions.

### Induced demand from real estate

The development of the real estate industry has created induced demands for construction materials, equipment, plant and machinery. This has increased employment in more than 50 industries including timber products, chemicals, electronics and so on. According to analysis of 1996 data, the multiplier coefficient of the real estate industry is 1.93. That is to say, when the input of the housing construction increases by ¥1000, the induced total output of its associated industries will increase by ¥1930. Clearly, therefore, real estate development in China has a significant impact on the national economy as a whole.

Apart from the direct stimulation of growth in other associated industries, the development of the real estate industry has also induced demand for a higher living standard. This has stimulated the consumption of consumer goods. According to one survey, when residents move into a new house, most

**Table 13.2**  Relationship between the development of the real estate industry and the development of the national economy (%).

| Year | Growth in GDP (%) | Growth in total invest-ment in fixed assets | Growth in total investment in housing construction | Increase in living area per capita in urban areas | Increase in living area per capita in rural areas | Increase in total area of newly constructed houses |
|------|------|------|------|------|------|------|
| 1987 | 11.5 | 21.5 | 21.4 | 1.7 | 4.6 | 0.7 |
| 1988 | 11.3 | 25.4 | 25.7 | 3.3 | 3.8 | 22.7 |
| 1989 | 4.2 | −7.2 | 0.6 | 4.8 | 3.6 | 13.2 |
| 1990 | 4.2 | 2.4 | −2.5 | 1.5 | 3.5 | −12.7 |
| 1991 | 9.1 | 23.9 | 21.7 | 3.0 | 3.9 | 25.0 |
| 1992 | 14.1 | 44.4 | 21.1 | 2.9 | 2.2 | 36.2 |
| 1993 | 13.1 | 618 | 58.8 | 5.6 | 9.5 | 75.9 |
| 1994 | 12.6 | 30.4 | 39.6 | 4.0 | −2.4 | 11.0 |
| 1995 | 9.0 | 17.5 | 24.4 | 3.8 | 4.0 | 6.9 |
| 1996 | 9.8 | 14.8 | 9.8 | 4.9 | 3.3 | 2.0 |
| 1997 | 8.5 | 8.9 | 3.3 | 3.5 | 3.2 | 5.0 |

*Sources: Statistical Yearbook of China 1998; Statistical Yearbook of Fixed Assets of China 1998.*

**Table 13.3**   Ratio of housing price to income in different regions of the world.

| Region | Ratio of house price to the resident's yearly income |
| --- | --- |
| Africa (excluding North) | 1.04 |
| South Asia | 6.95 |
| East Asia | 4.15 |
| Latin America and Caribbean | 3.06 |
| Europe, Middle East and North Africa | 5.03 |
| Industrialised countries | 4.7 |

of them will spend more than ¥10,000 on decoration. If 3,800,000 new houses are constructed each year, decoration expenses will reach ¥40 billion. The input will be even greater if we take consumer goods into account.

## High ratio of housing price to wages

It is important to consider housing price with affordability. According to a survey of 52 countries and regions undertaken by the United Nations and the World Bank in 1990, the reasonable ratio of house price to annual household income (see Table 13.3) should be in the range 3–6.

According to the report, *Human Settlement in the People's Republic of China*, the development objective of human settlement in China is to reach an average of 9 square metres of space per capita and an average living space of 60 square metres per family. Applying these standards, the ratio of housing price to household income in different provinces and regions in 1997 is shown in Table 13.4. In 1997, the average annual income of Chinese employees was ¥6470, while the average price of houses was ¥1789.8 m². If a family of two owns a house of 60 square metres, the ratio of housing price to annual income would be 8.3 – much higher than the international standard. Obviously there is an affordability problem in China.

It is interesting to note the discrepancy in the ratio of house price to yearly income between the eastern and western regions of China. There is a greater inter-regional difference of the ratio in the east than in the west. The relatively high ratio is skewed by higher housing prices in some cities and provinces in China. Ignoring provinces and cities with housing prices higher than ¥2000 per m² (Beijing, Tianjin, Shanghai, Guangdong and Hainan) reduces the average price of commodity housing by about 28% to ¥1268 m². Hence it is important that housing policy should be tailored to each region. On the other hand, there are also huge differences in wage levels in China. In 1997, wages in state-owned enterprises, collective enterprises and other economic

**Table 13.4**  Ratio of house prices to annual income in different provinces and cities in China (1997).

| Regions | Province/city | House price (P) | Average yearly income per capita (YI) | P : YI per family | YI of Party employees* (YIp) | P : YIp per family |
|---------|---------------|-----------------|----------------------------------------|-------------------|-------------------------------|---------------------|
| East | Bejing | 5,478.4 | 11,019 | 14.92 | 10,698 | 15.36 |
| | Tianjing | 2,133.4 | 8,238 | 7.77 | 9,420 | 6.79 |
| | Hebei | 1,350.8 | 5692 | 7.12 | 6,029 | 6.72 |
| | Liaoning | 1,518.1 | 5,591 | 8.15 | 7,096 | 6.42 |
| | Shanghai | 2,790.5 | 11,425 | 7.33 | 13,608 | 6.15 |
| | Jiangsu | 1,352.1 | 7,108 | 5.71 | 9,617 | 4.22 |
| | Zhejiang | 1,452.6 | 8,386 | 5.20 | 9,804 | 4.44 |
| | Fujian | 1,792.5 | 7,559 | 7.11 | 6,379 | 8.43 |
| | Shandong | 1,171.9 | 6,241 | 5.63 | 6,981 | 5.04 |
| | Guangdong | 3,149.8 | 9,698 | 9.74 | 10,705 | 8.83 |
| | Guangxi | 1,093.8 | 5,542 | 5.92 | 5,449 | 6.02 |
| | Hainan | 2,185.1 | 5,664 | 11.57 | 7,744 | 8.46 |
| Central | Shanxi | 1,009.9 | 5,320 | 5.69 | 4,874 | 6.22 |
| | Neimenggu | 960.8 | 5,124 | 5.63 | 5,582 | 5.16 |
| | Jilin | 1,207.7 | 5,664 | 6.40 | 6,591 | 5.50 |
| | Heilongjiang | 1,349.9 | 4,889 | 8.28 | 6,396 | 6.33 |
| | Anhui | 961.6 | 5,492 | 5.25 | 6,379 | 4.52 |
| | Jiangxi | 723.3 | 5,089 | 4.26 | 5,851 | 371 |
| | Henan | 877.1 | 5,225 | 5.04 | 5,505 | 4.78 |
| | Hubei | 1,251.8 | 5,401 | 6.95 | 6,230 | 6.03 |
| | Hunan | 928.5 | 5,326 | 5.23 | 6,307 | 4.42 |
| West | Chongqing | 1,016.9 | 5,502 | 5.54 | 6,068 | 5.03 |
| | Sichuan | 1,070.5 | 5,626 | 5.71 | 6179 | 5.20 |
| | Guizhou | 908.1 | 5,206 | 5.23 | 4,835 | 5.63 |
| | Yunnan | 1,235.3 | 7,037 | 5.27 | 6,966 | 5.632 |
| | Tibet | 138.6 | 10,098 | 0.41 | 11,959 | 0.35 |
| | Shanxi | 1,290.9 | 5,184 | 7.47 | 5,189 | 7.46 |
| | Gansu | 1,111.3 | 6,182 | 5.39 | 5,736 | 5.81 |
| | Qinghai | 1,137.5 | 7,091 | 4.81 | 7,803 | 4.37 |
| | Ningxia | 1,114.5 | 6,073 | 5.51 | 5,584 | 5.99 |
| | Xinjiang | 1,288.5 | 6,644 | 5.82 | 7,011 | 5.51 |
| Total | | 1,789.8 | 6,470 | 8.30 | 6,981 | 7.69 |

*Includes employees of government departments and of the Communist Party.

*Source: The Statistical Yearbook of China 1998.*

entities were ¥6747, ¥4512 and ¥8789, respectively. When compared with the national average of ¥6470, the ratios were 104.3%, 69.7% and 135.8%, respectively. Considering the wage level of workers in collective enterprises, the 'house price to income' ratio will reach 11.9, making these workers unable to afford housing without a subsidy. In short, in formulating housing policy, the government needs to take into account the different income levels of the various employment sectors.

*High vacancy rates*

Under the planned economy, housing was allocated to workers at a nominal rent. Housing was a welfare responsibility and production of housing consistently lagged behind demand; existing stock was fully utilised. Housing reform stimulated the rapid development of the real estate market. Vacancy rates for housing began to increase. By the end of 1997, the total area of vacant commodity housing in China was 71.35m m$^2$. All types of housing were affected, including high-class houses, ordinary commodity housing, and even the 'comfortable low-cost housing' developed for less wealthy families. However, ordinary commodity housing represented 87% of the overall vacancy rate. Vacancy rates also varied in different regions according to differences in housing prices. In small and medium-size cities, the development of new housing was relatively slow; as a result, the vacancy rates were not too high. High vacancy rates have become a particular problem in the large cities (see Table 13.5).

In 1997, the total area of vacant commodity housing in Shanghai was 7.06m m$^2$ (13.6% of the national vacancy rate). The corresponding vacancy rate in Shenzhen was 2.59m m$^2$ (5% of the national vacancy rate). In 1997 about 52% of the total area of the unoccupied commodity housing for the whole country was located in Guangdong, Shanghai, Jiangsu and Zhejiang. On the other hand, much of the vacant commodity housing was in fact incomplete new development, or obsolete, low-quality stock unsuitable for human habitation, or located in remote areas without proper infrastructure support. The problem of high vacancy rates was hindering the development of the real estate market and needed to be solved.

## Long-term development of the real estate market in China

*Review of housing distribution 'in kind'*

State Council Document No. [1988] 23 stipulated that, from mid-1998, the allocation of housing units should be stopped and progressively replaced by policies for allocating housing according to a monetary system (housing allowance). The local governments of provinces, municipalities and cities themselves should determine the time frame for implementation of these policies according to local circumstances. For some less developed regions and cities, the central government should, for the time being, continue the old system of housing allocation but with a view to phasing it out as soon as possible. The government should conduct surveys at the national level and collect relevant information for the formulation of long-term housing policies.

**Table 13.5** Vacancy rates in major cities (1994–1997).

| Housing type | 1994 Vacant area (10,000sq.m) | 1994 Ratio (%) | 1995 Vacant area (1,000sq.m) | 1995 Ratio (%) | 1996 Vacant area (10,000sq.m) | 1996 Ratio (%) | 1997 Vacant area (10,000sq.m) | 1997 Ratio (%) |
|---|---|---|---|---|---|---|---|---|
| Villa or top-grade apartment | 158 | 6.3 | 263 | 6.8 | 322 | 6.9 | 371 | 7.2 |
| Ordinary commodity housing | 2354 | 93.7 | 3409 | 87.8 | 4081 | 87.5 | 4549 | 87.4 |
| Comfortable housing | — | — | 210 | 5.4 | 259 | 5.6 | 282 | 5.4 |
| Total | 2512 | 100.0 | 3882 | 100.0 | 4662 | 100.0 | 5202 | 100.0 |

*Source: Ministry of Construction: China Real Estate Industry Statistics.*

## Formulating policies according to local situations

The discrepancy in the ratio of house price to salary between China and international standards has already been mentioned. The ratio is high in the eastern provinces and low in the western region but, even in the eastern region, a substantial imbalance exists. The ratios in Beijing, Guangdong and Hainan are above 9 while those in other places are between 5.5 and 8. This is attributable to the exceptionally high prices for housing in these cities. Excluding Beijing, Shanghai, Guangdong and those provinces with extremely high housing prices, the average price would be ¥1297 m². Subject to these exceptions, the average price of houses reduces by about 28% with a correspondingly low ratio of average housing prices to average family salary. Considering the scale of the cities concerned, house prices are so high in some major cities that purchasing a home is beyond the economic capacity of ordinary families. Policies should reflect differences between cities and regions and accept the need to pay special attention to some places.

## Housing allowances for government organisations

Housing subsidies in the form of cash allowances may be an effective way to cater for the housing needs of the Chinese people. In order to promote this policy incrementally, it may be tried out first out in government organisations (civil servants constitute 7% of the working population). This would enable the model for other collective and private enterprises to be established. Nevertheless, the housing allowance policy should contain greater flexibility, taking account of the interests of various social groups.

### Definition of housing standards

It is common practice for housing standards in China to be based on floor area of usable accommodation. Indeed, this was the primary benchmark for the allocation of welfare housing before the market reforms. Although senior staff have been allocated bigger houses, location is individualised and plays an important part in establishing prices. Thus, there is a trade-off to be made between size and location. The difference in property values in different locations is especially marked in big cities. For example, Beijing has five ring roads: the price of houses within the second ring road is ¥8,000–10,000 m². Within the third and fourth ring road the price drops to between ¥4500–6500 m²; between the fourth and fifth, the price drops to ¥3000 m² or so; in the suburbs beyond the fifth ring, the price drops to ¥2000 m². Thus, the allocation of housing based only on size cannot truly reflect the actual value of the properties. At present, housing benefit for individual workers is determined by rank and is known by everybody. The benefit is based on the size of the flat rather than the value of the flat. This has become a source of unrest and conflict between cadres and workers. Housing standards based on rank or status therefore should be determined carefully according to the actual values of the properties.

### Definition of the standard of housing subsidy

In establishing housing subsidies that are appropriate for local conditions every province, municipality and city should take account of local average house prices, the physical condition of the property and the salary of applicants. Although the subsidy should be about 25% of salary, individuals purchasing houses over a 20-year term should expect to pay no less than 15% of the family income. Subsidies in major cities can be as high as 50–60% of the house price. In medium-size cities, the subsidies can account for 30–50% of the price, while in small cities and towns the subsidies may even be unnecessary if the ratio of house price to the salary is reasonable.

## *Establishing a property rights system*

The policy of selling state-owned houses at discounted prices does not prevent the new 'owners' from re-selling their house in the private market after five years. However, the basis on which houses are sold by the State involves a sharing of the rights of possession. The quality of the individual's actual 'ownership' may be unclear. State-owned housing is normally sold to individual employees of state-owned enterprises. The property is transferred not directly from the State but from the state enterprise. The state enterprise is, clearly, not the absolute owner. There is some sharing of the rights of possession between the state enterprise and the new owner. The government housing policy gives the state enterprise the right to convey possession to the new occupants but, because of this sharing of interests between the state-owned enterprise and the individual workers who purchase the houses, the distinction between ownership and use rights has not been clearly defined. In order to ensure that the real estate market in China can be further developed, a clear property rights system must be established. Moreover a property appraisal system should be developed, supported by a property data archive, to provide objective valuations of property.

## Developing secondary and tertiary markets

The expansion of housing provision over the past 15 years has been largely achieved by the addition of new stock. Virtually all 'private' housing has arisen as a result of the government policy of selling state-owned houses. That policy incorporated a prohibition against resale within five years of acquiring the new housing. Over the past 10 years the volume of property that could be released into the second-hand market has grown. A true real estate market cannot depend entirely on new property. To activate the real estate market in China, it is important to develop secondary and tertiary markets in order to establish a true measure of supply and demand. This relates to the size, type and quality of accommodation but also location factors. Hence it is very important to set up guidelines for buyers of state-owned housing to resell their house in the private housing market. Many state-owned houses are now beyond this restriction period and many owners are eager to sell their houses in the market, hoping to purchase a new one. A vigorous second-hand market would also provide a bridge between the subsidised housing market and the 'commodity housing' market. This in turn would stimulate the market for property finance, particularly home purchase mortgages.

## Establishing a property tax system

According to experience in many cities, lowering the tax rate levied on property transactions is an important incentive in developing secondary and tertiary markets. To encourage householders to sell old houses and buy new ones, some cities have implemented incentive measures. Shanghai, for example, operates a policy of a comprehensive tax, payable by the seller, amounting to 5% of the price of the house. This includes sales tax (0.84% of the price); land value-added tax (2.22%); individual income tax (1.84%); tax for urban maintenance and construction (0.07%); and educational attached fee (0.03%). At the same time, stamp duty is reduced by 50% (about 3% of the purchase price). Many cities have imposed a similar comprehensive tax of 5% of the price payable by the seller. The purchaser is required to pay stamp duty (2–4% of the price), stamp tax (0.05%) and the registration fee (0.1–0.2%). Both the seller and the purchaser pay a handling charge for the exchange (0.5–1% of the price). The total sum of the taxes and fees paid by the seller and the purchaser equals 11% of the purchase price.

## Development of the rental market

The rental sector is a core component of the real estate market. The development of a rental sector is important in the overall development of the real estate market in China. In practice, there is already a 'latent' rental market in China. Some occupiers of state-owned housing have rented out their flats to other families in order to generate extra income. In particular, many of these leasing transactions are made between local citizens and the incoming transit population in large cities. This is actually a loss of national income as the state-owned housing was allocated to the workers as a form of welfare. Hence it is important to establish a fair and open rental market to make sure that there will be no loss of national income from this 'latent' rental market.

## Development of the housing finance system

Because of the apparent discrepancy between the high price of houses and low purchasing power of individuals, lack of support from the financial system hinders housing reform and the development of a real estate market. A robust system of real estate finance is an essential tool for managing and stimulating the development of real estate markets. Such a system was largely unnecessary under the planned economy. In general the development of real estate markets in China is largely limited by insufficient capital. Housing in China is still expensive in relation to the low average wage of the population. It is difficult for workers to buy their own houses without support from banks or other financial institutions. Real estate developers face a similar problem of insufficient funding for real estate projects. The development of a robust real estate financing system remains one of the major challenges in the development of real estate markets in mainland China.

## Acknowledgement

This chapter is based on the research project '*Research on Real Estate Market System in China Mainland*', funded by the National Natural Science Foundation of China, project no. 9470002.

## References and further reading

Che, Jianghong (2000) *Studies on the Real Estate Market Mechanism*. Shanghai Social Science Institute Press, Shanghai.
Cheng, Siwei (1999) *The Objectives, Models and Focus of Housing Reform in Urban China*. Democracy and Construction Press, Beijing.

Dong, Liming, Hu, Jianying, He, Shaoyi & Feng, Changchun (1995) *Real Estate Development and Management*. Peking University Press, Beijing.

Feng, Changchun (1999) *Real Estate Development*. Liaoning People's Press, Liaoning.

Liang, Yunbing (1996) *Development and Control of the Real Estate Industry in China at the Beginning of the 21st Century*. Economy and Management Press, Beijing.

Lin, Zengjie, Lu, Ping & Yu, Xiang (1999) *Studies on the Policies about the Marketization of Public Housing in China Mainland*. Remin University Press, Beijing.

# Index